SELECTED
CONTRIBUTIONS TO
PSYCHO-ANALYSIS

SELECTED
CONTRIBUTIONS TO
PSYCHO-ANALYSIS

By
John Rickman, M.D.

Compiled by
W. Clifford M. Scott, M.D.

With an Introductory Memoir by
Sylvia M. Payne, C.B.E., M.B.

KARNAC
LONDON   NEW YORK

Originally published by The Hogarth Press Ltd, London in 1957
Reprinted in 2003 with new Preface by
H. Karnac (Books) Ltd.
6 Pembroke Buildings, London NW10 6RE

British Library Cataloguing in Publication Data

A C.I.P. for this book is available from the British Library

   ISBN 1 85575 320 0

10 9 8 7 6 5 4 3 2 1

www.karnacbooks.com

ACKNOWLEDGEMENTS

The Editor wishes to acknowledge with gratitude permission given by the Editors to publish the late Dr. Rickman's papers previously printed in or by

The American Journal of Psychology
The British Journal of Medical Psychology
The British Medical Journal
The International Journal of Psycho-Analysis
The International Universities Press
The Journal of Mental Science
The Lancet
The Practitioner

CONTENTS

Preface   *page* 7

Foreword   9

Editorial Note   17

1 An Unanalysed Case. Anal Erotism, Occupation
   and Illness (1921)   19

2 A Psychological Factor in the Aetiology of Descensus Uteri, Laceration of the Perineum and
   Vaginismus (1926)   22

3 Discussion on Lay-Analysis (1927)   26

4 On some of the Standpoints of Freud and Jung
   (1928)   32

5 On Quotations (1929)   37

6 The Psychology of Crime (1932)   45

7 On 'Unbearable' Ideas and Impulses (1937)   52

8 Sigmund Freud: A Personal Impression (1939)   59

9 The General Practitioner and Psycho-Analysis
   (1939)   61

10 On the Nature of Ugliness and the Creative
    Impulse (1940)   68

11 A Case of Hysteria: Theory and Practice in the
    Two Wars (1941)   90

12 Sigmund Freud, 1856–1939: An Appreciation
    (1941)   95

13 Psychology in Medical Education (1947)   105

14 The Application of Psycho-Analytical Principles
    to Hospital In-Patients (1948)   115

15 Guilt and the Dynamics of Psychological Disorder
    in the Individual (1948)   119

16 On the Criteria for the Termination of an
    Analysis (1950)   127

17 The Rôle and Future of Psycho-Therapy within
    Psychiatry (1950)   131

CONTENTS

18 The Development of Psychological Medicine
(1950)   144

19 The Factor of Number in Individual- and Group-
Dynamics (1950)   165

20 Reflections on the Function and Organization of
a Psycho-Analytical Society (1951)   170

21 Methodology and Research in Psycho-pathology
(1951)   207

22 Number and the Human Sciences (1951)   218

23 A Survey: The Development of the Psycho-
Analytical Theory of the Psychoses 1894–1926
(1926–1927)   224

Appendix I. Need for Belief in God (1938)   384

Appendix II. List of Publications by John
Rickman   391

Index   397

PREFACE

JOHN Rickman was probably one of the most experienced editors I was ever likely to meet. He was insistent that writers should not only concentrate on the people or events that they were reporting, but that they should also describe the context in which they functioned and their relationship to other sources of relevant knowledge. He emphasized, too, that they should realize that as the observer they were also part of the 'picture'.

In this spirit let me sketch in the context of how I come to writing a preface to this most welcome re-issue of Dr Rickman's *Selected Contributions to Psycho-analysis*. At the 42nd Congress of the International Psychoanalytical Association in Nice, I was presented by colleagues with a Festschrift entitled *Within Time and Beyond Time* (published by Karnac Books) to mark my 80th Birthday. After I had returned to London from France, I was approached by Oliver Rathbone of Karnac Books, who offered me a contract for an edition of unpublished papers by Dr. John Rickman. He had been encouraged to do so by a friend of mine who knew that I had been engaged over a number of years in compiling and editing Rickman's papers. (My colleague Masud Khan had helped with the original selection of papers. I then did most of the editorial work on the papers, helped by an occasional consultation with Masud.) As well as completing this editorial task, I would be expected to accompany it with a scholarly contribution on the life and works of John Rickman.

In considering whether or not I could take on this task at my age, I knew that in addition to information that I had collected about John Rickman, the Archives of the British Society had a collection of 700 letters between him and other people, together with much information of his work on the main committees of the Society and Institute, some of which was accessible on our computerized retrieval system. I also knew that Rickman's daughter, Mrs. Lucy Rickman Baruch and her analyst husband were still in good health, and that they would help me with information about her father.

After some thought and discussion I agreed to accept this offer, and went on to discuss the relation of this new book to the collection of Rickman's papers, published in 1957, entitled

7

Selected Contributions to Psycho-analysis, but which had been unobtainable for some years. Karnac agreed that they would reprint *Selected Contributions to Psycho-analysis* at the same time with the publication of the collection of Rickman's unpublished papers edited by me. Hence the copy you hold in your hand today.

The wide variety of topics included in both books indicates Rickman's extensive range of interests and his inter-disciplinary contacts. The reader may, as it were, 'listen-in' to Rickman's attempts to understand and throw light on problems met with by many different professional groups including Psychoanalysts, Psychologists, Anthropologists, General Practitioners, the War Office Selection Boards, Teachers and followers of various religions including the Shamans and the Quakers, whose teachings were part of John Rickman's background. Looked at in this way, the two volumes provide an important context for each other.

Having completed the research work that I had to do in the archives and elsewhere in order to 'rediscover' John Rickman for myself, I realised that if I had learnt anything from John Rickman, he would have expected me to describe not only what he did during his life, but also to give equal value to the various contexts within which he lived and worked. This I have also tried to do, in my Introduction to his papers in my book, *No Ordinary Psychoanalyst*, under the title of 'The Rediscovery of John Rickman and his Work'. In the course of this Introduction, the reader may also rediscover John Rickman, as I had to do, as they consider John Rickman's life events and their influence on his writing and thinking. It therefore stands, as it were, as an Introduction for the two volumes taken as a whole.

PEARL KING
(July 2003)
Editor of
No Ordinary Psychoanalyst:
The Exceptional Contributions of John Rickman

FOREWORD

THE sudden death of John Rickman on July 1st, 1951, at sixty years of age was a serious blow, not only to his personal friends but also to the British Psycho-Analytical Society and the Institute of Psycho-Analysis. Dr. Rickman had been intimately associated since 1920 with the development of the science of psychoanalysis in England and with the foundation of the organizations concerned with its teaching and practice.

Dr. Rickman was a Quaker and came of Quaker stock. He was educated at a Quaker public school and afterwards at King's College, Cambridge, where he took a Natural Science Tripos and the first part of his Medical Degree. He completed his medical training at St. Thomas's Hospital, London, graduating in 1916. On qualification he volunteered for the Friends' War Victims Relief Unit in Russia, and later wrote a number of articles on his experiences when practising medicine amongst the Russian peasants. Certain of these articles, most of them published anonymously at the time of writing, have recently been revised and published in a book written with Geoffrey Gorer entitled *The Peoples of Great Russia*.

While working in Russia he met his future wife, Lydia Cooper Lewis of Philadelphia, who was working as a social worker with the American Friends' Service Committee. They were married in 1918 in Buzuluk, Samara Province, by Russian civil ceremony, the first marriage ceremony that had happened since marriage had become legal apart from the Greek Orthodox ritual. A daughter was born to them in 1921.

John Rickman did pioneer work in Russia of a kind which he was to repeat on more than one occasion during his lifetime. In the hospital in which he was working he organized the training of Russian peasant girls as nurses. His object was to teach the people something which might be carried on when the unit left the country.

On his return from Russia, John Rickman specialized in psychiatry. He held a resident post at Fulbourn Asylum, Cambridge, and there also he pioneered by holding lectures and seminars for nurses. His interest had been aroused in psychoanalysis by Dr. W. H. R. Rivers, who was in Cambridge at that time and on his advice in 1920 Dr. Rickman went to Vienna to see Freud and worked with him there. On leaving Vienna he continued his study of psycho-analysis and of psychiatry by joining the group of men in London who were interested in psycho-analysis under the leadership of Dr. Ernest Jones, and by becoming assistant to Dr. W. H. B. Stoddart in the psychiatric out-patient department of St. Thomas's Hospital. In 1926 he wrote his M.D. thesis on a psychological factor in the aetiology of prolapse of the uterus. At different phases in his career he worked with Freud, Ernest Jones, Ferenczi and Melanie Klein, and thus had had the privilege of contact with some of the most original research workers in the study of the unconscious mind.

Dr. Rickman, a tall powerfully built man with the traditional quiet courtesy of the Englishman, by his presence might appear formidable to those who had not the chance to approach him. Experience showed that he was invariably interested in other people's problems, and would take infinite pains to help colleagues as well as patients in difficult situations. In fact a survey of the work which he did in adult life gives evidence of humility and diffidence about his own intellectual accomplishments in the earlier years, and his readiness to urge a colleague to aspire to a position which he himself had an equal right to acquire. Other evidence of this character trait becomes apparent when the work he accomplished as an editor is considered.

Dr. Rickman's contact with Freud in Vienna and Ernest Jones in London led to his taking an active part under the leadership of Dr. Jones in the purchase of the International Psycho-Analytical Press, which held the rights of publication in the English language of many of Freud's earlier works. Collaboration with the Hogarth Press laid the foundation of the International Psycho-Analytical Press in England. Subsequently the Hogarth Press became responsible for the publication of the principal psycho-analytical books in England and has continued to do so, since 1924, in collaboration with the Institute of Psycho-Analysis.

His interest in publication persisted throughout his life, and was characterized by a technical knowledge of format, type, and printing, combined with a highly developed sense of the correct arrangement of the content of a publication. These gifts were used more in editorial work than in the publication of his own writings, although the papers he wrote were numerous and sometimes anonymous. One of the tragedies of his death was the fact that it occurred at the moment he had decided to give up administrative work in order to complete, revise and publish more of his own writings.

John Rickman's pioneer administrative work for the Institute of Psycho-Analysis was one of his most important contributions to the progress of the psycho-analytical group in England. It had a creative drive in common with his work in Russia. In the first place, in 1924 he assisted Ernest Jones to found the Institute of Psycho-Analysis, and his concern with legal documents led him to play a prominent part in formulating the legal constitution of the Institute. He found a suitable house and treated the first patient in the Institute in 1926 on Freud's 70th birthday, and was the first business secretary to the Institute, a post he resigned in 1928 when he went to work with Ferenczi. From this date until 1938 he did not hold office but was a valued member of the Board, Training and Publication Committees most of the time.

During these years he took a particular interest in the public relations of the Institute of Psycho-Analysis, and did as much as any other member to foster good relationships between psychoanalysts and other groups of psycho-therapists. The Medical Section of the British Psychological Society was the group in which contact with other psycho-therapists could be made. He was its hon. secretary for a number of years. Rickman was assistant-editor under Dr. T. W. Mitchell of the British Journal of Medical Psychology from 1925 until 1934, and on Dr. Mitchell's retirement in 1935 he became editor and held the position until 1948, when he took over the editorship of the International Journal of Psycho-Analysis; for some months he was editing both Journals.

Owing to the demands made on him in respect of his position as President of the British Psycho-Analytical Society he relinquished the chief editorship of the International Journal of Psycho-Analysis in 1949 but remained on the editorial board. During his years of Editorship he reformed the appearance of the Journal, which had not recovered from the restrictions of war economies.

Many psycho-analysts, academic psychologists and psycho-therapists can testify to the trouble he took in putting their papers into shape for publication, giving valuable advice on form and arrangement, and sponsoring new ideas, some of which are now basic.

At the start of the last war he joined the Emergency Medical Service at Haymeads Hospital, Bishops Stortford, and later worked at Wharncliffe Hospital, Sheffield. In these hospitals he was confronted with the problem of the rehabilitation of soldiers who had been through the Dunkirk evacuation. He was partly responsible for preparing and for introducing the use of Raven's Progressive Matrices, which tests were later adopted, amongst others, by the War Office Selection Boards.

In 1942 he transferred to the R.A.M.C. in order to join the teaching staff of Northfield Military Psychiatric Hospital and later took part in operating the methods of selection employed by the War Office Selection Boards. He was chosen to play the part of the psychiatrist in the official film sponsored by the War Office on the work of these Boards.

With Dr. Bion he did some original work on leaderless groups. Dr. Bion writes:

John Rickman had a great capacity for grasping the value of a new idea. I appreciated this when I found, during the war, that he had heard of some views I had expressed about the occupational therapy of soldiers in psychiatric hospitals and had then and there set about translating them, nebulous though they were, into action at Wharncliffe. I visited him there and he told me about it. It was a fascinating account, illuminated by flashes of humour, punctuated with generous tributes to the merits of what were assumed to be my ideas, but never once betraying the least awareness of how much the scheme he was describing was the child of his own creative imagination.

I remember thinking then at Wharncliffe and later at Northfield what a good combatant officer he might have made. He used his abilities and his knowledge to persuade the men in hospital to have a look at themselves and so seemed on the verge of achieving a new kind of leadership in which men were brought to face the unknown territories from which arise the diseases of a sick society. I do not know how far he might have gone with this had his health been good but even at Northfield he seemed to me to be grossly overtaxing his strength. He put his gifts at the disposal of anyone who genuinely sought help from him and did so with great cheerfulness and generosity. Indeed, had he not been so careless of husbanding his resources I think it would have been not only better for him but for the causes he had so much at heart. But I never heard of anyone who was able to persuade him to consider his own welfare.

In 1944 he became ill and had to leave the army for medical reasons, and he was soon immersed in psycho-analytical work—both in connection with the reconstruction of the legal constitution of the Institute of Psycho-Analysis and in the extension of its training programme as well as private psycho-analytical practice.

He accepted the office of Scientific Secretary of the British Psycho-Analytical Society for a time, and in 1947 was elected President and held the office for the maximum time of three years.

At this time the Institute of Psycho-Analysis was obliged to seek a new building owing to the extension of the work and the approaching termination of the lease of the house occupied at the time. Dr. Rickman took an active part in deciding on the purchase of the lease of the new building, and worked hard on the committee responsible for the repair, adaptation and redecoration of the new home of the Institute. He was particularly interested in restoring the beauty of the reception and lecture rooms, which contain valuable examples of Adam period decorations and ceiling moulding. One of the rooms now bears his name. His was a complex personality with wide progressive interests.

From the age of 29 he studied the work of Freud and read all Freud's writings and those of the other psycho-analysts. How well he knew the early psycho-analytical literature is shown in his publication of the Index Psycho-Analyticus in 1928. His later work therefore had the intensive study of psycho-analysis as a background. During the last period of analysis with Freud in 1924, his always active interest in the psychoses was intensified by Freud himself, who encouraged him to take psychotic patients in analysis and thus help work out the psycho-analytic technique of dealing with the psychoses. One result of this was his survey 'The Development of the Psycho-Analytical Theory of the Psychoses'.

During the post-war period of his life, two psychological

problems seem to have been in the forefront of his mind. It is possible to recognize the same interests earlier, but rather by implication than from evidence of active research work.

The first was his interest in the psycho-dynamics of groups, and the second was the emphasis he placed on the need to study the technique of communication between a speaker or teacher and his audience.

Throughout his analytical career he had supported those who wished to make contact with other groups interested in psycho-therapy and psychology. His work in the army had made it clear that it was necessary that a way should be discovered of applying the dynamic of psycho-analytical technique to group therapy, if the knowledge and insight gained through psycho-analytical experience was to be fruitfully employed for the treatment of more than one person at a time.

After the war he took an active interest in the reorganization of the Cassel Hospital, which under the Medical Director, Dr. T. F. Main, was becoming a hospital where the staff included psycho-analytical training amongst their qualifications, and where patients could receive psycho-analytical treatment or psycho-therapy depending on applied psycho-analytical principles. He was also associated with the Tavistock Clinic which was being reorganized by psychiatrists who, on leaving the army, had taken training in psycho-analytical technique. In this Clinic research into group treatment on psycho-analytical principles is one of the main activities. He took also a lively interest in the Tavistock Institute of Human Relations, whose staff were engaged in social psychological tasks and some of whom were being trained as psycho-analysts. His drive to do pioneer work is evident in the part he played in aiding the activities of these three groups of research workers.

Rickman's interest was not confined to the study of psychoanalysis. Certainly he was aware of, and was influenced by, the fact that scientific theory in the present day, particularly in the disciplines of physics and biology, is expressed in terms of energies and dynamic processes. Continuity of life rather than creation is emphasized. Theories of acts of creation are of historical interest only. The development of a science of statistics promises to take the place of a search for first causes.

Dynamic sociological, psychological and political theories show the influence of analogous trends. There is no doubt that

Freud's psycho-dynamic theory shared, if it did not anticipate, much of the same point of view and at the same time, throws light on the mental dynamics of the individual scientist who is producing these abstractions.

Developments in psycho-analysis at the present time emphasize the dynamic importance of the earliest forms of object relationships whether intrapsychic (phantasied) or external, and in technique the economic factor of interpretation is the criterion of correctness. [1] Psychological theories such as Lewin's 'Field Theory' obviously correspond to dynamic theories of other branches of science; Rickman was interested in the field theory but not satisfied. He said in his paper: 'Reflections on the Function and Organization of a Psycho-Analytical Society': (Chapter XIX) 'The dynamics of a multi-structural group is as yet without its Freud.'

The second psychological interest with which he was occupied at the time of his death, and which was obviously related to the deeper and wider interest already referred to, is the technique of communication between human beings, particularly in the form of speech. He developed conspicuously as a public speaker and broadcaster during the last years of his life and it seems likely that he would have gone further had he lived. He advocated extempore speaking rather than the reading of written papers (as Freud himself had done) and discussions rather than lectures for teaching purposes.

His interest in the 'art' of speaking went hand in hand with his growing interest in art as a whole and its relationship to unconscious drives.

He said: 'Those who think that psycho-analysis is a science and only a science may comfort themselves with the belief that everything is in the literature; those who regard the practice of psycho-analysis as something of an art (as well as employment of a scientific method) will have already learnt more than their teachers knew they were giving.' It is clear that he considered that the oral tradition in psycho-analysis should be carried over into the scientific meetings and that the speaker should by his technique promote the occurrence of transference phenomena in order to get into communication with the audience. It seems likely that, apart from the many arguments which can be put

[1] Note his paper on 'The Criteria for the Termination of an Analysis' Chapter XV.

forward in favour of extempore speaking, the Quaker tradition of 'inspired' rather than prepared speaking must have played a part in making his contention important.[1]

In so far as John Rickman's insistence on the importance of extempore speaking depended on the importance of establishing a positive transference relationship to the audience it is of interest to record that he laid special stress on what he called 'the here and now' situation in psycho-analytical technique, holding the view that interpretation of this situation was the essential dynamic in the treatment.

His interest in art was not confined to the art of oratory, and is shown in his paper on 'The Nature of Ugliness and the Creative Impulse' (Chapter IX) and in his membership of the Institute of Contemporary Art. He contributed to a symposium on 'The Significance of Primitive Art' at a meeting of that Institute held in 1948.

The papers chosen for publication in this volume are not confined strictly to the theory and practice of psycho-analysis although all show the author's interest in Freud's psychodynamic theory of mental functioning and the influence of this theory on allied disciplines and organizations. The intention is to show the breadth of his knowledge and understanding and the urge which he had to demonstrate the value of the application of psycho-analytical discoveries to medical education and various branches of medical science.

S. M. PAYNE

[1] His Lister Memorial Lecture to the Quaker Medical Society in 1935 was a psychological study of Quaker beliefs and practices. His brief paper read at the Fifteenth International Psycho-Analytical Congress in Paris in 1938 'The Need for God' grew out of this.

EDITORIAL NOTE

THIS volume contains Dr. Rickman's published papers on psycho-analysis. Students of social psychology will be glad to learn that another volume is in preparation which will include his unpublished papers and most of his papers on applied psycho-analysis. The second volume is to be published by Tavistock Publications under the editorship of Miss Pearl King and Mr. Masud Khan, who have also assisted with the present volume.

The original work of selecting papers for the present volume was carried out by Dr. Clifford Scott and subsequent editorial work has been done by Mrs. Rickman, Mrs. Baruch (Lucy Rickman), and by Dr. J. D. Sutherland.

All students of Freud know that the rapid growth of psycho-analytical thought during the past fifty years makes it essential to place each contribution historically. The papers have therefore been placed in chronological order with two exceptions. 'The Development of Psycho-Analytic Theory of the Psychoses' (1926) because of its length has been put at the end; 'The Need for God', read at the Fifteenth International Psycho-Analytical Congress in 1938 (Dr. Rickman's only Congress paper) has not previously been published and is added as an appendix. A list of Dr. Rickman's publications forms a second appendix.

I

AN UNANALYSED CASE:
ANAL EROTISM, OCCUPATION AND
ILLNESS[1]
(1921)

THE old man whose case is here given came under observation
in circumstances which rigidly excluded analytic investigation;
the facts given below were poured forth by the patient and tell
their own tale; this brief notice cannot convey the full impression his conversation left on the mind, his dramatic nods and
grimaces illustrated his story when words failed him.

The patient is now aged sixty-five. He said he had bowel
trouble for twenty-seven years, beginning with 'diarrhoea and
corruption and prolapse following the conception of my only
son'; he had 'no control over his bowels at all'. Since that time
(1893) he had not had a single solid motion. I asked whether he
had had treatment and what relief he had received. He replied
that when going to a doctor he always said, 'Now, doctor, don't
interfere with my bowels whatever you do!' Nevertheless he
went to a famous hospital and was treated for six months. He
kept 'fit' for twelve years and then became worse. At this point I
asked how fit he was during that time. He said he was fit enough
to work, he didn't *go* more than four times before he left the
house in the morning; once immediately on rising, the second
time after lighting the kitchen fire, then again after shaving and
last after breakfast just before leaving for his work. I asked if the
diarrhoea continued throughout the day and if his illness interfered with his work. He replied that usually he did not go more
than eight times in the day and that he always knew how hard
he was going to find the day's work by the way he went before
breakfast, 'more than four times and I know I am going to have
a bad day.'

[1] Reprinted from the *International Journal of Psycho-Analysis* (1921),
2, 424–6.
This case history was presented verbally to a meeting of the
British Psycho-Analytical Society on February 10, 1921.

In 1904, after twelve years of good health, his trouble became worse so that he was 'weakened in body' and he returned to the hospital. Here, he said, they fetched the doctors with the longest fingers and examined his back passage. It was said that the 'webs' which held his bowels up were weak and so his 'insides' had dropped down. He was in a bad way, they gave him six hours to live and advised that he should go to the infirmary. His wife would not hear of this, so he returned home and recovered without treatment.

Eight years later the trouble returned. In the interval he had poor sphincter control but could 'hold' better at some times than others. Again eight years later he had another bad turn and on this occasion went to another hospital where I saw him. I asked what the hospital had done for him this time; he replied, rather dolefully, that they had cut his bowels out. As a matter of fact a caecostomy had been performed and he had colon lavage daily. At the operation the pathological findings were: Enormous thickening of caecum and ascending colon. The blood serum agglutinated Flexner's bacillus in all dilutions and Shiga's partially. No amoebae were found in the stools; he received a course of emetine.

He did not volunteer anything else about his health so I asked him about his occupation. He was a labourer and worked for preference at unstopping sewers or in digging the foundations of houses and making the trench from the house to the 'main' (drain, of course). I asked if the smells in the sewers were bad, he replied, 'Oh no. Well, nothing in partic'lar. I never worked in compressed air'. It appears that some sewers are kept fresh by forced draught, it was in such that he had not worked. He had also been a bricklayer's labourer and had to mix the mortar.

He was next asked to tell about his bowel condition before the illness which began twenty-seven years ago and in particular his condition during infancy. He said he had been 'free in his motions as a young nipper but later had a costive nature' which caused him to miss a day or two, and he had had trouble to pass his motions, which were like green walnuts. However, at the age of sixteen or seventeen when he went to work at the gas-works his costiveness came to an end and he was 'free' again.

When asked what his relations had suffered from he replied that he had an idea that his father was troubled with his bowels, because he was frequently seen to stand with his legs crossed in an attitude as though he was squeezing himself up. Then the patient volunteered, 'I always advises my son, "if you feel it— GO! Never hold it back" '. His son is now 'troubled with kidneys and wind'.

The patient dreams at night that women are preventing him from going to the water closet.

II

A PSYCHOLOGICAL FACTOR IN THE AETIOLOGY OF DESCENSUS UTERI, LACERATION OF THE PERINEUM AND VAGINISMUS[1]

(1926)

GYNAECOLOGY is chiefly concerned with the physical condition and position of the genital organs. Sometimes psychoanalysis is able to contribute an interpretation of the phenomena in terms of libido and explain the present conditions in terms of the patient's past love attachments and his capacity to renounce infantile sexuality for an exogamous genital gratification. The physiology of use must be supplemented by a 'physiology of pleasure' (Ferenczi).

In the psycho-analytical literature we read of the genitalization of other organs and learn something of the changes so produced, but little has been said of the changes in the genitals themselves when not acting as the central erotic organ of the body. Recent investigations have led me to think that weakness of the pelvic floor and of the suspending ligaments of the uterus may be evidence that the genital stage has not been reached or maintained, and that loss of 'tone' in these tissues is a sign of 'degenitalization'. A case to illustrate this point.

A woman of twenty-seven, six years married, suffered from horror of intercourse—she feared something terrible would happen to herself and to her husband; she was also constipated, having no 'power' to expel faeces, and did not perceive the call to stool. She developed prolapse, and was treated with douches, pessaries and pads, but without relief; she was convinced the treatment would do her no good. In the course of time her fears diminished to some extent and consenting to coitus she had a child, but it died soon after birth. She conceived the idea that she had suffocated it *in utero* by pressing on the umbilical cord

[1] Reprinted from the *International Journal of Psycho-Analysis* (1926), **7**, 363–5.

with a vaginal nozzle used as an enema nozzle. Her dread of sexual relations returned, and the bearing-down pain and dragging sensations and heaviness in the legs grew worse. The analysis of the horror of intercourse led to the discovery of unconscious phantasies of strangling, squeezing, and 'nipping' her husband's and father's penis; any activity of the pelvic floor was sufficient to evoke these terrible thoughts, whether the activity was in sexual intercourse or in the contraction of the pelvic muscles when at stool. She felt it 'terribly wrong' to move these parts in any way, actively or passively. They suffered from a hysterical paresis. This may account for the beginning of the prolapse, but it does not explain one feature of her response to it. After the purpose of the treatment with pessaries became clear to her, she felt convinced that treatment would do her no good, for, as analysis showed, she saw in the descent of the uterus the possibility of obtaining a protruding genital which she had envied in her brother. The gynaecologists' efforts were being defeated by an unconscious wish, or rather several: the need for self-punishment expressed in the continuance of the pains, 'which were like labour pains' (and like them gratifying to the unconscious!) and by the cancellation of the castration-complex by growing the coveted organ herself. The case is interesting because it shows that in a branch of medicine where physical factors are usually regarded as providing a complete explanation of the condition, psychological factors prove to be of great importance. Are there other departments of the subject where psychical factors may be added to the aetiology of a 'physical' disorder?

No one acquainted with psycho-analysis doubts the hysterical basis of vaginismus, which is one of the most striking examples of lack of psycho-sexual adaptation to a partner. But in the whole period of pregnancy we find hysterical manifestations, vomiting in the early months and 'false alarms' at imagined parturitions in the later ones. We are therefore led to examine parturition itself to see what neurotic manifestations may be found there. But first a word on normal labour. The uterine contractions exert a force proportional to the resistance of the lower genital canal; 'the perineum is able to bear all the force instinctively exerted without injury', as Denman[1] wrote nearly

[1] Thomas Denman: *An Introduction to the practice of Midwifery*, London, Sixth edn., 1829, p. 135.

a hundred years ago; but if the woman, from excitement or from pain, begins to use all her force to end the labour speedily we know that there is grave risk of laceration of the perineum. At this juncture, if the diagnosis of a normal presentation has been made, and the course has been regular, the obstetrician begins to render active assistance, he calms the patient and directs her when to exert force and when to desist. In other terms, he supplies the allo-erotic element required to make a unified psycho-sexual response to the genital stimulus. For this reason no doubt many women who would choose a gynaecologist of their own sex prefer a male obstetrician. Some women in labour behave 'hysterically', as the saying goes, they exert their force at the wrong time and do not respond to the advice of the physician, they do not take the tempo of their voluntary exertions from the rhythm of the uterine contractions nor from the bidding of their obstetrician. The sexual element in the situation, the genital relation to a father-imago, places a greater strain on the super-ego than it will bear, the patient loses touch with him in the act of birth as she did with his forerunner, the husband, at the time of conception, and, disregarding injury and extra pain, she behaves regressively, expelling the child, as she expels faeces, with force and without delicacy. One writer[1] has found a correlation between laceration of the perineum 'abnormal resistance', and vaginismus, one which supports the theoretical view here put forward.

In a preliminary and short communication these remarks must suffice to indicate a new field of work awaiting exploration. In conclusion a quotation from a gynaecologist:[2] Wir alle empfinden es als unwissenschaftlich diagnostisch, von einem Tumor zu sprechen, erst die Art des Tumors gibt der Diagnose wissenschaftlichen Untergrund, aber wir scheuen uns nicht, von nervösen von nervös labilen und hysterischen Frauen zu reden, ohne auch nur den Versuch zu machen, den Zusammenhang zwischen diesen psychischen Abnormalitäten und dem Genitaltraktus feiner zu analysieren.' With the delicate scientific pro-

---

[1] Jean Antoine Remy Fétis: 'Des Ruptures de la cloison rectovaginale au cours de l'accouchement. Leurs rapports avec la résistance anormale de périnée et le vaginisme'. Thèse de Bateau, 1923.

[2] Professor Wilhelm Liepmann: Vortrag vor der 18. Versammlung der Deutschen Gesellschaft für Gynäkologie. *Archiv. für Gynäkologie*, 1923, Bd. 120, S. 271.

cedure devised by Professor Freud—the analysis of the transference in the psycho-analytical situation—a beginning has been made in the analysis of the relations between psychical abnormality and the disorders of the genital tract.

III
DISCUSSION ON LAY-ANALYSIS[1]
(1927)

1. Terms of reference
2. The requirements of analytic work
3. General educational principles
4. Legal aspects
5. Administrative
6. General considerations

1. *Terms of Reference*

(i) To enquire what pre-analytical educational standard should be required: and

(ii) What administrative measures will be needed if lay-analysis is to become a recognized professional activity.

2. *The Requirements of Analytic Work*

Analysis is at bottom a technique by which the analyst is able to investigate the mind of another person (by means of a modified introspection) and the patient to perceive, and so to control forces operating in himself which were formerly inaccessible to his consciousness. The difference between the two people lies in the superior power of the former to set aside resistances and to operate with smaller quantities of cathexis:[2] the aim of the analysis is to give to the patient in this respect the capacities of his analyst.

The aim in the education of the analyst is two-fold, first, to overcome his own resistances (this requires a personal analysis), and secondly, to develop his power to perceive the relations between objects existing in the outer and inner world respectively, i.e. first, to remove a libidinal inhibition, and secondly, to develop the capacity of an ego- (intellectual) instinct. In

[1] Reprinted from the *International Journal of Psycho-Analysis* (1927), **8**, 207–12.

[2] I.e., to perceive the beginning of the development of an impulse instead of having to wait till it develops sufficient force to overcome the resistance.

Ferenczi's terminology, we might say that both ends of the psychical function need to be dealt with, the genital and the intellectual. It is not sufficient that either one alone be the object of the educationalist's care; love forges bonds with the outer world and promotes action, whereas thought forges no bonds and promotes no action, but opens up endless new combinations of relationships without doing anything with them (Ferenczi's 'unconscious reckoning-operations'—'an auxiliary organ of the sense of reality'). A properly functioning mind oscillates between the libidinal and ego-cathexis, between an introjection of the outer-world guided by love followed by an unconscious process in which the introjected material is split up into its elements, these are joined by other memory presentations and recombined, the recombinations are sorted and finally delivered for preconscious and conscious reality testing. What is of importance here is that two quite different mental functions are involved. The analysis of the candidate effects removal of affective inhibition without adding to the intellectual function. [1]

It may be asked if there is anything in the intellectual sphere comparable in effectiveness with analytic solution of neurotic and characterological conflict and defect, and whether it is not vain to expect anything valuable to be done to the intellect after, say, the onset of the latency period; and if there is really nothing comparable in effectiveness with the analytic work on the libido, the question arises whether any preliminary educational standard is necessary at all, whether a peasant's mother-wit would not—if 'analytically' free—meet the needs of practice. The putting of this last question brings forward a new point, namely, that the pre-analytical educational standard is desired not so much that the candidate shall come well stored with facts of knowledge as that he should have had experience in handling data and of the methods employed in weighing evidence. But to return to an earlier question, whether any education can do for the intellectual function what analysis can do for the libidinal. The answer being in the negative leads to a fresh question, whether it matters what direction the previous education has taken. The answer here clearly involves early

[1] It may be urged that the candidate can watch the mind of his analyst at work, and that this must not be forgotten as a feature of intellectual education, but the transference disturbs this to the very end of his analysis, so it should be neglected in an educational scheme.

libidinal as well as intellectual preoccupations (e.g. theology and the Oedipus complex, medicine and sadism, chemistry and the anal stage, mathematics and narcissistic omnipotence). The moment the matter is put in this way it is obvious that as far as the libidinal aspect goes no logical rule can be formulated since theology is the least and mathematics the most scientific of the representatives just mentioned.

Our attention is turned to the purely intellectual aspects of pre-analytical education, and, always assuming that some standard is necessary, we may ask what are the criteria of desirability between say a training in science, classics, modern languages, literature or history. The criterion lies in the attempt made in the various mental disciplines in question to overcome the omnipotence phase of ego-development. Only in science is this found as a predominating characteristic, accompanied, it is true, by a tendency to an over-projection of the 'psychical reckoning-machine' as in the psycho-phobia of neurologists. In classics and literature there is no systematic attempt at overcoming this defect. 'Because all the results of science are obtained by a common method they naturally integrate into a homogeneous body of knowledge.' It is of the first importance that the candidate should have experience in the methods of integration in the physical sciences before he undertakes the more complicated study of the mental sciences. Psychoanalysis lies nearer to physiology, biochemistry and morphology, than to the laxer disciplines of literature, art and history. The candidate must, therefore, have taken a decisive step in the direction of scientific method before he can be admitted to the professional ranks of the psycho-analysts. As to the standard required in the science education, it is in conformity with practice elsewhere to require a degree, and this will ultimately have to be insisted on.

3. *General Educational Principles*

The aim of education in medicine is not so much to fit the candidate for the standards of work in general practice current at the time of his matriculation, as to furnish him with an equipment in the various branches that will enable him to follow intelligently work done in any of the 'specialities', not only in the present, but, to some extent, in the future. The same aim must hold in psycho-analysis. Because instincts are threshold phenomena between the psychical and physical, both psychical and physical worlds must be studied systematically. Because myths and dreams are possibly connected with racial history, and because the latter may influence the formation of instinctual and presentational groupings into diseases and symptoms, it is necessary to know something of pre-history, just as a course of zoology and embryology is included in the medical curricula to prepare the mind for meeting anomalies of physical growth. Professional education must always be planned on what may at first seem an unnecessarily elaborate scale, or the practice of the profession will suffer in the long run.[1]

4. *Legal Aspects*

The law in England (i.e. the judgements of the courts in an action at law) confers remarkably few privileges on the medical profession, but those few are precious, the two most important being; (a) the recovery of reasonable fees, and (b) the presumption that acts done in the course of professional work are done in good faith, i.e. without malice. A privilege is never accorded without an obligation, and this in the case of medicine, is less definite. It is probable that at the root of this obligation lies the acceptance and carrying out by the practitioner of the long prescribed course of medical studies, submission to the discipline of a special body appointed for that purpose and maintenance of the current standard of ethics.[2] Before a body of practitioners

[1] Analytical speculations give a clue to the reason for this: where satisfaction is allowed to run hot on the heels of impulse there is small chance of anticathexis having scope for its culturally beneficent work.

[2] Mrs. Riviere, who was shown the MS., comments on this paragraph as follows:

' "The obligation" of the medical profession is surely the generally assumed compulsion they are under to render assistance to anyone who needs it, when needed. I cannot see that psycho-analysis will entail this obligation; it is a question therefore whether psycho-analysts will enjoy these two privileges of the general medical profession. They will, of course, have other "obligations" quite as peremptory and disagreeable (e.g. self-effacement and complete disregard of personal reactions while devoting all possible attention to patients' interests, etc.), but when will these self-sacrifices be recognized as worthy of corresponding privileges?'

This is a strong point. I do not, however, think that his First Aid or emergency obligation (which coroners lay stress on) is the qualified man's chief title to his privileges.

of psycho-analysis (not being medically qualified) can claim professional rank, it must be clearly demonstrable that they have already accepted an obligation, and are therefore entitled to the privilege.

When the obligation is recognized, it will be time to start a register, not before.

5. *Administrative*

(a) The administrative measures required within the profession of psycho-analysis would follow the course now being shaped by the British Psycho-Analytical Society and the Institute of Psycho-Analysis;

(b) Those relating to other professions should probably comprise only three rules: (i) there is to be no transfer of patients without the consent of the former practitioner.

(ii) No patient to be undertaken for treatment by a person not medically qualified who has not been examined first by a medically qualified person; and

(iii) Refusal to meet in consultation persons who have not subscribed to a recognized obligation.

(c) The public would get protection from quacks in psycho-analysis; this can only be done if the practice of psycho-analysis is hall-marked as is the practice of medicine, surgery, dentistry, nursing, massage, law, architecture, surveying, accountancy, etc., by instituting a disciplinary body, an obligation and a register.

6. *General considerations*

In psycho-analysis therapy is to be kept sharply distinct from diagnosis; the latter must be left to medically qualified persons.

The question is whether the lay analyst should be classed as a nurse or masseuse, or as a laboratory assistant. In fact, neither of these categories fits, and this makes the matter difficult of comprehension to other professionally minded people. If psycho-analysis were a prescribable treatment like massage, there would be no difficulty; the physician knows a good deal about the anatomy and pathology of the part to be treated, and limits the therapeutic procedure he delegates to a narrowly prescribed process. But psycho-analysis is more like a highly complicated laboratory technique in which investigation of new disturbing factors plays a very large part in the process itself. In addition to this it is a particularly close human relationship (in which it approximates—to continue the analogy mentioned above—to nursing). The administrating bodies will therefore have to recognize all these features and not expect the physician who hands over the case to a lay analyst to be able to prescribe the course of treatment in minutiae, nor is it reasonable nor in the interests of public policy that he should be forbidden to hand on his patients to properly trained persons.

The question comes back again to education: the analyst (whether lay or qualified) has to exert the social tact of a nurse and the intellectual precision of a skilled laboratory technician. The training will therefore have to accord with these requirements, and it may be added that commensurate fees will have to be recognized as reasonable for a lay analyst to charge. He or she must not be pushed to a lower standard of living than is proper to a person of his or her intellectual training and social status. The tendency in nursing now is to raise salaries and improve the grade of candidates; among lay psycho-analysts the standard should be high from the start and maintained at a high level, and the administrative attitude in all professions must not countenance anything tending to lower status or performance.

IV

ON SOME OF THE STANDPOINTS OF FREUD AND JUNG[1]

(1928)

AT the 'Debate'[2] on 'The Standpoints of Freud and Jung' I employed my time in exposition of the discoveries of Freud and took occasion to remark that he had no viewpoint peculiar to himself but worked on that shared by scientists generally, namely, determinism. In science this same determinism they now say fails to explain some events in the atom, so we must now modify our dogmatism or rather dogmatic attitude—born of long success—and say that determinism is *not* now the one and only standard of science; but returning to the non-determined events in the atom, one wonders how they would have been discovered without a long application of determinist methods, so, for the sake of the future of science (to reduce the chances that people may erringly say a thing is not determined when it is) it behoves us all to work on with the determinist principle, counting it no loss but a gain if by our own efforts we are proved mistaken sometimes and thereby a philosopher is made happy.[3]

At the debate before mentioned the topics centred about sexuality. In his *Elaboration* Dr. Baynes has put his finger on the most important matter of *transference* on which I confess to have laid too little stress in my exposition. In this phenomenon the Freudian sees evidence of an automatic repetition of infantile attitudes expressing both a desire for sexual gratification and an inhibiting impulse (conscience—also acting automatically).

[1] Reprinted from the *British Journal of Medical Psychology* (1928), **8**, 44–8.

[2] A Debate on the Standpoints of Freud and Jung, held at the British Institute of Philosophical Studies on October 11, 1927, by H. G. Baynes and John Rickman.

[3] In his definition of science (p. 14) Dr. Baynes omits an exceedingly important element, if not the most important, namely the *principle of minimum hypothesis*. My chief complaint against Jung and his school is that they are in haste to introduce hypotheses with the largest possible scope and are negligent of hypotheses that are designed to explain particular groups of *otherwise unrelated* mental events.

What brings about the misery in the patient is that both these things (desire and inhibition) are acting at cross purposes and both are unconscious, the effect being to prevent the individual from obtaining complete discharge of instinct tension. I believe there is not a word of this description at which Dr. Baynes would cavil, though he and I might differ as to the emphasis to be laid on this or that point. But he would say it did not express enough, it did not for instance take account of a synthesizing element in the psyche. It does not, but of that later. In addition he notes in the relationship of physician and patient that 'new vibrations deeper than the personal are brought into play' (*vide* p. 25). On this matter I am not prepared with evidence as I have myself not experienced anything 'beyond' personal relationships (I count my relationships to myself—narcissism, self-love—as personal), but it would surprise me if these deeper than personal vibrations, if such exist, were not of the order of events in the atom, i.e. events of which we can have opinions but no knowledge till an analysis of mind has been carried into the region of the infinitesimal, which is the province of those analysts of matter, the mathematical physicists. Dr. Baynes should count the Freudians as his allies in bringing him a hope of definiteness in regard to these extra-personal relationships, just as he should regard the old school physicists as his helpers in establishing his non-determinism on an extra-philosophical basis.

In the *handling of the transference* the Freudian and Jungian methods stand in the strongest contrast. Every action of the patient in the phase of transference represents to the Freudian a repetition in action of an impulse once experienced psychically. It is the analyst's task to bring this to the patient's attention and get him to recollect the earlier psychical experience, in other words, something in the past has to be found to *match* the present experience. It follows from this that the less the analyst shows himself or his personality, the more he is a blank screen on which the patient may project his phantasies, the more exact will be the reproduction of the old experience. It will also be noted that the analyst has to do no more than detect and match two things produced, a new mental experience (centring on himself) and an old one (centring on some person in the patient's past). His self-effacement has to be as complete as possible in order that the patient's own characteristics may be thrown out in the strongest light.

B

The Jungian analyst, if I interpret Dr. Baynes aright, plays a different rôle. He knows where the 'buried treasure' lies hidden, i.e. in the 'collective unconscious', and he can put the patient in touch with it; furthermore, the patient knows of the analyst's power to do this, and his dependence on the analyst is a result of the latter's superior knowledge of these sources of power, just as a passenger is dependent on the aeroplane pilot who steers him over the Himalayas (p. 28). The stress falls here on the knowledge of the pilot and the ignorance of the passenger; but knowledge and ignorance of what? And what constitutes the difference between the two persons? We will take the latter question first. Dr. Baynes holds that the neurotic lacks a goal or value in life, so presumably—since the blind do not lead the blind—the analyst has a goal or value which he can communicate, and this leads us back to the first question, namely, the thing of which there is knowledge. I believe it resolves itself into a mystical experience, a sense of communication between person and person through extra-personal channels, namely, through the person and presence of God (the Creative Force of the *élan vital* school, a supreme psychic value, according to Dr. Baynes) in whose keeping lies the Future Determination of present events. If this rendering of Jung's position is correct, it becomes at once apparent that his view is separated from Freud's by the widest of gulfs, for the latter can at best promise the patient a limited improvement (namely, that which can result from straightening the patient's past entanglements) whereas the former (Jung) offers him the unlimited possibility of attuning himself to the Collective Unconscious, the medium through which the Divine is made manifest.

In the Freud-Ferenczi theories the mind is conceived as divisible into two polarities—the ego or integrating part which is in touch with the outer world, and the id (libidinal in Freud's narrower, not Jung's wider sense) which is instinctual, has no particular integrating quality and is not directly in touch with the outer world. Dr. Baynes lays stress on the psycho-analysts' preoccupation with the libido and overlooks the great importance which they attach to the ego functions. For instance, the notion of the transference as an *automatic* repetition of past experiences is derived from the interpretation of the ego's part in the business. The integrating functions of the ego are, in psycho-analytic practice, not found susceptible of direct influence, the most that can be done being to remove hindrances to their action. 'Psycho-synthesis' in the Jungian sense is not practised because no one has yet found a way of doing it (or if he has he has not published his technique). The synthetic power of the ego manifests itself in transference in the form of *inactions* rather than actions, its failure is most clearly seen in the neurotic subservience to infantile claims for indulgence in the transference, where 'reality-testing' and adaptation are of secondary importance to repetition and infantile pleasure-gain, just as they were subservient during the patient's illness. So the analyst abstains from playing an active rôle of protector, guide or father-imago, not only in order that the correctness of the patient's phantasies may the more easily be assayed, but in order also to force him to try for himself to achieve his own adaptations to life and to instinctual outlet. Another reason for the analyst's non-interference in the patient's life has also a reality-basis. He *does not know* what is best for the patient, not even after the most extensive analysis. He may know what will be bad for him, he may surmise which of two may be better, but in the end the patient has to carry out the job of living for himself, and the more he relies on his own resources the better. From first to last the analyst has one goal before him, to make the patient aware of himself, not to make him aware of the good, the true or the beautiful, not God or Humanity, but only himself. If he achieves a knowledge of God or of ultimate things, that is the patient's concern, and it may possibly be to his gain—one never knows—but it cannot be a duty of his analyst's. To the analyst there are no 'germinal realities' (p. 27) but only practical ones, because the work of analysis is to relieve the patient of practical hindrances which he must be got to understand, by means which he must be got to understand. Freud's ideal is to let the patient leave the analysis understanding the seriousness of the illness from which he suffered and how he came to suffer from it, to the same extent that he (Freud) understands it. It is a joint piece of work, both being at the end equally master of it. Jung's I gather is different: it is to lead the patient to the less definite goal of apperception of the extra-personal sources of power. On this difference I shall make two comments and then close my part of the discussion: first I regard the Jungian method as depreciative not of human personality in general but of the *particular* personality under treatment, because it divides attention between what the person brings with him and what the Jungian analyst sees or thinks he sees of God, of ultimate things, of the Collective Unconscious. If these high things are ascertainable by one mortal (the analyst) who is freed from his fixations, they are potentially ascertainable by the patient too *after* he is freed from his fixations. If these views about God and the Collective Unconscious are a myth, themselves a sign of infantile thinking and emotional fixation, to bring them into the analysis is only to perpetuate the infantile. My second comment is that the Freudian method is more precise than the Jungian in that it attempts to match present transference phenomena with past mental experiences; the Jungian on the other hand I gather attempts to match the present phenomena of transference with future mental experiences, which is far more ambitious. I regard the former as the occupation of the scientist, the latter as the prerogative of the Deity. The followers of Jung divide their interest between the actual personality of the patient under treatment and the indefinite entity of the Collective Unconscious or God or whatever it may be called, and this I myself hold to be a depreciation of *human* personality. In contrast to Dr. Baynes I further believe that it is the determinism of the Freudians which leads them to an *exclusive* attention to the *person* they are treating, since with this 'dogma' to guide them they have nowhere else to look but to the patient's past experiences for an explanation of the symptoms and modes of behaviour.

Finally, whether Dr. Baynes is right or wrong about 'new beginnings which are not historically determined', 'new vibrations deeper than the personal,' and the like, he will never *know* that he is right (as distinct from *believing* that he is right) without the labours of the Freudians or others with more exact methods. Freud is not infallible, but without work by his method it will not be possible to *demonstrate* that Jung is right. If such methods of verification are of no particular interest to the followers of Jung, they should unequivocally announce their view-point as extra-scientific, and then if they acknowledge their work to be religious they will have made a step toward definiteness for which the world will be grateful.

V
ON QUOTATIONS[1]
(1929)

1. Introduction
2. Three motives for making a quotation. Quotation and hypnosis. The difference between quotations and examples. The first quotation. Virtuosity in quotation. Exhibiting a new idea as a quotation. Compulsive quotations. Quotations in dementia praecox. Compilations. Improving quotations. Parody. Priggishness. Plagiarism, open and concealed. The aversion from quoting. The acceptance of quotation. Mimicry
3. Conclusion

1. *Introduction*

SOME years ago I entertained the hope of being able to make the analysis of quotations from poets and novelists, but particularly from poets, into a new instrument for literary criticism. Lines are quoted to us that have impressed themselves on the minds of our analysands and are brought forward in a setting of associations which is usually free from the peculiar self-conscious atmosphere which aesthetic criticism frequently both generates and wilts in. My hope was that a significant connection would be found between the quotations from the great poets and important features in the patients' infantile experiences, but though I had a 'run of luck' in this respect which nearly evoked a paper for the British Psycho-Analytical Society, my evidence over a longer period gave me no ground for thinking that we have in the correlation of quotations and recollections of early experiences an index of the poet's merit as it is usually judged. Owing to over-determination in the selection of passages it has not been possible to separate the aesthetic merits, the personal associations to the content, the respect for the poet and the mood or tone of the poem of which a part is quoted from one another with sufficient distinctness to form the basis for a

[1] Reprinted from the *International Journal of Psycho-Analysis* (1929), **10**, 242–8.

definite statement. While disappointed that my curiosity about the content of the quotation and its relation to the patient's mind did not lead in the direction expected, I found more scope for inquiry when attention was turned to the occasions when a quotation is used.

2. *Three Motives for Making a Quotation*

When we suspend the train of our own thoughts in order to introduce those of another person we may well ask ourselves what motive we have for abandoning for the time being the pleasure in exploiting our own ideas. The motives can be reduced to three, either to win over a listener or reader, or to overwhelm him, or through fear to conceal from him what we are really thinking; or in terms of the pleasure-pain theory of mental action the pleasure derived is due to the fact that the sense of helplessness is averted; we have risen to the occasion, albeit with the help of another. Just as the dream representing our wishes as fulfilled ministers to our need for the illusion that all is right with us and our world, so the quotation restores the sense of control over a situation that has been in danger of passing out of our grasp.

If we study the motives which give rise to the quotation we generally find that they are mixed in any given case; for instance when our patients quote Freud they are as a rule really thinking, 'I dare not knock you on the head but I can say that Freud says . . .' and thus they try to overwhelm us, and at the same time they conceal their own opinion about us and Freud and analysis. Again we find Freud quoted by psycho-analysts to each other, sometimes to win over, sometimes to overwhelm the listener. We may go further, and following Ferenczi compare the two motives, which often give character to the tone in which the words are uttered, with the two types of hypnotists' behaviour according as it approximates to the father-identification (commanding, severe and abrupt) or to the mother-identification (persuasive, soft and long-suffering). The outstanding difference between the hypnotist and the person who quotes is that the hypnotist exploits a father- or mother-identification which he himself makes quite unconsciously, whereas the person quoting is fully aware that he is taking upon himself the words of another; they are alike in that they are neither of them aware that these identifications are made to enable them to escape from psychical embarrassment, the hypnotist not venturing to be naive with his patient through fear of him, and the speaker or writer not allowing himself to know that he has got out of his depth.

Just as the psychological processes of hypnotism are not fully comprehensible without a study of the mind of the patient, so those of the person quoting are not to be understood without considering the listener; the important common factor in all four persons is found in the survival of the positive libidinal bond between parent and child in the unconscious. To make this point clearer it will be necessary to consider the differences between a quotation and an example. The example is drawn from life, is usually objectively verifiable and invites further inspection; it suspends the train of the speaker's thoughts only to give greater strength to his ideas and has the purpose of leading the listener back to his own experience of the outer world. A quotation has none of these qualities inherently; I admit that the distinction is sometimes hard to draw, as, for example, when in a medical paper someone else's published case-records are used to illustrate the topic treated; the main difference is that the essence of an example lies in its close relation to objective experience, of a quotation in its dependence on transference.[1]

Those whose experience in early life has led to a restriction in the disposition of their libido are particularly susceptible in many cases to a like regressive flow of interest in others, for though such regression may be attended by painful consequences it is better than supporting the discomforts and dangers of completely free libidinal desire; thus we find patients whose

[1] When discussing the topic of transference in this connection with Major Daly, he suggested that at first quotations were confined to the classics, using this in its widest sense of the Early Fathers, the Vedas, Holy Writings and Holy Sayings. This is probably correct and can be verified. If we throw up the reins and let imagination go gallop we may suppose that the first quotation was made when that ancestor (unknown but yet beloved by psycho-analysts), the youthful male of the pre-human horde, approached a group of females in the night. If he let his footfalls be the only herald of his approach they might regard him merely as one of those pestering youngsters whom they could box on the ears, but if he imitated the guttural and determined notes of his sire he prepared their minds for a submission which may have spared him in the moments preceding his triumph considerable physical effort.

capacity for libidinal satisfaction is restricted are pleased either to succumb to or to resist the advances of the hypnotist, whereas those without castration anxiety and parental fixation find in his performances something odd and objectively interesting; in the same way those who are interested in a subject without restriction of imagination are not intrigued by citations from authorities but treat them as they treat everything—objectively. Some essayists are prized for their virtuosity in poetical quotations, the present explanation being that those who admire these exhibitions of scholarly discrimination prefer in their authors a guidance along paths made safe by inhibition rather than the impassioned leading of vigorous and original minds. In everyone there is something which beckons out the quotation as a relief from the strain of attending to ideas that are new, just as in everyone there is a pleasure in behaving like a child; but in most people there is a critical faculty which demands that the quotation shall be good enough to justify the temporary relinquishing of a current personal relationship, just as there is in most a critical faculty causing a doubt whether the pleasure of being treated as a child (being hypnotised) could compensate for the loss of adult relationships.

We may note in passing a widespread habit in social intercourse of congealing the free-flowing stream of conversation with a story; sometimes these narrations are prefaced with the name of the author, whereupon we are supposed to become immediately submissive; sometimes they recur and recoil with such frequency that the talk turns into a battledore and shuttlecock game, called 'capping yarns', and, as a game, is a substitute for the serious work of love-making or aggression; it is a sign of mental embarrassment when it becomes compulsive. Orientals are particularly prone to this form of conversation. In 'milder' cases of dementia praecox we occasionally find our every approach to the patient met with a quotation, a sign of supreme embarrassment. I think they are mistaken who regard these patients as having had their personality destroyed by the disease; the sufferers may be saying in this instance, 'I do not think you are worth talking to,' or else (less embarrassing to our vanity unless we are analysts), 'Such is my fear of betraying my inner feelings to the cold winds of your criticism that I prefer to hide my thoughts behind this mask of quotation,' or else they may be saying, 'Since my gestures, which you call stereotypes, and my persistent statements, which you call verbigeration, are not intelligible to you, take this quotation, which is not mine, into your consciousness and try to perceive that in spite of all your denseness and my pain I am trying to communicate with you.'

The readiness to take a deferential attitude to quotations is made use of by young or timid persons when they put forward their own ideas or epigrams in the disguise of quotation marks. Such action clearly comes under the third category of motives mentioned above—to conceal the writer's own thoughts or at least to conceal their paternity. A variant of this trick (having analogy with concealed plagiarism) is for a compiler of other people's ideas slyly to introduce some of his own thoughts into his Summary; in this way he can get a respectful attention to his views without having to stand up to the dangers of isolated statement. Thus the aggressiveness of the public and the scrutiny of critics and reviewers, which is always ready to spring up in the presence of youth or weakness, is tricked out of its satis-faction, and the author can hold up the world to secret ridicule by exploiting the hunger adults display for repeating nursery attitudes in place of intellectual objectivity.

At the opposite pole to this rather impudent way of dealing with our weakness for quotation is the trick some conversation-alists employ to misquote but improve on the original; it can be classed as a trick because by beginning with well-known words we are reduced to a more or less uncritical state, and then when weakened by transference a new idea is forced forward for our acceptance. By this device two aims are achieved at one stroke: the speaker has stolen the listener's affection for the author in order to give prestige to an idea of his own, and the author is humbled. It is a risky trick, because the listener may suddenly become vindictively critical of the new idea out of a revived loyalty to the injured author and resent the intrusion.

Another literary trick, which employs displacement of affec-tion from an old to a new author and from a well-known to a new work, is parody; but in parody it is assumed by both writer and readers that no real malice is intended against the author. He may, in a gentle way, be made to look a fool, but he must not be made to say anything contrary to his ego-ideal; for instance, in the parodies of Hiawatha involved and repetitive nonsense can be indulged in to any extent without giving offence on any topic so long as it is not obscene; for since no one can associate Hiawatha with coarse, salty verse, the parodist must submit to the same censorship as was exercised in the poet's mind when writing the verses. When violence is done to a poet's verses by aggressive sexualization of them the reader is aware, in a peculiarly heightened degree, of the sadism of the parodist's game. However, the chief mark of parody is that it is quotation turned back on the person quoted with an ironical comment, as if the parodist said, 'I and all my readers really think this of you, that you deserve not to be taken so seriously, that you are nearly the clown these unflattering imitations make you out to be.[1] The parodist leads an attack on the author which we are ready enough to follow; he expresses for us, but not too sharply, a resentment at having to acknowledge the superiority of the poet, the boldness and openness of the attack shielding us from any too conscious acknowledgement of humiliation at our perpetual submission before the masters of our language. It is quite otherwise with plagiarism, which excites the anger of the public nearly as much as parody excites its admiration.

Plagiarism is of two kinds, the open and concealed. In the open kind one author takes the expressions or ideas of another without acknowledgement; the concealed kind is technically not plagiarism at all, i.e. acknowledgement is made, but in a half-hearted way, by footnote or by a slight reference. Both are psychologically related to that character-trait of never under any circumstances quoting at all; the plagiarist does not want to quote either, but his painful sense of the weakness of his own ideas compels him to snatch those of another; for even though he will be disgraced if caught the impulse to win the admiration of his public overrides all his fears. It is literary kleptomania, the impulse being to steal something symbolic of the genital in order to restore the illusion of potency.

The case of the person who refuses to quote others at all betrays a great but unconscious submission to authority; the defiance is determined not by a wish to overmaster the authority,

---

[1] I sometimes wonder whether those extremes of 'good' behaviour, the priggishness of childhood and sententious moral uprightness of adult life, are not maintained with such enduring zeal because these exhibitions are regarded by the unconscious as loud-voiced parodies of parental injunction. Parents too can enjoy the parody so long as they are not aware that it is parody, hence grotesquely priggish behaviour can go on for generation after generation.

but to avoid contact with him. The fear of being passive accentuates in consciousness an activity in the direction of originality that is not sustained by object-love (desire for the mother, to win the approval of the public), but by object-dread (fear of the father). This type of personality may be set off against that of the individual who is willing, i.e. not afraid, to use quotations, namely, one who is concerned before everything to present his thoughts clearly, one who can tolerate a temporary dependence on another person without dreading to lose his individuality for ever. It bespeaks a degree of objectivity which castration[1] anxiety never permits, an objectivity extending even to the self. It is after all no disgrace to be out of one's depth in the realms of thought or to acknowledge the need for help in expression as well as classification of ideas; those who are fortified by an unshattered or restored self-confidence do not anticipate with dread moments of helplessness.

We find in mimicry a theme related closely to quotation, but with the accent laid on the personal attributes of the original, not on what he has written. It presupposes an affectionate relationship between the original and the audience, but not an unrestricted awe. As in the case of parody, we rise by identification with the mimic to a point of almost equal strength with that great being whom once we dreaded.[2] Further, we are pleased by the physical courage of the mimic who dares in his own person to challenge the powerful with his ridicule; but we are quick to detect in the mimicry the signs of disarming submission and resent the spoiling of aesthetic pleasure which that involves. Masochism spoils more otherwise good art than does sadism. We always demand of the histrionic artists who amuse us the high courage we lack in ourselves—to submit our bodies to the ravages of emotional passion without yielding up our independence.

[1] I have constantly to remind myself that repetition of a word never clarifies and usually diminishes its meaning; I think, as regards myself at any rate, that this caution is particularly necessary with such technical terms as castration-anxiety, castration-complex, castration-wish, castration-threat, etc.; and I suspect when I use them that I am making a pretence at being care-free and bold in using the most terrifying thought in the psycho-analytical armamentarium when really my mind is dodging its only duty, viz., plain thinking.

[2] Mimicry of the weak arouses the reactions of anger and pity, anger at the mimic and pity for its victim.

Those who dare not mimic for fear of being thought mere weak imitators are not at peace in themselves; they fear to betray a restriction of libido-disposition because for them to acknowledge imitation is to admit their mental slavery to a past defeat.

3. *Conclusion*

It is usual to try to authenticate a psycho-analytical paper by stiffening the thin framework of the ideas contained with an accretion of technical terms or else to give scraps of case-histories to which the theories refer. I have no apology to make in this paper of all others for not quoting more technical terms, which I regard in the present stage of psycho-analytical development as too frequently a hindrance to clear thinking; and, in respect to the analytical case-material on which this paper is based, as I have drawn it from a source that is likely to be more convincing to myself than to anyone else I shall give no details— the person concerned is myself.

VI

THE PSYCHOLOGY OF CRIME[1]
(1932)

THE discussion has brought out three points which we commonly meet with when lawyers and other intelligent laymen consider crime: first their surprise that the criminal cannot give a reasonable explanation for his act, secondly the compulsive element in crime, and thirdly that criminals often do not in fact appear to be so aggressive as they are commonly regarded by the general public. On each of these points the psycho-pathologist is ready with an explanation, though from the nature of the case it is not very convincing to those who have not his special opportunity for investigation.

As to the first two points, they are shared with the neurotic, who also cannot explain his peculiar behaviour, which is often also compulsive; for our present purpose the centre of interest attaches to the third point; something peculiar has happened to the criminal in connection with his aggressive impulse.

If we view the criminal not in respect to his place in society but as a person with a peculiar way of dealing with his instinctual energies, he appears to us to be endeavouring by his acts to rid himself of an almost unbearable internal tension; his crimes, viewed in this way, are attempts at relief from the intolerable and because they serve this (to him) useful and apparently remedial purpose the criminal views with suspicion those who want to treat him for his criminality. The intolerable mental tension is not due to a simple increase of aggressiveness or destructiveness, but to a weakening of the controlling part of the mind and an incapacity to temper this aggressiveness by admixture of the impulse of love. The love impulse is present in every case and this gives rise to the conflict from which they suffer. We can revise the previous formula and say that the criminal endeavours by his act to solve an intolerable internal conflict,

[1] Reprinted from the *British Journal of Medical Psychology* (1932), **12**, 264–9, the fourth of five articles on the 'Psychology of Crime', the other articles being by T. S. Good, H. A. Field, T. Christie and E. Glover.

adding that he is literally unaware of the true nature of that conflict.

In the search for the true nature of that conflict the psycho-pathologist looks for a representative situation in the life of the individual which contained elements of all subsequent experiences and all subsequent inhibitions; the situation must not be a theoretical schematic construction but an actual experience shared in its main features by everyone, yet capable of individual differences; his aim must be a scientific not an *ad hoc* explanation.

Such a situation is found in the triangular relationship of father, mother and son in early childhood, commonly referred to as the Oedipus situation; the boy must learn to endure separation from his mother and the renunciation of libidinal gratification from her, and endure frustration at the hands of his father without becoming too rebellious or too submissive; he must experience frustration without distortion of desire and without apprehension. If the early experience referred to could be apprehended by a child in its second, third or fourth years with emotional detachment, the task of the psycho-pathologist would be an easy one, but the child cannot be detached. His emotional world is principally made up of the relationship of these two persons to one another and to him, and is based on his conception of their behaviour in their most intense moments, i.e. in sexual intercourse. His conception of the world is not a true picture but a composite of what actually exists in his home and his own instinctual urges. This mixing-in of his own instincts is exceedingly important, and shows us how the aggressive element in the criminal distorts his life, viz. by preventing him from having a belief in love and tenderness as a trustworthy and permanent bond between persons and towards work.[1] It is found in every one that the conception of personal relationships undergoes profound changes during development, at one time it is dominated by sadism, only later is it established on a basis of tenderness. The importance to the child of wise and wholesome parents is not least that they give him an opportunity to pass through the sadistic stage without guilt (which they cannot do if they deny the same in themselves) or without confirming him in the suspicion that there is really nothing but brutality in the world; and an objection to a bad home is not

[1] An appendix (A) touching on this matter is printed at the end of this paper.

only that it inculcates bad habits but that it facilitates the retention of sadistic phantasies.

But sadistic phantasies and bad homes are the lot of many neurotic and unhappy persons; the central feature of the criminal's life is a split in his mind,[1] not in the sense of two organized personalities as in the famous case of Sally Beauchamp, but rather in the more circumscribed field of instinct discharge. One part appears normal and deals adequately with relatively small amounts of libidinal or aggressive excitement; thus the criminal can often get through school and even apprenticeship fairly well but breaks down when in the open field of competition: from the exercise of this normal part comes his conscious enjoyment of life. Of the other part he is wholly unconscious (for the reason that it is associated with his most painful memories) and this is concerned with two peculiar and powerful modes of instinct discharge, the direct and the indirect. In the direct mode of discharge the criminal, feeling himself to be in a world of violent people, and all relationships to be basically violent, meets the dangers which he phantasies to be about him by violence, either to persons, property or society. In the indirect mode of discharge the criminal tries to master the vehemence of his instincts not by attack upon others but by utilizing their aggressiveness against himself, i.e. by getting himself punished; his mind is obsessed by the need for punishment,[2] not for wrongs which he has actually done, but for what he unconsciously regards as his wrongful tendencies. Many neurotic persons suffer from a compulsion to manipulate the circumstances of their environment so that their lives are wrecked and thwarted; the criminal of this type differs from them in that what he rouses against himself is more sadistic in character, he differs from the 'compulsive dupe' in that the means to his goal gratify his phantasies of sexual activity, whereas those of the dupe's are passive.

Emphasis is laid by the psycho-pathologist on the criminal's failure to integrate the aggressive impulse into the structure of his mental life, and on the fact that the break from the normal path occurred very early in life. This early failure in integration

---

[1] An appendix (B) discussing this assertion is printed at the end of this paper.

[2] The phrase 'need for punishment' is a clinical description rather than an ultimate analysis of a mental state.

is the specific causal factor in crime, and this may be influenced by an hereditary emphasis of the aggressive instinct, or by weakness of the co-ordinating mechanism, or on the other hand it may be due to an unfavourable environment, e.g. lack of love from the parents which hindered or prevented him from realizing that love is a bond in personal and social life which is strong and enduring.

The specific causal factor is to be sharply distinguished from contributory causal factors such as current temptation.

Perhaps the psycho-pathologists' most valuable contribution to the study of crime lies just in this clarification of aetiological factors, for when these are confused the work of the lawyer, eugenist and sociologist is painful, uncertain and wasteful.

Appendix A. Relating to the emotional difficulty which criminals experience in applying themselves to everyday work

In the normal person the discharge of instinctual tension is carried out in the fields of sexual relations and work. Those who have grown up in the belief that love plays a relatively small part in the permanent bonds between persons, usually experience a sensitiveness in respect to their sexual function which the Freudians call 'castration anxiety'. This anxiety (which is not just a conscious dread of the loss of the genitals by amputation or mutilation) is found to have the widest connections in the unconscious mind, and manifests itself among many other ways in dread of having an inferior position or of being given a woman's job.

In everyday work the rôles of male activity and female passivity are combined or alternate, e.g. the employee must submit to the direction of a superior and the executive must go through a productive 'gestation' stage of absorbing ideas from others and devising a policy which does not involve too much compromise—both feminine attitudes; in these cases the male keeps his 'position' and masculine character, however much he may be ordered about in the one case or become a thoughtful organizer in the other. Work therefore requires a pliancy in respect to activity and passivity and a capacity to be swayed from one to the other without the worker developing anxiety. The criminal in many cases lacks this pliancy; he must work alone, he cannot take orders from others or work harmoniously with them. He feels it degrading to be 'bossed about' and soon shows his latent anxiety by either 'chucking his job' or becoming quarrelsome—Adler would call this the 'masculine protest'. Above all, in the case of work the outlet of aggressiveness must be modified to suit the material in hand; this is accomplished in the normal person by fusing aggressiveness with love to form an interest in the task undertaken and a desire to bring it to a successful conclusion. The criminal has little capacity to form this tender relationship to his task, the instinctual excitement in him must come out in massive discharge and often in the relatively pure form of destructiveness; only thus does he feel relief in action, and as the fear of society and the feeling of guilt keep him back from his action as long as possible, the impulse to commit the act is apt to be explosive, it is liable to be repeated because it is never done in freedom from anxiety.

Appendix B. Referring to the assertion that the central feature of the criminal's mind is a split in his mental life

This dogmatic statement, not unsuitable in a ten-minute paper, should not, when time and space allow, go unchallenged. Psycho-pathological theories concerning the specific aetiological factor in criminality may be placed in two groups, those which class it with the neuroses and those which class it with the character traits; there are grave objections to accepting either without qualification.

Criminality as a neurosis. Many criminals are also neurotic; in the days when no neurotic symptom was understood it would have been only natural that that other symptom, the crime, should also be regarded as part of the same disease; though, oddly enough, this view was rarely held then, largely perhaps because the criminal was thought of as wicked, not as ill. His inability to give a rational explanation for his act, combined with the compulsive nature of the deed, appears to place the criminal in the group of obsessional neurotics; in support of this we recall the singular lack of affect which both show, and the fact that in both there is an increase of the aggressive impulse. One objection to this view is that the neurotic substitutes thought for action, whereas the criminal does not. A more deepgoing objection is that the criminal's action appears to be an instinctual outlet without the distortions and the displacements of libido which we observe as the results of repression. Repression has seriously miscarried in these cases; this fact leads us to consider another type of case where repression plays a smaller part than in the neuroses.

Criminality as a character-trait. The character-trait is a stereotyped mode of responding to an external situation on the pattern of behaviour which afforded libidinal gratification at an early stage of development, e.g. the character traits of obstinacy and delay which can be traced to the enhancement of anal excitations by retention of faeces. Such obstinacy is looked on by the ego with pride and not, as in the case of the neurotic, as a symptom acknowledged with regret. So with many criminals their narcissism seems to be bound up with the trait in a particularly strong way, so that they lack insight into it as an abnormality which impedes their progress and impairs their happiness.

Reverting to the notion of a split in the mind, it might be represented more accurately by saying that in the development of the child a change occurred when sensory experience was interrupted by shock or unbearable terror; from that time onwards one part of the personality remains fixed to the experience of that episode with its highly narcissistic character and with the jealousies and pains of the Oedipus situation unsolved and perpetually rankling, the other part 'carries on' with development but it has a more shadowy nature; the sense of actuality in respect to the operations of this other part is never complete, it makes an apparently satisfactory adjustment to life but the patient is more obviously 'strange' to outside observers than is his behaviour strange to himself—he lacks insight.

This notion reintroduces the concepts of fixation and dissociation in a way rather different to their early use by Freud, and is taken from the recent views of Ferenczi. Dissociation is usually regarded as an introjection of two different groups of incompatible objects, which come into play alternately or when internal or external conditions change. It is thought to be a rare occurrence, and in the Sally Beauchamp exaggeration it is, but if we assume that one of the personalities has a very primitive organization, so primitive that it has made almost no introjection of a loved object and that there is almost no super-ego developed (in Professor Freud's use of the word, not Mrs. Klein's—the difference largely being that he uses it in respect to persons and she to 'part-objects') then we have the basis of the 'criminal part' of the criminal's personality. The 'other part' is less connected with the *Me*-feeling and is more pliable, more educable and weaker.

We can, however, view the matter in a more orthodox way and say that the anxiety regarding the phallic phase of the Oedipus situation proving too great, there was an extensive regression to the earlier sadistic satisfaction; this view has a further observation to support it, viz. that aggression is found clinically to save the effort of repression. In all these cases a certain amount of object libido is dealt with after the manner of normal or neurotic persons.

I am aware that traumatism of the ego is now usually classed among the frustrations, and as such I have treated it in the body of the paper, but in its original meaning it should not be omitted as a possibility in these cases. Throughout this discussion of aetiologies one point has not been stressed, viz. that the different factors are seldom incompatible and usually re-enforce one another.

I do not think that the neuroses or psychoses, still less the character cases and epilepsies, will be properly understood until we know more about the 'toughness' and the sensitivity of the ego, and the nature of 'tension' and of shock. Ego psychology lags behind our knowledge of the instincts and of the social responses. This is a private comment for psycho-pathologists; to others I would add that enough is already known to form some estimate of the value of our own work and that of lawyers, eugenists and sociologists.

VII

ON 'UNBEARABLE' IDEAS AND IMPULSES[1]

(1937)

I F at some future date, a student wished to survey the development of psychology in the last fifty years he would find much to guide him from a study of this Journal, which is remarkable not only for its scope but for the fact that it has given an early welcome to so many ideas which have exercised a lasting influence on our science.

Before about 1900, psychology was in the main concerned with the phenomena of consciousness, with introspection and cognition and with such experiments as would throw more light on these problems. The question of pain, when considered at all, was treated as a mode of sensation, it did not include 'mental suffering'. But suffering is to the ordinary man most closely associated with mental phenomena, physical pain is a rare and unwelcome visitor and the victim of it hastens for help or takes care to avoid the occasion of it. In the case of mental suffering the victim does not call in aid till he must, indeed he often seems compelled to take the very path to meet it and even at times to welcome it. It would be hardly an exaggeration to say that to the ordinary man a study of the mind that did not in any great measure deal with the *sufferings* of the mind would be regarded as dealing with an abstraction. This view is not held as a reproach to the psychologist by the ordinary man, for experience shows that the moment that mental pain is the subject of study he takes up a contrary attitude, saying that the topic is being mishandled and emotion is given too great prominence to the belittlement of reason. Another factor which contributes to the difficulties of studying mental pain is indeed a strange one. Though willing enough to speak in general terms of misery as an inevitable part of our human lot or to call an individual 'shallow' or 'inhuman' who has no understanding of mental suffering, yet

[1] Reprinted from the *American Journal of Psychology* (Golden Jubilee Number, 1937), **50**, 248–53.

the moment that this suffering is an object of investigation its victims are regarded as abnormal, for 'psycho-pathology' is thought of as a science of mental disease rather than the study of mental suffering and its deductions are regarded as in no way valid for the normal mind or the normal man, who of a sudden is pictured as guided by reason and predestined to a life of pleasure. Even psychologists have shared these contradictory views.

The rescue of psychology from the predicament is due almost entirely to the work of Freud, who gave an account of his way out of the difficulty in this Journal twenty-eight years ago in 'The Origin and Development of Psycho-Analysis',[1] which was, one is specially glad on this occasion to recall, the first general exposition of psycho-analysis ever published.

Psychologists as a rule not only choose their field of study but can within limits regard the person whose mind they are going to investigate as 'laboratory material'; the research worker is in more or less complete control. In the case of clinical psychology it is otherwise, the person whose mind is to be investigated is usually in a nervous state and does not know what is the matter with him. He resents or is suspicious of 'interference' and yet is driven by mental pain to discuss with his physician the most distressing ideas from which he suffers, much though he would prefer that his mind should be 'let alone'. At first sight the situation seems unpropitious for discovery, and indeed if the psychologist behaves in a clinical situation as if it were a laboratory, that ends the chances of his keeping the 'laboratory material' within view at all—the patient goes to someone who will 'understand him'. That is to say the physician interested in research and the patient interested in relief from suffering appear to pull in opposite directions; the divergence of aim can however be resolved. If the physician keeps one point clear in his technique, things cannot go hopelessly astray, viz. when a patient is told to say anything that comes into his mind, keeping nothing back on grounds of its apparent irrelevance or on any other pretext, there *is* a connection between his associations even though it may not be immediately obvious. The patient on his part will have but little interest in research, and it is invariably found (if the physician does not interfere with the free flow of the patient's ideas) that the patient will keep the personal side of the relation-

[1] *American Journal of Psychology* (1910), **21**, 181–218.

ship to the fore, showing either warm affection or bitter hostility or a mixture of both to the person who is treating him.

Experience shows that if the physician can give equal attention to every manifestation of the patient (friendly or hostile, 'interesting' or 'irrelevant') he will discover that the patient is struggling with 'unbearable' ideas and impulses, and is also struggling with a double tendency, to bring these ideas and impulses into the open at the same time being full of apprehension about doing so. The physician for his part, perhaps not unnaturally, often finds within himself (if he has any capacity for insight) a great aversion to dealing with unbearable ideas and impulses. If he glosses over these or belittles their importance the therapeutic effectiveness of his work falls, and he gets no results in his cures or in his research.

The important field of psychology that deals with unbearable ideas and impulses was no man's choice, therapeutic necessity forced it on the physicians, and one instantly assumes that these ideas and impulses are thrust on the patients by illness. A great deal that is important for the future of psychology hangs on that assumption—it may be wrong.

Research in psycho-pathology does not in essentials differ from other kinds of research; the important thing in every case being the removal as far as possible of the influence of factors which cannot be observed or controlled. The research situation in the case we are considering, which is also a therapeutic one, consists in the patient being given the most favourable opportunity under observation of giving free play to his associations; this means that the physician must keep himself and his own ideas in the background and confine himself to pointing out connections between the patient's ideas which the patient himself fails to observe.

It is found that a situation then arises in which the patient finds himself in an 'unbearable' position. Ideas and impulses come to the mind which are 'intolerable', and a great deal of manoeuvring takes place in order to reduce the mental strain. It is a close observation of this manoeuvring which has made psycho-pathology such a fruitful field of discovery. If the physician's attitude of benevolent detachment is not changed by the behaviour of the patient, i.e. if he can retain his objectivity, a new situation arises. The patient is found to be responding to an *imagined* environment as well as to that which exists objectively, and the imagined environment is conditioned by ideas and impulses which as later work would show belong to the period of the patient's infancy. It is at this point that the investigation usually gets out of hand, the physician often begins to tell his patient that he is not distinguishing between reality and phantasy and that in fact he himself is not as his patient imagines him to be. This may be true objectively but the thing of importance is that the patient has such an idea at the moment about his physician, and that is what has to be explained. No amount of hedging about the 'irrelevance of' a mere transient thought will do in psycho-pathology any more than the mere transience of a flash can be brushed aside when investigating an electrical circuit.

Only if the physician can tolerate the intrusion of these intolerable ideas and impulses into the intricate personal relationship which the patient's attitude creates will he be rewarded with an insight both into their origin and the part they play in the patient's symptoms and mental development.

Clinical View of 'Unbearable Ideas'

If we carefully use the special instrument of clinical research mentioned above for investigating the deep levels of the mind, we find a type of mental function quite different from the conscious adult one,[1] and our present subject—unbearable ideas— takes on a new aspect.

An idea or an impulse is unbearable when it inevitably involves total loss of security. This definition applies both to conscious and unconscious modes of mental function, and it is valid for actual, i.e. objective, and for imagined, or subjective, sources of insecurity or danger. Freud distinguished between fear,[2] where the source of danger is known to the conscious mind, and anxiety where it was not known; in the former case the appropriate response was flight or some manipulation of the external situation (Rivers' 'manipulative activities'), in the latter case no activity directed to the external world removes the source of mental tension.

---

[1] The most concise yet full statement of this is given in 'A General Selection from the works of Sigmund Freud', *Psycho-Analytical Epitomes* (1937), **1**, The Hogarth Press, London.

[2] *Op. cit.*, last section.

The feeling of *mental insecurity* belongs to the latter category of events. If the danger to life (or to what is regarded as precious) is external, the mind is not benumbed—unless for reasons to be given later it is inhibited by the unconscious—and it deals actively with the trouble. The sources of danger which give rise to the 'unbearable ideas' lie in the unconscious. These may be summarized under two headings, loss of satisfaction from the object (due to a change in the object as it is conceived in the unconscious) and loss of the capacity to love (due to a change in the self); either of these will bring about an unbearable situation and the mere thought of it is felt to be intolerable.

We must distinguish carefully between conscious and unconscious modes of object relationship when using this simple formulation; it is not a case of loss of satisfaction from *any* object, but from that object which lies in the focus of the unconscious desire. Our orientation to the problem must be guided by the subject's unconscious phantasy.

If we make use of the researches into the early mental development of the child, for which we are principally indebted to Melanie Klein,[1] we shall have a clearer understanding of the character of loss of relation to the object which is so intolerable.

The infant, whose impulses swing with uncontrolled strength from love to hate and hate to love, is at first oriented to one object—the breast—and this object is loved with a consuming love or is made the point of unbridled attack in its phantasy. In a gust of hate it destroys in its imagination the very object on which its life and its satisfaction in life depends. Its ambivalence and the fact that it is a mouth-governed creature cause its strong impulses to be a source of danger to itself—not in an objective sense but in its phantasy, for imagination begins early. In other words the experience of the small infant leads it to regard its own impulses as dangerous to its security, for in its phantasy-experience, which to it is a part of reality, love and hate both tend to the disappearance of the object of desire.

We are not here concerned with the steps by which the sense of security is built up, but only with the continuing effect in the unconscious of the early dangers to a sense of security. Man's

[1] Melanie Klein, *Psycho-Analysis of Children* (1932), 1–393, The Hogarth Press, London; see also M. Klein and J. Riviere, *Love, Hate, and Reparation* (1937), **2,** The Hogarth Press, London.

behaviour may be described as the resultant of his response on the one hand to the current, objective, conscious situation in which he finds himself and on the other hand to a series of past situations, which are for the most part unconscious but which colour his subjective attitude to his environment; further his response to the present and past situations is determined by two factors, the (external) influence of the environment and his (inner) instinctual forces. There is thus in the adult a double object, the actual objective or conscious one and the image of a past object reactivated in the unconscious; and a double orientation, towards the (external) object, only existent in the present, and towards the (internal) image persisting in the unconscious from the past. It is necessary to consider both if one is to understand the nature of the unbearable, because the threat to the object which causes the intolerable mental pain is in all cases the phantasy of attack upon the image of a 'good' or helpful, i.e. satisfying, object of early experience. The unbearable sense of sin from which the melancholic suffers with such severity is to be explained, not as a remorse for past *deeds*, but as the self-punishment under a load of guilt for *phantasied attacks* upon the person who in the past was most loved, most needed and most hated. In the same way we can trace the sense of utter desolation which afflicts the paraphrenic, that universal chaos and destruction of all good and living things, as the experience (in phantasy revived during the crisis of illness) of those early sadistic phantasies in which the living were bitten up, torn to bits, and annihilated.

The major mental illnesses provide us with the most conspicuous examples of unbearable ideas, but if we carry the analysis of mind to its deeper, i.e. unconscious, levels, we find even in the normal person evidence that he also passed through a period in which he strove with mental pain that proved well nigh unsupportable.

The consequences of these discoveries are likely to be momentous for psychology. In the first place man's colossal appetite for destructiveness is shown in a new light, for though it undoubtedly springs from a destructive impulse, it belongs in the main to a period of development when the instinctual impulses are not integrated. Secondly, man's enormous capacity for guilt is found to be part of a reaction against the destructive tendency, and, thirdly, man's unique capacity for constructiveness is found to be stimulated by a wish (guided by the impulse of love) to restore and re-establish what had been in phantasy attacked and smashed in the phase of unintegrated instinctual expression.

This conception of the part played by unbearable ideas in the development of 'normal' impulses in normal people is of assistance to us in understanding the 'drive' in artists to produce 'eternal' or 'living' works of art. It seems at least likely that the creative impulse is spurred on to even higher achievements by the need to re-establish the sense of 'indestructible life' partly at any rate because of the experience in the (unconscious) phantasy of the unbearable pain caused by the destructive phase.

Postscript

It is gratifying to recall at the time of a Jubilee that within the first decade of the period in question psychology extended its boundary to include territories of the mind cut off from consciousness because the ideas and impulses in that region were unbearable, and now in the last decade of the period we are beginning to understand not only more about mental pain but also to realize that the mind can recover from its travail and use its bitter experience in the construction of its highest and most precious achievements.

VIII
SIGMUND FREUD: A PERSONAL IMPRESSION[1]
(1939)

In Professor Freud two characteristics were present in the highest degree: his friendly simplicity towards one as a human being and the prodigious power of his mind. The combination of these qualities made one feel to be in the company of a new kind of being—an ideal for human nature. Freud accepted his transcendent intellectual gifts as a phenomenon of nature, a thing neither to be personally proud of nor of course concealed; they belonged as much to the universe as to himself. Lesser men might have used such power for their own aggrandisement, but he was immune to the temptation because his protagonists were not his fellows but the obscurities in human nature. The confusion in man's mind was an affront to him and he set about to get to terms with his enemy. Characteristically, and here he gave a lead to his followers and to the world, he turned first to the obscurity of his own mental processes, patiently exploring that seemingly chaotic and unprofitable region—the world of dreams. He always referred to the results of this ten years of labour as a piece of good fortune that was not likely to come twice in a lifetime and seemed to be grateful to the generosity of nature for disclosing to him such valuable secrets. He gave the rest of his life, from about forty onwards, to the detailed working out and consequences of the laws he had in fact himself discovered. That such discoveries were changing the outlook of psychiatry, anthropology and sociology, giving a new understanding of the forces in art and religion, and indeed likely to change the mental outlook of the human race, was but evidence of his good luck to be in at the beginning of a new world of thought. He knew full well the part he had played in bringing about the changes, but never forgot how small was his discovery compared to the infinity of detail and complexity into which some day order must be brought. His unshrinking modesty be-

[1] Reprinted from *The Lancet* (1939), **2**, 813.

fore the vastness of Nature led him to measure the praise of men by a scale that fitted both the framework of our knowledge and the universe of our ignorance. The application of this standard proved discomforting to flatterers—with whom he was not popular.

A personal analysis in his hands was in the fullest sense of the word a joint undertaking. He never moralized nor gave dogmatic instruction but rather showed to the best of his ability what was going on at the moment in the mind and personality that was being studied. He implicitly trusted in good results following from a greater understanding of what is present in human nature. The human mind and human impulses were not of his creating and he found in them neither cause for self-congratulation nor self-reproach. He studied them closely, patiently and with singular lack of prejudice. Though intellectually so detached he was sensitive to every shade of emotional expression and feeling, and with this capacity for receptive understanding went patience which could afford to wait for the development of the best in those whom he held in affection. Intellectual power and constructive imagination in such degree contained within a nature essentially gentle and patient was a revelation of the heights to which the human spirit can attain.

IX
THE GENERAL PRACTITIONER AND PSYCHO-ANALYSIS[1]
(1939)

IN two recent issues of *The Practitioner*[2] some problems connected with psychology in general practice were dealt with. As this is often connected—in the minds of patients, at least—with psycho-analysis, it may be well also to give some account of this subject. The term 'psycho-analysis' was first introduced (Freud, 1896) to indicate a particular kind of treatment of neurotic patients which, although hypnosis was dispensed with, relied on mental means for curing emotional disturbances of the mind. As this was done by a detailed examination of the patient's symptoms, the name came to be applied to the special method employed in the making of this examination; and since these studies resulted in the discovery of a set of data concerning those parts of the mind which are unconscious, the term was employed also for the branch of science which deals with those data. The term 'psycho-analysis' therefore denotes (according to context) a method of treatment, a research technique, or a branch of psychology which deals with a part of the mind more or less inaccessible apart from the special technique. When a patient says, 'I think I need some psycho-analysis,' he may be interpreted as saying, 'There is something bothering my mind, I do not know exactly what it is, but I want it dealt with!' and the practitioner, even though he may not be trained in the technique, should know from this that his patient is referring to, and is worried by, something definite but as yet unplaced, and therefore probably not capable of full solution by ordinary introspection or interrogation.

Early History

The beginning of this work was as follows. In 1880 Breuer, a Viennese physician, was experimenting with methods of treating

[1] Reprinted from *The Practitioner* (1939), **143**, 192–8.
[2] *Psychology in General Practice* (July, 1938), and *Sexual Disorders* (September, 1938).

neurotics. He discovered that if he questioned his patients when under hypnosis about their symptoms, these were found to be related to episodes in the patient's past life which gave rise to them. Further, the symptoms were related only to experiences in the life history of the patient when strong excitement had been roused but had not been dispersed by appropriate action. Investigation showed that in every case there was an alteration of consciousness, viz. the scenes in question were *forgotten* and could not be recalled by conscious effort. The next discovery was that it was not as a rule one episode alone that was traumatic, but a series having the same bearing on the patient's emotional life. Treatment consisted in recalling these scenes and allowing the emotion to become re-attached to them. This 'talking cure' (called a 'mental catharsis') was not a simple process of letting the patient 'talk it out', but a detail-by-detail interrogation under hypnosis.

Freud's first improvement of this technique was to dispense with the hypnosis and attack the amnesia only from the side of consciousness. A force was then found to be at work in the mind of these patients opposing the recollection of painful episodes, and this force, or 'resistance' as it was called, had to be overcome. How then can one discover something which practitioner and patient alike know nothing about, and which the patient has a 'resistance' against recollecting? By continued urging, some of the forgotten scenes were recollected and some not, but enough was recovered to show that the experiences and episodes were not really lost from the mind.

A closer study showed that the experiences thus 'actively forgotten' or 'repressed' were wishes and impulses which had once been roused, but which were in conflict with the rest of the personality. The conflict roused guilt feelings, and the dread lest the impulses should dominate behaviour caused mental pain and anxiety. The value to medicine of these discoveries lies in the fact that for the first time a neurotic illness was explained in terms of the patient's past mental experiences (i.e. in terms of mental pathology). It was no longer necessary, as had hitherto been done, especially in France under Janet's influence, to ascribe the major part of the altered consciousness to such sweeping but rather nebulous conceptions as hereditary weakness.

Transference

Some of the forgotten experiences, however, were found to manifest themselves not by conscious recollection, but by the patient's re-enacting in his relation to the physician his earlier emotional attitudes, suspicions, desires and fears; i.e. the patient 'transferred' on to the physician a rôle which had once been significant in the patient's past. The very reproaches that the physician was unsympathetic, cruel, amorous, jealous, indifferent or stupid, were found to belong to forgotten events and relationships, which, however, preserved their power to influence the patient from the side of the unconscious. This 'transference' to the physician of early emotional attitudes provided Freud with an opportunity to study in detail those parts of the mind which were hidden from the patient's view. The delicate emotional situation between physician and patient which allows this transference to develop without distortion is of the greatest value in mental research and therapy. It is the 'instrument' by which further knowledge of this part of the mind is obtained and also by which the patient is enabled to gain a deeper insight into his troubles and his past experiences. Further, it gives him the conviction that these are influencing him at the present time, and an understanding of the way in which they still mould his life helps him to get control over a part of his mind that was dominating him.

The main difficulty in using this 'instrument' or technique is to avoid any distortion of the picture of the patient's mental past which it affords. It is obvious that since the things which come to light cause the patient to experience anxiety, guilt and shame, he is bound to find relief in any obscuring of the situation which if re-enacted will cause apprehension or embarrassment. Most people on finding themselves drawn into the network of a neurotic patient's emotionally disturbing impulses would feel somewhat reluctant to continue in such a delicate situation, and physicians are no exception to this. This reluctance on the part of the physician is comparable with the resistance on the part of the patient to face the facts of his own emotional past without distortion. That this is not a mere conjecture is shown by the experience obtained when training psycho-analysts; viz. when the pupil overcomes a repugnance to face something in his own inner experience he is not disturbed to find himself in a situation where this very impulse or feeling is ascribed to him by his patients: knowing what part it has played in his own life, he is ready to face the issues again, this time with the advantage that the problems are now conscious and therefore under his control.

Qualitatively the emotional life of neurotic and normal persons is in many respects alike, there being neither impulses nor ideas in one that are not in the other, and quantitatively they are far more alike than people commonly imagine. The neurotic has not more 'force' in his emotional life than the normal. The difference lies in the *distribution* as between the conscious and unconscious, and in the *manner* in which the two major impulses of love and hate shape the mental attitude to those who stand emotionally nearest to the patient. The clinical problem is therefor not that of looking for something in the mind which ought not to be there, as one would look for a septic focus, but of surveying the mental outlook of the patient and observing by a most detailed study of his life history the way in which he has responded to his environment and sought to impose himself upon it.

What has just been said about the quantitative and qualitative differences between neurotics and normal people, and the way their life history may be regarded, is common to every form of psychotherapy. What is peculiar to psycho-analysis is the use that it makes of this 'transference situation' in elucidating the unconscious (i.e. the 'actively forgotten') parts of the mind and the drives to action found there, and it is found in practice that it takes at least four years' training to give a proper grasp of this therapeutic and research technique. (The only place in Great Britain where this training is given is at the Institute of Psycho-Analysis, London).

Use of Psycho-Analysis

It is sometimes said that everyone does psycho-analysis on his patients in these days. This is no more accurate than to say that everyone does brain surgery in these days. The fact is that brain surgery and physiology have revealed more of what goes on inside the skull than was known before, and if the possibilities of a brain tumour are being considered in a given case, knowledge that the brain surgeon has made available is thus being used. The physician does not perform the same operations as the brain surgeon although he uses the knowledge gained by this means. So it is with psycho-analysis. The exploratory work of Freud on adults and, in more recent years, of Mrs. Melanie Klein on children, has added greatly to the understanding of the mind, but the employment of that knowledge in clinical work for a better diagnosis and understanding of a case is not the same thing as using the special technique, i.e. psycho-analysing a patient. The contribution of psycho-analysis to general practice is not therefore a special therapeutic procedure that may be more or less rapidly acquired and easily administered, but an understanding of the suffering of the mind, which helps in diagnosis and in the handling of the patient who is troubled. Psycho-pathology is not a science of mental disease so much as a science that is concerned with mental suffering. Much suffering seen among patients, marital unhappiness for instance, cannot be classed as a disease, nor are the patients by ordinary standards neurotic, but they experience mental pain in the non-fulfilment of their expectations from love, and, from the guilt due to their unloving and hostile impulses towards those they desire to cherish, they may live in misery. To put the matter in this bald way is to ignore one consideration—whether these mental processes are conscious or not. But in this connection it must be remembered that the force of an impulse is no less strong if it operates in the unconscious.

If psycho-analysis had done no more than contribute to an understanding of the causes of mental pain in the mentally normal it would have deserved well of the medical profession, but it has increased knowledge of those conditions which are characterized by anxiety. Anxiety of the mind always has a cause, just as bodily pain always has a cause. If the factor causing the pain is not at once recognized the physician does not dismiss it from his mind but, on the contrary, redoubles his efforts to find it. So it should be with anxiety. Now anxiety is by definition a condition of nervous apprehension in which the cause is not known. If the feeling can be 'placed' in connection with an object or situation, the proper term is fear. When dealing with patients who exhibit anxiety it is irrational for the physician to expect that the explanation offered for the condition (if given at all) will be necessarily rational or comprehensible. If the patient could explain it properly he would not go to his medical attendant about it. The patient's less comprehensible worries, doubts and suspicions, his querulousness and even his emphatic prejudices, must therefore be met with a specially sym-

c

pathetic attention, because he is trying to rid himself of a burden and is using the occasion of his visit to his physician for the purpose.

Phantasies

If the practitioner could give the time to the investigation and could avoid foreclosing the discussion of painful but important topics—not an easy matter, as has been hinted above in con-nexion with the four years' training—he would discover that the patient's emotional life was being influehced not only by his present environment and the instincts appropriate to it, but also by *phantasies* which do not belong to the present but to the re-mote past. The nature of these infantile phantasies, which exert such a profound influence on subsequent character, and indeed on mental health, is, of course, not fully known to the patient owing to the amnesia which hides the early years. So, when the physician is listening to the narration of symptoms, he has to reckon with an unknown factor which, nevertheless, contains the key to the problem, and this calls for special forbearance and patience. If it were only a matter of listening the problem would not be so difficult, though it does consume time; what is awk-ward is the way in which the practitioner is woven, usually without his realizing it, into the pattern of these phantasies, and plays a rôle in the patient's life not of his own choosing. The neurotic, without exercising a deliberate intention, indeed with-out knowing he is doing so, is in his relation to the physician and towards all who stand near to him, engaged in a double task. He is trying to get satisfaction both for present needs and at the same time for those unfulfilled and unconscious desires of the remote past. These are incompatible and because they are he suffers mental pain. It is not the purpose of this article to dis-cuss the treatment of the neuroses nor in any detail the handling of the neurotic patient, but this much should be said: however incomprehensible the symptoms may appear, and however aggravating the patient's demands on his physician may be, that practitioner will deal with them best who can realize that behind the confusion and the clamour there are definite con-flicts, the solution of which would ease the mental pain, and whatever the patient's demands may be, he will be helped best if the physician can preserve an attitude of detachment without coldness, and friendliness without prejudice for or against the wayward impulses at work.

The impact of the phantasy life of one person on another is always strong—the creations of the artist, the power of the lover, the deeds of the criminal, and the symptoms of the neurotic hold the imagination through the phantasies thus roused. In meeting the neurotic on his own ground of passions unfulfilled, of anxieties and of guilt, the physician shoulders a heavy task. On this, his own ground, the patient lives, and only on this ground can he be cured. Sympathy will ease him, but only knowledge of the sources of his pain will help to rid him once and for all of his illness.

REFERENCES

Freud, S. (1932): *Introductory Lectures on Psycho-Analysis*, London.
—— (1937): *A General Selection from the Works of Sigm. Freud*, The Hogarth Press, London.
Klein, M. (1932): *Psycho-Analysis of Children*, The Hogarth Press, London.

X

ON THE NATURE OF UGLINESS AND THE CREATIVE IMPULSE

(MARGINALIA PSYCHOANALYTICA. II)[1]

(1940)

1. Introduction
2. The Etymology, Meaning and Uses of the Word 'Ugly'
3. An Experiment on the Feeling of Disgust
4. Some Factors which influence Æsthetic Appreciation:
    (*a*) A missing part
    (*b*) The attitude to deformity, to defective growth, to a 'foreign body' and to unfinished work
    (*c*) Fettering of interest to periods, cultures and antiquity
    (*d*) The relation of limitation of æsthetic appreciation to inhibitions in love life
5. Dream-Work and Art-Work
6. What is it that is Satisfying in Art?
    (*a*) Sensuous pleasure
    (*b*) The solution of conflict
    (*c*) The 'eternal' factor
7. What is Ugliness?

1. *Introduction*

The study of Æsthetics presents difficult problems and the solution of them is made more arduous if the field of observation is unduly constricted. So long as Æsthetics is confined to an examination of Beauty research is likely to prove as sterile as is a study of Behaviour which confines itself to the single factor of

[1] Reprinted from the *International Journal of Psycho-Analysis* (1940), **21**, 294–313.
The second of a series of notes marginal to the already full pages of psycho-analytical literature. The first appeared in an issue of *the International Journal of Psycho-Analysis* honouring one of Ernest Jones's decennial birthdays Vol. 10, 42 this appears for the same purpose ten years later.

pleasure. Human psychology made greater progress when it
gave recognition to the factors of mental pain, anxiety and
guilt; it would therefore seem prudent to accord more significance than is commonly done in the literature to these disturbing but powerful forces in our æsthetic inclinations, and to
see whether the underlying impulses of destructiveness, which
give rise to these painful feelings, do not provide a substratum
to Art as they do to everyday life. It is even possible that by representing in a neutral medium the interplay of creative and destructive instincts the artist can help us to comprehend a better
solution of the conflicts that press within us than we could do
for ourselves unaided, with nothing interposed between us and
our passions but the medium of our unstable flesh. The artist
provides more than a momentary consolation for our miseries;
he goes behind the veil which screens the source of our dejection
and brings back evidence for the triumph of the creative impulse over the forces of destruction; he can do this not by the
denial of pain but by facing it with a determination to master it.
If we are to learn anything about Æsthetics we must be ready to
follow the path he takes.

It cannot be said of the psycho-analysts that they study only
the pleasant things of this life, and we should expect that their
contributions to æsthetics would be full of the struggle between
the contending forces in the mind. Oddly enough the subject
has suffered a relative neglect and when mentioned attention is
given in the main to those factors which have contributed to the
content of a work of art rather than to the meaning to the artist
and his audience of the underlying forces of love and hate, of
creativeness and destruction, which possess us in the depths of
our being; perhaps it would be more correct to say that the
deeper strata of conflict are implied rather than made explicit.
The strain that man suffers from the double task of adjusting his
love and hate to two objects at a time, both being loved and
both hated, and, what is more, both being related to one
another—a difficulty in orientation and emotional adaptation
which analysts call the Oedipus Complex—has of course found
much exemplification in our literature. Ernest Jones' 'Hamlet'
(1910) is an excellent instance; and the way in which, owing to
the unbearable nature of our unconscious ideas, if appearing un-
disguised in consciousness, our minds disguise the crude and
horrible, so that these will not disfigure the more gracious

intentions of our thoughts, has been often illustrated; again we can refer to Ernest Jones' work, particularly his 'Madonna's Conception' (1914). The lead in this direction of research was given by Freud in his *Delusion and Dream* (1907) and *Leonardo da Vinci* (1910), he also wrote the only paper by a psycho-analyst which deals solely with the aspect of æsthetics that is usually neglected—'The Uncanny' (1919).

The research into our mental life which takes into account not only man's double orientation and ambivalence to objects but which also brings into prominence the employment of projection and introjection, not as mere and occasional expurgatory or masterful acts, but as the basic behaviour of the immature psyche, and stresses the continuing activity of the extroject and the introject in the outer or inner world respectively, and the interplay of these in the mind, and, as it seems, the body of the infant and of our unconscious grown-up selves— these new researches, which we owe to Melanie Klein, throw fresh light on æsthetic problems, and are illustrated in her 'Infantile Anxiety-Situations reflected in a Work of Art and in the Creative Impulse' (1929). What follows here is a marginal note to that paper, and to her 'Contribution to the Psychogenesis of Manic-Depressive States' (1935).

2. *The Etymology, Meaning and Uses of the Word 'Ugly'*

Skeat tells us something which at once carries us deep into our subject. He defines *ugly* as

frightful, hateful. It comes from a root connected with *ugg-* (Icelandic) meaning *fear* and with *-ligr* meaning *-like*. The main root is traced in the Gothic *ogan*, again meaning to *fear* and *ogjan* meaning *to terrify*. The Scandanavian *oga* (dread) is connected with the O.H.G. *egiso* = terror and the Gothic *agis* = *fear*, anguish and the Irish *aegal* meaning the same thing. These words are derived from the same root as the Greek ἄχος meaning *anguish* and *affliction*.

In the columns of the O.E.D. under *Ugly* we find the following:

Having an appearance or aspect which causes dread or horror; frightful or horrible, especially through deformity or squalor ... offensive or repulsive to the eye ... morally offensive or repulsive, base, degraded, loathsome, vile, later used in weaker sense as offending against propriety, highly objectionable ... offensive or unpleasant to taste or smell ... causing

disquiet or discomfort, of a troublesome awkward nature . . .
somewhat hazardous, perilous . . . suggestive of trouble or
danger . . . cross, angry, ill-tempered.

3. *An Experiment on the Feeling of Disgust*

Although in this paper we shall not refer again to the contributions of Experimental Psychology or Experimental Æsthetics to the solution of the problem of Ugliness—nor for that
matter to any other work but psycho-analytic—the researches
of Petö (Budapest, 1935) cannot pass unnoticed. They are valuable not only because they deal with the rather neglected field of
Osmics but chiefly because they show that the subjective
response may vary with the age of the subject, a point that does
not find much mention in works on æsthetics.

Various substances (spices, flowers, fruit, resin, fumes, and
smells of putrefaction—assafœtida, polysulphides) were ex-
hibited to nearly 300 children, aged from one month to sixteen years, who were divided into three groups, under five,
five to six, and over six years old. 89 out of 92 under five
showed no disgust or disagreeable feeling, one showed disgust
towards some smells, two reacted as grown-up people would
have done. Of the 39 in the five-to-six-year group 11 behaved
with indifference or said that disagreeable smells were good
ones, 19 showed disgust like grown-up people, 9 showed
partly a satisfied or indifferent, partly a dissatisfied reaction.
In the over-six group of 164 children, 127 showed dissatisfaction or strong disgust, 13 indifference, 24 a mixed behaviour. Only the children of five years and over distinguished
between agreeable and disagreeable smells; before that age
there was no aversion; over six-years children made the adult
distinctions.

Petö rightly points out that in view of the light which psycho-
analysts have thrown on the latency period and also on the
building up of the super-ego, with accompanying changes in the
mental outlook, at least among civilized peoples, the main
alteration in æsthetic response in this instance may be ascribed
to changes in the vita sexualis and to consequent altered outlook of the mind.

4. *Some Factors which influence Æsthetic Appreciation*

(a) *A missing part.* Some people feel uncomfortable in the
presence of ancient statues which are incomplete; they say that

these would be beautiful if they were not mutilated, but as now seen they are horrible and sometimes in their injured state they are even called ugly.

When such people come as patients to us for analysis— usually of course for other reasons than a disturbance of their æsthetic sense—we have an opportunity of finding out some of the factors which influence their appreciation or disappreciation of these objects. Analysis does not provide much material for æsthetic study, but the smallness of the number of individuals who bring forward material bearing directly on these problems is compensated for by two factors: first we observe the æsthetic judgement or appreciation in the same setting as we observe all other mental activities of the patient, i.e. in the framework of his free associations in analysis, and secondly we are able to observe the changes in æsthetic appreciation running parallel with the changes in mental outlook in other directions, in the patient's love life, work and sublimations generally.

Returning to the statues: it appears that the subject identifies himself with these objects, i.e. he has thought of himself as a mutilated person, or he has identified the statue with someone whom he has in his thoughts mutilated. It would be more correct to say that the sight of the statue rouses unconscious phantasies of re-mutilation, because the phantasy is not roused for the first time by the statue. Its injury awakens the impulse to carry the destruction a stage further. These phantasies can be traced back to the patient's early years and have undergone many modifications, submergences and resuscitations. An important fact confronts us at this point: the reawakened phantasy is more disturbing than the defects in the object itself; the phantasy, which is one of aggressive action, remains unconscious, the affect of fear or horror becomes attached to the external object so that the person does not realize his secret wish; the phantasy is kept from consciousness at the expense of the richness of the subject's emotional relation to an external object.

The reason for thinking that the affects roused by the phantasy are more disturbing than those roused by the defects in the object is found in the effects of treatment; when the wish-phantasy of mutilation is brought to consciousness and the patient is able to bear an examination of it, and has traced its origin in its relation to loved persons, it is also found that his contemplation of mutilated statues is now not affected by his anxieties; he can enjoy them as a 'composition' or a 'unity' and is not distracted by the defective or defaced parts. It is perhaps hardly necessary to say that the change does not come about through 'discussing the statues', nor from any talk about æsthetics, but solely as a by-product of work necessary for the treatment of a neurotic trouble.

It may be objected that this first example is a trivial and neurotic reaction and that it cannot be made the basis of a general criterion of ugliness. I should consider the objection sound were the response to mutilation not so very widespread; mutilation phantasies play a large part for instance in the inhibitions of love life, and I should be loath to exclude them from a discussion of æsthetics, because their elaboration in the unconscious part of the mind and the impetus they give to exertions of an opposite character—restorative and creative— may on further examination be fruitful in our understanding not only of æsthetics but of our social life.

(b) *The attitude to deformity, to defective growth, to a 'foreign body' and to unfinished work.* It is not regarded as surprising when people say that they regard deformity of body or defect in growth, whether generalized or localized, and whether seen in the flesh or in a representation, as ugly. Though we accept the statement readily enough, the reason for this view may be quite complicated. There is a component derived from the anxiety about personal mutilation which comes from an identification with the victim of the distortion; but since the mind resists the idea that the self is ever horrible this factor of identification with a dreaded sight cannot in itself lend much strength to the feeling that the object is ugly. There is, however, sometimes another component derived from an identification with the aggressor who has produced the distortion; such pleasure as is harboured in the unconscious on this account is manifest in consciousness as discomfort due to guilt, the direct perception of guilt feelings as such being suppressed. In the case of a work of art the aggressor is clearly the artist, so that the contemplation of his work puts us in a position where we are faced in our phantasy with two objects at the same time, the producer and the object produced, which in the unconscious is always regarded as a person. It is possible that the production and enjoyment of art is dependent on this capacity to cope simultaneously with ambivalence to two intimately related but yet separate objects. The eagerness in the young to produce what in any other animal would be properly regarded as a biologically useless activity, the drawing and plastic work, rhythmic noises and tunes, and the variation in intensity of these impulses with the phases of sexual development, suggests that a close connection' exists between the employment of art-work and the personal and social problems derived from this double orientation, because in the young the task of experimental manipulation of love and hate impulses towards objects, internal as well as external, is almost its sole occupation. (Those who apply the Theory of Dialectical Materialism to art and who emphasize the dependence of creative art upon the social impulses, have also to consider the possibility that these spring from a common root: those who hold true to the theory will readily accept this; those whose inner strains call for immediate application of their views in political action commonly overlook it.)

Returning to the distortions and to unfinished work: these have in common the effect of rousing in the imagination the thought of what might have been. Just as the distortion rouses guilt at our complicity in the deed or anger at a potential good thing being deformed, so on contemplating unfinished work some feel cheated by the artist and react to the frustration with hostility—using the judgement of ugliness as a cover for their resentment. Others of course respond in the opposite way, feel grateful to the artist for that part which he has given them and enjoy the opportunity to share with him in their phantasy in the completion of a lovely production. There is another characteristic which sometimes excites the judgement of ugliness, viz. where the onlooker finds what he regards as a 'foreign body' in an otherwise acceptable work. If this particular figure was not in the composition or this cloud was not in the sky the picture would be all that could be desired; as it is it is spoiled by this alien thing and the picture is reckoned ugly. This is the antithesis to the 'missing part' objection, it is the presence of something bad which renders the whole intolerable—a neurotic reaction, surely.

(c) *Fettering of interest to periods, cultures and antiquity.* The foregoing considerations have roused in our minds the impression that these factors which limit æsthetic appreciation are neurotic manifestations, and that perhaps no true art lover is influenced by them; in a word that the investigation of those things which produce aversion are calculated to disclose neurotic behaviour, and that it does not take much gumption to surmise that neurosis is likely to disturb art appreciation in some way or other. Maybe this is so; nevertheless the way in which the disturbance comes about should not be neglected by psychology.

Leaving aside the aversions, let us consider some factors which limit the scope of what is felt to be attractive in works of art. Certain periods in history and certain cultures have as we say an appeal for us, we think we should have felt at home in them, and anything which reminds us of them gives us pleasure so that we readily respond to their influence. If we examine this attitude more closely we commonly find that there is a connection between the conception of the culture or period and the day-dreams or phantasies which serve as the background of our mental life. The links between the culture chosen and the day-dream can be traced if we follow the history of the significant content through the course of development of the patient's phantasies, but the awakening of the association by a work of art need not be direct nor of course need it disclose its Œdipal roots; indeed it need not be direct at all, e.g. the general treatment or style of a picture may evoke some echo of that world we people in our day-dreams. An artist seems to be able both to convey by an economy of means denied to lesser folk a wide range of associations, more particularly of the emotions, which the whole composition and the details of his work evoke, and to control them so that they shall not scatter wide but by subtle focussing reinforce one another and penetrate deeper and deeper into the mind of the onlooker; at least I take it that some such process occurs, analogous to the interplay of elements in a dream.

These preferences for particular periods or cultures are apt of course to pass over to a possessive appreciation of the chosen field with depreciation of others—a characteristic of nursery preferences, but one which leads directly to interest in external objects. In contrast there is the type which can only enjoy or venerate the antique. One patient whose family was of a 'respectable antiquity' was fascinated by any work (artistic or political) of the period when his family 'began'. I think the reason which some antique-fetishists put forward, viz. that objects which have been preserved through the ages against the carelessness and resentment of succeeding generations must have some merit in them, contains a truth, but a truth which they use as a rationalization. In this connection we must remember those who are unable to see in an ancient work of art anything that commends it to their favourable notice, i.e. a quality as intrinsically irrelevant as antiquity is used as a mark against it. The truth is that there is a fashion in these matters, and people are influenced to a far greater extent than they are aware in their æsthetic appreciations by social habits. Another instance of this is the relatively recent enjoyment by civilized nationals of the art of primitive tribes; it would seem likely that this is a case of diminution of æsthetic inhibition coinciding with a greater tolerance of other sexual customs and social codes than their own and resulting in an increased æsthetic enjoyment: anxiety is the chief inhibition of enjoyment, whether it be æsthetic or other.

(*d*) *The relation of limitation of æsthetic appreciation to inhibitions in love life.* The parallel between these two kinds of restriction is striking—the preference for newness or for age, the satisfaction in completeness and intolerance of a missing part, deformity, a 'foreign body', the pleasure in private possession of the prized object and numbing of the senses in a public collection, the proneness to be disturbed from the enjoyment of the whole if anxiety is roused by a part—all these peculiarities are in the person approaching an object whether it be artistic or sexual. The legend of Pygmalion reminds us that from classical times the connection between the two impulses was recognized and that a bridging of the gap might be abnormal. And yet there is a ready transfer of emotion from loved persons to works of art in normal people and many feel a refreshment of spirit from a work of art similar to that which they experience when they make the acquaintance of an inspiring person. It seems to be stronger than a mild narcotic and provides more than 'a temporary refuge for us from the hardships of life' (Freud, 1929). Though its influence may 'not [be] strong enough to make us forget real misery'—the same may be said of love—yet it has the power to penetrate beneath the surface of our minds and both assist us in our struggle with despair and help us to grasp those things which seem to triumph over death.

It seems that since we left the illuminating pages of Skeat and the O.E.D. we have drifted away from the subject of ugliness and have hardly touched on the creative impulse at all. Perhaps that will come later, but we must consider first some more general problems connected with what may be going on in the artist's mind when he is engaged on his work.

5. *Dream-Work and Art-Work*[1]

'Dream-work' is the best known instance of the interplay between unconscious impulses on the one hand and perceptions and memory traces on the other. In the dream the unconscious wish uses sensory perceptions and memory traces in order to express thoughts that cannot come to consciousness on account of repression; the dream work consists in transforming the arrangement of images so that they have one meaning for the unconscious part of the mind and they may or may not have another sort of significance or interest for the conscious layer of the mind. Since the aim of the dream is to provide unconscious satisfaction to the dreamer it is as a rule a matter of relative indifference whether the manifest content of the dream makes sense for anyone else; there is the familiar analogy of the play written by and performed for an audience of one—the dreamer.

Dreams differ in respect to the degree to which the manifest content shows the influence of the primary processes of thought (condensation, displacement, absence of contradiction, etc.) or 'perception identity', or reveals the influence of the secondary processes of thought or 'thought identity'. Perhaps this difference in dreams could be employed also in æsthetics. Some works of art give the appearance at first meeting of being confused and formless (Surrealist pictures for example), others show at first sight at any rate the opposite tendency, viz. an effort to achieve exact representation of detail (Frith's 'Derby Day' is an instance of this). Just as orderliness of the manifest content of the dream is not its most important characteristic for the analyst, so conventional forms are not the most important thing to the artist. The Surrealists deliberately imitate the dream but only of course the visible characteristics of the manifest content. On the analogy now being pressed, their work will be strong only so long as the force attaching to the latent content can be given full scope. Also on this analogy it would be as rash to judge an artist's work by the standard of his own theories as to value the

[1] The substance of this section was sent to about a hundred members of the British Psychological Society in December 1936.

significance of a dream (as a thing giving a key to important aspects of the dreamer's inner life) by the importance he attaches to its neat arrangement or its incoherence.

Both dreamer and artist strive to reduce mental tension; an important difference between the two work processes lying in the different 'audiences' for whom the elaborate phantasy is produced.

We should try to relate the aphorism 'A dream is a play with an audience of one', to the saying that an artist does not produce for himself but for the whole of humanity. Ferenczi (1913) in one of his brilliant asides put the question 'To whom does one relate one's dreams?' and quotes Lessing's couplet

Alba mihi semper narrat sua somnia mane,
Alba sibi dormit; somniat Alba mihi.

(It is just as charming in English: Alba always tells me her dreams in the morning; she sleeps for herself, but she dreams for me.) Sachs (1920), recalling our attention to the fact that the day-dream is a preliminary stage of poetry, considers that 'day-dreams in common', in which two or more persons co-operate by giving up their closest ego-interests, should further our understanding of the production of poetry. He found that a common feeling of guilt leads the players of the story-telling game to seek and to find 'relief in the working-out of a day-dream, since in it lay an unconscious admission of the same guilt of the other party. . . . The artist's own person has to step into the background for the sake of the effect of the work!'

We could therefore arrange the dream series as follows: first the dreams for oneself alone, then the dreams for a particular person, then the day-dreams-in-common for the group playing that particular game. To apply this to art is no great step, but our explanation must also take into reckoning that the artist feels that his work is for the whole of humanity and for 'all time'. We achieve a simplification if we say that the 'inner audience' for whom the artist works is the super-ego. This may influence his work on three levels: the least important super-ego element is derived from the art school where his technical accomplishment was in some measure shaped, where his work had to pass muster. It is a late acquisition, a conscious or pre-conscious level of mental operation, which guides the hand rather than fires the spirit. Another audience is that of the cultured people of his generation whose influence he absorbed during his formative years. The first influences his technique, the second commonly influences his choice of subject, neither have much to do with that which will make his work live. I suggest as a guess that there is a third kind of 'audience' composed not of memory traces of actual people's actual behaviour but of those compounds of external experience and inner phantasy which following Melanie Klein we call 'inner objects'. A work of art is composed for them in the sense (to be elucidated more fully later) that they are the objects who are intended to be influenced; they both give impetus to the creation of the work and are the objects to be influenced by it. Before we deal with this there is a general question to be touched on.

6. *What is it that is Satisfying in Art?*

Three answers to this question will be discussed; first the factor of sensuous pleasure, secondly the relief of tension that comes when a conflict is solved, and thirdly an aspect which we may call an 'eternal' factor, borrowing the term from common usage.

(a) *Sensuous pleasure.* It is usually held that the mere representation of a sensually attractive object does not constitute great art. The wide diversity of object-choice in the love life of man, and in its derivative the beauty-loving life, is so great that the attractiveness of a particular object exactly reproduced is bound to have a restricted appeal. At best this so to say photographic representation of the attractive recalls past gratifications; what 'movement' it possesses is retrogressive, and even the recall of past pleasures is limited. Its effect is psychologically unstable, it cannot recall a moment from the past without recalling all of it, its pain and its guilt as well as its joys; the avoidance of discomforting aspects of experience does not re-animate experience but fosters illusion. Such art is a 'flight to beauty'; it reminds us of the struggles of the psychotic to conceive of a world more and more saturated with goodness so that he may cherish the illusion that evil does not exist in it at all. But anxiety and guilt cannot for long be denied, the attempt to evade them leads to an ever increasing emphasis on the charms of the object, till the point is reached when—in the case of a work of art—the observer can feel neither identification nor loving object-relation with the thing represented and dismisses it—as he would dismiss a person who had such a one-sided disposition—as insipid and uninteresting.

And yet sensuous pleasure lies at the very centre of art. It is clear that sensuous pleasure of the positive or attractive kind is not enough; the artist who is in flight to beauty creates an illusory world and does not help us much to face the pain of the real world nor does he endear it to us. I take it that I have been describing 'Escape Art' and its limitations.

(b) *The solution of conflict.* In work where this plays a large part the artist faces the problem of anxiety and guilt. The mind finds rest when it has first mastered pain and then turns to pleasure. This factor is easier to state than to demonstrate, but an example is seen in 'Hamlet' in which as Ernest Jones (1910) pointed out the playwright carries us into the painful situation of the Oedipus conflict and depicts various aspects of its solution. Drama deals with the tensions of triangular situations in the medium of the relation of living people; in the case of other arts the analogous interaction would be that of part-objects and the interplay of constructive and destructive tendencies. There is little I can say in support of this notion beyond the statement that it strikes me as somewhat plausible. Just as our adult emotional life is a great elaboration and synthesis of the primitive phantasies of childhood, so one would expect our adult art to be a similar elaboration and synthesis of the graphic impulses which in our early years gave expression to our need to exercise power over objects with the magic of drawing, and our need to externalize and fix those ever-changing images and moods which disturbed our peace of mind. To the child's phantasy a line *is* a parent figure, another line crossing it is the other parent or is a knife hewing the first in two. The pencil is a magic wand giving power over the figures to do good or ill as the mood is at the moment. This is a primitive expression of what the 'infantile artist' *feels*, it bears no relation to what he *sees*. When a higher stage of graphic skill is reached there is a desire to bring under the dominion of the magic pencil objects seen in the outer world.

One might hazard a guess about the development of the graphic impulse having three phases: first the expression in the magical action—drawing—of primitive impulses directed against external objects, without regard to the accuracy of the representation of those external objects in the drawing—a depicting of inner phantasy, perhaps of the relation of inner objects to one another. In the second phase attention is paid to the depiction of the form of the external object, interest being driven to it perhaps through anxiety as to the fate of its inner counterpart, but the treatment of details is governed by part-object interests. In the third phase the element of 'composition', always present even in the first phase though then rudimentary, now develops, perhaps as a result of the increasing capacity to separate the elements in the combined-parent figure; this is the phase in which the interaction between inner and outer objects ceases to be wholly magical and acquires some of the characteristics of thought—delayed discharge of mental tension allowing for the matching of the product of the mind with the objects dealt with, whether these are external events and processes to be co-ordinated by the formulation of a law (as in science) or the matching of the feelings experienced on viewing an object after its exteriorization, with those experienced by the ego resulting from maybe unconscious introspection (as in art). Composition is probably always a synthesis of elements which the mind has decomposed or torn asunder, an effort of construction after a mental act of destruction.—This is a modification of Ella Sharpe's view (1930).

We may get a little further if we consider the nature of the instrument in the unconscious phantasy by means of which this magical control is exercised, and by considering the artist's relation to it. Sometimes we hear an artist say, 'If I am an artist, I live; if not, I am dead. Unless I am creating, I am nothing!' There is felt to be something inside but separate from the self which is essentially creative, it produces 'art-children' out of the artist, who is in a way passive to its power but active in response to it. If we follow carefully the early history of this mental experience we find it expressing a passive relation to a creative image of infancy, the father figure, and to the part of him which is both capable of creating and of entering another person. The creative power is in phantasy an inner possession because in phantasy its corporeal prototype was originally desired by the child for the purpose of incorporating it in the self, and thereby he could obtain control over his world, father, mother and all future children and rivals. But the incorporating process cannot be selective against the inclusion of the unpleasant; the ambivalence felt against the external object follows it into the inner sanctuary. Hate jeopardizes it in the one place as in the other. 'If I am an artist, I live' can be interpreted, 'Unless I have evidence that this object within me is alive and active in the creation of good things, there is nothing to live for since my hate against it will extinguish the producer of all that is good and desirable.' In such a case—perhaps in all—the production of a work of art takes away the sense of guilt arising from the fact that death wishes are streaming towards and stifling the good object which was once external and now in phantasy is harboured within the self. Artists sometimes feel that they are the trustees of a great treasure, this accounts for their modesty; at times they feel so close an identification with the great force within them that they reckon themselves as gods. In this connection and in view of the infantile origin of the notion of god and of creativeness the arrogance of some artists is not a thing to be wondered at.

(c) *The 'eternal' factor.* Of one thing an artist is certain when he has achieved his highest purpose: that its power to affect the heart of man will last for ever. It is not a sufficient explanation that his work will give satisfaction beyond his lifetime and that in the reckoning of time after our death we count a thousand years as but a day; the imperviousness of the unconscious to thoughts of personal extinction and to the gauging of time do not bring us to the correct position, as it seems to me, to value this feeling of the 'eternal' in art. Nor I think should we lean overmuch on the thought that through the most intimate contact of the artist's mind with generation after generation of men he extends the duration of his influence to timeless dimensions. Such a pre-conscious thought may make an artist the readier to speak of his own or another person's art as of everlasting value, but the same motive cannot influence us who merely look at and appreciate his work.

A work of art appeals to us in proportion to the depth of the emotional level which is stirred in our minds; the artist cannot take us where he himself has never been. If we limit ourselves to what might be called the biographer's life of the artist we cannot explain the power these people have to affect nearly the whole of mankind. But if we take into consideration the intensity of infantile pain, the enormous courage and 'endurance of the child in the face of what it feels to be great dangers to itself and to loved ones, its passionate belief that in spite of the fact that its world is reduced to chaos nevertheless it will and can put things right, its good humour due to its belief that in spite of its own evil impulses it has the power to restore and recreate a good world again and that its good objects will remain, if we reckon with the fact that the child goes through periods when the face of familiar things is changed and all that it loves and trusts is crushed by its own violence and befouled by its hate, and if with all this we reckon with the influence and power of infantile phantasy and experience upon our adult perception and emotion: then we may see how the artist can lead us into and out of the world of suffering. His creative activity is the Beginning of a New World built on the ruins of the old; those strokes of the brush in his phantasy build up bit by bit the good objects which he has destroyed and make them come to life. (I do not mean to imply that all great art is done in a paroxysm of nervous breakdown, but that unless the artist can reach down to the experience of deep anxiety and find the way out his work will not give us a deeper understanding of ourselves or a fuller enjoyment of life.)

But to return to our question. Time is not really the point of discussion, *death* is the thing referred to. The immortal work of art is not one which has merely survived through the ages from the carelessness and indifference of other people, but is a living proof that the artist himself has stayed the course of havoc and has himself made life come out of dust and confusion. In all nature death is the only irreversible reaction, the triumph and the illusion of art is that it can turn back the dead into the world of the living.

It is not so really. It is believed to be so. But artists feel it this way, and because we wish for the same outcome we give currency to the conception about the eternal value of a great work of art. At least this much is true, that these treasures are the nearest to the eternal that man can make, and in fact both in antiquity and in the reverence they compel they can meet the challenge of the everlasting hills.

We have been speaking about works of art to the neglect of that to which the term beauty is most applied—the human face. Of its beauty we say that it contains an undying loveliness, though we know that half a dozen decades will end it. Do we only mean that we hope that the satisfaction we get from the contemplation of the beautiful face will never be erased from our memory by pain or destroyed by hate?

I would like at this point to refer to a curious experience. A patient in deep depression came for analysis. She was dressed in black and wore knotted round her neck a long scarlet rope of silk, her face was hooded with a large black hat. She wore black gauntlets of shiny kid, but her fingers which kept up a twisting angular movement seemed too small for the gloves so that the thin leather creased and bent as if it were the loose scaly covering of a bird's claw. Her face was made up in the livid purplish colouring of a corpse; her mouth was curved almost to deformity and was usually drawn in, but it opened and closed slowly as the tip of the black kid claw pulled down the lower lip. Her brow was drawn and her eyes stared intently at nothing. All this while she uttered soft groans, saying to herself 'Oh! Oh! Oh!'. In the course of a session a commonplace interpretation was made; instantly she changed to a new creature. The angular movements of her fingers gave place to a smooth stroking of her body, the claw turned to a soft caressing hand, the hunched shoulders relaxed, her brow smoothed, her eyes brightened, the hollows in her face filled with smiling cheeks, her expression was radiant. The thought crossed my mind, 'Why, my goodness, she is beautiful!'

Reflection showed that in repose (I am not speaking of the expression in melancholy) and even when smiling, which had great charm, the attribution of beauty might perhaps be an exaggeration. My first idea was that my mind followed the quick return of animation, and, possibly in relief of strain, overshot the due mark of appreciation. But to that view another and less psycho-mechanical explanation can be added. For the moment my words—so I then regarded the episode, or so my unconscious phantasy ran—had brought this living corpse to life. It was a miracle, and the description 'beautiful' was applied because that is what we think of life when we expect death, that is what we think when we see the signs of triumph over death.

Since having this experience I have wondered whether some of the special power to hold a lasting position in the memory which some film actresses possess, I think of one in particular, is not due to the fact that in repose she has at times the appearance of enduring an almost unbelievable burden of inner misery and mental pain, and not once but several times in each film we see that 'miracle' occur—under the influence of her partner or from the upwelling of her own emotion that bare skull grows soft and human.

One of the characteristics of beauty is its power to convey the feeling that struggle is over, that peace has come at last. Though we may go into the depths of pain and depression again and again we carry with us the assurance that through all violence and evil there has remained this marvellous witness to the endurance of life over death. Once deathless is deathless ever more!

In all this only one aspect of beauty is touched on, that which leads to the reduction of anxiety and pain, not that which leads to the heightening of pleasure and desire. Or should one say that which leads directly to the heightening of pleasure and desire? It is doubtful whether the direct paths of the mind are as straight and simple as they seem; maybe we only wish they were so, so that we need take no reckoning of the way our mind is shaped by pain.

What, it may be asked, has all this talk of Beauty to do with our topic—Ugliness? Only this, that it does not do to try to answer over-simple questions on the terms of reference which wishful thinking too readily provides. This paper serves merely to emphasize a possible genetic connection between the pain due to destructive impulses and the paramount need to create lasting goodness and wholeness from what had been in phantasy injured and rendered bad. The urge to Reparation is, owing to the strange nature of human mental development, probably an integral part of creative activity; the horror of the ugly and the wish to change it is that *vis a tergo* which thrusts us into constructive work in art, in science and even in the humble tasks of our daily round.

7. *What is Ugliness?*

Ugliness has power over us, we cannot treat it with indifference. It rouses our deep-set emotions and its horror lingers in the memory. The etymology of the word shows that it is closely connected in men's minds with fear; but we also find on closer viewing that it rouses anxiety and guilt. A sailor may call a cloud 'ugly' but he means only that it forebodes the dangers of a storm; as an artist (on land) he might regard its splendour with admiration because its threats will not assail him; as an ordinary being he might find relief, as many do, at watching the development of an *external* tempest, which being none of his making can be viewed without rousing inner alarm or misgiving. If there should be horror we can safely say that it is due to the arousal of early phobias and phantasies in which the raging elements are surrogates for persons whom he himself has lashed to fury, and that he dreads to witness the external fulfilment of his own secret wishes or to see spread out before him the awful chaos which lies within himself.

The case of a cloud called 'ugly' is really too simple to help us much; but what do we mean by an ugly face? Is there a face that all mankind would call ugly; an awfulness that strikes chill into the heart of every soul? A configuration of chaos, a sense of something destroyed, of hate embodied in or indelibly marked upon human flesh, that we have no power to transform? As eternal beauty is a challenge to destruction and a triumph, is ugliness a challenge and a victory, but to the other side? Ugliness is not merely displeasing in the highest degree, a cause of mental pain, giving no promise of peace, it is something which stirs phantasies so profoundly that our minds cannot let the object alone; it does not feel as if this thing has merely 'happened' but that it is something done to hurt. I believe that the fear which ugliness rouses is due to the irrefutable evidence which it provides that the will to destructiveness has been let loose; and we turn from it in part through dread of the temptation of complicity, in part because we cannot bear to contemplate what in our unconscious phantasy we have already done to something that was and might again be good. Those whose lives have been shaped by restitutive impulses, the Sisters of Mercy, nurses, and those who minister to the incurables, and also those who are fortified by the desire to fulfil a special office, the priest giving extreme unction or relatives attending to the wants of the dying, do not notice or are seemingly unaffected by appearances which all others would call the ugliest manifestations of deformity and disease; and such is the power of affection, often supported it is true by the process we call 'denial', that persons whose character and conduct seems of the ugliest are to those dear to them people who are only troubled in spirit and struggling with difficulties.

The word 'ugly' is used as a judgement upon an object or as the expression of an emotional response to it, and always denotes a disturbance, present or latent, of equanimity in the presence or at the thought of the object. If we are dissatisfied with a description or definition of the term which allows for so much subjective bias, it means, I think, that we are trying to make our intellectual judgements an absolute criterion, like an act of mensuration where both end points can be tested with complete freedom. But if we must be content, as I think is the case—and we can only be satisfied with it if we are convinced that it is true—that in the emotional life of man there is always a point of reference, a zero on the measuring scale, that lies in the unconscious part of the mind, then we must adapt our mode of research, or at least one part of it, to a closer understanding of the unconscious factors which influence if they do not govern our æsthetic judgement and appreciation.

(If one end of the measuring scale is buried out of sight we must forgo absolute standards and use the concept of quantity only so far as it applies to what we can observe. In this connection I have made no attempt to apply the dialectical conception of a change of quantity producing a change of quality; this cannot for long be ignored in respect to the problem of anxiety though so far few analysts have dealt with this.)

Man, it has often been said, is a religious animal; this notion is used to support the view that there must therefore be a God, an Absolute of Creativeness and Initiation, towards which we poor mortals must inevitably turn in our moments of need and to whom we must give thanks for our blessings. Man, it is less often said, is an Art-needing animal, and by the same process of ratiocination it is thought that there must be an Absolute of Beauty to which as the lodestone draws iron we half blind mortals turn for a criterion and for refreshment. Both views express a lofty if rather childish aspiration but they are hard to reconcile with man's position in animal creation. If we were oriented, as I imagine the animals are, in a relatively simple way, to the objects which excite our interest; if we desired without doubting our love and hated without qualm; if our periods of rut and non-rut were more or less separated, and the sexual impulse only thrust itself upon us when we were independent of parental care and capable of achieving coitus and reproduction after the manner of those who produced us; if the litter in which we were born was not confused and encumbered with the still dependent but vigorous offspring of the litter before us, and we had no ground for jealousy of those that came after us—if all these things were so, I doubt if we should have deep rooted in our mental life our load of anxiety and guilt. But then we should not be human, and, as Freud said, none of us would change places with the creatures in an animal community however much we might feel discontented with our human civilization. The reason for this, I surmise, is that, these experiences having become engrained, we need to work over the tangle until it is straightened out. There is a limit to the process of denial; under strain or throughout weakness we can deny a part of the reality of our inner life, but not all of it. Born into a human world we shoulder a burden characteristically human that cannot be laid down.

The mark of our humanity is the depth of our capacity to love and the agony which overwhelms us when our loved ones lie in danger from our own aggression. The strongest passions arose when we were weak and least able to control them, and our minds were flooded with phantasies which roused—and still rouse—our horror and excite our sensual cravings. On this foundation our mental lives and our civilization are built.

In the works of man, as in those which we separate and call the products of nature, we see creative and destructive forces in active interplay. When we discern the influence of creation predominating we are moved by something we call beauty, when we see destruction we recoil at the ugly. Our need for beauty springs from the gloom and pain which we experience from our destructive impulses to our good and loved objects; our wish is to find in art evidence of the triumph of life over death; we recognize the power of death when we say a thing is ugly.

REFERENCES

Ferenczi, Sándor (1913). 'To Whom does One Relate One's Dreams?' *Further Contributions*, Chapter LVI.

Freud, Sigm. (1900). *Interpretation of Dreams.*

Freud, Sigm. (1907). *Delusion and Dream in W. Jensen's 'Gradiva'.*

Freud, Sigm. (1910). *Leonardo da Vinci: A Psycho-Sexual Study of an Infantile Reminiscence.*

Freud, Sigm. (1919). 'The Uncanny,' *Collected Papers*, Vol. IV, The Hogarth Press, London.

Freud, Sigm. (1929). *Civilization and its Discontents*, The Hogarth Press, London, p. 35.

Jones, Ernest (1910). 'A Psycho-Analytic Study of Hamlet.' *Amer. J. Psych.*, **21**, 72, and in *Essays in Applied Psycho-Analysis*, The Hogarth Press, London.

Jones, Ernest (1914). 'The Madonna's Conception through the Ear.' *Essays in Applied Psycho-Analysis*, The Hogarth Press, London.

Klein, Melanie (1929). 'Infantile Anxiety-Situations Reflected in a Work of Art and in the Creative Impulse.' *Int. J. Ps.-An.*, **10**, 436.

Klein, Melanie (1935). 'A Contribution to the Psychogenesis of Manic-Depressive States.' *Int. J. Ps.-An.*, **16**, 145.

Petö, E. (1935). 'Contribution to the Development of Smell Feeling.' *Brit. J. Med. Psych.*, **15**, 314.

Sachs, Hans (1920). 'Day-Dreams in Common.' *Int. J. Ps.-An.*, **1**, 349.

Sharpe, Ella (1930). 'Certain Aspects of Sublimation and Delusion.' *Int. J. Ps.-An.*, **11**, 12.

XI
A CASE OF HYSTERIA—THEORY AND PRACTICE IN THE TWO WARS[1]
(1941)

GOOD fortune sometimes sends us a case which aptly illustrates some view of illness we are interested in; occasionally we find one which enables us to make a brief historical review of our theories. Such is the case of a soldier of 28 who received superficial gunshot wounds of the right arm and leg on active service and thus incommoded made his way to the coast during the retreat wandering about for five days unable to get treatment. After a few weeks in hospital he recovered from his wounds and went on sick-leave. On returning to his depot he developed a glove anæsthesia in the arm below the wound and hysterical paralysis. This condition continued for many months during which he was morose and dejected. When seen he had an evasive manner and spoke in clipped speech with 'Yes, sir.— No, sir.—I'll answer any question you put, sir,' volunteering no information.

Viewed in terms of the last war's psycho-pathology we would say that there was a break in the representation of the limb as an active thing in the mind, because, in the struggle between the impulse to duty and that of self-preservation (the fear of injury or of extinction in active service) self-preservation had won: he had no occasion to experience the fear while protected by his hysterical paralysis. Though it came on after leave and on return to duty, he was unaware of the relevance of this factor in its causation because—the symptom having solved it—he was now unconscious of the conflict in his mind. That he was an unstable fellow lends support to the view that the dissociative mechanism of escape from conflict is often found in those with some hereditary degeneration; his evasive manner might be ascribed to a psychopathic disposition due to the same cause.

[1] Reprinted from *The Lancet* (1941), **1**, 785–6. Read at a meeting of the medical section of the British Psychological Society at Nottingham on April, 1941.

The fact that he had seen active service in the Far East and only broke under the strain of the battle in Flanders also shows that even trained regulars can be pounded into dissociation if the threat to life be severe enough. Treatment would have followed within the framework of reference of the psycho-pathology. Since rest, massage and electricity had failed, his esprit de corps would have been stimulated, his sense of shame touched on, under hypnosis he might have been shown the limb in movement so that that break in the representation in the higher centres would have been bridged. It would be possible to extend the theoretical exposition with other views and evidence. This man of marriageable years roved through life single, refusing promotion so as to keep the equal camaraderie of his friends, unspoiled by differences of rank. But self-love, heightened by danger and stimulated by the injury, awakened fears of other injuries and threats from the infantile past and pulled him away even from loyal companionship. Regression, once begun, ended in the focusing of all attention on the flaccid limb. 'It is all I can think about,' he said. It would not be discordant to common knowledge among psycho-pathologists to see in the helpless right arm both a symbol and a visitation of punishment. He is impotent to defend himself; guilt now contributes to the maintenance of the symptom since with it he must leave his companions, just as a sense of guilt must have contributed to its origin when he failed them on return to duty. And further by being thus incapacitated he stays in England. The regressive pull to home and security would tend to keep him ill 'for the duration'.

Viewed clinically, yet other considerations presented themselves. It was observed that he nursed his arm, it was all he could think about, he stroked it and tried to make it warm (it was blue and cold). The clinical handling of the case was guided by the simplest of all rules in psychology but one that is commonly neglected—that when anyone just lets himself talk at random, whatever two things are mentioned (or even indicated by gesture) in close temporal association have also a common link in meaning to the patient. It was soon clear, when he was got to talk, that the 'poor arm' represented in his thoughts a person who was dead, and one for whom he would have given his right hand—his best companion in the dreary first winter of the war for whose sake he had refused promotion. He mourned his friend, who was killed in the action which also wounded him, and he nursed his own damaged self at one and the same time. When those two dreadful events happened his feelings for his friend were numbed, he paused a moment by his side (or he did desert him at the end? He could not bear to think of those times) and betook himself to the coast. When, on the basis of his own associations, it was pointed out to him that his mourning was being carried out within himself in the much nursed dead arm, he became resentful and said flatly that it was the doctor's idea and not his own. The point was not argued since the links between two contiguous ideas are not necessarily conscious, and one cannot argue in any hope of a fruitful outcome with forces hidden by an active defence from the patient's own consciousness; but he was persuaded to speak often of his friend, and it was remarkable how his arm and his friend were linked in the associations of his mind. And as he thus spoke he began to tremble and showed signs of grief and need for sympathy, a contrast to his earlier suspicious and impervious politeness. No new memory was obtained, no removal of amnesia, only—but that was much—an increase in feeling. For a week or two he remained depressed and then took up his military interests again. His pleasure in small-arms drill, its briskness, those resounding right-hand slaps on the butt of his good rifle, proved a stimulus to recovery. In the hospital there was a system of 'para-military training' in which military exercises, the equivalent, for soldier patients, of occupational therapy, were blended with psychiatric testing of the patient's response to situations calling for various degrees of quickness, assertiveness, exertion and discipline. Under these conditions his improvement as a soldier could be watched with the same care as his progress as a patient.

He had opportunity to resume his military interests from the moment he entered the hospital, but he did not do so until his mind was partly unburdened of its load of grief. He was shown no sympathy beyond that common to the professional relationship of doctor to patient. The change which occurred was not due to the mere provision of military drill or to any endeavour to win him over to better morale; such effort as was expended (adding all the interviews together they amounted to about an hour), was directed—following the lead given unwittingly by his own words and gestures—to disclosing to him the thoughts and feelings that were hidden in his mind. When a connection was made between his past experiences and his present existence, when he was enabled to bear the burden of his mental sufferings and see them in the context of his still developing emotional life, then and not till then could he resume interest in his environment, look into the future, become accessible to the feeling of pride in military accomplishment, and make friendly contact with his fellows on equal terms.

It will be remembered that he quickly recovered from his physical injury and fell ill of his hysterical paralysis on return to his depot. Here the sight of familiar faces awakened in his mind the memory of those he had lost in battle. Perhaps the disturbance and dissociation came not so much from the fear of injury but from the tension of mind due to this unassimilated experience of death, though it was not his first bereavement. When he had begun to adjust his feelings to the loss of a loved person his soldiering could be resumed, and he could face danger to himself and valued friends again.

Then and Now

The contrast in psychiatric theory between the two wars rests principally in the views taken of the emotional aspect of the patient's mental life. In the last war the important consideration was the conflict of instincts: those of self-preservation versus those of the herd (social attitude and duty to others). There is almost no mention of grief, mourning and depression in the psychiatric literature of the last war. In this war attention is directed to the kind of emotional bond existing in the patient's mind to objects (people) in whom he is interested, and to those representations of instinct (which we call phantasies) in the more primitive, but none the less important, levels of the mind which are not conscious. We do not see the conflict in abstract terms of instinct but in terms of concrete object relationships, historically determined for each individual by his past experiences, including his phantasies. These experiences affect his capacity to adjust himself to the changing conditions of his present life. The case quoted illustrates only one of the many aspects and causes of mental illness in war, and so may seem to over-emphasise it.

There is also a contrast in practice. We now assume that since the causes of the trouble are to be found not at one moment or phase of his life history only but throughout his development, our therapy must aim at presenting that development to the patient himself as it has been revealed to us in his anamnesis and his associations. Probably in the last war the link in meaning between contiguous associations was generally regarded, in theory, as a valid basis in investigation, but it was commonly neglected in clinical work; in this war we find our psychiatric experience enriched when we pay attention to this simple guide to therapy and research. But if we ascribe the change in theory and practice chiefly to the good use made by psycho-pathologists of the association rule, we must not overlook additions to knowledge made in other fields of psychiatric research.

XII

SIGMUND FREUD 1856–1939: AN APPRECIATION[1]
(1941)

FREUD's death marks the close of an epoch, and his life's work was the foundation of a new one. He was the last of the great nineteenth-century scientists, he inherited their tradition and their methods, and on their foundation he built a new edifice.

Born in *anno Darwinii*, he gave a new dimension to biological thought; *The Origin of Species* showed man's physical relation to the brute creation; within fifty years Freud's corresponding work on *The Interpretation of Dreams* showed the way in which impulses of instinctual origin (in the mental sphere the part of us nearest to the animals) find representation in our imagination and are transformed into the bonds which unite us in our cultural life.

To every thinking man and woman now living the death of Freud was a personal event. The ideas which he formulated have become a part of our everyday thought, and though the number who read his works is comparatively small, the recognition that they touched the inner life of man gave him a position in our regard which we can accord only to the great leaders in history. However little was known of his personal life, mankind has recognized and respected a fellow-being who endured calumny and lived to receive honour. And all men admire the energy and creativeness of a pioneer. His death in exile, and after many years of great physical suffering patiently borne, brought him within the horizons of our own imagination and experience, for the kinship in pain and affliction is more easily felt by our common clay than the sweeping movement of spirit and creative imagination which carries us away from our accustomed thoughts to new visions of the universe and to rediscoveries of familiar things. So all men drew breath and paused at Freud's death: the moment witnessed another and

[1] Reprinted from the *British Journal of Medical Psychology* (1941), **19**, 1–8.

irrevocable move made by the Fates on the field of human destiny.

The period of history in which we live has been called The Age of Science; it would be more modest and more true to say that in this generation science has made another step forward. In large measure this expansion of vision is due to Freud's work. The growth of Science, as a writer in *The Lancet* has recently remarked, has influenced men's lives in two directions: it has given man greater power over the forces of nature and has thus raised his standard of living. It has also increased the range of rational thinking; this second result if less spectacular is no less important. The researches of Newton, though immediately concerned only with the laws of motion and physical forces, by their simplicity and range united in men's thought the structure of the whole universe; what was true of a candle's beams must also be true of light from the sun and the most distant stars. There are no islands of local truth in a dividing sea of chaos, but one rule of law stretching to the boundary of human discernment and beyond it. The indirect effect of this realization of the unitary character of the universe was a confidence in reason in the face of an ever-prevalent human tendency to superstition. The spanning of the stretches of interstellar space by man's measuring devices strengthened his belief in the active power of his mind, so that it did not quail before the apparently more elusive mysteries of his mental life. In the age which Newton founded, the Age of Reason, the realm of magic and superstition was attacked with a self-confidence previously lacking, and blind wonder at the terrifying incomprehensible gave place to a determination to clarify and map out, if only by slow stages, this last remaining *terra incognita*—man's too emotional ways of thought.

Freud's work extended the domain of law to every aspect of the human mind. The concept of man as the product of a separate act of creation, an island of humanity in a totally different creature world, had as regards his body been abandoned, but the mind and the soul remained outside the laws of common nature; as they said at one of the seats of learning, there was Natural Science and Moral Science. To Freud belongs the distinction more than to any other man of giving us the beginning of the laws which in time will clear away the confusion between these two ways of regarding the universe without and the world of feeling and values within the mind of man.

Freud gave us two things of inestimable worth for increasing our power to understand the complexities of the human mind: an instrument of research (free association in the transference situation) by means of which the unconscious forces in the mind which mould social behaviour may be observed, and also a few rules, simple in theory though requiring years of training in their application, which enable an observer to trace the connexion between conscious and unconscious modes of thought (in his *Interpretation of Dreams*). All the rest of his work, and that of the hundreds who employ his methods, follows directly or indirectly from these two contributions. His work on dreams showed the way in which present impulses and past experiences find representation in current thought, i.e. how picture building and verbal expression become the vehicle of mental forces; his discovery of the transference situation enables an observer to penetrate beneath the surface of consciousness and bring forgotten past experiences within the scope of immediate observation. He himself reckoned it a piece of good fortune to have found the way to the meaning of dreams, but comparatively few of those who use his theories recognize their dependence for the development of the genetic and social branches of mental science on the exploitation in the spirit of research of the transference situation. The supreme importance of this research instrument lies in the power it gives the user of it to check the validity of theories, Freud's or anyone else's, concerning the relation of thought to impulse and the quality of the 'social forces' in the unconscious. He or others may be right in their views, but they will not *know* that they are right until they are verified by a method of observation which supplies a new set of data to corroborate or correct the notion being tested. So far there has not been any fundamental advance in research technique comparable in importance with that just mentioned. The inclusion of the study of children's behaviour within the framework of the technique of the transference situation is a most valuable extension of the same general principle. This research, which Freud left to others to carry out, provided new data of a hitherto quite unexpected kind that have corroborated the main lines of his theory of mental functioning.

Freud's work was received with incredulity because it dealt with unconscious forces in the mind, with horror because he broke the silence regarding infantile sexuality. He pointed out in plain language that the development of the sexual impulse

D

does not start at puberty and is not only present but is most active even in early childhood. The mode of expression of this impulse is of a different nature in infancy to that in adult life, but its effect on the orientation of attention and thought is if anything more powerful than in later years. Mankind had found the burden of adult sexuality hard enough to bear and its joys to be so unlike any other experience that for a two-fold reason sex was given no comprehensive study but was treated either with over-estimation or with cynicism or condemnation. In the course of time the essential fact which he established (of there being two kinds of sexuality, an infantile and an adult) was seen to bring much clarification of thought not only to the subject of sex but to that of the neuroses and of cultural life as well. It also established the child as an object of study in its own right so to speak and not merely as an immature adult; when children to the mind of science became the equals in importance of their grown-up counterparts, a new era dawned for the social sciences. From the knowledge obtained by the study of children man may obtain power and control over yet another aspect of nature—his own. That province cannot be won until the causes of the amnesia covering infancy are understood; we owe to Freud both the recognition of the amnesia and the significance for personal and for cultural development of what was hidden.

The advance in therapy which he made rests on the same basis—the discovery by the patient himself in the transference situation of the early experiences of desire, mood, thought and deed, which belong to these early and impressionable years. He not only made therapy possible where hitherto it had either failed or had been uncertain (the comparison with Lister's work has been made), but he also provided in his psycho-pathology a framework of reference covering great fields of experience that had hitherto been almost uncharted. Many have rejected his charts, but they owe to his bold initiative not a little of their courage to face new problems of the mind, whether they try to use his technique or not. It is a great pity that the position of this research instrument is not more widely realized by scientists. We regard Freud as a master thinker; his main claim to regard in the world of science, however, will in the future lie not so much in his theories (powerful though they are) as in his method of research, a technique which gave as its first fruits *The Interpretation of Dreams.*

It is not an easy task for a contemporary to attempt to estimate the extent of Freud's influence, but there are precedents to help us. Newton's work impressed itself on his own generation for the reason that it strengthened men's resolution to attack new problems, it seemed to put an end to chaos. Freud's work divided the world; those who saw in it the beginning of order where there had been confusion and those who dreaded an exploration of the warring forces in the mind, between those who had faith that reason did not destroy and those who clung for their temporary peace of mind to the familar rafts of their own conscious experiences while denying the possibility they could be drifting or blown by invisible currents. Freud compared himself to Copernicus and Darwin when considering the blows that man's vanity had received from men of science; but the likeness to Newton is nearer in that as a lawgiver he has fortified the mind of man by pointing out harmony existing in what had seemed to be diversity. (It is characteristic of him that he made this point clear in a study of his own confused thinking —in dreams.) It is true that he administered the third great blow to man's vanity, but he gave at the same time a *method* by which man's mental affairs could be examined and so set in order.

When a man appears among us who widens our horizons and shows us the unmistakable connections between events which had hitherto been thought of as belonging to separate worlds and who gives us a new medium of thought, we naturally wonder what forces were at work within himself which gave him this power to command and arrange and simplify the baffling complexity. One answer to this question, which will occasionally rouse the curiosity of mankind for many generations, is perhaps to be found in his peculiar attitude towards death. A single example will have to serve.

One of his pupils returning from the Near East called on him, then on holiday in the Semmering, for a talk and to discuss the fresh impressions from new fields of travel. The old man listened. He had the rare power to absorb silently, endlessly, and without effort to the speaker or distortion of the narrative by the force of his own special interests. And when the account was finished he asked for news from England. There was none, for the mails had gone astray in Constantinople; so after preparing the way he broke the news of James Glover's death. There was silence, each absorbed in his own reflections. Then Freud, as was often his habit, began to murmur his thoughts aloud: 'First Abraham, and now this fellow . . . there ought to be some Law, there ought to be some Law!'

It seemed as if he was conversing and gently expostulating with the Powers of Destiny at having been cheated of a final secret which transcended all others in importance.

How he loved Life! How bewildering was Death! Death stood for the untimely interruption of growth and being, of love and fulfilment. It was the last object of man's hatred and the first that he should face. He personified its force—this Titan 'Thanatos'—and pictured the struggle of the Giants, not in the sky beyond the sight and reach of men, but deep in the very cells and tissue of their nature. Silently, invisibly, Thanatos pulled down the work of his opponent 'Eros'. Love, the builder, had only this one dreadful master who always won the contest, but only after a long-drawn-out battle. Since Death could not be curbed, at least it must be mastered with the understanding. This was the struggle calling for a man's full strength, enabling him to disregard the temptation to petty quarrels with his fellow-men and to concentrate on the great task of producing by his creative power a theory, a book, a work of art, a battle, or the smooth running of a daily life, that would stay the hand of the Destroyer for oneself and give to this and the coming generations a further impetus in the eternal struggle with the inner seed of death.

The extension of the concepts he originated to the field of hypochondria, and its relation to persecutory and depressed conditions shows that his essential ideas can be employed fruitfully in psychiatric conditions where even he doubted their efficacy. His working model of the ego had surface experiences rather than contents, accordingly it did not go quite 'deep' enough when applied to the psychoses, though it was lively enough to serve a purpose for the psycho-neuroses. Thanatos, the Seed of Death lying in the very core of Being, did not become a vital part of his working model, indeed he found it hard to apply clinically.

Seldom can a man have given less occasion for recrimination. At a time when he was almost universally and most bitterly attacked no one could quote a single mean or petty remark made by him, and it was interesting to observe that when his detractors were faced with the fact that they were producing no evidence for their personal venom some of them turned the situation upside down and remarked, 'Ah! but you should have heard him years ago when he was a young man!' His voice had a richness and flexibility that equalled his wit and his remarkable gift for narrative. He could hold a group, great or small, in any society as soon as he began to talk. Perhaps some envy came into it too; there are many who will not recognize greatness, and as many who will not acknowledge quality in a contemporary, or will delay their admiration until their disapproval is conspicuous. Freud responded to the abuse by withdrawing from public controversies and giving his energies to his work and to writing. He did not try to raise himself up by attacking his fellows and profit by their failure, but by adding to knowledge and discovering the sources of ugliness he put his vast resources of mind and spirit to a task that would give a longer satisfaction than the echoes of personal triumph over a fellow-mortal.

This combination of immense strength coupled with an essentially gentle disposition had inevitably an effect on those who came into contact with him, at once inspiring and benumbing. A person so remarkable in personal endowment and profound in thought ran the risk of becoming an Oracle to his followers, so that what he said became a part of Truth (since it emanated from a source of almost dazzling inspiration). Freud himself knew the risk but was powerless to avert it. He warned his 'School' against accepting as members those whose infantile wishes had not been experienced again in their personal analysis; but the influence of the 'Master' (the image in the mind of a perfect Father) is always hard to eradicate, since through weakness and guilt human nature clings so tightly to the concept—the invention—of omniscience and perfection. He respected those who had an independent mind and groaned aloud, though not in public, if it were pointed out to him—which he knew all too well—how his readers followed the letter of his writings to the neglect of the spirit. An enthusiastic pupil asked him once why he did not take on some of the functions of a Director of Research and so stimulate others in profitable lines of thought and investigation; he replied that research could not be directed, a man might count himself fortunate if he had a flow of good ideas and was wise if he pursued them with courage, but that was a task which could not be done for anyone by another; and (this was said before the word 'training analysis' was invented) if any one wanted to do research in psycho-analysis he should take the trouble to start with an experience of his own analysis. It is better, he said, to focus attention on the things which hinder clear thought and creativeness than on planning tasks for other people without knowing (and without their knowing) what their limitations are. Although he held this view, he was generous in his time and thought when discussing problems that were put to him by his pupils; no one more than he was an encourager of research.

He was before all things a scientist, and if we are to benefit by his work we must follow the methods of science which he pursued with such patience and skill. His theories about mental functioning are there for the world to read in a dozen large books, and there the number will stop. Volumes of 'Freudiana' will appear to illumine or beguile the leisure hours, but whatever they may give to *belles-lettres* they will add next to nothing to the book of science. The future of his science lies in the development of his method of research rather than in reference to his findings.

Just after the last war an eager young pupil went to him for a personal analysis (it was not called a training analysis in those days, and at that time there were no bibliographies and no *Collected Works*) and asked him for the name of his publishers in order to get and study his writings in chronological order. He replied: 'Don't bother. Learn to read in the Book of Nature— your own analysis here—then you can turn whatever other pages you like and will profit more from them.' A noble answer from an old man to a young, and it contains a pointer to the source of all future developments of his science. The transference situation is a research instrument, *the* research instrument of the analyst, for disclosing forces in the mind of which the person himself is unconscious and for tracing the connection between the unconscious forces and the development of the personality as a whole; by developing its resources this science will progress, and as far as one can see at present there is no other method to compare with it in efficacy. So long as there are people who make it their chief interest to use this instrument of research into the unconscious, the essence of his life work will live on; if that spirit were to vanish, then the science which he founded will become static and will soon congeal into a philosophic-religious cult, a thing which he most loathed—perhaps the only thing he loathed—of the works of man.

The last of the great nineteenth-century scientists, he held their belief in the value of reason. He trusted implicitly in good results following a greater understanding of what is present in human nature.

The capacity to produce so much, and with an elegance of style and a feeling for values and beauty, arose from a singularly clear and noble spirit. Malevolence did not drag him down because he had so little of it at loose within him. His wisdom and strength were freely given to his fellow-men because to mankind he felt that true friendship which owes nothing to sentimentality, overestimation or condescension. In trouble and in joy he met his fellow-creatures as friends; he had come to terms with his own Thanatos and so could approach others with a clear mind and spirit.

His imagination was an inspiration and his friendliness an encouragement to all who knew him, his scientific integrity is a legacy to mankind. One instance of this integrity of spirit, and an event momentous in the history of psychology and so of human destiny: by means of the technical procedure which he employed he found (about 50 years ago) that many of his neurotic patients had in early childhood been the victims of seduction, their sexual partner being usually a parent or other nearly placed elder. Then he discovered that in fact these seduction scenes had not taken place. At first he was completely at a loss, his confidence both in his technique and in its results suffered a severe blow. And yet the subject-matter of those scenes was unquestionably related to the symptoms from which his investigations started. In the face of this quandary he examined his technique again and found that he had not suggested the seduction episodes to the patients but that they were the products of the patients' minds of great significance to the patients themselves: they were not physical facts but psychological facts—phantasies—and as such had as much right to a place in scientific esteem and usage as physical facts. No event in his career was so important as this, and none needed so much courage to assimilate. The priority given to tested evidence over previously held opinions and the holding to a research technique even though its results may be baffling and embarrassing are the qualities of a scientist. It is both the burden and the privilege which his science puts on his followers to endure a continual test, for the nature of the material (concerned as it is with mental pain) calls for frequent self-examination: a person does not just become a psycho-analyst, he has to keep on being one; there can be no lasting contentment with the data or the method of its acquisition. The enormous body of new facts which he discovered are relatively static, they cannot of themselves increase in diversity or 'meaning'; the spirit of his work is dynamic and his research methods if used with his sincerity and love of truth will continue to disclose the nature of the life and mind of man.

XIII
PSYCHOLOGY IN MEDICAL EDUCATION[1]
(1947)

AN important event in the professional life of every medical man, if not the most important event, is his dealing with patients in the first months of general practice. It is the first test of the young practitioner; it is also of course a test of his professional education. This article will discuss some of the difficulties, and the reasons for the difficulties, in the transition from student to practitioner, with special reference to the acquisition of professional skill in and understanding of the relation of a sick person to his medical adviser.

Changes in Medical Education

There are two ways in which a doctor can get instruction. He can be taken by his teacher into the patient's environment and be told there what factors have led to the ailment, what difficulties lie in the way of the remedy, and what chances there are, all things taken into consideration, of recovery. The teacher and his pupil make an entry into the patient's life, they enter his region of 'social space' and do what they can to bring some easement within it. The apprenticeship was an example of this kind of medical education. The second, the more modern way, is different: the patient is drawn into a region where he is isolated from usual social contacts and interests, and is examined by a number of hospital departments which have specialized on one or other aspect of the mechanism of his body or mind. The criterion on which the laboratory departments report is basically a statistical one: the findings lie within the normal limits for the age group of the patient examined.

Contrasting these two generalized methods of instruction and calling the former 'individual or apprenticeship' and the latter 'statistical or hospital', we can see advantages and disadvantages in each. When there is but one instructor, usually unsupported by the large and complicated apparatus of a hospital organ-

[1] Reprinted from the *British Medical Journal* (1947), **2**, 363–6.

ization, the latest discoveries in physiology and pathology are apt to suffer some neglect; there is pressure exerted on both teacher and pupil by the environment of the home to consider before all things the present emergency, including the social and financial strain of having a sick member on their hands. The patient is seen in the world in which he lives. Under such conditions it is admittedly not easy to examine in detail the workings of his various organs, but it is difficult not to see the way his life is tied in bonds of affection and dislike, in aspiration and despair, to his relatives and the social group of which he is a member. The apprentice to the general practitioner penetrated into the home and stood both to gain and to lose by that medical relationship.

A patient sent to hospital (to use the usual phrase) enters an unfamiliar region of social space. Within that organized system of research and therapy the easiest objects of study are the 'parts of the machine'—those portions of the individual patient which are most susceptible to test and measurable reaction. In such an environment of isolation from the personal and social forces which act upon the personality it is difficult to get a comprehensive understanding of the personality of the patient. An over-all view is a greater achievement of clinical synthesis in a hospital than in a house; a thoroughgoing mechanistic analysis of the patient is more difficult in the home than in the ward.

The task of medical education is to develop fully the capacity both for clinical synthesis and for mechanistic analysis. The questions arise: What conditions most favour this double development? What factors make those first few months of general practice something to be anticipated with dread and looked back on with relief as a thing long past? That many practitioners are eased in this transition by the senior partner of the firm they join, and thus enjoy a postgraduate apprenticeship, shows that the present—we do not know yet about the future—organization of medicine can allow the filling up of this gap in technical education.

How does the Doctor Spend his Day and his Energy?

Odd though it may seem, there has never been a 'job analysis' of the doctor's working day, or, if such an investigation has been made, it has received almost no publicity. It would appear that medical education has developed without a detailed reference to the job for which the student is being trained. How much of the doctor's time and how much of his skill are employed in the diagnosis and therapy of injuries, disorders, or normal processes—for example, confinements? How much of his day is given to specific planned acts of therapy, how much to diagnosis, and how much to travelling? Nor do we know how his time is divided between the age groups, the occupation groups, the income groups, or disease groups, or how far the proportions vary with urban and rural and other social and geographical divisions.

Important as these facts would be, one would think, both for teaching and for planning the future of a health service, even such an investigation of the relatively easily measurable units of time would ignore the subtler but perhaps more important factor of 'concern'. The doctor has concern for his patient: he is worried if he does not know what is wrong with him or how to bring him relief for his suffering. It is this concern which makes him feel the personal and human value of his work in the social —or, if you will, the spiritual—life of the community; it is something which makes him regard the financial return as only a part of the reward of his profession.

This factor, so important to the vitality of the profession and to its growth, cannot easily be brought within the scope of the mechanistically oriented education of the student. One does not have this concern-feeling for organs but only for a person, a fellow human being; one cannot book-learn it, it comes from a personal relationship.

The worries of the first few months of the general practitioner's life, or even the first few years, spring not from a need to harden his heart to suffering but to soften it so that he can feel his way into what the patient is going through in his suffering and yet keep his head. It is the attribute of professional competence to appraise the feelings of the patient, through sympathy with him, without losing objectivity and judgement of the situation as a whole. To get this over-all appraisal of the situation is often one of the main motives which lead the patient to seek professional advice, and the doctor cannot give it unless he has faced all the issues which confront his patient.

Though the patient may have to move into the 'hospital area' of social space and the doctor may have to move into that of the 'family area', the appraisal can best take place in the neutral ground of the doctor's consulting-room. He must make it neutral to all influences and prejudices if it is to act as a 'diagnostic and therapeutic area' in which patient and practitioner can both move with ease and mutual understanding.

The Medical Interview

One thing must be assumed in medical work: a patient never consults his doctor without good and sufficient cause. He may make a great fuss over what seems a trivial complaint, or he may dismiss as trivial symptoms of the gravest significance, but the cardinal fact is that he has come to a point when he cannot manage by himself something concerning himself—there is a breakdown in adjustment processes. Let us leave on one side those seemingly easy cases—for example, a cut hand needing a few stitches (though even such events may be indicators of accident-proneness or some such short-cut solution of a long-standing trouble)—and all of those cases which occasion the doctor no concern. What remain? Just those cases— and taken over the year how numerous they are!—where the physical-mechanistic solution to human suffering has failed.

Two questions the practitioner has to put to himself: What is wrong? and, no less important, How ill is the patient? A repetition of a visit to the surgery with the same worried expression about the same 'trivial' complaint, or a new one equally trivial, is a distress signal: the degree of the maladjustment is not to be measured by the degree of dysfunction of the organ system complained of—the patient is more ill than his body gives warrant for. What should the doctor do—judge the situation by the sole criterion of physical disability and dismiss the rest as 'imagination', or assume that where there is much complaining there is something paining? And if this be the case, how does one discover the cause if it is not in the body? Is the registered medical practitioner to have traffic with the woes of the soul? Perhaps he need not go quite so far.

It was said that the consulting-room should be a sort of neutral ground where everything can be considered dispassionately (which is not the same as cold-heartedly) and without prejudice. If the patient has some worry on his mind his original complaint may be only a point of entry to the consulting-room, where he wants to get rid of his burden. Then the important thing is not only to let him talk but for the doctor to let himself listen. When it has been acquired, the art of listening is not a tedious one-way traffic but a technique of getting the patient to unfold the life-history of the suffering lying at the root of his present complaint as it is to be seen in the framework of the development of his personality as a whole: a history-giving rather than a history-taking. How can this art be acquired?

No Research without Therapy; No Therapy without Research

This is rather a grand way of saying, among other things, that between patient and practitioner there must be a two way traffic.

The sufferings which lead to 'trivial or pointless complaints', no less than an easily spotted neurosis, are basically hidden from and are confused for the patient himself; they are bound up with the development of his personality and are an expression of conflicting trends within it. If their solution were easily within his capacity he would have solved them long ago; the fact that he comes to his doctor is sufficient evidence that his powers of adaptation have for the moment at least broken down. He cannot cope with the present problems of his life because he has to solve and satisfy unresolved and uncompleted emotional situations of the past. The aim of the interview is to allow the patient to disclose as fully and as freely as possible the history of his development. This disclosure the doctor must meet with sincerity of purpose and dispassionateness, and he must not lose patience in the face of failure.

These qualities are among those which are prerequisites in the research worker. The solving of the problem of mental pain in the individual patient is not possible without this research quality in the therapist, and his greatest contribution to the two-way process is less often advice than an understanding of the problem at issue.

Research workers who try to invade the private lives of human beings to wrest from them answers to abstract research problems seldom get far with their researches into the cause and cure of mental suffering, and their work usually remains in the academic library for which it was written. People can disclose the sources of their mental suffering only during the actual experience of relief of that suffering. The so-called 'normal psychology', which takes no account of the influence of pain, anxiety, guilt, and grief on human behaviour, need not for long detain the medical student in his preparation to deal with people and their problems in real-life situations.

Is Psychiatry yet Another Speciality?

When a patient comes into a consulting-room the doctor has before him only the small segment existing in the present of an organism with an extension in time. This organism, as was recently said by a writer in *The Lancet*, began as a speck of jelly and will end some day as a life-size corpse. It grows by constant interaction with its environment, passing through different physiological phases and as many different psychological and social orientations. The egoism of the infant partly gives place to the passions of love and rage of the child (both, often and most embarrassingly, directed to the same person), and later to the stormy mixtures of adolescence, then to a fairly stable maturity, and finally shrinking in body and mind in old age (Shakespeare has said that better, but it bears repetition). Each age and stage has its problems, which when unsolved are never completely left behind: the doctor has to listen for the murmur of those old and unresolved complaints beneath the apparent preoccupation with present ills.

The study of these problems is called psycho-pathology; the application of such knowledge to the sufferings of the individual is a part of psychiatry (and of groups, 'sociatry'). The training of the student to elicit a history (the much-guarded history of the development of the personality) is one of the duties of his psychiatric teachers. Training for the assessment of the retardations of development, intellectual and emotional, is also part of psychiatric teaching.

The whole range of neuroses, marital maladjustment, character disorders, delinquency, and insanity; the wider range of so-called psychosomatic affections, and the still wider range of mild and temporary worrying upsets (which are partly due to misery of spirit or insecurity, to lack of love or incapacity to give and receive affection and find rest of body and mind)—all these are medical problems which get help from psychiatry, and sometimes only there. Is psychiatry a speciality? It stands outside the physical-mechanistic separatism which was till perhaps recently the prevailing convention in modern medicine, for if it is to do its job it must take a wide and time-spanning view of the personality in its social setting: it is of course no less a speciality than medicine itself.

On Bringing the Student to the Patient

(*a*) The medical student should be brought at an early stage in his career into relation with patients. For example, when dissecting he should have periodic turns of duty as a dresser in the casualty out-patients department; even a sprained wrist or ankle should be seen in relation not only to anatomy but also to social disability. The young student should be relieved of some of his load of corpses and learn to carry live burdens. (Some of the apparent immaturity of the medical student is a reaction to the abstract and impersonal nature of his studies, which frustrate his clinical inclinations. It is a sad thing that the student's first 'patient' is a corpse.)

(*b*) Much more time should be *lived* in medical institutions. Even in the pre-clinical years the student could learn some of the routine of the ward as a student orderly, both to have an insight into how patients behave and what they feel when doctors are not present, and to get some first-hand knowledge of the ward as a community. A few weeks in epileptic and mental defective colonies, in tuberculosis and other sanatoria for chronic cases, would widen his understanding of the chronically sick. His status on some of these visits would be nearer to that of the nursing than the medical staff; on others he should go as assistant to the doctors.

I might illustrate the value of the good nurse's approach to a case by the following example: A patient in a public ward suffered from nocturnal attacks of respiratory and other kinds of distress. His house-physician and the registrar were asked by a doctor patient in the same ward, as a matter of professional interest, what precipitated the attacks. They did not know; medical examination gave no clue. The patient's nurse was asked and gave an answer without hesitation: the attacks followed the visits of a particular relative. Two comments here: first, the nurse, whose knowledge of anatomy, physiology, pathology, and clinical medicine was of high nursing standard, used that knowledge in a quite different way from the house-physician and registrar: the latter made it the sole theoretical instrument of aetiology and diagnosis; the former (perhaps freer because she had no self-imposed duty to limit her thinking to what she read in books) was able to observe the facts as a whole. The doctors had not asked about the effect of visitors; it had not, presumably, come into their theories of aetiology. The second point is that the nurse observed the patient in a wider region of biological activity, that of the family—that is, in a social setting. The doctors saw only what lay in the bed, not even what came to the bedside. Which, in this case, was the more clinical and which the more veterinary observer? Of course, such a question should not be put: it is a question framed with reference to 'academic subjects' and not to scientific method. Rather let us ask, Which of the two provided himself or herself with the greater number of frames of reference, and used them in an integrative way?

Speaking aphoristically, the best medical instruction is clinical—that is, bedside. If the patient's illness and not 'a disease entity' be the subject of instruction, the best bed for this purpose is the patient's own, the next best is one that the hospital pupil has to be responsible for, the third best is that which is in hospital and which someone else looks after: the first educates the G.P., the second the nurse; the medical student in this respect comes off third best. I am referring to learning about the illnesses of actual people, not about diseases; and, further, I am saying no more than that this kind of bedside or clinical experience—though it does not come into examination-ridden curricula—is important for the student and the young practitioner.

(c) He should at first be taken by almoners and psychiatric social workers, and later go alone, on follow-up visits to a selection of the patients he has seen and treated as out-patients and in the wards. He should realize how large is the gap between the 'social space' of the family and that of the hospital, and he should be taught the techniques for lessening and bridging that gap—for example, the endeavours made increasingly nowadays to create within the hospital and convalescent home transitional communities where the recovering patient can make an effective rehabilitation.

(*d*) He should have experience in all branches of the mental out-patients department, in intelligence testing, in the social workers' department, and above all in the practice of psychiatric interviewing.

(*e*) He should interview relatives of patients with the same care as patients themselves—time spent on learning interview technique is repaid a hundredfold in his general practice.

(*f*) Anything that brings the student to the patient, to his home, to his factory should be welcomed, and will help to make the transition from medical school to professional life as easy and as fruitful as possible.

(*g*) Medical education should proceed on the principle (hard though it be to apply) that knowledge gained through the shouldering of responsibilities is the best sort of medical knowledge to have.

On Using the Ex-student's Experience

A sample survey might be made one, two, and five years after leaving medical school, asking general practitioners what comments they would like to make on the curriculum of their training. Such opinion-taking would be specially useful to estimate the desirability of continuing experimental changes in the curriculum and dropping those that were not expedient.

The Doctor-Patient Relationship

An experiment is in train to evolve a national health service. The stability of the profession *vis-à-vis* the patient population will ultimately depend on the doctor's capacity to meet the patient's need to be understood as a person. If treated as a merely physical mechanism composed of parts and system the patient will turn more than ever to self-medication or to unqualified persons. The existence of quacks[1] is a reproach to the

[1] A quack may be defined as a person who seeks to establish a quasi-professional relation to a client (or patient) without having first submitted himself to a course of training regarded as adequate by the teachers in that profession; who makes no consistent endeavour to integrate any discovery he may make in the exercise of the profession to the body of knowledge already existing—to the end that the range of experience of the next generation of students may be improved; who when in a difficulty with diagnosis or treatment does not call in a brother-practitioner, laying before him all the facts

training and to the practice of the regular profession. (A survey of medical needs and medical aids, if realistic, would have to include the activities of the quack, his clientele, and his method of work.)

The remedy for the problem of unqualified practice lies in better medical qualification—a training which meets the needs of those worried and distrusting patients who cannot define their ills and who turn from one adviser to another till they find a listener.

The organization of a national health service will fail of its purpose if scope is not given in fullest measure for the relationship between doctor and patient to be one of personal trust and confidence and for that continuity of interest in the individual patient which springs from professional 'concern'.

known, being ready to accept the advice offered, or who would not be willing, if called in by a brother-practitioner, to put his experience fully at his disposal and return the patient to his own practitioner, not trying to keep him for himself; and who is unwilling to submit himself to the discipline of the organizations of his profession in matters affecting his ethical relations to his patients.

The definition turns on four things: on the willingness to learn in due humility from an older generation, to give without arrogance to the next generation, to treat one's own generation with generosity as equals, and to submit to a social code.

Most of the articles on quacks and quackery enlarge on the practitioner-patient relationship; ought not more consideration to be given to the relation existing between persons in the same field of social activity—namely, brother practitioners?

XIV

THE APPLICATION OF PSYCHO-ANA-
LYTICAL PRINCIPLES TO HOSPITAL
IN-PATIENTS[1]

(1948)

W E are met to consider the application of psycho-analytical
principles to hospital in-patients. Before we consider the applications it would be well to consider briefly, and have some
agreement on, what those principles are.

First, the whole fifty years of psycho-analytical experience
shows that one cannot separate research from therapy in this
field of work. The technical aim of the therapy is to enable the
patient to disclose as fully and as freely as possible the history of
his development, including not least that of which he has been
unconscious. This disclosure the doctor must meet with sincerity
of purpose and dispassionateness, and he must not lose patience
in the face of failure. These qualities are among those which are
prerequisites in the research worker. The discovery of the
causes and the solving of the problems of mental pain are not
possible unless the patient experiences relief of that suffering in
the course of his treatment; then he will co-operate in the research and in the therapy. This can be briefly summarized by
saying 'No research without therapy; no therapy without research', i.e., the patient's personal and particular difficulty has
to be the subject of a special and personal investigation, personal both to the patient and to the doctor treating him.

The second point is that there is invariably a strong but unconscious defence set up against the resurgence of the past
emotionally-toned experiences, and these defence processes
operate both in the patient and in the doctor treating him; if
the latter has not worked through his own past experience he
will unwittingly co-operate with the patient's defences in
greater or lesser degree, and this will nullify both the investi-

[1]Reprinted from the *Journal of Mental Science* (1948), **94**, 764–66.
A contribution to a Symposium at the Royal Society of Medicine
[Section of Psychiatry] March 9, 1948.

gating process and the concomitant therapy. This work cannot be learnt from a book; it is a piece of living, i.e., an always changing experience.

The third point is that invariably there is disclosed a disturbance in those aspects of the patient's object relationships which in the widest sense we can call sexual and which, again, are unconscious. The kind of object relationship thus disclosed originates in infancy, and tends towards behaviour which is incompatible with the ordinary adult or conscious or social relationships.

The fourth is the most important of all for our present discussion. It is invariably found that the patient's behaviour is determined by two classes of tendency: the one is to adjust to his present environment (of this he is usually conscious), the other is to use the present situation to work through uncompleted emotional experiences of the past (of these he is invariably unconscious); these two tendencies operate simultaneously. The aim of the psycho-analytical procedure is to discover and to facilitate the patient's re-experiencing these uncompleted and unconscious emotional situations in the relation existing between patient and physician and make them conscious. It is a new kind of social relationship which Freud devised and called the 'transference situation', which is at once the instrument of research and of therapy. A therapy which does *not* give the development of this transference situation the highest priority (and the working out of present findings in it in terms of the patient's past experience by free associations) is by that much not using psycho-analytical principles, i.e. the measure of 'psycho-analyticness' of a therapy depends on the degree of priority given to this process.

Now I have gone into these preliminary details, which after all are well known, because something important must be said which is not so widely realized; these are positive statements about what occurs in psycho-analytic treatment, not about what must not occur. There is nothing in all this that is incompatible with the exhibition of sedatives, shock-therapy, surgical interference with the brain or other organs, not even with the restriction of social locomotion (certification). Any or all of these things are compatible with psycho-analytical therapy of the patient *provided*—this is a most important provision, particularly, most particularly, for the analyst—provided that every event is referred back to this peculiar kind of social relationship called the transference.

The more that the analyst discloses his own opinions or personality, the more difficult is it for him and the patient to discern what is transferred from the unconscious into the situation. For this reason the analyst and patient do not meet socially, nor does the analyst give advice. Further, it is a relation between two people. In out-patient analysis this is possible.

With in-patient psycho-analytic treatment there are complications because more than one doctor comes simultaneously into the doctor-patient relationship; from a two-body it becomes a multi-body situation; for example, the Medical Superintendent, the House Physician and the analyst *vis-à-vis* the patient. How does this affect the application of psycho-analytical principles? In essentials not at all, it only makes the unravelling of the transference phenomena more difficult. The role ascribed to each of these persons in the patient's current phantasy life has to be discerned separately and with their interconnections and interpreted to the patient. This is more difficult for the analyst than in the usual out-patient treatment, because with in-patient work these other doctors are in fact playing a social role in the analyst's as well as the patient's life. So both parties to the analytical relationship have more to cope with, but the principles of the work can be applied just the same.

We could summarize what I have said so far almost in three words: the work of analysis is essentially—like all scientific work—a-historical. True we deal with the reconstructions of the patient's past, but we see them 'here and now' (the three words) in the present, here before us in the transference situation, now. It is the discovery of *all* the ingredients in the 'here and now' on the part of patient and analyst which constitutes the essence of this work. Its success depends on the power to concentrate on the details and their inter-relations in the 'here and now'. 'There is no middle position' as an aphorist said, 'between the "here and now" and the "cut and dried".'

Before I conclude I want to add one word about co-operation between analyst and other doctors who are also involved in the medical care of the case. Such co-operation is not easy because in the transference situation itself the other doctors can play no direct part; frustrated curiosity is always hard to bear. But when the patient (as may well happen) plays one doctor off against another the situation is apt to be exasperating. In the long run this usually rights itself if the doctors concerned can see the value of referring, and letting be referred back, everything that occurs to the cardinal situation of psycho-analytical research and therapy—the transference situation. What really counts is not where the work is done, but how thoroughly the essential principles are grasped and what priority they are given.

XV

GUILT AND THE DYNAMICS OF PSYCHOLOGICAL DISORDER IN THE INDIVIDUAL[1]

(1948)

In this session of the Conference we shall hear the topic assigned to us discussed from several aspects, medical, legal, ecclesiastical and philosophical. Within each of these disciplines there is, as is well known, diversity of opinion, which is a healthy sign; between these disciplines there is even greater diversity, probably because the method of professional approach to persons suffering from guilt is different in each of these learned disciplines. What I shall say from the viewpoint of a psycho-pathologist will be an attempt at a combination of not altogether incompatible opinions.

In addition to the doctor's general responsibility for the physical and mental welfare of his patient, the psycho- pathologists have, since the early pioneering days of Freud, a common method of work which is shared, so far as I know, by no other profession: they listen to whatever the patient may say in free association about his pains, griefs, dreams, aspirations or joys; they regard no two ideas as irrelevant to one another if the patient has brought them—however unwittingly or however unwillingly—into the same stream of associations. Thus the psycho-pathologist sees guilt in a wide context of personal experiences: not in relation to religious beliefs and ethical codes as the clergy inevitably do, not in relation to abstractions as the philosophers choose to do, but as the patients find and feel it within themselves.

The psycho-pathologist—as a result of intensive study of people who, though comparatively few in number, are of wide diversity of type, and each patient seen for very many hours under the same conditions of observation—is in a position to place into a frame of reference the various theories of guilt and

[1] Reprinted from the Proceedings of the International Conference on Medical Psycho-therapy (being Vol. III of the *Proceedings of the International Congress on Mental Health* (1948)), London, 41–7.

its relation to the dynamics of psychological disorder. The frame of reference he uses is based on the development, as he sees it, of personality in the human being.

Guilt is sometimes thought of as a painful tension arising between an individual and a code of behaviour. Sometimes this code is regarded as of human origin, e.g. the social conventions (including laws) in which he is brought up, sometimes as of divine origin, e.g. the dictates of conscience implanted by God in the individual. Most, if not all, psycho-pathologists regard guilt as a manifestation of tension existing within the individual but arising, as we shall see in a moment, from the interplay of the person with the environment: from an absorption of a part of the environment into the self.

I should add that there has been a continuous development of psycho-pathological ideas in the last fifty or sixty years, which is itself an instructive object of study. At first, guilt was thought of as a sign of tension between the individual and the social code, then it was found that this social code, as far as its effects on the individual are concerned, was derived from the child's relation to the father and mother, i.e. conscience was an incorporation within the personality of parental injunctions. And these injunctions were accepted by the child and incorporated as a part of itself into its ways of mental behaviour in order that it might keep in good relation to its parents, both of whom were loved though one of them was a rival in its erotic life. Disobedience to the now incorporated parental injunction gives a pang of conscience or guilt and produces a fear of retribution; furthermore, disobedience to the dictates of conscience now causes a sense of separation between the child and its parents, and, therefore, of loneliness and depression. The pain of guilt thus viewed—and it is only a first approximation—is compounded, among other things, of depression and retribution-anxiety.

Guilt cannot, however, be considered in isolation; it is one kind of psychical action in a complicated, inter-connected set of psychical actions which appear to serve the purpose of keeping the organism in a quasi-stable equilibrium. Anxiety is as important as guilt in the formative—or deformative—influences on the growth of personality, and it is sometimes difficult to distinguish clinically a pang of guilt from the persecutory anxieties which also limit the freedom of action of the individual, and inhibit his social and personal growth.

If, taking a general view, we consider the various kinds of deep-rooted but secondary mental distress, we can single out two that are specially relevant to our discussion: the one is characterized by a feeling of depression, the other by a feeling of being attacked or persecuted. (But Nature, never obliging to the theoretician, inconveniently provides us in the majority of patients with a mixture of the two elements.)

The depressive sort of deep-rooted mental pain is experienced when we feel somewhere in our minds that we have done an injury, or intended an injury—albeit only in phantasy—to a love-worthy object. We do not feel any defensive guilt if the object we injure is felt by us—and felt unwaveringly—to be worthy of our hate, nor do we feel depression at its loss. The persecutory sort of deep-rooted mental pain arises when a person projects on to the outer world feelings of hostility which he cannot tolerate within himself: he then feels the outer world to be bad and aggressive, and he himself, by contrast, to be innocent.

If people and objects could be sorted out conveniently into either love-worthy or hate-worthy, and if there were no intermediate class towards which we had mixed feelings, life would be simple; but then it would not be human life as we know it. To repeat, we feel guilt when we do an action that will bring ourselves the isolation from love which follows from parental disapproval, or derivatives of that disapproval, and the punishment of their displeasure. Also, we feel guilt when we do or intend an injury to a loved person; but, as guilt is an almost intolerable burden, we repress the experience and it can only with great difficulty be faced fully and examined. This is true for almost all stages of our development.

When an emotional situation involving ourselves and those whom we love and depend on is disturbed by too much pain, and is repressed, it still continues to influence our mental life, and there is an urge to resolve or complete that uncompleted situation, even though, through repression, we are no longer aware what it is we want to complete. Indeed at each stage of our lives we carry the past over into the present; i.e. we not only live in and for the present, but are urged also to complete—here and now—what was unresolved in the earlier stages of our development, particularly our early childhood's difficulties. Perhaps the Fall of Adam from grace and Man's inheritance of his guilt is a myth derived from the experience we all go through of incurring guilt from our relation to our creators and those who nurtured us—our parents. Not that we ever experienced an age of Innocence, however; far from it, those mixed passions of love and hate, both turned to the same persons in our environment, were there from our earliest years.

Let us review the matter once more. In our infancy, on whom did we lean for life, for love, for guidance? Who, when we were most impressionable, could put us in a barren land by the withdrawal of love, and by giving love could fill our lives with contentment? Perhaps the question if put in this way leads to a too simple answer. The first person who fulfils this rôle in our lives is the mother. But from an early age we have to come to terms with two people at once: the two parents. The double (love and hate) impulses originally directed against one person are transferred to this three-cornered relationship, and in this 'Oedipean situation' the sexual impulses, now more focused than before, suffer their acutest frustration. In the case of the boy, for instance, the father is hated because he stands between himself and his mother; but the father is also loved and admired. The hate against him is a source (a main reservoir, so to speak, outflowing into subsequent experience) of guilt.

It is the invariable discovery of this early love-and-hate-ridden relation to both parents together (found by analysts of all schools) which leads us to ascribe both the climax of guilt feelings and the focal point in the development of stability in the personality to this experience in the earliest years of life. It is the reactions to the guilt of the early period of life which gives us our proneness to mental illness and instability, to crime and also to our loftiest aspirations and achievements—in a word, which makes us human.

The reason that depressive guilt—which contains a large element of love—is, in suitable measure, culturally valuable, is that it leads to a change in the direction and object of both loving and aggressive impulses. Henceforth, a part of the aggression is turned against the self instead of to a loved person in the outer world, and this in-turned aggression provides energy for that which, when conscious, we call conscience, but which is better described by the more inclusive term, super-ego. But the super-ego draws strength from the loving impulses as well. The wish to seek approval from the parents is not only due to dread of their displeasure and fear of their attack; it embodies also a wish to draw closer to them in identification of interests, behaviour and outlook. Later, for orientation to the parents, there is substituted an orientation to the community. Henceforth the child becomes a social animal, sensitive to the opinions of others. Without this sensitiveness, which is stimulated by a small but tolerable amount of (unconscious) guilt, the personality would not develop an increasing social capacity.

The persecutory element in guilt leads to propitiation and an undue value attached to conformity.

To sum up, to develop and simplify what we have considered so far, and are going to consider: if man had no aggressive impulses he would not have feelings of guilt. The pang of guilt is of two kinds: the one is in the last analysis depressive, due to misery at injury done to a loved object and the pain of isolation; the other is persecutory, and occurs where there is projected hostility returning upon the self as dread of punishment. These components are commonly mixed.

But there is always aggression, and there is always love (ambivalence is one of the outstanding characteristics of the developmental period in the human young), and so there is always a reaction to the aggression. The guilt I am considering is not a sort of reflex jerk on the feelings because of some specific act, but a quite complicated process, involving the whole of the personality, with continuity from the weaning period, probably reaching climaxes at about five years of age and puberty. The unresolved guilt feelings from one period of life are carried over to the next, so that it is expedient to give priority to consideration of the early guilt-ridden experiences when estimating the influence of guilt on the personality and its maladjustments.

The kind of reactions we are considering go far beyond the awareness of the twinges of guilt that are usually spoken of in non-psycho-dynamic literature: first, the process is for the most part unconscious (another name for it might be 'a need for punishment' though that is an incomplete description); second, the process does not end with a painful intrusion into consciousness—there is a continuous need to do something about it.

The reactions to guilt—the need to do something about it—may take various forms: (a) a drive to *restitution* in the external world for the injuries done or intended in phantasy against the loved object (this guilt reaction to the depressive element leads to a reinforcement of the impulse of creativeness); (*b*) a compulsive urge to *propitiation* of an aggressor and to an undue amount of *social conformity*—a reaction to the persecutory component; (*c*) a *denial* of the aggressive tendency (thus leading to a 'superficial' personality of the extravert type): (*d*) a brooding absorption in and at the same time *repression* of the aggressive tendency (leading to a 'profound' personality of the introvert type—with creativeness that is primarily in the intra-psychic field); (*e*) *compulsive behaviour* where the tendency is to get rid of the tension due to guilt by courting punishment (as is found in some criminal types, where the main guilt *precedes* the crime for which the courts punish, in the accident prone, and in some sexual perversions); (*f*) in the same direction as above, not individual acts, but the whole life may be one long spread-out *expiatory existence* (the masochistic character type); (*g*) the wide range of cases of *sexual anomaly* in which the sexual act is felt to be an injury to the partner or at least a degradation (leading to impotence or frigidity or to a Don Juan-like compulsive change of lover); (*h*) those elaborate *compromise formations* which we find in neurotics and psychotics; and though it is only on the borderline of our present subject I should like to add (*i*) man's *interest in religion* and charitable organizations.

If we turn to the psychological disorders in the individual that are conveniently but usually too rigidly classed as psychoses and neuroses, guilt appears as a frequent symptom. This is particularly clear in the manic-depressive disorders, at least in the depressive self-accusatory phase; but in the manic phase careful examination shows the active denial of guilt, and with it a denial also of all values in the inner world of phantasy. This 'manic defence' affects far more people than could by any stretch of classification be called psychotic, and indeed is a common feature in certain cultural areas in the world today. These people, those with 'manic defence' as the nucleus of their character, do not appear to be as ill-adjusted as they really are because their reaction to guilt is obscured by the fact that their mode of defence against intrapsychic tension is the customary one of their country or class. I have singled out this type of defence for special mention because it seems to me to be one of the signs of maladjustment in our civilization and a threat to its stability. (The reason why I think Religion to be weak in the face of the disorders we are considering, and why it has thrown so little light on the origin of guilt—though it has talked enough about it, Heaven knows—is that it started with an hypothesis which has paralyzed its power of investigation: it usually assumes both a God and a Devil, or it assumes forces one of which is all-good and the other all-bad. Thus it fails to grapple at close quarters with man's seemingly eternal problem of love and hate for the same person—with ambivalence, which to many is an intolerable mental burden. Religion has not yet recovered from its initial and perhaps intrinsic mistake of dividing God and Devil. Thus the problem of the ambivalent relation to the great creative Father is left unresolved and insoluble on the premises it employs. Religion and law provide evasions of the solution—they institutionalize the mental defences. The primal act is not punishable at the time of commission, because the guilt-evoking aggressive intention works intra-psychically; but as in the unconscious part of the mind there is no Statute of Limitations, debts against the conscience are never remitted).

The only sure way of removing the burden of guilt is to bring the sufferer back, against terrific resistance, to recall, to re-experience the pain, grief and guilt of those early—and heretofore unresolved—emotional situations of ambivalence, and to get him to readjust himself to the new understanding of himself and his inner world and to the world of people about him. This slow and painful therapeutic task, which involves not a dabbling in generalities but a re-experiencing in the close personal relation to the physician of the very problems he flinched from before (an undertaking which is not, however, infallible) is clearly not a panacea that can be used at present at any rate, for the mass of mankind. Fortunately most people are not in urgent need of psycho-therapy; but at least those who deal professionally with the human sciences, the advisers to our culture—though the advice is seldom taken—need to know, when they deal with human problems, how widespread is the influence and how deep-rooted is the origin of guilt.

If radical treatment is so slow and laborious, if the number of people it can directly affect is so small, it may be asked whether the psycho-pathologist is not both impotent and gloomy at the prospect facing mankind; can the benumbing and distorting effects on guilt of healthy growth be mitigated in any way? The most important act of prophylaxis is to face the facts, and the most important fact to face concerns the up-bringing of children.

It is hard for a child to grow up in a broken home or a potentially broken home without acquiring an extra burden of guilt. Because of its ambivalence a child will always feel some responsibility unconsciously for the broken home. A home is potentially broken if one parent uses the child's affection as a weapon of offence or defence against the other parent. In a word, the child needs to see in its parents people who respect each other and can get on well together; this helps him to overcome his ambivalence and it diminishes his ever-active guilt. (A great part of the work of Child Guidance Clinics is that of dealing with the painful results of broken and potentially broken homes.)

In respect to the child, there is one cardinal point to make: its guilt begins early, and so does the considerable cultural restraint of its aggressive and other a-social impulses; certainly by the time it is four years of age it is a cultural unit, though not yet a stable one. This fact should be borne in mind, and also the the fact that the child has its own pace of cultural and mental growth. A child needs very little teaching about what is right and wrong: it is greatly helped if it is left to find its own way to a good relation even to not-so-good parents. A parent's failure to recognize the child's capacity for guilt is a failure to recognize that it is a human being.

In this paper I have stressed the depressive aspect of guilt rather more strongly than the retributive or persecutory aspect because the ill-effects of parental harshness in increasing the child's sense of guilt are so well known. The depressive component of guilt produces a great deal of man's apathy in the face of remediable suffering, and robs him of his initiative to make the best of his circumstances, but the reaction to this depressive component strengthens the tendency to reparation and creativeness. The persecutory component, being more influenced by hate, has less wholesome reactive consequences both in personal and, I suggest, also in international life.

This Conference does well to give its attention to a subject which—through its painful character, to be sure—people strive to avoid.

XVI

ON THE CRITERIA FOR THE TERMIN-
ATION OF AN ANALYSIS[1]
(1950)

THE lack of a systematic follow-up of our cases several years after treatment is ended makes difficult an accurate assessment of the criteria for termination. We know something of the cases which come back for more analysis and the reasons for the incompleteness of the first therapy, but we do not usually know enough about those who do not come back, though we sometimes get favourable accounts of those whose analysis was terminated before we, at the time, thought advisable.

There is a second reason for hesitation in defining the criteria. The class of case now treated, speaking generally, is more of the character analysis type than the simpler hysteria and obsessional with which psycho-analytical work in the main began. Both our frontiers and our method of work are changing, and also our criteria.

In an analysis two parties have to be satisfied, the patient and the therapist. The patient is often satisfied too early with the results obtained in the procedure, while the therapist has his own and less subjective criteria. One of these can be given a sort of code name, 'Irreversibility;' i.e. the process of improvement in personality-integration and adaptability, which has been reached thus far, should be of such a degree and kind that, even without further analytical aid, there will be no reverse process or regression on the cessation of treatment—granted of course that no enormous stress is put upon the patient after treatment ends. The matter can be viewed in another way, viz. has the treatment removed the major obstacles to the action of the integrative processes which operate within every living organism, so that these integrative processes will in the end get the upper hand without further analytical aid?

[1] Reprinted from the *International Journal of Psycho-Analysis* (1950), **31**, 200–201.
  A contribution to a Symposium of like title given at a meeting of the British Psycho-Analytical Society on April 6, 1949.

Such general considerations I believe to be fundamental to our topic this evening. When looking more closely at specific criteria, we can single out a few of undoubted importance:

(a) the capacity to move smoothly in memory (and to let old feelings surge up on occasion) from the past to the present and back again, i.e. the removal of infantile amnesia, which of course includes a facing and working through of the Oedipus complex,

(b) the capacity for heterosexual genital satisfaction,

(c) the capacity to tolerate libidinal frustration and privation without regressive defences, and without anxiety,

(d) the capacity to work and to endure unemployment,

(e) the capacity to tolerate the aggressive impulses in the self and others without losing object love in its full sense and without guilt, and

(f) the capacity to mourn.

These are listed in the order, I believe, in which these criteria have appeared in our periodic literature.

These various factors, though subject to quantitative change, are combined by the clinician to form a pattern of action which is or should be assessed, not in respect to an ideal personality, but to one which will not disintegrate or regress under instinctual pressures or privations. The point I want to stress here is that the ultimate criterion (singular) is a *pattern* combining many factors each of which may have quantitative variations and each of which has a 'point of irreversibility'.

Thus far I have not spoken of transference phenomena. I will come to them in more detail later; we know these phenomena are the source of our greatest insight into the depths of the patient's mind and at times are also a source of confusion as to the way in which he is actually shaping in the external world. This last is for several reasons:

(i) because of the thoroughness with which the ego is oriented in analysis to the working through of the unsolved emotional problems of infancy,

(ii) because of a self-punishing tendency not to appear to the analyst to be 'good' when the patient feels himself to be evil,

(iii) because of a wish to cling to the analyst and so perpetuate an infantile situation and to keep future patients from the couch.

For quite a variety of reasons the analyst is presented with the disintegrative aspects of the patient and often less clearly with the integrative ones, for which reason it has been remarked that 'Psycho-pathology says more about what is yet to be done than what has been done, because a large part of what has been done is a silent process of integration which is also carried on in the unconscious but is manifest when the occasion calls for it in the external world.'

Now to come to a point mentioned earlier. The week-end break, because it is an event repeated throughout the analysis, which is also punctuated by the longer holiday breaks, can be used by the analyst when making the integrative pattern before referred to in order to assess the development of the patient.

The patient, who early in our work pictures his analyst spending the week-end with nose deeply buried in books and never stirring save to go to a library to get still more books, later in the analysis pictures him going to the theatre and eventually enjoying family life.

The patient who, on the contrary, pictured her analyst as spending even week-ends in America in pursuit of a wife or lover, eventually pictured him in domesticity in London.

The week-end and holiday interruptions of the work forced up transference phantasies; as the work continued these changed in character in correspondence with the internal pattern of forces and object relations within the patient. The point of irreversibility could be given when, despite upheavals in the patients' lives, the picture of the analyst's week-end remained a balanced one and included the sixfold capacity I have mentioned.

Some patients react with dread to the coming week-end break so that after Wednesday they dare not 'let themselves go' because they cannot bear the great wrench of leaving on the Friday. Every week-end to such patients is a bereavement. But as the analysis proceeds it becomes first a sadness, then a relinquishment, and finally the analyst moves freely in and out of their life space. Where is the point of irreversibility? I know of no fixed and definite criterion, but when there can be sadness, no matter how poignant, without the *gestalt* of the analyst changing in the patient's mind, then I think it can be said that that point has been reached.

I do not want to go into more detail about the week-end response but to refer again to a previous formulation: the ultimate criterion is a *pattern* combining many factors each of which may have quantitative variations and each of which has a 'point of irreversibility'. The clinician is a person who has to match the pattern of 'the patient as a whole' against the pattern of normality which might be described in terms of self-adjusting equilibria. It is further suggested that the criteria for terminating should be considered in relation to the criteria for beginning the particular treatment of the particular patient. The presenting symptoms, which should be kept in mind throughout the analysis, in nearly all cases are the result of a long defensive process and therefore are a guide, though not a complete guide, to the structure of the personality, no matter what other symptoms develop or what other psycho-pathological phenomena are disclosed during the course of the analysis. In this final and most clinical—I would not deny the use of the word clinical-intuitive—assessment the removal of the roots of the initial symptom complex (not its suppression) is of outstanding importance.

XVII
THE RÔLE AND FUTURE OF PSYCHO-THERAPY WITHIN PSYCHIATRY[1]
(1950)

1. IT may be well to begin by delimiting the term psycho-therapy; to me it has two aspects:

(a) It is a procedure of verbal interchange between patient and doctor in which the phenomena presented by the patient to the doctor during interview are interpreted by the doctor to the patient—to the end that the patient's mental pain shall be relieved (by the interpretation) and he shall have an increased understanding and mastery of the impulse-laden, unresolved, emotional conflicts in his own personal past experience, and a better insight into his own personality.

(b) Psycho-therapy is also a procedure in which transference phenomena are manipulated by the doctor, whether or no he is conscious of the nature of those phenomena within the patient or in himself.

This double-channelled definition is positive, i.e. it states what happens, but it does not exclude the simultaneous or alternating use of non-psycho-therapeutic procedures such as induced hypoglycaemia or narcosis or fits (which are sometimes given the lordly title of biological treatments). This definition also covers most of the procedures of Group Psycho-therapy, which I shall discuss in more detail later.

2. It may also be well for a moment to discuss Psychiatry, within which it would seem psycho-therapy has both a rôle and a future.

Psychiatry used to be a circumscribed area of medical activity into which one class of troublesome people were sent when their behaviour was conspicuously odd (prisons, to which the other class of troublesome people were sent, were for a time, strangely enough, reckoned outside the boundary of psychiatry). Now-a-

[1] Reprinted from the *Journal of Mental Science* (1950), **96**, 181–9.

A contribution to a Symposium given at the Inaugural Meeting of the Psycho-therapy and Social Psychiatry Section of the Royal Medico-Psychological Association on April 13, 1949.

days psychiatry is an area of activity which people actually seek to enter of their own accord, because they feel at odds with themselves and because they know that they can be helped to help themselves. Who would have guessed, say, forty years ago, that insight would *increase* the demand for psychiatry?

These changes in the relation of psychiatry to the community and the demand for psychiatric help are due in such large measure to the influence of psycho-therapy within and without the profession that one would almost suggest a title for another evening's discussion: 'The Rôle and Future of Psychiatry without Psycho-therapy.'

3. If we enquire into the reasons which have given psycho-therapy such influence I think it can be summed up quite simply: (*a*) psycho-therapy has *methods* of research and therapy which can be taught, and the results of the psycho-therapist's investigations can be brought within fairly generally understood frames of reference; and (*b*) there is a sort of professional morale question involved—both the patient and the doctor invest in the same business and both therefore have an interest to make it a going concern. The patient risks his future happiness and a good deal of time and money in the therapy, the doctor invests a good deal of his time and his reputation. The extent to which this enterprise will continue to yield dividends depends on the extent to which both parties can learn to face unpleasant facts in the present. The most important feature of any psychiatric investigation is the influence of mental pain upon the course of human behaviour, and a study of the vigorous defence which is put up by patient and psycho-therapist against the acceptance of the unpleasant has to be given a high priority in their joint undertaking.

4. It is a mistake to think that the founder of modern psycho-therapy merely by action of intellectual genius hit upon a series of ideas useful in the relief of mental suffering. It is never thus in the progress of the human sciences. Each step has to be won at the cost of overcoming painful personal resistances, the dissolving away of carefully guarded defences involves an expenditure of effort in self-mastery; progress in psycho-therapy is not an intellectual achievement only, nor mainly, is it a morale issue. Like military morale in time of war it involves facing an enemy, this time an internal one—one's own disruptive and destructive impulses, and one has to keep on being on the

watch for their influence on current behaviour. But psycho-therapists are not the only people with a professional interest in the relief of mental pain, the clergy are much concerned with the pain of guilt. One of the reasons why the Church has not in the last thousand years or so added materially to our knowledge of mental pain lies in the fact that the clergy have not devised a technique for the investigation of mental pain, nor had psychiatry until recently.

5. The psycho-therapist's work, like that of the scientist generally, is essentially a-historical. The data that bring conviction to him and to the patient are those memories and personal attitudes which arise in the immediate present, 'the living present'—that four seconds of *now*—in the presence of the psycho-therapist. Anamneses are events recalled, history-taking is a collection of data which by itself adds but little to the patient's experience of himself in his unpleasant, disruptive aspects. Self-knowledge does not come by recollection but by re-experiencing; unless the recollection impinges on a personal relation in the present, and the interrelations of the memory and the current personal relationship are explored, mere recall does not make an almost irreversible effect upon the person concerned.

The technique of the psycho-therapist consists in the management of the interview so that transference phenomena can appear with the least possible distortion to the end that the patient can match against one another the attitudes and ideas which emerge from the past and those that are seen to exist in the present—it is the example of the testing of reality as far as possible under controlled conditions. I call the analysis of free associations in the transference situation the 'social instrument' of research and therapy. (Unfortunately, to learn the use of this 'instrument' requires several years of training.) The other 'instrument' is that simple collection of rules for the elucidation of unconscious thought processes which Freud gave us in *The Interpretation of Dreams*. By thorough and patient application of these two techniques to the minutiae of the patient's utterances and gestures the great advance in psychiatry has been made, the psychiatrist gains a new quality of interest in his material, and many patients have been given good grounds for believing that their condition was not incurable.

6. So far I have mentioned only the therapy of individuals

taken one at a time. Group therapy is of two kinds: (a) a number of people are assembled together for purposes of explanation of their condition or for exhortation, or for that 'companionate therapy' which comes when groups are formed mainly for the purpose of social amenity; (b) the other kind, to use the famous phrase of Dr. Bion, its originator, makes 'the study of intra-group tension the task of the group', i.e. the members of the group study the group-cohesive and the group-disruptive forces operating within themselves as individuals and in the group. This latter kind of Group Therapy has that quality of a-historical research which characterizes science and which in individual therapy has given us most of our ideas and data.

With any kind of psycho-therapy, individual or group, there is one question it is most useful to ask oneself: what proportion of the time and energy during therapeutic sessions is given to the study of the defences against personal or group disruptiveness? According to the answer to this question the various kinds of therapy can be ranged in a sort of rank order; my guess is that those high in the scale furnish most to psychiatric research and give the more satisfactory therapeutic results, those low in the scale have a shifting population of adherents, are least keen about integrating their findings with those of other research workers, and the range of their therapeutic successes is less.

7. In speaking thus far of psycho-therapy stress has been laid on pain, disruptiveness and similar disquiets of the mind. There is no such thing as 'Psychiatry without Tears' and it is as well to face the fact. In good psycho-therapy, however, an equal attention is given to joy and creativeness, but this aspect can never be treated in isolation from its opposite.

It would be a mistake to ignore the valuable by-products of psycho-therapeutic work, namely, the insight gained into the structure of the personality; research on this matter, however, cannot be isolated from the general problems of the patient, no matter how clever or ambitious the research worker may be. In the human sciences pure research is usually a stultifying self-delusion, there is only operational research. If a research worker goes to a patient to get answers to his own questions he does not get far in the exploration of the underlying problems of human personality—his research can be left in the library, it is usually of but little use to the clinician. A thesis, however learned, however much it is stuffed with statistics, tells us but little about the woes of the suffering patient if it does not treat at first hand with anxiety, guilt and despair.

In the other kind of research—operational research—the patient (or a group) calls in the therapist and there is that mutual investment of energy to which I have already referred. In this case the patient's (or the group's) own questions have top priority and the research worker's questions and curiosity have second place. In the field of the human sciences research and therapy are inseparable, for a patient cannot disclose the deeper levels of his mental pain unless he has the experience that the process of exploration gives relief to his pain. I believe this is true of groups too, though some group therapies seem to give more relief than they actually do; both kinds of therapy have to guard against the denial of painful problems and see that there is not an escape into temporary and unstable solutions.

8. Now as to the rôle of Psycho-therapy within Psychiatry:

(*a*) Its emphasis on the inseparable connection between research and therapy is a necessary reminder to psychiatry that it is quite as much dependent on the human sciences as on the physiological and other non-human biological ones.

(*b*) The genetic studies of the development and malformation of the personality, inevitable in any thorough-going psycho-therapy, will help psychiatry to see more clearly the inter-relation of individual development and the social cultural patterns in which that individual grows up.

(*c*) The free-association studies of the psycho-therapist in the a-historical transference situation give to psycho-therapy a research instrument which no other branch of psychiatry affords in anything like the same potency.

(*d*) The fact that the psycho-therapist is compelled to face the most painful issues of human maladjustment without resort to evasion such as placebos, gives to psychiatry an almost automatic index of its own professional morale, since a repudiation of serious professional attempts to deal with serious clinical problems cannot be made without those thus exercising their indifference becoming somewhat conspicuous in a world of suffering humanity.

(*e*) Not least psycho-therapy has proved successful in restoring to full capacity patients who were formerly incapacitated by neurotic disabilities that did not respond to other forms of therapy. Its rôle in this direction is extending, and these extensions of remedial power have raised not unwarrantable hopes in the patient population and made the practice of psychiatry more interesting to its practitioners.

9. As to the future of Psycho-therapy within Psychiatry:

(*a*) This depends on the freedom of locomotion given to the psycho-therapist within the psychiatric field. Any move towards limiting psycho-therapy to the neuroses is retrogressive. Both out-patient and in-patient facilities should be available to the psycho-therapist even if for years he does not show much in the way of improvement in his cases.

(*b*) Even though the disposal and direction of the psycho-therapist's time and energy are—or seem to be—dictated by the enormous number of cases calling for quick therapies, every psycho-therapist should be free, and indeed, be encouraged, by the organization he serves, to have at least one case on which he can spend an unlimited time. I can testify to the effect of such a permission on the raising of psychiatric morale, for during the war, on the advice of Brigadiers J. R. Rees and Sandiford, every Army psychiatrist in therapeutic work, no matter how vast his patient load, was allowed a case on which he could spend an hour a day for as long as the psychiatrist himself thought necessary.

I would go so far as to say that the future of psychiatry depends on such measures, which conserve the research and therapeutic impulses of the psychiatrist and give him some hope and a little scope.

(*c*) Since this is a section of social psychiatry (which is a relatively new idea) as well as of psycho-therapy (which is half a century old—how time flies!) and since it is the inaugural meeting, I would like to add a word about the scope and possible future of social psychiatry based on experience of psycho-therapy.

It is a field for operational research, not for quizzing by ambitious workers who want new worlds to conquer. The psychiatrist will have to earn his entry into this field by being able to serve its deeper needs. Research and therapy must go together here, and we must freely acknowledge that so far no one with the genius of Freud has arisen among us to give us even the most elementary advices for interpreting the data we are faced with; it is both imprudent for ourselves, unfair to psychiatry and grossly unfair to the public to lay claims we cannot amply fulfil.

The exercise of psycho-therapy upon individuals teaches us, to say the least, the prudence of humility; the temptation to offer to humanity in its present distraught state more than we can give is one which we need to bear in mind. We do not know the remedies for the ills of our society because our notions about the aetiology are still so dim.

The technical methods of this new research and therapy may well be different from those we use with sick individuals, but the basic principles of the work will probably be much the same: to give priority to the client group's need and let the doctor's curiosity and therapeutic ambition come second; 'difficulties' in the way of the research have to be considered as part of the field of therapy and research; the study of resistances and the careful painstaking overcoming of them will probably yield more research data to the doctor and more relief to the client group than any other method of approach. The way of individual psycho-therapy has been hard enough, but though hard, rewarding; the way of social psychiatry will probably be even harder, let us hope it will be still more rewarding.

May I conclude with a passage from Walt Whitman which Churchill quoted on the radio in one of the dark days of the War:

'Now understand me well, it is provided in the essence of things that from any fruition of success, no matter what, shall come forth something to make an even greater struggle necessary.'

APPENDIX

The paper to which this is an Appendix contains nothing new and, though perhaps suited to an Inaugural Meeting, would not be worth printing were it not for the fact, as the discussion following it showed, that its statements were generally misunderstood. An explanation—to be sure unusual in a paper that contains no original thought—may nevertheless be useful, and a personal note may perhaps be excused.

One of the striking things about the discussion, to me at any rate, was the fact that several members referring to this paper said it was all very well, *but* they were not psycho-analysts, nor could they spend unlimited time on a single patient. This clearly indicated that the paper had misfired.

The crux of the matter lies in the psychiatrist's conception of the function of, and his rôle in, the psychiatric interview, that is to say, in the technique of management of the two-person relation which is created when a patient asks for help because of a psychiatric complaint. Fact-finding can be separated from therapy, but—such is the nature of the human mind—the *range* of the facts thus made available will be more limited than would be the case were therapy and fact-finding given a more equal priority. To say this is not to belittle the scientific value of research and deduction within the limited field, nor for that matter to deny the fact that the range of data is unlimited when therapy is given first place. The important thing is that mental pain benumbs the faculties (call it repression or resistance if you will), and the research worker, if he is wise, will reckon on the fact that the range of his data is restricted by factors of which his informant is unconscious and to which the researcher too may have just as active an aversion.

This by way of preface to the psychiatric interview—the best gift of psychiatry to medicine. To put it too briefly, the psychiatrist should first get clear in his mind and then disclose to the patient at the appropriate moment (timing is an art, fact arrangement a science) the relation between two sets of facts or sequences of facts. The one sequence is the chronological unfolding of the events of the patient's 'history', so that both he himself and his doctor can get a picture of him as a person who has changed and developed in the course of time and through the impact of his impulses and environment. The physician is naturally tempted to complete this picture sequence as fully as possible in the time allotted to the interview, i.e. to get 'the history of the person' as well as the history of the complaint. In the course of listening to the history, at the back of the physician's mind, there may be a most active sorting of data into categories, a veritable whirr of Hollerith, and the classifying frames of reference can be the most various and scientific. By long practice this sorting and matching process—particularly matching against the pattern of other case histories—can go on so smoothly that the machinery of the doctor's thinking goes unnoticed by his patient; when the thinking is smooth the doctor's intrusions and interrogations upon the patient's narrative is also usually smooth. But the physician, in the interest of research no less than of therapy, must give ear to another sequence, viz. the events occurring in the consulting room itself.

This is the a-historical part of the investigation. When, on one occasion, a patient burst into a psychiatrist's consulting-room with the remark, 'Doctor, my sister has played no part in my life,' he was voicing not only a piece of history, albeit with a negative sign attached to it, but he was behaving in the a-historical present. He knew his doctor was 'one of those Freudians' and he wanted to 'clear away a lot of that nonsense' from the very beginning. This is a gross example, but it illustrates, perhaps almost to exaggeration, that the current interlocution is manipulated by the patient, and unless he himself is on the watch, the physician too tends to be manipulated in order that unconscious needs may be satisfied which, though dating from the past, are also active in the present. The patient just referred to 'gave the game away', a fact which any psychiatrist could observe. But when the game is not given away, when the deflection of attention is unobtrusive, the physician must be on the alert for any deflections caused by the patient or himself.

A good psychiatric interview has something of the atmosphere of conversation among sensitive and well-mannered people, at least on the doctor's side. In polite society at least half of a person's attention is directed to the mood and the slight indications of a wish to change the subject on the part of the interlocutor, while the rest of the attention is given to the topic and to its pleasing development on a conscious rational plane. In the psychiatric interview the objectives (what Konstantin Stanislavsky called the super-objectives) lie outside the usual topics of conversation or customary thought; they concern the structure of the personality and the failures of its function. The patient always, and the physician too, unless he is on his guard, steers the conversation so that nothing shall arise which tends to threaten or disturb the structure and function of his personality, which is at best in a condition of quasi-stable equilibrium. The physician's duty is to discover and disclose the factors which threaten the equilibrium without upsetting it. The comparison between the psychiatric interview and conversation in polite society, though it is incorrect in respect to *aim*, has a certain usefulness when considered as a *technique* of perception of personal feeling and thought. If psychiatry is to give a lead to medicine in the matter of interviewing, I think it important that we should be clear that there is no question of an entirely new skill being employed, but that a skill (which is widely distributed in the population, particularly in the 'interviewing professions', i.e. medicine, law and the Church) is in the case of the psychiatric interview developed to a far greater extent, and to a 'depth' that is not only comparatively little employed, at least consciously, but is hardly dreamt of in professional circles outside of psychiatry with a psycho-dynamic orientation. Put briefly, we do not do things in or with our interviews which other people are incapable of doing, but we are guided by considerations which others, to their loss, tend to ignore. We on our side also endeavour to guide the course of the interview and are, of course, influenced by our theories of psycho-dynamics and personality development; but though we are so influenced we have, nevertheless, to give the patient such freedom of expression as to allow of spontaneity both to his utterance and to his underlying mood. This freedom is important because it allows data to appear which the physician is not looking for (thus, his theories can be checked and corrected), the patient feels that the dignity of his personality and individuality is being respected (a point of growing importance when medicine is becoming more and more a Department of State), and by the establishment of a two-way channel of communication the physician is given an opportunity to feel his way into his patient's capacity for (or the restriction of) social relationships.

The psychiatric interview can be—should be—a sampling technique for discovering the quality and flexibility of the patient's social relationships. The physician by the exercise of care and discernment (if he has an appreciation of psycho-dynamics) can uncover elements in the patient's past history of which he himself is and was unaware; I refer particularly to his conflict-ridden relation to parents and siblings. If the physician has trained himself to discern the rôles which the patient, all unwittingly, thrusts upon him in the course of the interview, he will when taking the history get some light on the patient's relation to people at critical periods of his life (critical periods, when conflicts are left unresolved—and being unresolved are carried over and unbalance the equilibrium of subsequent years—these are of special importance to psychiatric interviewing).

There are two sorts of facts in a psychiatric interview, those that the psychiatrist needs to know to make a diagnosis, and those he needs to know in order to get on with the treatment.

When obtaining the former the psychiatrist's mind has to be predominantly and actively concerned with norms of behaviour, disease syndromes and neuro-psychiatric processes that have not yet been given a clear definition—he has, as it were, to feel his way into the body (or body-mind if you will) of his patient. When obtaining the latter sort of facts that he will use in psycho-therapy, the psychiatrist's mind has to be more passive and receptive and to be predominantly concerned with feeling his way into the social and emotional life of the patient. By social, I mean his relation to people as distinct from his psycho-physiological constitution and the vicissitudes of bodily maladjustment. The facts required in this category are mostly of a kind that cannot be obtained by question and answer, they emerge as a result of the social and therapeutic setting of the interview itself. The distinction between these two sorts of facts is arbitrary but may be useful as a rough indication of the kind of contribution that psycho-therapy has given to psychiatric interview technique.

In the discussion at the meeting it seemed to me that some who took part assumed that because they were not psycho-analysts the principles outlined in the paper were not theirs to apply. If this is a legitimate inference the paper failed badly in its main purpose. Perhaps the difficulty lay in the meaning given to the words (§ 8) 'the analysis of free associations in the transference situation' (the 'social instrument' of research and therapy). I am aware that when this procedure is given the highest priority and is pushed to its limit the term psycho-analysis alone is justified. It may be remarked that the general principles can be applied in any degree of concentration and there are usually moments in most psycho-therapeutic interviews when, if the psycho-therapist is alert to the possibilities, these general notions can be used—to the enlightenment of the patient and the intellectual satisfaction of the physician.

When writing this paper I tried to keep in mind the title of the Symposium of which it was a part and to use only such concepts as were at the same time fundamental, in my view, to psycho-therapy and common to all schools of thought. Freudians, Jungians, Adlerians and the inchoate host of eclectics may rebuke me that I have not said enough, but none of them I hope will reprove me for having said too much.

When it comes to that, what is all this business of psycho-therapy about? The neurotic's trouble is a misfunctioning so persistent that the very structure of his personality seems to be affected by it—more boldly, we may perhaps say it *is* affected by it. The psycho-therapist's task is to change the functioning so that the 'set' of the patterns of behaviour shall be consistently more flexible, i.e. adaptable and effective. (Effectiveness in this sense is not to be equated with extravert efficiency—though with people in the Western culture that may be frequent—but with a decrease in dammed-up tensions, blocked of outlet, with corresponding strain.) Here I wish to put in a personal opinion, but one that is shared wholeheartedly by many psycho-therapists, and halfheartedly—perhaps because of the terrific implication—by many more. I cannot see how a maladjustment or constraint of personality that has persisted for years, and broken out conspicuously for the first time, maybe, in adult or adolescent life, can be readjusted except by the re-experiencing of the original conflict situation and thus working out a new and better solution.

'But surely,' you may ask, 'there are psycho-therapies, and ones that are worthy of the name, which do not aim at or involve this re-experiencing and working through process? Hypnotism, for example, which does not necessarily employ the interpretative activity to which reference is made in the first paragraph? Are you going to deny to these therapeutic procedures the name of psycho-therapy?'

Perhaps this fair and reasonable criticism was in the minds of the contributors to the discussion who said that they were not psycho-analysts. It touched on the major omission of the paper.[1]

---

[1] The second, and minor, omission, was pointed out by Dr. Bierer in the discussion, viz. that not *all* of psycho-therapy is a verbal interchange. I should know that: in the course of an analysis of a very disturbed schizophrenic with depressive features the patient hid herself within her only garment, a blanket, so that only the eyebrow showed; nothing daunted I continued the conversation from where we left off last time and noted the changes in that eloquent but only visible member, which changes—a frown, scowl, surprise, a flicker of amusement, a softening of the curve—indicated the changes of her mood and thought. My surmises proved correct, for when next she displayed her face and used her voice she corroborated the general trend of my guesses as to what had gone on in her mind. That session was no verbal *interchange*—it might even be called an 'eye-brow'

What I have tried to conceptualize is the process of radical change in the structure and function of the personality, i.e. the attainment of a point of irreversibility in the process of change. The ameliorative procedures such as hypnosis, indeed, most of the 'short term therapies' (how well named!) do not reach, or attempt to reach, that point of irreversibility; but they have claim, I admit, to the term psycho-therapy.

So the lop-sidedness of my paper is apparent, but on the other hand I am loath to use two general names for psycho-therapy. That a scale could be drawn—or several—is beyond doubt; the drawing up of such scales, with their correlates (see § 6) may even be useful, particularly if attention is paid to the causes of failure in effecting 'irreversible change' in the procedures studied.

But to return to the general discussion. The title is too narrow; 'The rôle and future of psycho-therapy within *medicine*' would provide occasion for a useful link between general medicine and psychiatry because inevitably it would bring out in clear outline the technique of the psychiatric interview—that modern discovery of the dynamics of the doctor-patient relationship.

analysis—but there was an endeavour to verbalize, to conceptualize and make concrete 'in the here and now' what was occurring concurrently in her mind.

XVIII
THE DEVELOPMENT OF
PSYCHOLOGICAL MEDICINE[1]
(1950)

THE half-century which this series of essays is designed to cover also spans the history of modern psychological medicine, which is also the history of a new skill. Every advance in medical science can be related to the development of skills—in clinical observation, in the design and use of apparatus of research, in the interpretation of data obtained by the use of the apparatus, and above all in conceptualizing the problem that is being faced. To this general rule the development of psychological medicine is no exception; but since the data differ so greatly from those of the physiologist and pathologist the means by which the facts are collected also are different. Both kinds of research are concerned with answers to the fundamental question, 'What goes with what?' If the data of the pathologist cannot be immediately linked with the data of the psychopathologist and psychiatrist, and vice versa, it simply means that 'total medicine' has not yet found a theory which combines the two.

This article does not touch on the development of psychiatry but tries only to outline some of the changes in thought and practice that have resulted from the study of the psychological problems which patients present to doctors for solution. To summarize in a short article the changes in the last fifty years would exhaust the general reader and weary the specialist, but a description of how it all arose from simple if subtle consulting-room work (without appliances of any kind whatever) and how the range of case-taking has been extended in penetration and in helpfulness to the patient may deserve a place in a story for doctors of doctors' work in this half-century of ferment and growth.

Doctors are not so confined as they were fifty years ago to the province of physical disease, and laymen are more ready to as-

[1] Reprinted from the *British Medical Journal* (1950), **1**, 30–37.

sume that their medical advisers are prepared to listen to any complaint, whether of body or of mind. If an examination of the body does not reveal a demonstrable disorder a doctor now hesitates before he says that a person with a multitude of complaints has nothing the matter with him. Where there is much complaining there must be something paining: if an organ does not show that there is anything amiss the person does.

Modern psychological medicine has arisen from the development of clinical skill in the doctor-patient interview, which in this specialist field is different in content, range, and effectiveness from what it was in the last century. At the beginning of this century psychiatry was under the influence of the German school of Kraepelin (1856–1926), which clung to the notion of disease entities and was absorbed in problems of description and classification of patients under certificate. Later in the 1920's another German psychiatrist, Kretschmer, working with neurotics, developed theories of the relation of disease entities with bodily types. These two schools of thought contributed ideas to psychiatry and gave the practitioner classificatory frameworks, but did not give a coherent body of theory which would integrate the enormously varied mass of phenomena in a practical way.

In America the main development of psychiatry was due to the psycho-biological outlook of Adolf Meyer (b. 1866). His approach laid great emphasis on the interview, which was to be so conducted that the unusual features of the patient's psychology had rather to be avoided than explored, and the not inconsiderable experiential knowledge of man by the interviewer should be used to study what was known about the patient's behaviour in terms of actual overt performance open to anyone who cared to look, without making what was thought to be a fruitless search for what was going on 'behind the scenes'—that is, in the unconscious. The merit of this approach is that it is available to every practitioner who takes a little trouble. The case history is examined with a thoroughness unknown to previous psychiatry. The collection of data regarding the 'speechless years' (up to about age 2, obtained from parents) and the childhood years from 2 years to adolescence, and from then onwards (including, where relevant, the involutional years), is done with meticulous regard to detail and accuracy. An interpretation of the data thus collected is based on general views such as anyone of experience might form of the events and facts as found, together with a readiness to include ideas about the patient's purpose in life. It is necessary for the doctor, on his part, always to consider multiple-interrelations in the causal factors of disease and health, to make an intelligent selection of leading items when making his assessment of the case, while at the same time recognizing the need for consistency in face of the great diversity of data and of causation. (See Muncie, *Psycho-biology and Psychiatry*.) The psycho-biological school, though it has improved skill in interview, has added very little to the understanding of disease processes or, for the matter of that, normal psychology, for the reason that it avoids theorizing—it lacks conceptual skill and is without challenge.

We must now turn to the vast amount of work which has been done in the last fifty years in the development of the theory, technique, and application of psycho-pathological research. The emphasis here given to the rise and development of psycho-analysis is certainly not due to the number of patients treated by that method (for that is comparatively small, and will probably always so remain), but because this theory has given a new dimension and therefore a new starting-point for thought. It requires no apparatus in the ordinary sense and is based on a clinical observational technique which centres on social phenomena to be found, if care is taken, most clearly in the doctor's consulting-room. Further, the psycho-analytical theory has proved so wide-ranging and integrative that (though naturally with a time lag) it is now employed creatively outside the field of clinical medicine, and is using and feeding back into academic psychology, anthropology, and education ideas which provide new starting-points for research.

A Basic Assumption

The basic assumption on which the whole of modern psychological medical research rests is simple; furthermore, it sounds plausible and one is ready to give it at least a theoretical approval. It is just this: When any two ideas come together in temporal association in the flow of one's thoughts there must be some link or links of meaning. It is one thing to toy with this notion; it is another to press it to its practical conclusion. In the psychological laboratories experiments with word associations had been carried out for many years, but the results of the research did not disturb nor did they cure anyone. Though some of those research workers had medical degrees, they had no medical responsibility for the subjects of their research, for in those days patients did not go to laboratories for help. The reasons for the sterility of this well-planned research appeared only later, and in the unlikeliest place—in the consulting-rooms of neurologists who were dealing with what was then generally regarded as most unreliable data, the outpourings of neurotics. The revolution came when the basic assumption above referred to was taken so seriously that the aetiological study and therapy of very ill people was made dependent on it, and—dependent on this—the professional reputation of the physicians undertaking this unpopular field of research and therapy turned not only on the correctness of the basic assumption but on the vigour with which the implications of it were pursued. The last is important, for, despite the reasonableness of the basic assumption, patients resist its implications—at times everyone, including the physician, tries to evade them and persuade others to do the same. Progress in psychological medicine has been made in the face of persistent opposition to the application of scientific methods of investigating mental phenomena; indeed, strange though it may seem, it is by the study of resistance to investigation that most advance has been made. The opposition of medical colleagues to this kind of investigation and therapy, which is now not so great as formerly, was a lesser hindrance—needed less courage—than the inner resistance of the medical psycho-therapist to face and overcome the objection within himself to the acceptance of unpleasant ideas. In the long run it never pays to ignore unpleasant things: they return if not dealt with.

Freud's Ideas and Discoveries

In the 1880's Josef Breuer discovered that neurotic symptoms had a meaning. Janet made the same discovery, but did not push his observations beyond saying that the symptoms were an expression of *idées inconscientes* possessing the patient's mind; he arrived at a generalization (as had the psychiatrist Leuret before him) but did not give particular or personal significance to the symptoms. The concept of 'meaning' here implies a relation—a relation in respect to detail—to the patient's previous life. But to return to Breuer: in 1880-2 he had as a patient a girl who suffered from numerous neurotic symptoms which came on after she had nursed her father during his last illness. She had periods of dreamy confusion in which her mind was far removed from present reality and occupied with her own thoughts. It was possible to hypnotize her and get her to talk without such confusion; her mind then kept going back to ideas and impulses which she had to suppress while nursing her father, and her numerous symptoms were related to these suppressed thoughts. When the patient recalled these thoughts and 're-lived' in imagination these scenes she was for a time rid of her symptoms, but soon relapsed, so that the process had to be repeated over and over again. In the repetition the scenes dwelt on shifted farther and farther back in her life; eventually all the symptoms were removed. The cure seemed to result from re-living the emotional experiences which for various seasons she had avoided feeling in the first place. The theory of the cure was that the 'accumulated emotion' which maintained the symptom found an outlet, a 'catharsis', in the treatment-room of the physician—that is, when it was brought to consciousness the patient got better. Freud developed this technique by abandoning hypnosis and getting the patient to talk freely, to say whatever came into his mind, holding nothing back because it might be thought to be irrelevant or distressing. The 'free association rule' is the foundation on which not only psycho-analysis but modern psycho-therapy rests, and it makes its demand on the psycho-therapist too, for if the patient must not consider anything irrelevant neither must his physician, and the latter has the added duty of making sense of it and also of convincing the patient of its meaning.

The history of psychological medicine is bound up with the development of Freud's ideas and discoveries. These may be said to date, first, from the abandonment of the use of hypnosis as a means of extending the range of exploration of the patient's mind; secondly, from the persistent study of 'resistances'; and, thirdly, from the analysis of the phenomena arising between physician and patient.

In the course of the kind of treatment we are now considering two things are invariably met with: the first is 'resistance'. The patient's mind seems incapable of taking an objective view of the procedure, 'forgets' the free association rule or pleads that certain ideas should be made exceptions to it, and becomes preoccupied with what the analyst must be thinking about the thoughts disclosed or about to be disclosed. In the hypnotic treatment the patient was urged to remember, and the amount of effort expended in recalling painful ideas and experience gave a measure of the 'resistance' to their recall. In the free association treatment there is no urging, but attention is directed to the reason for the tardiness of the mind to master its own content. It becomes apparent (to both parties eventually) that something is happening in this social relationship of two people, physician and patient: the patient cannot recollect directly— the resistances are too strong—but he is 'transferring' on to the analytical situation some of the undischarged emotion which he could not deal with in the critical phases of his development. This is the second of the things invariably met with. The therapeutic co-operation between two adults has superimposed on it all kinds of emotional cross-currents from the past of which the patient was consciously quite unaware, or to a strength that he could not believe possible. This past situation, transferred to the present and dominating the physician-patient co-operation, is 'the transference situation'. The treatment consists in disclosing to the patient the operation of these early and buried impulses and seeing them in their past and present setting; the art of the treatment lies in the maintenance of a quiet, interested, objective personal relationship throughout the storms and confusion of these transference phenomena; 'the science of the treatment', so to speak lies in the employment of the simplest possible technical (theoretical) aids to the understanding of what is going on.

We may at this point consider an essential feature of this kind of research and therapy—namely, the capacity to listen: to listen without preconceptions and without impatience. This is a difficult accomplishment and takes years of practice. The physician needs to be utterly passive to impressions and to be not unduly hastened to action by a therapeutic urge (diagnosis and exploration must come before therapy), nor must theories intrude and bias contemplation of the facts.

The data provided by following the free association rule (and the transference phenomena) are given some sort of order if the basic assumption is really made basic to the work. (The patient's 'resistance' frequently challenges this assumption; it is usually, if not invariably, a counter-attack to cover a sore spot.) Out of the experience of this rule and this simple notion Freud was enabled to construct a theory which gave meaning to neurotic symptoms, to hallucinations, and even to dreams.

Freud's Theory of Dreams

Without the basic assumption dreams would have remained an unsolved riddle, and without a solution of the dream problem neuroses would have been left without their key. In the first place it is necessary to distinguish between the manifest content of the dream and another, latent or hidden, content. The former is what the dreamer remembers of his dream—it is in consciousness; of the latter we will first assume that it has sense if we can but find it. Employing the 'basic assumption' and free associations to elements of the remembered or manifest dream, it becomes clear that the dream elements represented a focal point in a number of trains of thought—that is, the dreamer makes a condensation of a number of thoughts all of which are represented in a single dream element. Another feature of the dream-work is the tendency to shift the accent from an important theme on to a trivial one—that is, there is a displacement of the emotion. A further peculiar feature is that a thing may be represented by its opposite; that is to say, it seems as if there is a part of the mind which can tolerate contradictions; and, finally, there seems at times to be a process at work to make the jumble look sensible and coherent. The importance of this study of dreams lay in the fact that by these simple devices of interpretation—that is, of undoing the disguises employed in the dream-work—light was thrown on the processes going on in the unconscious mind, or, more strictly, we are helped to make inferences about the interplay between different parts of the mind. The manifest dream is that part of the total dream process which is accessible directly to the conscious mind, but, by employing the basic assumption to free associations to the dream elements and the devices of interpretation above mentioned, thoughts are disclosed (and their relation to the manifest content is recognized by the dreamer) which seem to belong to another part of the mind and personality—to the unconscious. Something like a force seems to be keeping the two apart; the urging to remember painful episodes in the hypnotic treatment and the 'resistance' to freely associating justify the use of some such concept. Freud's most simple rules for the unravelling of the meaning of dreams may be described as the main tool of research and therapy in this field. They have often been challenged; some think they have added materially to them, but no one has found in them anything superfluous. Freud's theory of dreams provides the main conceptual structure on which psycho-dynamical research is built, and therefore on which therapy is based.

The Problem of Treatment

When the urgings of the hypnotist were abandoned in favour of a passive observation by the therapist of just whatever the patient liked to say or to impute to him (or to try to manipulate the relationship between them) the focus of attention of the therapist is turned to the forces in the patient's mind as the immediately significant data, and these data in strangely large proportion are apparently irrelevant to the immediate situation. The therapist is pictured by the patient to be playing all manner of rôles; and it soon becomes apparent that these rôles have relevance to periods and episodes of frustration in the patient's past life and even to early childhood.

When sufficient care is given to detail, and the phenomena to be observed are not blurred by the impatient interferences of the therapist—how difficult that task is, as beginners only later discover!—a new sort of mental functioning becomes apparent: primitive, infantile, and unconscious. One of its important features is the part which bodily impulses of the most element- ary kind play in the personal relationship which the patient's fantasy elaborates. It is not a simple 'falling in love' but a complicated mixture of love and hate, tenderness and aggression —put simply, both attraction and repulsion, 'ambivalently' mixed; it is a mode of a relationship which is strange to adult ways of thought. It seems that the free associations in the trans- ference situation disclose two new things: first the way in which bodily-centred impulses of instinctual origin (in the mental sphere the part of us which is nearest to the animals) find representation in our imagination and outlet in our action, and also how they become transformed into the bonds which tie us in love and in hate to those nearest and dearest to us, and also by displacement to our kind generally—this throws light on our cultural life and may provide a clue to that great gap which separates us from the animals. We are not only more intelligent than the beasts, but we have a more flexible emotional life; if we are frustrated in our love (and who is not?) we displace our longing to another and seek satisfaction from a new source. Animals pine for a lost companion; man uses his frustrations, for the most part, to build, under the pressure of painful loss, an inner world—a private zone of culture—where he can work through his privation, however long and devious the path, to a solution of his longing. The richness of that inner world, which animals seem to lack, is the result of overcoming mental pain; we seem to differ from the animals, too, in being able to share with others the benefits we gain from our private zone of culture.

The second thing that may be observed is that, though there are in fact only two people in the therapeutic situation, the patient frequently behaves as if there were three or more—that is to say, he takes the analyst as the object of his impulses and also feels a constraint as if another person's rights and feelings had to be taken into account at the same time. It seems as if from an early age of personal or mental development the individual cannot help dealing with two people at a time; if the third party is not actually present the mind unconsciously imagines him or her to be there. The character of the behaviour, and indeed the mood, of the individual and his confidence or diffidence in life generally, as well as his capacity to co-operate with his fellows, are greatly influenced by his relation to this third party. (The obscurity of these last statements may be perhaps diminished in a later consideration of this important topic.) With a perhaps aphoristic inexactitude we may say that the barrier between human psychology and sociology is broken down when account is taken of the unconscious influence of 'the third party' in the relation between two people. (As this touches on society, it may be one of the most momentous discoveries in social history.)

By taking a few liberties with dates it is possible to arrange the dominant ideas into four periods.

First Period (1896–1914): Development of a Libido Theory

As has been said, one of the things disclosed by the free associations is the strange unadult nature of the impulses which the unconscious harbours. They are primitive and erotic and the conscious mind repudiates them; indeed, much of the above-mentioned 'resistance' is a manifestation of this repudiation. Man appears to be unique in having two types of sexuality: an infantile kind, which persists in the unconscious, and an adult kind, which 'crystallizes' at puberty. It is the persisting influence of the infantile type which leads to abnormalities of a sexual nature in the adult and largely accounts for unhappiness in married life, and it is also one of the elements in the causation of social maladjustments, including neuroses.

The sexuality of the infant—the erotic desire for another person or part of that person—is in the early days characterized by a mouth-to-nipple relationship. The infant is predominantly a 'mouth animal': what it does with its mouth is exciting to it and has greater emotional value than have other activities. In fantasy the mouth activities give it control over the object of its desire and thus minister to its sense of power; they also give that feeling of access of pleasure, even ecstasy, which is characteristically erotic. Later in infantile development defaecation and urination (unlike the early oral and later genital activities) do not necessarily involve physical contact with another person, but in the infant's fantasy they provide a means of doing something to people. A personal and bodily substance is held in control at an orifice and then is expelled, not into the void—the child's mind peoples every cranny of its world—but towards those on whom its thoughts rest. A bodily substance and bodily action which biologically have nothing to do with sexuality are used by the imagination as the medium of erotic play and personal relationships. In the course of development the genitals take the primacy. These organs above all others have the power to discharge the sexual tensions of the body and at the same time to bring the individual psychically into a specially close relation with another person. The increasing urge to sexual mastery and possession of the desired object, in imagination as well as in the act, brings with it a new, or rather an enhanced, source of danger—that of rivalry with another person of the same sex, typically a parent figure in the unconscious. There is rivalry in the earlier ('pre-genital') activities also, but the unification of erotic activity and the clarification of sexual objects and aims, which reach a climax with the primacy of the genital organ, increase its influence in personal relationships. The

Oedipus complex—that is, sexual attraction to the parent of the opposite sex and hostility to the one of the same sex—is the earliest social relationship which the individual experiences. This difficult period of development is reached and usually in good part solved by the age of five. These stresses are veiled from adult recollection by an involuntary and active forgetting, but they reappear when the effort of urging under hypnosis overcomes the resistance, and, as has been said, spontaneously and with less distortion in the transference to the therapist.

Extension of the Theory

In the course of his work Freud found that his neurotic patients remarkably often presented scenes of seduction in infancy, in a detailed and precise way, and these scenes fitted into the picture of the symptoms; but on trying to get objective verification Freud found no substantiating evidence. This was at first felt to be a blow to his previous findings—that a disturbance of the development of the sexual impulse due to active interference was one of the main factors in causing neurotic illness. Then he took a courageous and momentous step in his theoretical constructions: these events had not occurred objectively but subjectively—that is, they were occurrences in the unconscious, they were fantasies which were important to the child at the time. These fantasies were repressed but retained their urgency, not to say clamorousness, in adult life—not, of course, that the adult is aware of the cause, but he is aware of the effect, the inner unrest. A new dimension was thus given to scientific thought by this extension of theory—what happens in the world of imagination obeys the laws of that world and can influence behaviour and a person's outlook on life; medicine and science need no longer be confined to the physical realm but had a new field to explore and conquer.

An indispensable addition to the theory was introduced with the notion of 'cathexis'—the concentration or accumulation of 'mental energy', the nature of which is obscure, in some particular channel. When an object is 'cathected' that object has a particularly strong interest for the person. This energy may be displaced from one object to another—for example, from a father figure to a representation of the father in later life: first on to those who stand *in loco parentis*, such as schoolmasters, and later to office chiefs, rulers, and so forth. Combining this concept with that of the unconscious, it is clear that the object in which the mental energy is invested need not be in the focus of conscious attention, nor need the person be aware of how much he is tied in bonds of interest (love and/or hate) to the object. Further, there is a linking of the cathexes in the unconscious, so that the characteristics of the early cathexes tend to persist in respect to later ones in the same series—that is, the patterns of behaviour which characterize early object relationships tend to be repeated in later object relationships of the same type.

Second Period (1914–23): Aspects of Ego Development

The ego itself, it was thought, could be the focus of this interest or cathexis, and the love-impulse, or at least a part of it, might take the self as its object—as happened in the myth of Narcissus. But 'narcissism' is not only a peculiar and somewhat perverted manifestation of the love life; it seems apt as a descriptive term of a phase that the young usually pass through, when attention is focused on the body's strength or its graces. Closer observation showed that it describes also an attitude towards those who are derived from the self, such as one's children, or objects with which there is a close, but maybe quite unconscious, identification: a self-love flows over to them and they are enjoyed less for what they actually are than for being an embodiment in the external world of what the self once was or would like to be. From this last point it was but a step (but not all steps are easy to take) to see in the attitude to an idealized object of the ego some of the primitive, but by displacement loftily aspiring, relation to the self. An 'ego-ideal' thus absorbs some of the available object-cathexes, so that those whose ego-ideals are overstrong display a restricted capacity for an adaptable and kinder object-love—'reformers' trying to shape the world to their own (often rather over-simple, if not infantile) ideas seem to exemplify this tendency.

The notion of cathexis leads to the view that the distribution of mental energy in the field of psychic life may be considered quantitatively; in the instance given the quantity of 'devotion' or love is portioned out between the persons ostensibly served and the image upon which they are being moulded. To the reformer himself his conduct seems to be one of selfless devotion to others, while to the rest of the world he may seem rigid in manner, self-centred, and ungenerous. Both views are in their way correct—the frames of reference are different: the first takes its reckoning from the energy put into the ego-ideal, the second from the meagre amount of personal love (object-love) displayed. This notion of the distribution of the quantities of mental energy is not to be restricted to that which is, so to say, visible in overt behaviour: the artist and scientist, the mystic and the lunatic—for that matter all of us—have inner worlds of fantasy in which are deployed and expended considerable quantities of mental energy. Whether that inner labour results in anything which is socially applauded or has social uses varies with each individual. But, useful or not socially, it is a source of gratification to the individual; it gives, if it is in low degree, that meed of pleasure without which mental life of human standard seems not to operate; when in high degree, it gives that rare sweeping 'oceanic' exultation of spirit and creative ecstasy which the artists, of all men, can best communicate to their fellows, and which it is our humble duty here merely to explain.

Third Period (1923–32): The Ego and the Id

How do we animals come to have an ego-ideal? Of what experience is it a product? Is it universal and invariable or confined to idealists? Do 'really normal' people possess one, or are the 'really abnormal' alone of mortals without one?

Reverting to the early work again, the patient's unconscious mind was found to contain active elements which resulted from incompletely solved emotional experiences; these, to be sure, were foci of illness, but the same principle is seen—depending on the circumstances—to be operative in a constructive or 'ego-cohesive' direction as well as in a neurotic (and particularly in the psychotic) 'ego-destructive' tendency. In the early stages of our development, perhaps because of an underlying bisexuality, the individual is oriented to two people at once, typically the two parents; the amount of positive or friendly cathexis which is attached to the parent of the same sex becomes incorporated in and attached to the ego, which henceforth acts as an internal representative of a once external object—a parent—guiding and supporting the ego in its struggle with its own unruly impulses. Born of a longing for the parent's approval and affection, the ego seems to split into two functions—an executive part (the ego proper), and a critical, parent-derived part (the super-ego), which watches the ego's behaviour respecting the crude impersonal instinct-driven part of the personality called the 'id'.

When referring to the treatment situation it was said that the patient attributes to (or 'projects' into) his doctor all kinds of rôles, and at times behaves as if a third party were present from whom the communications about to be made must be kept secret. We are in a better position now to 'place' these phenomena—they are manifestations of those parts of the unconscious mind with which the ego is dealing—namely, with the id and the super-ego. The task of therapy is to bring about a reorganization of these three elements of the mind so that they work together in harmony; it comes about when they are confronted with one another in the present—that is, when the patient comes to recognize that, though his id is primitive and amoral, it is a tolerable part of the total personality. At the same time there occurs an amelioration of the severity of the super-ego which, though, broadly speaking, is patterned on a parent figure, is in fact in its early stages based not on what the parent actually was but what he was fantasied to be—another instance of the influence of fantasy.

(A study of the ego-ideal, or super-ego, is of importance for understanding some of the phenomena of hypnotism and even of autosuggestion: the hypnotist is endowed with the qualities of an ego-ideal and there is a consequent compliancy towards him. The more disguised form of suggestion, such as with placebos, probably follows this pattern—that is, on to the person of the doctor there are projected infantile fantasies concerning his magical qualities. In the long run this sort of patient-doctor relationship proves a hindrance to the acceptance of a more rational medical co-operation between physician and patient.)

Fourth Period (1932 to the Present): Aspects of the Development of Object Relationship

The severity, the sometimes fantastic severity, of the super-ego led to a closer study of the aggressive component in the personality. Going back to the early days of personality development, it seems that the infant has to effect a working arrangement between two opposed tendencies—of love and hate—and furthermore that his love and hate are directed to the same objects—once again the parents. When our feelings towards any object are such that we wish more of it, want it closer to us, and hope that its like will never perish from the earth, we may be said to love that object, and to us it is a 'good object'. When our feelings are the reverse, when we want less of it, want it farther away, hope it and its like will cease to exist, we may be said to hate that object; to us it is a 'bad object'. For love and hate, good and bad, we may, on this viewing, substitute the simpler concepts of motion towards or away from, more or less, construction or destruction. These two opposed tendencies are at work in the infant's relation to its first love object—the mother's breast. On this it lives; hate for it brings inevitably the pangs of hunger: emotional conflict is from the beginning a desperately important thing. Frustration magnifies the hate—that is, makes the object still more bad—and yet the need for the breast make the infant desire it as a thing which stills physical discomfort, so it is at times thought of as a 'good thing'. At this stage the child is a 'mouth animal'—that is, the instrument by which it attains dominion over its object is that which incorporates the object within itself: mastery of an object entails internalizing it. The self thus becomes filled with 'good' and 'bad' objects—'good' if the mood at the moment of internalization is friendly; 'bad' if it is hostile. There are therefore dire and, indeed, lasting consequences from the use of the expedient of 'projecting' its own emotional state upon the object. 'Good' and 'bad' have at first no moral connotation; that may come later, but can be expressed in terms of movement nearer, a desire for more, etc., or the opposite: we are dealing here with the pre-moral stage and pre-social stage of development. When the self is filled with 'bad internal objects' its greed for more and more 'good' ones increases, to neutralize the bad; hence a vicious circle is developed, because greed begets guilt. As development proceeds these internalizations take on more and more the character of the actual objects, so that, to jump several stages, the person feels that he embodies the attributes of his parents. In passing we may note that savages, still in this animistic stage of object relationship, imagine that if they eat a lion's heart they will be imbued with courage; the idea is found also in some religious rituals.

Speaking descriptively, the ego is a boundary phenomenon

between an internal world (an 'internal society', it might be called, since the unconscious seems to be almost exclusively preoccupied with personal relationships) and an external world revealed through the sense organs. Behaviour can be viewed as the result of the ego being driven by (id) instinct-impulses but curbed by that representation within itself of parental authority (the super-ego), while at the same time the ego has to adapt itself to and master portions of the external world. But behaviour may also be regarded (and without contradiction) in a rather different way—namely, as a container of cathected objects which may work in a unified way or which may show oscillating, unstable, divergent tendencies according as the grouping of forces within the ego is cohesive and unified or disruptive and diversified. These internalized objects (or superegos) may be pictured as having an arrangement in depth; the most primitive are the most deeply buried, but with each 'layer' (representing a phase of development) influencing the deposition of, and the freedom of, movement in the more superficial layer above it; and, furthermore, and more difficult to conceive, in each 'layer' the same objects (the parents, siblings, and other relations, or their surrogates, are always the central figures) recur again and again. So we find, for example, parent-regarding tendencies of differing degrees of primitiveness (or, on the other hand, of complexity) interacting with each other, the resultant influencing behaviour. The 'cathected internal objects' should be distinguished from mere memory traces. The unconscious is not a sort of card-index drawer of photographic images; a better analogy would be a group of objects (people or bodily parts of people) being constantly rearranged and manipulated in moods of love and hate, but unconsciously, by the individual concerned, while at the same time he is similarly manipulating objects in the external world, in the 'external society'. There is a constant interplay between these two manipulations; achievements, no matter how sublime or base, are made not alone for their effect on contemporary society or posterity, but also to adjust the relationships in the 'internal society', that intrapsychic constellation of social and personal forces which is an ever-present and inalienable heritage of our past experience and development.

Now to return to the early stages of this eventually elaborate object relationship: there is stability in our emotional orientation to, and hold upon, objects when we are able to recognize at the same time their 'good' and 'bad' qualities, when, despite anger-rousing frustration, we can keep our orientation to them and our good regard unchanged. One of the several ways by which this mature attitude is achieved is by turning against the self part of the aggressiveness which the frustrating object rouses in us; we then become severer with ourselves for our aggressive impulses towards objects that we hold to be good, and the object is spared at the cost of the self; we suffer pangs of guilt. Pain thus caused is, as it were, cherished by the self (or at least there is 'resistance' to its disclosure and removal) because it is part of a device for protecting a good object. Another way by which the mind is eased of its load of guilt is by 'restitutive acts'—that is, making good the damage done in moods and moments of anger. Sometimes 'restitution' thus based is the main motive of an adult's life; the indefatigably, almost wearisomely benevolent people commonly react lifelong to impulses of great strength which once operated at a nodal point in their emotional development, and as the whole process is unconscious it pursues its course usually unchanged by time and circumstance. Apart from more extreme cases, the restitutive reaction to unconscious guilt plays a large part in the drive towards creativeness which differentiates us from the animals, whose work usually perishes or becomes indifferent after the act of eating, of copulation, gestation, and lactation. Man combines with his fellows in his restitutive work, as he sometimes combines with others in his destructiveness. From this recognition of the need in ourselves and in others to restore and create, from the unconscious feeling and sharing of the guilt of destructive impulse, rises a community of feeling for the restitutive and constructive urges: in these feelings we find some of the roots of religion, art, and science.

Other Workers in the Field of Psycho-therapy

Two names are, or used to be, commonly coupled with Freud's—Jung and Adler. The latter employed the genetic method of approach—that is, he tried to find out how the patient's present condition and symptoms can be explained by reference to his past experience; but he narrowed the range of his theory unduly by an over-emphasis on the will to power. His ego psychology was too simple to be professionally useful, though it helped many others to write popular rather than scientifically penetrating articles. Jung's work is different. In so far as I understand his complicated and seemingly mystical theories, Jung holds that in addition to the influence of past personal experiences there is also and always the influence of the collective unconscious shaping the destiny of the individual. This may of course be true, but from the point of view of science (and therefore its application in medicine) such general theories are of less importance than a step-by-step process of explanation of the influence of events that can be traced in a sufficiently thorough investigation. In the thirty-five years in which Jung's views have been developed in detachment from the history outlined above they have never attained such strength of articulation as to embody a quarterly journal or any cohesive library series of books; the absence of such collective and conscious utterance puts the views of this school at a disadvantage.

Returning to the main line of psycho-pathological development, which for vigour and imagination is almost exclusively psycho-analytical, mention may be made of four workers beside Freud (1856–1939). Sandor Ferenczi (1873–1933) was also a clinician of the highest imaginative capacity who grasped the full implications of the transference situation and thus widened the range of therapy; his study of the part played by the homosexual impulse in the aetiology of paranoia and the developmental stages of the sense of reality were useful in the study of the psycho-pathology of the psychoses. Karl Abraham's (1877–1925) work on manic-depressive disease did a similar service to the psycho-dynamic study of that disorder. Melanie Klein, using the extended application of transference analysis employed by Ferenczi to the study of small children, developed theories of object-relationships and depressive and schizoid conditions which have proved of great value in the study of neuroses and psychoses. That the last-named person is not a doctor or an educationist or a psychologist by training and yet has added to the specialist literature in a region of considerable clinical difficulty emphasizes the fact mentioned earlier that in research work the acquisition and employment of special skills are of paramount importance: old skills alone do not break new ground. Ernest Jones more than any other worker than Freud has applied psycho-dynamic ideas to a multitude of fields.

F

Value of a Common Frame of Reference

At the close of the last century there was a lack of a medium of communication between doctors in respect to the aetiology, symptomatology, and therapy of the psycho-neuroses, and the same was almost true of the psychoses. One man's guess was as good as another's, since none of them produced a theory wide enough or elastic enough to act as an integrator of thought: a general psycho-pathology was lacking. The value to medicine of the ideas outlined above lies chiefly in the fact that they provide a frame of reference, a means of communication between practitioners and students. One person may put more emphasis on one aspect, another on another, but at least everyone who studies the subject at all will know where his views fit in, and where they do not, in a widely ranging theoretical structure.

The practical professional consequences of this general theoretical structure are of considerable importance. First, there can now be a greater mobility of professional personnel—for example, from in-patient mental hospital work with psychotics to out-patient work with neurotics; the child-guidance and delinquency clinics need not be separated from the hospital work by lack of common ideas. Secondly, the young practitioner who takes up psychiatry has got a lively body of ideas to bite on, to struggle with, master, and improve—it would be no longer said to a beginner proposing to go into a mental hospital, as was asked of me. 'Is it beer or whisky which brings you so low?'; nor do young psychiatrists when considering a change of job ask first of their young colleagues what are the sporting facilities of the other hospital, but what are the opportunities for study or research in psycho-dynamics. Flexible theories vigorously applied improve morale.

Applications and Effects of the New Ideas

The provision of a technique for the study of the development of the human personality, carried on with vigour, courage, and discrimination over a period of fifty years, leads almost inevitably to the practical application of the findings in as many fields as the theory covers and there are research workers ready to use the new material. Perhaps the reason why practitioners of psychological medicine are asked so often to contribute to technical discussions held by professional men in other disciplines than medicine is because a clinical study of psycho-dynamics inevitably leads to investigations of the interaction of the individual with the institutions of society and to an attempt to discover the motives which lead to the individual's interest in science or art and his need for religion, politics, and sport.

The work began with the need to cure adult hysterics and obsessional neurotics, but it soon became clear that there were infantile neuroses which reappeared in early adult years (the first psycho-dynamic treatment of a child, by a sort of child-guidance technique, was undertaken by Freud in 1909); the application to psychotics in and out of institutions came later.

The barriers which separated medicine proper from insanity and the neurotic from the normal have begun to break down. Clinical medicine, which has never been blind, has acquired a new interest and grasp in listening not merely to the sound of organs but to the voice of the whole personality seen in a social setting. If the contribution of psychological medicine to general medicine could be summed up in a single sentence, one would say that it has given a new dimension to the medical interview. The study of psycho-dynamics has progressed step by step with the improvement of clinical skill applied to discourse between doctor and patient: as in science generally, so in psychological medicine, progress consists in an ever-developing scrutiny (in this case without the aid of apparatus) of what lies in the field of observation. Nowadays we can get more out of a consultation than could be got before—that is to say, clinical skill has been increased.

Conclusion

It was said the psycho-dynamic ideas outlined above have given a new dimension to medical thought; in no branch of medicine is this more true than in psychiatry. That the child is father to the man and that the child models himself on his parents have long been guessed, but how the process worked was not realized. These studies have led to a way of looking at the growth of personality in health and disease which is valuable because it provokes further thought (one of the best criteria for assessing the worth of a theory); psychiatrists, while developing other techniques for the empirical treatment of mental disease, find themselves, wittingly or not, when trying to explain the behaviour of their patients, employing some or most of the ideas here so briefly sketched.

On this occasion it may not be out of place to recall that the key idea to this great advance in medical theory and technique was published just fifty years ago: Freud's *Interpretation of Dreams*. A clinician, without laboratory aids or other such devices, by the closest attention to the material before him, unpromising and the least worthy of scientific care as it was then thought, changed his speciality out of recognition and raised the potential of every doctor's clinical interviews.

XIX
THE FACTOR OF NUMBER
IN INDIVIDUAL- AND GROUP-
DYNAMICS[1]
(1950)

THE term 'Group-Therapy' can have two meanings, and it is well to keep the distinction clearly in mind. It can refer to the treatment of a number of *individuals* assembled for therapeutic sessions, or it can refer to a planned endeavour to discover (and so make accessible to the understanding, and thus control) the forces which operate in the participating *group*.

The first is primarily a therapy of *individuals* (group behaviour and its study being a secondary but important consideration); the second is primarily a therapy of a *group* (individual behaviour and its study being a secondary but important consideration). These two may blend.

The first is found in several forms which we can name according to where the dynamic emphasis is laid. One kind is based on general explanations of the nature of neurotic trouble; this may be called *didactic* group therapy. The physician may, however, be less concerned with explanation and more interested in giving comfort; this may be called *reassurance* group therapy. The comfort and companionship may be carried far, that is, the aim may be to produce such a degree of happiness in the group as to deserve the name *companionate* group therapy; or the technique may be that of catharsis by a sort of public confessional in which case we may speak of it as *confessional* group therapy (without confusion with the other and older use of the word 'confessional'). There is another kind of group therapy in which transference interpretations are given of the behaviour of individuals and by inference of the group, called *analytical* group therapy.

Let us now consider the second kind of group therapy, which

[1] Reprinted from the *Journal of Mental Science* (1950), **96**, 770–73.

A contribution to a symposium on 'Group Psycho-therapy' held at a quarterly meeting of the Royal Medico-Psychological Association on February 22, 1950.

we owe to Dr. Bion. This, if I understand him aright, is primarily concerned with the behaviour of the group as a group, and less with the behaviour of individuals in it. The difference is very important theoretically, and therefore, in the long run, practically.

One of the characteristics of individuals, as distinct from groups, is that individuals have an infancy characterized by a long development from immaturity during which they are physically and socially dependent: if groups, *as groups*, have anything comparable with this we know as yet very little about it. Very gradually we are beginning to know something about the integration of individual personality; we know that it is both threatened and stimulated by unresolved emotional conflicts during infancy, and that its final achievement, which we call maturity, is never as rigid or as stable as the instinct-ridden 'personalities' (if we may use the word) of the wild members of the lower species. Following, and perhaps developing, Freud's theories in 'Group Psychology', we can see one way in which the psycho-dynamics of the individual influence the behaviour of the group—the dependent state during human infancy and the unresolved problems of that three-person relationship called the Oedipus complex (in both direct and inverted forms) leads to a search for and veneration of Leaders, who are identified with the ego-ideal, and to a bond through positive identification with those who share the same ego-ideal figure, and through a negative identification a hostility towards those who do not.

Such concepts, which are now so much the common stock of our daily thought that we find them in leading articles of our newspapers, give a valuable theoretical structure to those group therapies which concern, explicitly or implicitly, the treatment of several individuals assembled for remedy of neurotic disturbances, but I venture to think that such concepts deal with only a portion of the operative *group* dynamics.

If we were to divide the kinds of psycho-dynamics according to the number of particles or bodies or persons concerned, we could speak of one- and two-body psychologies which deal with reflexology, with the 'higher neurology', and with those strange researches using the brass instruments of psychology which study persons in sound- and social-proof rooms of our laboratories—all this is one- or, at most, two-body psychology. A three body psychology deals with all of the derivatives of the Oedipus complex, and this, as we have seen, is very useful in group therapy. There is perhaps—I repeat, perhaps—a multi-body psychology, which would, if it were articulate, that is to say adequately conceptualized, deal with the psychological forces operative when several or many individuals are together.

If, in an endeavour to understand the psycho-dynamics of a group, we employ as a model for our thinking the three dimensions of space, one co-ordinate can be represented by the one- and two-body psychology, another by the three-body psychology, and the third by the multi-body psychology. On this reckoning the three psychologies are complementary; but there is a corollary, viz. that an event (if, indeed, the theory is right) can only be 'placed', i.e. accounted for, if cognizance is taken of the forces in all three psychologies, or, as one might call it, the three regions of psychological space.

At this point I expect to be challenged with the question—am I not advocating a herd instinct, and is not the psychology of the individual and of the horde (to quote Freud's term) enough? My answer is that horde psychology carries us a long way, and usefully, but I suggest that it carries with it a 'field determined' limitation. It is based on research done in the two-body situation of the psycho-analysis of single persons who have failed to master the complexity of the three-body (Oedipal) situation, and who therefore *transfer* into every other situation those as yet unresolved three-body problems. This is likely to be particularly evident where individuals, still Oedipally handicapped, are assembled for remedy of three-body problems.

When groups of people, having already a structured relation to one another, call in a psychologist because of their discontent with their group relationship and wish it bettered—when this occurs we shall have a situation in which multi-body psychology can be studied more easily, though, of course, the investigation will be complicated by the two other psychological factors. Without Freud's three-body theory, an examination of a multi-body situation becomes unmanageably complicated; in the study of human society Oedipal factors will always have to be reckoned with.

To return to the challenging question—about herd instinct. I see no objection to it; many animal species exhibit it; man certainly shows a tendency to shoal, or herd, or group together. Perhaps—again, perhaps—the herd impulse provides a matrix within which the multi-body as well as three-body forces operate. The trouble is that we lack as yet a wide-sweeping theoretical framework for multi-body psychology, without which group therapy (in the second sense I described at the outset) will lack its backbone of theory.

I am well aware that I have said nothing but commonplaces, and have added nothing whatever to the theories which may help us to explain in detail the behaviour of groups. My sole excuse for occupying your time with these banalities is that in our absorption with the tasks of applying three- and two-body theory we tend to overlook that groups, like animals, have, so far as we know, nothing like a human infancy.

[Transference, and transference interpretations, depend on the carrying-over into the present of past situations that have a different quality from those now existing. The child is different from the adult both structurally and functionally; Freud laid stress on this about fifty years ago, when he emphasized the importance of infantile sexuality, and subsequent researches have in no way diminished the importance of that discovery. Interpretations which only compare similar structures and functions are not 'mutative', to use Strachey's term, and it does them undue honour to call such interpretations explanatory, because they miss the point; they are not, in fact, interpretations in the strict use of the term. Another feature of human infancy is that its most important behaviour and character-influencing qualities are repressed; there is something preventing 'closure' to the unresolved conflicts; there is an amnesic gap in the experience of the individual which has to be filled in (not merely bridged by explanations) before the patient can obtain his full maturity. Furthermore, the therapeutic work with individuals mainly concerns the restitution of processes of growth within an organism whose boundaries can, generally speaking be defined, and whose changes occur within a biological time scale proper to the species—'three score years and ten', as the Bible says. The art of interpretation lies partly in conveying to the patient the present operation of concurrent but discrepant patterns of behaviour which belong to different periods or positions in the time scale of that patient's growth. It is with these considerations in mind that one can say a group has no infancy, that the term 'group interpretations' does not consist in filling in a gap between structurally and functionally different phases of an organism living in, and bounded by, a well-recognized and highly relevant time scale, and that such 'group interpretations' are not intended to remove an amnesia. All this notwithstanding, it is possible that groups have phases (perhaps, indeed, lasting in some cases throughout their existence) characterized by such instability of behaviour, such apparent unawareness of threats to their very existence, such unmindfulness of their relation to other groups and the community of which they are a part—because of these things it is tempting but not useful, to speak of groups as being infantile. Our lack of a comprehensive picture of group life inclines us to lean overmuch on analogies.[1]]

One of the main tasks of research, at least one that lies nearest to hand, is to discover the limiting factors in the operation of three-body psycho-dynamics in a multi-body situation.

[1] The portion in brackets was added to this paper as a result of the subsequent discussion.—J.R.

XX
REFLECTIONS ON THE FUNCTION AND ORGANIZATION OF A PSYCHO-ANALYTICAL SOCIETY[1]

(1951)

1. Introduction
2. A brief survey of the field
3. An experiment in co-operation between organizations
4. An arbitrary classification of research areas in the field of psychology
5. On the nature of a profession
6. An approach to the sociology of psycho-analysis
7. Will the former opposition to analysis return?
8. The distribution of psycho-analytical publications
9. On the presentation of papers to a psycho-analytical society
10. On the oral tradition in psycho-analysis
11. A personal note about the organization of a psycho-analytical society
12. Table showing membership and associate membership, medical and lay, in 1932 and 1948

1. *Introduction*

NEXT to a total lack of contributors and of subscribers nothing is more dreaded by an editor than that the organization he serves should establish a precedent that addresses from the chair and such-like speeches for an occasion should be published in his Journal. Knowing this both as an editor and as an ex-president of one of the Branch Societies of the International Psycho-Analytical Association (the British one) I have tried to avoid embarrassment to the editor and I hope to readers by removing from the addresses from the chair given in July, 1948, 1949 and 1950 all references to current events which do not have a general bearing, and am placing before the readers of this journal some reflections which, though based on the experience of only one Society, may perhaps have a little significance for all.

[1] Reprinted from the *International Journal of Psycho-Analysis* (1951), **32**, 218–37.

It is proper at this point to say that to remedy such defects as are apparent to me in the three original reports I have revised them and in places added to them considerably. Naturally I offer them with hesitation because they are discursive and do not derive exclusively from that area of research which it is the profession of psycho-analysts to explore.

Readers are kindly asked to imagine themselves to be members of the British Psycho-Analytical Society in the reconstruction phase following a world war—a Society which has grown in numbers to about one hundred with about fifty students; also to realize that among the students in one year there were more lieutenant-colonels than any other category, i.e. that students and members had been busily and responsibly employed during the years of war struggle in many and diverse psychological duties; also to recall that the Society is about thirty years old, its Institute (the organization which manages its trust funds, arranges for the housing of the Society, the clinic and the library and the training) is twenty-five years old and is undergoing a reorganization in order to enable it to function more efficiently under the wide and generous regulations governing such charitable organizations in England.

2. *A Brief Survey of the Field*

A survey of psycho-analysis in the first fifty years of its existence cannot be separated from a consideration of the field of forces in which it operates. In a world that has changed so much in the half-century, it is surprising to discover how little in essentials psycho-analytical work has altered in that time: the use of the simplest concepts—how profound and revolutionary they are, we are still daily discovering—those concerning our capacity to translate unconscious processes into conscious ones (or to undo the dream work and symptoms and see what lies beneath) and our 'social instrument' of research (the transference situation) have undergone but little fundamental alteration in this period of world-wide transformations. Freud laid his foundations well, and fortunately for us lived long to build on them.

Though the essential work of analysis has not altered radically (and to say this is not to deny the extension of theory and practice but rather to afford a criterion for distinguishing the continuity and fundamental identity of all psycho-analytical work from that in other fields) the direction of pressure exerted by the community upon psycho-analysis has changed a very great deal. We all know that formerly to be a psycho-analyst was to be thought an oddity: it was a hindrance to professional progress, and all of the propulsion in the psycho-analytical direction came from within the persons concerned. A group of people reckoned as eccentric is never given professional status, they are thought of as outsiders. Today, within a generation, the situation has largely changed. Professional status is expected of us— that we know by many and by no means small signs—and the Institute has to face that pressure.

The reason for the change in the public and professional attitude to psycho-analysis lies in the fact that the analysts have in their research and therapeutic technique an instrument of great power: what happens in their consulting rooms will give a new direction to the thoughts of mankind. Though hardly more in number than one in a million of the population, what lies within the analyst's field of research will eventually influence that million. We may therefore with seriousness and in all modesty give consideration not only to the phenomena which it is our professional duty to explore but also to the sociological aspects of our work. We may be sure that if we do not consider the sociological implications others in some ways less fitted for the task than ourselves will do so. This is justification enough for considering the function and structure of the psycho-analytical society, which will here be examined mainly as a means for fostering and transmitting ideas relating to what seem to me to be the essentials of psycho-analysis.

The concept of the transference situation is one of our great inheritances. It is a social situation demanding the utmost of the two participants, and it is to be expected that the use that is made of that research and therapeutic opportunity will never be quite the same in any two decades, or perhaps even in any two years. It is also to be expected, and the event justifies the surmise, that the inferences drawn from behaviour in that situation will vary from individual to individual. A new idea, a re-viewing of an old idea, will change the pattern of behaviour in that situation, if the idea is real—i.e. if it has effects.

Transference (and counter-transference) deals with forces within the participants which have not established perfect equilibrium and are in conflict with one another. It is a situation calling for constant vigilance. Vigilance is a part of the analyst's habit of mind, and in this task he is considerably aided by a social institution which keeps before him a useful mirror reflecting both himself and the contemporary world of similar experience, viz. the discussions in the meetings of his psycho-analytical society. They are few in number and heroic in endurance who can thrive and remain supple without the aid of these colleaguely meetings; perhaps even research workers, except those of the highest flight, benefit from them. The clinical discussions give opportunity not only to acquire new ideas and to see new meaning in the old ones, but also for the listener to feel his way into the relation arising between another analyst and his patient, to penetrate the boundary wall of someone else's consulting room.

The differences in behaviour in the transference situation which discussion discloses are one of the healthy signs of our work. Discussion of these is fruitful in proportion to the energy given to the task of seeing just what tools of his trade the speaker is using and how fully he is using them; it fails in usefulness if not guided by a friendly participation in the total *situation* being disclosed.

Though differences in behaviour in the transference situation are to be expected and their discussion welcomed, the institutionalizing of these differences must be undertaken with considerable caution by the group, and with an equal hesitation by the individual. The corrective to the tendency to institutionalize differences, as far as the group can influence the attitude of the individual, lies in the conduct of the scientific discussions, particularly of case material. The mental participation in the analytical work of a colleague is a very personal affair. It is based on an identification with him in the doctor-patient relation being discussed; it involves an understanding of his frame of reference with a full and lively sense of its potentialities as he himself feels them—only after this full participation within the speaker's frame of reference can the listener profitably add his own opinion to the discussion, or to a wise consideration of the topic.

There is probably no field of activity more difficult to discuss intelligently than ours: the material itself is elusive, the observation of the material is not shared by another person, and the concepts employed in explaining a class of phenomena never provide enough dimensions to enable the events to be given a final 'placing' in the world of human experience—the marvel is that our discussions are as fruitful and as coherent as they are. They are useful in proportion to the energy given by those participating in the acquiring of new identifications and different frames of reference to the problems we meet in the isolation of our own consulting rooms.

The scientific meetings, however, provide another and perhaps not lesser benefit. They can, if the assembled members are so minded, provide a 'climate' favourable to the germination of ideas. The great pioneers, to be sure, do not need this—they are capable of producing superb work without such aid while the majority cannot—but everyone likes warmth of heart towards his ideas, and is fortified by constructive criticism.

In the preceding paragraphs there has been a transition of topic from the transference situation to discussion in the scientific meetings, rather as if there were a close connection between these two kinds of social contact. It is just this connection which gives a special quality to our scientific meetings and which makes them so different from other kinds of discussion groups. The common experience, the starting point and reference point of the whole work and movement is the same, or nearly the same, to all analysts, and only analysts can share it.

All that has been said so far concerns a group of people who need have no organization binding them together, indeed they need not have met personally; the communication is through the medium of the common experience of handling transference phenomena with the aid of the simple but penetrating ideas given us by Freud. This is always the position of a new and unprofessionalized, of a creative but not potentially unstable, community: but it lacks organs of contact.

The problem before every growing psycho-analytical group, sooner or later—and they all seem to grow, though some may be destroyed—is that of retaining the fresh and intimate exchange of ideas on the scientific side while developing a structure capable of resisting internal and external pressures. It may be an insoluble problem, but it is not wise hastily to assume that this is the case. It probably requires the analogue of the analyst's vigilance—the Society's or Institute's self-examination, making sure that it is conducting its affairs so that its creative potential is given the greatest means of outlet and its organization only the attention needed to keep it supple and responsive to changes.

An organization such as ours passes through two phases. In the first, while it is struggling into existence, it is mainly concerned with the problems of its own maintenance; in the second phase, the one in which we now are, its own maintenance is assured, but it becomes an organization of which is demanded satisfaction of the needs felt not only by the individual but by other organizations.

It is becoming evident to a number of people outside our society that the training which the Institute provides gives the person so trained something which even a personal analysis does not supply. One reason for this may perhaps be found in the earlier paragraph of this paper when considering the relation between work in the consulting room and discussions in our scientific meetings. Our training affords practice in the process of making identifications with people who are in this special kind of social contact we call the transference situation, i.e. people so trained acquire a flexibility probably not to be obtained by any other professional means. The student analysand takes on a case under supervision while he is himself undergoing personal analysis, and this gives him an opportunity, denied to the patient coming for therapeutic analysis, to feel the operations within the transference situation from both aspects more or less simultaneously. It is this duplication of rôle in a situation which deals with the inhibition of growth and stability (i.e. which examines the hindrances to the development of emotional relationships in new situations) that puts the person trained by us in a position of greater demand than those who are only analysed by us. This double experience of being analyst and analysand gives a specially clear occasion to become aware of the interplay of forces, positive and negative, conscious and formerly unconscious, working to the consummation or disruption of the projects in which he is participating.

In years gone by we reckoned it an advantage to our science that a few of our members should be interested in anthropology, education and others of the mental sciences. The theories we receive from Freud we thought should be carried into fields other than the therapeutic so that a broader basis could be given to our understanding of human affairs. In recent years, and stimulated by war, which promotes experiments, attention has been given not only to the application of psycho-analytical theories, but also to the observation of the tensions and conflicts occurring in specially created temporarily closed communities (the analytical transference situation being an instance of a temporarily closed community, albeit of only two persons). It is too soon to speak of the theoretical outcome of these investigations, but they have already yielded some interesting and encouraging practical results.

According to those who were responsible for the technical work involved the following enterprises owe a part, and in some cases a considerable part, to psycho-analysis: the War Office Selection Boards, the Civilian Resettlement Units, certain Group Therapy experiments, and numerous technical procedures for assessing and promoting a good military morale. Since then some of the underlying ideas in those experiments carried out during the war have been applied, and are being increasingly applied, in the civilian field, so much so that it would be no rash prophecy to say that in ten years' time, if we were so minded, we could fill as many candidate vacancies in lay non-therapeutic fields (that were never before the war considered particularly relevant to psycho-analysis) as we now give to medical therapeutics.

In addition to the new fields of enterprise, we are being asked to train psychiatrists whose life work will probably lie in mental hospitals and psychiatric out-patient departments; this is in itself nothing new, but the increased emphasis under the National Health Service on full-time service will inevitably change the later professional life of a number of our candidates.

Dealing with this last group first, it would not be expedient to make any restriction on the post-training activities of our candidates; rather should we welcome the opportunity for research and therapy in a branch of psychiatry which is so difficult and which needs such clarification as we can bring. The State Medical Service may indirectly and by inadvertence, one might say, induce us to have a special or advanced training in the psycho-pathology of the psychoses, mental defect and delinquency—a development that would be indirectly helpful to child and to adult therapy.

Returning to the training of lay persons who will take up non-therapeutic activity, the three following points merit consideration: first, a welcome should be given to enterprise wherever it is found; we do not know what additions to knowledge, or to our science in particular, may come from such enterprise; secondly, since there is pressure on our teaching staff, it is expedient to conserve a good proportion of people who will do clinical work over a long period of years (it takes years of clinical work before an analyst is fitted to be a teacher of analysis and no amount of theory reading or work outside the consulting room can substitute for that done inside it): a clinical cadre is necessary to keep the teaching going; therefore, thirdly, only a small proportion of the applicants who may spend their post-training years in the non-clinical field should be admitted to our training. It is assumed that these considerations only affect the selection of candidates, and that the Institute will continue its policy of not laying any obligation on its candidates to undertake any particular activity after they have passed the course. In this respect we are educators, not directors of labour.

In 1948–49 the National Health Service came into operation and the Act of Parliament founding it gave the Minister of Health the right to 'claim' any hospital or clinic which might be useful to that Service; the Act also gave the Governing Bodies of the hospitals and clinics thus claimed the right to petition to be 'disclaimed': it was an honour to be claimed and a privilege to be allowed to be disclaimed. After much deliberation it was agreed to request the Minister of Health to 'disclaim' our Clinic. This he has done, but it may be put on record that our request to stay outside the Health Service was looked on with regret by a number of psychiatric colleagues in the region into which we would have been drawn.

The attitude of our psychiatric colleagues is cordial, their interest in our training is one of appreciation and they wish to have our candidates in their hospitals. This is satisfactory, as it means our students will be given facilities and not as formerly discouragement when they come to our Institute to study.

3. An Experiment in Co-operation between Organizations

In 1921 a proposal was made to the Governing Body of a world-famous Mental Hospital by a candidate for the post of Medical Superintendent that the patients should be put in a 'climate' or 'social field' where everyone had been analysed, i.e.

all the persons in contact with a patient (not only the doctor in charge of his analytical therapy) would be in a position to recognize and not be unduly reactive to the deeper sources of conflict which heavily influence the behaviour of the patient; thus the expression of the patient's troubles would be less hindered by lack of understanding and he would not feel so socially rejected. To begin with, the experiment would be confined to a single ward, much later perhaps to the whole hospital. It may be worth noting that the candidate was not given the post for other reasons than his enthusiasm for psycho-analysis; indeed about twenty years later the unsuccessful candidate was asked by a member of the Governing Body of that Hospital if he had been able to carry out the project elsewhere—the idea had certainly not been forgotten.

Without the members—save one—having any knowledge of this episode this Institute has come near to fulfilling this project. Within the candidate-intake over a period of nearly two years a large proportion came from the Tavistock Institute of Human Relations and the Tavistock [Out-Patient] Clinic, both in London, which for our present purpose may be considered to be the same organization. Our Institute invested heavily in the training of practically all of the senior staff of this organization. This was done, as the saying is, 'without strings attached', i.e. as in medicine, the law and the Church, those responsible for education make no conditions regarding the use to which the training will be put, neither did our Institute.

The return to psycho-analysis from this large investment of time and money will in part be direct in that there will be an increase in the number of practitioners of psycho-analysis, in part indirect in that the application of dynamic psychology to areas of human science other than the treatment of patients will, because it adds to psychological knowledge, facilitate combined research. Although psycho-analysis is based on the transference relationship in its direct research area, it is part of the broad progress occurring in the human sciences which includes direct research in relationships, equally complicated, in the function of groups.

Such experiments as the one mentioned above, which was only partly in the clinical field, cannot be lightly undertaken nor can they be often repeated because the centre of psycho-analytical research—this is both its strength and its limitation

—is that it is a two-body situation, so that most effort must be given to the direct development of the potential of that situation. But there is scope for the application of intensive co-operation with other organizations without leaving the strictly clinical field. When only ambulant patients are taken on for a particular kind of treatment, which is nevertheless suitable for non-ambulant persons, there is necessarily a restriction in the scope of the research afforded by that treatment. So it is satisfactory that an important proportion of our training and clinical effort can flow into the Cassel Hospital where psycho-analytical treatment is given to In-patients, many of whom need hospital care at some time in the course of their illness, and who, following discharge from Hospital, can be treated as Out-patients by the same doctors.

The association of our Institute with the Tavistock and with the Cassel Hospital is not an affiliation in any formal sense, it is one that is purely functional and not structural. It is therefore of a type which can be extended or diminished as occasion demands without altering our independence and without restricting our liaison with other institutions. These points are very important. With regard to the National Health Service, though in some ways we may lose by staying out, we gain only in proportion to our freedom to give in directions where our contributions have most scientific power; in assessing this we have always to reckon on the cumulative gain where several workers of like mind and training can form a 'climate of opinion', an atmosphere in which new and incompletely formulated ideas can germinate.

One feature of the two organizations named of outstanding importance is the emphasis placed by them on the 'feed-back' process in group dynamics, an operational idea and action derived from psycho-analysis, which with its transference interpretations is *par excellence* a 'feed-back process' in a two-person relationship.

4. *An Arbitrary Classification of Research Areas in the field of Psychology*

As has been said elsewhere and in various contexts[1] the field

[1] E.g. in the *Journal of Mental Science, British Journal of Medical Psychology* and the 60th Birthday Commemorative Volume to Géza Róheim (none of it published at the time of this writing).

of psychology may be broken up into areas according to the number of persons essential to the research under consideration. Thus introspective psychology, the psychology of the special senses, of reflexes, learning processes, etc. may be called a One-Body psychology. Psycho-analysis is a two-body psychology with an immense lot to say about three-body dynamics and about sibling relationships, making a four-body psychology. But when we come to five- (or multi-) body dynamics the psycho-analyst has less *direct* evidence to work on, in fact as psycho-analyst he has almost none at all.

(Freud's excursion into group dynamics was almost exclusively confined to the derivatives of the Oedipus situation, i.e. to parvi- not multi-body dynamics). If we look at this arbitrary schedule more closely we see that predictions as to behaviour become less certain as we make inferences from a lower to a higher category; thus who would, from the basis of laboratory research into one-body psychology, have predicted the findings of the two- and three-body transference phenomena? Again a knowledge of one-body psychology is an aid to the understanding of the early stages of ego development (when one-body processes are paramount), but who can say to what extent the later phases of the ego's development are not influenced, perhaps largely, by multi-body dynamics, which is outside the range of *immediate* observation of the psycho-analyst?

Such considerations as these come to the mind when reflecting on the policy of our Institute when it invested its educational resources so heavily in the enterprises of the two organizations previously named.

It is impossible to predict, perhaps for a decade, what the outcome will be of having a *group* of persons trained in academic psychology, psychiatry and professionally concerned in group dynamics who are also trained psycho-analysts. Our Institute has made an experiment which may not be repeated for years, but it is in keeping with a broad, and may one be so bold as to say 'university-like', policy of education to encourage integrative studies provided that these are based not on armchair speculations but on the acquisition of professional skills by research workers in several psychological disciplines. Our Institute, however, may have to endure the reproaches of those who say we scattered our resources too widely. One thing is certain—it is impossible to predict where the growing points of science will next bud out; and one thing is imperative—creative imagination, no matter how inconvenient to our complacency, must be given the fullest scope.

5. On the Nature of a Profession[1]

The demand for persons trained in psycho-analysis leads to the questions: what is a professional man and has psycho-analysis any right to call itself a profession?

A professional man is a person (i) who has submitted himself to the discipline of an education in the theory and practice of his occupation by the teachers of that occupation; (ii) who, when himself a practitioner, will endeavour to correlate what discoveries he may make with the body of knowledge formed by his predecessors, his teachers and fellow practitioners, and will keep no discovery to himself but will share it with his colleagues; (iii) who, when he has reached a sufficient level of maturity to be made a teacher of his profession, will withhold no knowledge from his pupils so that the next generation will be at least as widely and well informed as he is himself; (iv) who, when in a difficulty of a professional nature, will call in a brother practitioner stating his problem fully, and if consulted by a colleague in such circumstances will give the best advice he can, keeping nothing back, and will not try to take away his colleague's practice from him in respect to the case in question, and (v) who submits himself to the ethical code of his colleagues in respect to his relations to his clients and colleagues.[2]

This five-fold definition links the generations of teachers, practitioners and students and is based on the relationship between equals and includes an ethical code; it applies widely to doctors, lawyers, priests, architects, but it will be noted that it

[1] This section was not included in any of the three annual presidential reports referred to in the Introduction.

[2] In the case of the medical profession there is a feature which is not found to the same extent in the others and that is the sense of personal responsibility which the practitioner should feel for the welfare of his patient. The problems raised by State Medicine, in which the practitioner has two masters, have not yet been solved, nor have they been discussed at any length or depth by psycho-analysts, perhaps because our conception of one of the parties to this problem —the State—must remain somewhat confused until such time as there is formulation and then clarification of multi-body psychodynamics.

does not include a Professional Register. How far does it apply to psycho-analysts and if so at what stage in its development can psycho-analysis be said to have started to be professional? Clearly on this basis psycho-analysis could not have been called a profession before the systematic training began to link the generations since such cultural transmission is essential to the definition. The question arises whether since there are medical and lay analysts there is no true equality among colleagues which the definition demands? The definition does not lessen the status of lay analysts because point 4 speaks only of referral within a group who share a common training and an ethical code. The fact that the lay analyst is under an obligation to keep in touch with the referring doctor does not put him in an inferior status since there is the same relation existing between consultant or specialist and the referring general practitioner.

In one sense psycho-analysis is not in and of itself an independent profession *vis-à-vis* other professions, for it is dependent on medical practitioners for its professional status, but within the orbit of the medical profession it can be regarded as a profession on the basis given in the definition. There remains to consider the Register Question. Who has the privilege of compiling a Professional Register and for whom is it compiled?

Clearly the only persons who can compile a professional register are those who have to educate the students and to assess their technical competence; but this answers only half of the question—an equally important thing is, who will recognize the register when compiled as having any social or professional significance? A register is not compiled for delectable perusal by those whose names are on it, but for the scrutiny of those who are excluded from it. The people who refer to the list of psycho-analysts is steadily increasing in number and in range of professional interests. Recognition of the List or Register is a slow—rightly a slow—process which has to be earned by those whose names are on it; the earning of recognition is done by the establishment of a high standard of training and assessment of professional competence and by the maintenance of a strict ethical code.

6. *An Approach to the Sociology of Psycho-Analysts*

Only those who make dreamland their habitation can dispense with a view from the window; those poor souls who are responsible for an organization in a quickly changing world must upon occasion look about them. One way of doing this is to follow the ways of thought of the sociologists.

In the United Kingdom there are at the moment about seventy-five psycho-analysts in therapeutic practice (a few have retired or are in non-therapeutic activity). That is roughly one for every 650,000 of the population. If we compare this with other occupations in which there is a fairly intimate personal relation between the professional man and his client we have the following comparisons (the figures are only approximate). Psycho-analysts 1:650,000; Medical Practitioners, 1:540 (this does not take into account the many doctors who are not in clinical practice, e.g. married women, those engaged in physiological research and in clinical laboratories, in administration, etc.); Solicitors, 1:2370 (again this figure is too low because many qualified solicitors have no personal or client relationship because they are employed in administrative posts, etc.); Church of England clergy (this is a very difficult figure to compute): about 1,850,000 people take Holy Communion in Easter week according to the rites of the Established Church, and there are about 25,000,000 on the nominal rolls of that Church; there are about 40,000 ordained Anglican clergy, but many of them are schoolmasters, are retired or do no parish work—1:625 is perhaps a fair figure for present comparison; in the Ministry of the Methodist Conference 1:168 (but this figure is again too low because it includes 'supernumerary ministers'); Roman Catholic priests about 1:400. (The ratio for the Jewish faith is at present difficult to compute because of the movement of population after the Nazis came to power.)

Turning to the medical profession: it has been suggested that the Psychiatrist ratio should be 1:25,000 or about 2,000 for the whole of the United Kingdom. (I give this figure because it has been used, though not officially endorsed, in high-level administrative discussion; it seems to me too low.)

When considering these figures it is prudent to take account of the rate of increase that is practicable as well as the number that is desirable. Psychiatrists, and still more so, psycho-analysts, take a long time to produce; but whereas a fairly large increase in the number of psychiatrists can be made without overburdening the teaching staff, in the case of psycho-analysts this is not the case because the training of each student takes about 1,000 individual tutor-hours—a time factor without parallel in any other profession.

The table of the world distribution of psycho-analysts (given at the end of this paper) does not disclose the interesting distribution within the countries named therein. If we assume, as indeed is reasonable in respect to private practice, that a psycho-analytical livelihood is not likely to be made except in fairly large centres of population and that since that livelihood must be made out of annual fees from each patient amounting to about one-eighth of the analyst's gross earned income, then it follows that the *size* of the population in the centre where the psycho-analyst settles is not the only, or indeed the main criterion; the more important criterion is the number of persons with a surplus income over immediate needs or a capital sufficient to support one-eighth of a psycho-analyst, so to speak. If these basic assumptions operated alone, one would expect in the case of the United Kingdom that the distribution of practising psycho-analysts would be roughly equal in the metropolis and the rest of the large industrial and academic cities put together, for these in number and in wealthy citizens are together nearly equal to the figure for London; in fact the proportion is about 70 to 5 in favour of London. If we examine the distribution in other countries we find that in 'decentralized' countries like Switzerland (cantonal organization and loyalties) and the United States (one of the most politically and economically decentralized of all highly industrialized modern states), the analysts are fairly evenly spread over the centres of urban wealth; in Holland, which culturally has been largely influenced by rival cities of roughly equal wealth and power, the analysts are (or are rapidly becoming) spread according to urban wealth; in France, as one would expect, the political prestige and economic domination of Paris is reflected in the distribution of the analysts. (Austria and Hungary before the Second World War came under the same category as France. Germany, before the Nazi *régime*, was on this reckoning about midway between France and Switzerland but with an analytical distribution nearer to the former.) In addition to the cultural factors already mentioned as influencing the distribution there are probably others both of internal and external origin; the former would include the cultural habits of the personnel concerned (e.g. perhaps a certain tendency to gregariousness found among Jews)

and on characteristics of the leadership of the pioneers of analysis in the various national or cultural areas. The factors of
external origin would include the influence of the extravert
culture of almost purely industrial cities on the rate of assimila-
tion, or rejection, of such a point of view as that of psycho-
analysis which has 'nothing to show for its work' and which
deals with disorders which cannot be seen post-mortem.
Another such factor is the tradition of university leadership or
professional prestige. In the industrial cities of England, for
instance, this is low, in Scotland very high, but despite this fact
there is only one psycho-analyst in Scotland. This tardiness on
the part of Scotland—so forward in every branch of scholarship,
of psychology and of medicine—is a strange phenomenon which
has not yet been explained.

The psychological aspects of the uneven spread of psycho-
analysis seem to me to merit attention, indeed their neglect—
among psycho-analysts of all people—should itself make us
wonder why there is this unmindfulness of serious issues.

7. *Will the former Opposition to Analysis Return?*

In its early days psycho-analysis met with a certain amount of
opposition, and some psycho-analysts think that the present
phase in which psycho-analysis receives a certain amount of
recognition will give way to a return to disfavour. This general
opinion cannot be disproved since it concerns the future and
because it does not specify the new cause, or give reason for the
return of an old cause of disfavour. It might be argued with an
equal or even greater plausibility that the disfavour which was
once accorded to psycho-analysis will move to another study of
dynamics, viz. those of the group.

The opposition to psycho-analysis in those far-off days was in
part due to the disturbing nature of the ideas themselves, in
part to a certain tendency among the exponents of our subject
at times to place less value than usual upon tact when presenting
startling opinions or in dealing with opposition. Indeed psycho-
analysts occasionally gave the impression that they were even
more persecuted by their opponents than in fact was the case.
The patience and discrimination which they possessed when
confronted by resistance to new and unpleasant ideas in the
consulting room were less easy to attain and maintain in

scientific societies, public debate and in published writings.

We may surmise that among the reasons for this state of things one point of importance was the fact that the intimate two-person relationship of analyst and patient gave a limiting pattern to psycho-dynamics as it was then understood, and in those early days we must also remember the frame of theory for the dynamics of conflict was thought to be adequately resolved by reference to the ego and the sexual instinct. With the introduction of the notion of the super ego a new dimension was given to theory and—unless I am mistaken—an increase in tact in respect to the public behaviour of psycho-analysts when in debate. I.e. before *Group Psychology and the Analysis of the Ego* appeared, the technical guidance which the analyst received from theory was concerned with individual and two-person dynamics on the one hand and on the other with quite general anthropological speculations (*Totem and Taboo* for instance) and not with the dynamics of face to face relations within groups. In other words in those early days the technical guidance from theory was quite inadequate to deal with such opposition as came from organized groups or society. It was at times a matter of surprise to me not that the opposition was so severe but that it was so restrained.

Another reason why the tact of the psycho-analyst in the consulting room lessened somewhat outside it lay in the fact that when in consultation the analyst and patient were both aware—at least at times—that they were involved in a joint investigation, a sort of family situation, and although as everyone knows there are things which upset families, there are also things which make this 'in-group' feeling an important force. The professional bond between the analyst and patient was reinforced by a special kind of in-group tie. Before the accession to theory from Freud's exposition of super ego psychology it was hardly possible for the psycho-analyst to orient himself to a group in at all the same way as to a patient if *he were using his theory as his only guide*: for his theory had no place for group ties. There was yet another thing of importance; apart from the fact that the exponents of the new ideas were regarded as threatening the prestige and economic security of those who were content with pre-analytical psychiatry, the analysts were thought of as merely unprofessional persons, mere free-lance raiders without a sense of responsibility. If it were not for the organization by various psycho-analytical societies of systematic and rigorous training programmes the opposition to psycho-analysis on grounds of its free-lance character would in my view have lasted much longer, indeed might have lasted indefinitely.

The reader will have noticed that there has been a shift of emphasis from public opposition to professional opposition; that difference must be clarified. In what may be called the free-lance days, before psycho-analysts took steps to become professional (in the sense outlined in section 5) all opposition was 'public'. Because the ideas presented were objectionable it was thought proper to attack them and the exponents of those ideas could be picked out for opprobrium one by one or be lumped together as a nasty muddle of misguided people; at gatherings of learned societies it was not thought necessary to use learning, reason or even courtesy as weapons against the new psychology. When, however, the psycho-analysts showed not only clinical acumen and effectiveness, not only expounded penetrating but useful and coherent ideas, but also could organize themselves without external support and command loyalty to their organization, then the organized professions were faced with a structure they could understand, and with a discipline they could respect and even envy. In all of this no mention is made of the content of analysis to which exception was taken. Its emphasis on the influence of sex in neurosis and everyday health, the worse than bawdy notion that children not only suffer perturbations of libido but even experience enjoyment from it, the pangs of incest, the overriding of untrammelled wishful phantasy by the constraints of a determinist philosophy—all of these factors played their part and have been discussed by psycho-analysts for years.

The effort which psycho-analysts give as a matter of course to patients who resist the analyst's endeavours to elucidate their problems finds warranty in psycho-analytical theory, but our theory does not cover at all adequately the dynamics of group relationships; we must therefore acknowledge that we cannot predict with any degree of certainty whether psycho-analysis, now that it is an organized body, will meet with anything like the severe opposition it once received. (It was said of the Reformer—it is not true of the Revolutionary—that he has only one certain ally, the Angel of Death, who removes to safer spheres those who oppose his reform—leaving the ground clear for those who with changing circumstances may not need that particular reform any more.)

The question whether or no the opposition to psycho-analysis will return can be viewed from another aspect. When psycho-analysis was born the organization of society and its various institutions seemed fairly safe, world wars had not seemed possible, revolutions of any importance, in the larger countries at any rate, had not occurred for half a century and the Individual —that product of the Italian Renaissance—was thought of as an isolated Special Creation personally related to his God, personally endowed by God with Conscience, answerable to God for the exercise of his Will, a Master of the Microcosm, the self. Psycho-analysis weakened these illusions and reinforced other influences that were working towards elimination of absolutism in personal and political concepts. Psycho-analysis was also regarded as a threat to the stability of society because the very illusions it weakened were thought to be essential parts of the structure of society, though they were not of course seen to be illusions.

Two world wars, several revolutions, and the rise of fanatical ideologies, have forced upon modern civilized man the need to re-examine the foundations of his corporate existence. The study of the individual's weakness holds less terror now, indeed it is often thought of as a relief from the strain of enduring our unstable economic and political lot. What is thought of as dangerous now is a study of the shaky foundations of the institutions of society—if *group* disruptiveness is brought to light then nothing is secure. On this ground among others the focal point of the public apprehension may well have shifted from psycho-dynamics to socio-dynamics or rather to a study of those forces which result in disruption in the areas of group action.

Painful ideas can be endured if they can be put in an abstract form, but if they are considered in a 'social enclosure' they are greatly dreaded. Psycho-analysis works in a social enclosure and a small one at that. The events in what has been called 'the here and now' (the analysis of transference phenomena is another name for it, though not a synonym) are by analysts made the chief if not the only topic of consideration from which they allow no escape; 'there and then' studies (such as psychiatrists commonly employ) are considered less dangerous because tensions can be dissipated without being fully faced. The studies of group dynamics made by those who have been trained in or influenced by psycho-analysis, have the 'here and now' quality of immediacy and inescapability and are dreaded. The organization that calls in the student of group dynamics has a comparable dread and for probably basically the same reasons as had the patient in days gone by who sought the aid of the psycho-analyst. Students of group dynamics will in my view get the brunt of such attacks as used to come to us; in terms of social danger we are not only safe, we are safety valves. But if we turn our considerable experience of unconscious processes to a study of the intra-group tensions within our own society (the risk of our doing this seems to be small) or to a study of tensions in other face-to-face groups then we shall get a return of public disapprobation, but in my view not otherwise.

The dynamics of a multi-structured group is as yet without its Freud; it lacks a conceptual frame of reference which is both useful and resilient, its analogue with metapsychology is vague and shapeless. It is possible that psycho-analysis as such has not much to add to this branch of the human sciences, but it is likely that a training in psycho-analysis will always be an advantage and may in time be considered a prerequisite to its professional study. Anyway, if there is a tendency for psycho-analysis to return to disfavour we shall have trained allies in the field of socio-dynamics to warn us and advise us in difficulty— that is if we reckon other human scientists as allies worthy of our confidence.

8. *The Distribution of Psycho-analytical Publications*

Speaking only of the United Kingdom and during the twenty-five years of the Institute's existence the number of psycho-analytical books sold (including separate issues of the Journal) is over a quarter of a million. It goes without saying that these are not distributed evenly over the population but at least 50,000 homes have a copy of one or more of Freud's books in them. Probably one in 500 of the population has read one or other of Freud's books. About a half of these book purchases have been made since the beginning of the second war, and this at a time when book and journal production worked under the severest handicaps of paper restriction, deflection of labour to war purposes and bombing.

9. *On the Presentation of Papers to a Psycho-analytical Society*

Any audience, scientific or popular, is composed of two kinds of people, those who grasp new concepts most readily from reading and those who take them in best by means of verbal, more especially spontaneous communication. The two types are here described in extreme form; there are of course mixed types, and also people who vary according to content or other factors in the matter under discussion. Neither of these two types get the best out of the method of presentation usually employed in the larger psycho-analytical societies.

A paper delivered to our Societies is usually written with a view to publication and is read almost verbatim from the script. The written word differs from the spoken one. (Royal Commissions permit their witnesses to do a moderate amount of editing of the style of their evidence—though not of course the content—otherwise the text would be almost unreadable, though when verbally given it was understandable; similarly many papers, excellent in print, are 'unhearable'.)

This is a well-known fact, and its importance is endorsed by the remarks made in the subsequent discussion that the hearers of the paper, even the ablest and most experienced ones, would like to read the paper before giving an adequate response to it. This is not the only objection to reading from script. Those who deliver from a typescript seldom take the precaution to get advice on how to deliver a paper. Any radio producer will say that the slight pauses in conversation do not always come at the full stops of written constructions, and that the rhythm and pitch of delivery must not be taken from the harsh parallels and spacing of the typewriter. In over twenty-five years of listening and editing I recall only two papers which read well in print and 'heard' well in the lecture room. The late Ian Suttie's typescript was scored like a sheet of music for time and stress, a most artificial looking object and yet when delivered it flowed with an easy grace to the ear and when printed without his scorings it was agreeable to the eye; the other was from the late J. D. Unwin who took the trouble to learn his paper by heart and spoke with a spontaneity that astonished only the few who had the galley proofs before them.

This is not an unimportant matter. A paper delivered occupies during the evening from fifty to a hundred listener-hours; these good people assembled have a concern that the occasion should be fruitful and give their best; too often the narcissism of the speaker, or a clumsy convention, hinders the occasion's proper development.

To the proposal that papers should be circulated in advance, it has been objected (a) that only a few coming to the meeting would read them, (b) some would read them instead of coming to the meeting, (c) that it is hard to get a paper written two weeks in advance of a meeting, (d) the prior circulation would spoil the uniqueness of a first delivery, (e) that when the content of the papers delivered is case material it is undesirable to have it in unrestricted circulation.

The last cannot be gainsaid, but the clinical parts could be reserved for the evening itself. The uniqueness of first delivery is not to be refuted because the first is always unique; what is important is the effectiveness of the delivery. (Perhaps analysts may unwittingly identify themselves with Freud who gave many of his greater papers to the Congress—but he did not read them, and his power of clear conceptualizing and graceful phrasing in writing and in verbal delivery were exceptional. Freud, by the way, likened verbatim delivery from a manuscript to a person inviting his friend to accompany him into the country, and then he himself rides in a carriage while his friend trudges on foot—it cannot be expected that there will be an easy companionship on such a journey.)

The first three objections to prior circulation of papers also concern the matter of morale, or rather a 'negative morale' within the Society. If this be so the state of morale is worth attention and the causes of the weakness should be sought. But there may be two other reasons why there is a wish to have typescript papers read aloud, the one is a simple wish to be read to— a carry over from an earlier, a much earlier, experience, i.e. a revival in a multi-body situation of the two person relation of mother and child. And then, reverting to the morale question again, it is possible that the shared experience of submitting jointly to a verbally delivered statement acts as a 'group-cohesive' when the group attains a certain size. It is worth considering whether the increasing size of the group does not call for increasing demands for evidences of group cohesiveness of a rather formal kind. If there are not these formal evidences of unity members assembled cannot believe that the whole company is ready to assimilate the new ideas; with some, perhaps many people, this is a precondition to the acceptance of new ideas. The foregoing is put forward as worth consideration despite the fact that in our two-body studies we cannot get *direct* evidence of it.

Some of the objections and many of the advantages of prior circulation of papers can be met if what is sent round is a formal structure, giving the references to prior work with the theme as then expounded, and at the meeting itself the speaker delivers shortly and informally and from notes how he came to the view he is now presenting, what points he would like discussed and where in his own opinion lie the difficulties which he himself has been unable to resolve. It has been objected that this proposal robs the speaker of certain of his privileges in presenting the paper as he wants. It is not part of this proposal to hamper the freedom of members, but it is important to use the occasion to the best advantage.

In the preparation of a paper contributed to one of our scientific meetings it is possible to distinguish two phases or stages. In the first the speaker has to clarify his own mind on the issue under discussion, and this we all know is usually a difficult thing to do. It is a piece of intrapsychic work which is intimately related to his own—and indeed largely unconscious—experiences. In the second phase he has to make contact with and communicate something to his audience. This is a piece of work with a predominantly social orientation, i.e. he does not speak unto the void but to human beings about whom it is an unwarrantable assumption that they and their thinking and feeling processes are identical with his own. As a part of this task of communication he has also to remember that when presenting a portion of a patient's behaviour he has to shape his description so that his audience will see much the same things as he himself saw and in the setting in which he saw them; this calls for descriptive art of a high order because the facts we are concerned with relate to the most complicated phenomena in nature—man's behaviour. His description has to be imaginative and at the same time precise. The less effort he puts into the creative process of description the more effort will his listeners have to exert in discovering what he is talking about: facts do not speak for themselves save in a setting of clear conceptualization—this is equally true of science and of art.

There is another matter of probably great importance when

considering the problems of a Society like ours: very likely two quite different needs must be fulfilled. The one is that the scientific contributions should help us to consolidate our belief in the correctness, or at least in the passing utility, of the concepts we employ (an 'establishing function'); the other is that the contributions should force us to unsettlement of our complacency, to a shaking of our convictions as to how right we are (a 'revolutionary function'). This is no new notion: a very well-known psycho-analyst once said that among others we needed two types of case, one which exemplified our theories and one which upset them.

A moment's reflection will show that what has just been described is also a part of the social function of Art; there are thus considered two kinds of Art—that which consolidates the cultural achievements of its time, and a 'revolutionary art' which breaks down conventional ways of looking at things and at life and death. Everyone will prefer one or other according to his passing need, and if he is free in mind he will at various times and crises within himself or in his environment go to both. So it may be with our scientific discussions. It may at first thought seem to be a contradiction or a strange distortion of established usage to compare the deliberations of a scientific society with the social function of Art, but the fact is that our work is half science and half art. For the most part we do not measure, we observe and match and manipulate patterns, and this is one of the features of art. The display of this process before an audience calls for selection of data based on logical and on intuitive mental processes, and the reception of the communications by the audience calls for a high degree of empathy with the speaker's approach to his subject and an equally high degree of critical capacity for assessing what he says. As in art, so in our science, the two kinds of contribution are needed, and at any moment it is foolish to try to say which is the more valuable to *the growth of science in the world of contemporary scientists* (the italicized words relate to a single thing or process) because scientists taken as a whole, and being human, require both sorts of food.

The matter is made more complicated by the fact that a contribution may 'establish' in one part of the theoretical field and 'revolutionize' in another, so that what to one part of the audience seems to be satisfactory as 'establishing', another part of the

G

audience will find encouragingly 'revolutionary'. The discussion of the contributions in such case get confused because the praise or the blame, the positive empathy or the withholding of empathy, is not related to the whole pattern of the paper in the setting in which the speaker is at the moment working but to parts of it which the listener at the moment needs for his own immediate purposes.

The whole process is more clearly seen if the behaviour of a Committee is studied. There are always two sorts of Agendas: there is the Written Agenda which each committee member has in common with the other members, and there are as many Unwritten Agendas as there are committee members. An opener of discussion in a scientific meeting contributes to the Written Agenda, those who follow always contribute to their own, and frequently to one another's Unwritten Agendas. The Unwritten Agendas are filled with items, not always conscious, which the speaker has on his mind. Thus committees move towards, around and beyond the ostensible point of discussion, and their final resolution is a resultant of the forces centring on the Written and Unwritten Agendas.[1]

As in committees so in our scientific meetings, the discussion wanders—as indeed it often should. But there is a difference: a committee is set for action, a scientific meeting for thought. It is often pretty clear when a speaker in a scientific discussion is unwittingly trying to give the assembly a committee orientation, i.e. to action, to the thrusting forward and acceptance of one key idea, or when he is trying to extend the range of thought; in the former case he is aiming to bring every one to his own view, in the latter to widen the range of appreciation in his listeners of the manifold complexity of the subject matter being treated.

Perhaps in the foregoing sufficient stress has not been laid on the frequency with which we hear those scientific papers which, after beginning with a general survey, show the growth of the

[1] Prof. Lionel Penrose, who kindly read the proofs, points out in respect to the Unwritten Agendas, that the total number of topics of discussion including the Written Agenda is two to the power n, where n is the number of Committee members who stay awake.

The practical importance of this formulation is that it gives a hint, perhaps a strong hint, that the enlargement of a small committee even by one member produces a greater effect than *arithmetical* proportions would suggest.

particular idea to be singled out for special consideration. It is perhaps true to say that aspiration at times exceeds performance, and that what to one listener seems to be a completely satisfactory account of the development of psycho-analytical thought on the subject discussed, to another seems one-sided and inadequate. There is probably no branch of science calling for more mutual forbearance among its members than ours and—perhaps because of the field of observation being one that we cannot directly share with a colleague—none where the technique of exposition in our scientific discussions needs to be more carefully studied.

Earlier in this section of this paper Freud's analogy of a journey was referred to. We may return to that with the question whether there is any importance attaching to easy companionship in the journey of discovery? I think the answer varies greatly according to the temperament of the listener. Some people react against pleasure when learning from others, some require much of it.

Is the main thing during the meeting the experience of mutual discovery or a didactic attitude from speaker to audience? Or, if both are desirable upon occasion, how can they be combined? When answering these questions—if indeed they are thought worthy of answer—we may perhaps bear in mind once again the extraordinary complexity of our subject matter and the peculiar, almost cloistered nature of our field of observation (the consulting room). Perhaps we can get furthest with these answers if, for a moment, we shift the whole discussion to a new direction, a consideration of the function of leadership in a scientific society.

A person who is given the privilege of reading a paper to be considered at a scientific meeting is undoubtedly accorded a leadership rôle. The way he uses the evening is dependent among other things on his notion of how that rôle should be fulfilled. There are conventions of different kinds which he can follow: (a) there are the derivatives of the 'Disputatio' of the Mediæval Schoolmen in which a proposition was put up and defended. Science owed much to this discipline for it gave precedence to intellectual clarity; but the combative atmosphere thus created tended to obscure the value of the less tough-minded persons whose gift lay more in seeing, perhaps at first dimly, the patterns of relationships which could not yet be codified by the constructs accepted by the Schoolmen. The 'Disputatio' finds among its modern descendants the ceremony of the M.D. Thesis in some of our ancient Universities and the 'reading-in' process (in lieu of examination) for full membership of our Society. The assumption underlying the 'Disputatio' is either that a student is fighting his way into a closed community or that he is fighting for a place for his ideas in an established body of thought, i.e. that his ideas are revolutionary. (This description of the 'Disputatio' refers to behaviour based on the Unwritten as well as the Written Agenda of the deliberation.) (b) There is an alternative assumption which may form the basis for a consideration of our problem. The model for this may be found in the 'Report on Work in Progress' given by one research worker to a meeting of the research team of which he is a member. Here the task of the group is to make an adjustment in the pattern of the hypotheses on which the research is based so that the findings outlined in the paper can be given their most effective place. This is best done if the underlying assumption is that all research workers are of equal competence (until the contrary be shown) and that no research worker can cover the whole field. The leadership rôle here shifts with each exposition of the problem, the evening's deliberation being centred more on the problem than the particular paper delivered to the gathering. But for the Research Conference meeting to be a success it is desirable that several persons should be prepared for the particular line of thought which the initial speaker will pursue, for in the measure of the importance of the idea presented so must the basis for it and its implications be thoroughly considered: the title of the paper is not enough to appraise the audience of the content.

It is beyond question that the former of these two methods increases the sense of importance of the reader of the paper and ministers to his narcissism and it is also beyond question that the latter involves more preliminary work both for the initial speaker and for the audience, and it is a fair guess that the latter in a scientific society is generally more profitable. The first speaker in a Research Conference has at least two things to prepare, first his written statement which would be circulated in advance, and then the short verbal statement in which he is addressing those persons actually present on that particular evening. The two statements would of course not be identical;

the first should lead up to the second, which should point out particular problems and the attempted solutions. If the speaker lacks conceptual precision this soon becomes clear. In the procedure where the reader of a paper wearies his audience by reading verbatim from typescript his lack of conceptual precision is at times obscured by reason of the fatigue of his audience.

This leads to a further matter for our consideration, viz. the desirability of having more preparation for the evening discussions. When the emphasis is on A Person Reading His Paper a preliminary 'Working Party' is naturally almost an infringement of prerogative rights: but if the notion of a Research Conference is to be the basis of the evening's deliberation such preliminary work by a Working Party would be quite a natural thing. It would also help if such a Working Party were composed of persons with different views and willing to see the 'growing point' in research that goes on a different line from their own. The amount of time thus occupied in preparation for each meeting might at first seem to be a deterrent, but if our main consideration is the improvement of communication with one another the question of the best method of presentation must be faced.

Before we consider the methods of communication of psycho-analytical ideas to a psycho-analytical society it would perhaps be well to give a little thought to the classes or categories of ideas which may be communicated. These may at the moment be grouped under two headings: those which *alter the horizons* of our thoughts and those which *rearrange* (and thus clarify) the phenomena and the exposition of the theories which we deal with. The former are rare events even in the life of such a powerful and original thinker as Freud. The group of concepts contained in his *Interpretation of Dreams* is the best instance of 'horizon moving' ideas, the concept of transference (Gestalt Closure in interpersonal relationships, it can be described—as can the second law of thermo-dynamics—in a number of ways), infantile sexuality, the structuring of the mental apparatus into ego, super-ego and id, and the concept of quantity in psycho-dynamics (which includes the notion of force or urge both libidinal and destructive, Eros and Thanatos) —these great notions clear away confusions and bring about major syntheses. Without them the 'rearranging ideas' would not be effective. The whole of Freud's Theory of Neurosis is on this reckoning placed among the 'Rearranging' series not in the 'Horizon Moving' series; similarly his group psychology is derivative from his concept of super-ego functioning; homeostasis, a concept which Freud imported into psychology with such great effect was originally a 'Horizon Moving' idea, but in the field of psycho-dynamics it was a 're-arranging' one. The instance last given, if this classification may be reckoned useful at all, discloses a further problem: the idea came to Freud as a great revelation; he even noted the date and felt it to be an historical event (which indeed it was); the idea was transplanted and in its new site acquired a new strength. So we can add a third category, viz. 'Transplantations,' which are of course of great importance to the integration of the sciences. Those who like to employ a rather old-fashioned dichotomy would refer the 'Horizon Moving' ideas to the realm of the Pure and the 'Rearranging' ideas to that of the Applied Sciences, but this should not be done in any spirit of depreciation of Applied Science as the instance given clearly shows.

These points are mentioned because of their application to a possible attitude to papers delivered to our Scientific Meetings: a 'Horizon Moving' idea springs from the deeper levels of the mental experience of its author and is a tremendous event for him and for the world of science. Despite the excitement and often the depression which such an event causes in its creator, perhaps just because of the accompanying dismay at the magnitude of the consequences, a special clemency should be extended to him in the process of his expositions, which may spread over years. If one is watchful one notices that the new idea adds a burden to its creator as well as to the listener which is hard to endure, as well of course as providing a stimulus which makes the burden somewhat lighter. The travail produced by a new idea is easier if it is shared by an understanding audience, and the audience is usually more ready to accept it if its author can convey in his exposition something of the hesitation, even the feeling of modesty, which accompanies the act of creation. (The Latin tag given on the title-page of *The Interpretation of Dreams* if read in its context is felt as a *cri de cœur* as well as a challenge to high Heaven.)

The birth of such mighty ideas are occasions which do not lend themselves readily to the Working Party 'working-over' to which reference has been made, for one reason that such ideas usually take years to assimilate; but all other ideas would in my view benefit from the method of Reporting on Work in Progress, and I think it is probable that the Scientific Meetings would be more profitable if the time was spent more than is now usually the case in discussing from many aspects the concepts which lead to, which relate to and which may be derived from the major topic of the evening.

Still using the now triple classification ('Horizon Moving', 'Rearranging' and 'Transplantation') we may consider the relation of the Working Parties to 'Transplantation' of ideas. The discussions of these relate usually to pure theory and are re-examinations of our everyday material in the light of concepts employed in other disciplines. The burden of new ideas here creates a slight sense of resentment at what seems at first viewing to be a needless importation—'we have got along without this notion, why bring it in at all, and besides it isn't "pure psycho-analysis".' But, despite vexation, a new approach to familiar things, though the horizon is not altered, is often useful, not least because the philosophy of science is in constant process of change and our younger members are often more familiar with them than are their psycho-analytical teachers. Working parties will lose much of their effectiveness if they do not span the generations. 'Transplantations' are more often done by the younger generation, who, after all, will in the next decades be the persons who will use them most. The pioneers of psychoanalysis were mostly young when they started analysis, and many of them stayed young in this sense till they died.

Ideas of 'Rearrangement' also lend themselves to Working Party treatment. This category includes the vast majority of the papers submitted to our societies. No horizon is altered, no concept is transplanted, but within the familiar field of action new applications are made of already known ideas, new data in support or modification of theory are disclosed and the general theories are given a closer link with observation. It is most useful, indeed quite indispensable, work in a growing science and is full of surprises.

It may be well to consider why the present, often somewhat inefficient and occasionally very tedious method of arranging our scientific meetings is adhered to, i.e. the verbal delivery of one-hour papers from typescript, when other ways of communicating ideas are within the experience of all members.

(1) Many people object to anything in the nature of organization, the idea of having a topic for the evening instead of a Member's Paper smacks of Planning and is thought to stifle spontaneity. With people whose work is as individual as is the analyst's this is understandable enough.

(2) A more serious objection is that the speaker is robbed of the opportunity of what I think may be called Surprise if he has been one of the initiators of a Working Party to prepare the topic of the evening. A paper is a sort of gift to colleagues and a gift loses some of its emotional quality if its specification is sent in advance. I think this factor of gift plays a considerable part in the Speaker-Audience relation in our meetings, and, despite disappointments, it is one which sustains a mode of organization which was more suited to small gatherings of a dozen or so than to the larger ones now assembling. It is pleasant to see a colleague on his feet meeting the challenge of the Society; this is particularly true of an Associate 'reading his Membership Paper' as it is called; but with the increase in numbers in a Society the opportunity to make a wide contact with colleagues in this way is reduced.

Related to the loss of Surprise there is a further objection to the Working Party idea and that is the risk, which some would feel more acutely than others, of having their ideas 'borrowed'. The value which persons place on having concepts attached to their name, or rather of having their name attached by colleagues to ideas, of course varies greatly, not only with the personalities of members, but with the morale in the Society as a whole. Here again the factor of number comes in; a uniformly high degree of sympathetic support for a partially formulated idea as the product and possession of a particular person is more likely to be found in a community numbering a dozen than in one of a hundred.

(3) The pride in originality and authorship is a human quality which has to be kept ever in mind in arranging the meetings, and though at times rigorous scientific pride may find itself alloyed with other sorts of pride this is a risk that must be taken by the Society. This is sometimes, but not always, related to another quality which may at first sight be thought to be threatened by the Working Party idea, viz.—

(4) The Leadership Rôle in delivering a paper to the Society. I do not believe the leadership function is closely connected with

the delivery of papers as such, but rather with the support given to discussion in an intelligible and constructive way.

To conclude, I think the flow of ideas from one to another would proceed with greater ease and effectiveness if more attention was given to the way our meetings were arranged, to the factor of size (even of seating [1]) and the preliminary preparation of the papers either verbally or by prior circulation.

I recall that about fifteen to twenty years ago it was thought by some members to be an undesirable thing that there should be meetings of small groups of members to discuss topics which interested them since such private gatherings were likely to foster cabals and to lessen attendance at and interest in the general meetings of the Society. Whatever may have been the reason in the past for deprecating such gatherings it is worth considering whether they should not be fostered now. Indeed such meetings have already begun: a meeting has already been held in London of Associate Members only; a move, surely, to be encouraged. There is one criterion for admission to any meeting of members and/or associates held in the premises of or under the auspices of the Institute which should in my opinion be insisted upon. Just as there is no justification for the expulsion of any member or associate on the ground of his holding any particular view as to the philosophy of science, medicine, psychology or even psycho-analysis, so it is my earnest hope that there will be no such grounds for the exclusion of any member and/or associate from any of the Discussion Groups that may be formed by or under the Institute. This is a negative criterion. The positive criteria in any Discussion Group that may be formed are, I suggest, for the Group itself to decide, and freedom should be given to such persons as desire to participate; they are particularly to be encouraged if they assist in the preparation for the scientific meetings and for the pages of the Journal. Indeed I look forward to the time when the first Wednesday in the month is given up to a full-scale meeting to give expression to the work of preparatory meetings (plural)

[1] The arrangement of rows of seats all facing a rostrum does not facilitate the fluid development of discussion; the amphitheatre plan, where people can see nearly everyone else face to face, would seem more appropriate to the building up of ideas in a small community. But this is, of course, a matter of taste for no doubt some find an invigorating stimulus in the lectern-and-pew arrangement.

held on a previous second Wednesday in the month. Again speaking personally I should be disappointed if in all of the preparatory meetings or any other 'Discussion Groups' or Working Parties' or whatever they may be called and held under the Institute, all views were not well presented because parties with divergent views commonly have so much to give to each other and to the Society.

10. *On the Oral Tradition in Psycho-Analysis*

Some sciences deal with more or less isolated objects, and inspection of these, even the peering eyes of a host of observers, affect the phenomena not a whit. Comets do not blench at the staring multitude nor do animalculæ establish reciprocal relations with the biologist; but a psycho-analyst can hardly look at his patient without producing, though maybe but for a moment, a change. The psycho-analyst's material of observation and his mode of looking at it is, accordingly, a very subtle one, and it is therefore not surprising that though there are reams of description of case material and a lot of papers on technique the essence of the experience is more often than otherwise just not there. True, the written descriptions give sections of the events observed which are of use to the psycho-pathologist, just as microscope slides are of use to the somato-pathologist; but slides alone do not give a clinical picture, nor do most of the descriptions of the interplay between analyst and analysand.

When we reflect on the source of our keenest understanding it will I think generally be found in the verbal instruction we have received from our great teachers. It may be well to consider this in some detail, for much depends on our preserving the oral tradition if we believe at all in its value.

An essential feature of oral communication in the sense here employed is that the speaker does *some* of his thinking while he speaks and that that thinking has reference to the actual audience before him. He does not give utterance in a universe of discourse to the whole world of science nor does he consider in the true humility of a teacher's love for his pupils that his dicta must and will stand the scrutiny of eternity: he speaks to those who are listening now and here before him, speaking to their groping need to understand the subtle experience he desires to communicate *to them* and, listening himself to their response, shapes his discourse to the uncovering of their understanding.

Whether the occasion be a seminar of students or a meeting of the Society in essentials it is the same. In the seminar the person at the moment speaking, 'who has the floor' to use a parliamentary phrase, is given a leadership rôle whether he be teacher or taught; in the Society meeting the leadership rôle is emphasized by delivery from a rostrum, but, if the basic pattern of the discussion is that of reporting on research to a gathering of equals, the speaker will have in mind that his pleasure and his duty will lie in an encouragement of his hearers to clarify their own research ideas which may run on lines different but perhaps no less fruitful than his own: leadership in both cases wanders about the room as it were, no one holding it longer than is necessary for the exposition of his own notions or to lead the way to the elucidation of those of others.

To give free play to the process of thinking while speaking is difficult at any time and particularly so when the audience is not in complete sympathy with the speaker. It requires the compassion and imaginative gifts of the audience to be exercised with generosity to a considerable degree, and often an exercise in self-restraint, which is taken for granted in the consulting room more often than in the meeting room. The fact is that the rostrum ministers to the speaker's egoism and when this governs his discourse or overrides his capacity for adaptation to his audience a counter-egoism is evoked in his hearers and a rhetorical dialectical struggle ensues. This spells death to an oral tradition, or rather to a consistently creative one.

To say that a person thinks while he speaks is not to deny him thought on the subject of his discourse before he speaks, but rather that since he has an audience now before him, a group of particular persons eager for his ideas, he must re-examine his subject *with* them, in their presence, so that they may be in a sense participant observers of the event in progress, viz. the elucidation of his thoughts. It must be acknowledged that the capacity to think, or re-think, spontaneously in this way is by no means uniformly distributed throughout the population, but it will be conceded that its occurrence is more frequent when the atmosphere is friendly, and of course in the assessment of the climate of opinion the speaker's projected hostility may exert a disturbing influence.

(The size of the audience plays a considerable part in the ease and the intimacy of oral communication. This is a strong reason for breaking up the gatherings of a large psycho-analytical society into small 'working parties' which can combine their findings for reporting later on to the full assembly.)

It is only persons with a special gift for this kind of intimate verbal communication who can exercise it with force in the presence of a hundred persons. Though mechanical means may enlarge the range of the voice, no device is yet known which will bring a speaker as close to his audience as is social life across a dinner table. The physical distance between the speaker and listener is not the only factor, another is the 'accessibility' of the speaker to his audience, perhaps the freedom with which he allows them in phantasy into the workshop or studio of his mind and his tact in removing their shyness when entering this territory.

Thus far when considering the oral tradition our attention has been turned to the pre-conditions for its occurrence, not for its content. If this could be defined I am sure that it would have been written down and published and thus would no longer be oral. Those who think that psycho-analysis is a science and only a science may comfort themselves with the belief that everything is in the literature; those who regard the practice of psycho-analysis as something of an art (as well as an employment of a scientific method) will have already learnt more from their teachers than their teachers knew they were giving. It is not a mere passing on of anecdotes about the great ones who are no longer with us, anecdotes have almost nothing to do with this transmission. Anyone will be able to give a final explanation of the Oral Tradition when he knows all there is to know about Cultural Transmission generally and Family Tradition in particular—the Oral Tradition in psycho-analysis comes somewhere between these two.

11. A Personal Note about the Organization of a Psycho-Analytical Society

It is not practicable to give in an International Journal even an outline structure of a Scientific Society because local custom varies greatly from one country to another. But I think it would be desirable, perhaps in the form of a Preamble to the Byelaws, to include three maxims, which if followed might limit somewhat the tendency to woodenness found from time to time in Committees.

(1) Where there is any ambiguity in the wording of these Byelaws or other Regulations of this Institute, they shall be interpreted in the light of common sense.

(2) The Council, the Training Committee and any other Committee set up under these Byelaws will best serve the interests of science and this Institute if, where there is a conflict between a new idea and an old custom, they take a risk with the new idea rather than take shelter behind precedent, and where it is thought that the risk cannot be taken they put as much energy into a re-examination of present usage as went into the creation and exposition of the new and rejected idea.

(3) An Institution, even though its aim be the advancement of science, has no intrinsic right to the expectation of a long life; it must every day earn the respect it receives and be content with less esteem than it deserves: to this general rule (which extends to the tenure of its Officers) this Institute is no exception.

If the term organization includes Officers and Committees, and their mode of election, tenure of office, etc., then the key to that structure in my view is given in Section 5 of this paper. I.e. the organization centres on the transmission of knowledge and power to the next generation, and it does this by preparing that generation by giving it first the benefit of its own experience and then trusting itself to the increasing control of the younger generation. One of the dominant ideas in the mind of every officer should be that of Progressive Abdication to trained successors, of every Committee, in the words of Bacon: that 'It would be an unsound fancy and self-contradictory to expect that things which have never yet been done can be done except by means which have never yet been tried'.

Table showing Membership and Associate Membership
(Medical and Lay) in 1933 and 1948

CONTINENT Location of Society	Full Members Medical + Lay = Total (1932) 1948	Associates Medical + Lay = Total (1932) 1948	Total Full + Associates Medical + Lay = Total (1932) 1948
EUROPE Austria	(40) 7+(10) 6=(50) 13	(11) 0+ (3) 0=(14) 0	(51) 7+(13) 6=(64) 13
Belgium	(1) 2+ (3) 3= (4) 5	Nil	(1) 2+ (3) 3= (4) 5
Great Britain	(25)38+(17)22=(42) 60	(20)32+(12)13=(32) 45	(45)70+(29)35=(74)105
France	(13)15+ (2) 4=(15) 19	(9)12+ (4) 8=(13) 20	(22)27+ (6)12=(28) 39
Holland	(23)29+ (1) 1=(24) 30	(3) 5+ (2) 2= (5) 7	(26)34+ (3) 3=(29) 37
Italy	(2) 2+ (3) 5= (5) 7	(3) 5+ (8)10=(11) 15	(5) 7+(11)15=(16) 22
Sweden	(5) 7+ (0) 1= (5) 8	(3) 5+ (0) 1= (3) 6	(8)12+ (0) 2= (8) 14
Switzerland	(14)14+ (6) 7=(20) 21	(8) 8+ (7) 9=(15) 17	(22)22+(13)16=(35) 38
NORTH AMERICA Chicago	(14)49+ (0) 3=(14) 52	(2) 0+ (0) 4= (2) 4	(16)49+ (0) 7=(16) 56
Detroit	(0)19+ (0) 2= (0) 21	(0) 1+nil= (0) 1	(0)22+ (0) 2= (0) 24
Los Angeles	(0)17+ (0) 1= (0) 18	Nil	(0)17+ (0) 1= (0) 18
New York	(57)124+(1) 0=(58) 124	(4)22+ (3) 0= (7) 22	(61)146+ (4) 0=(65)146
Philadelphia	(0)12+ (0) 1= (0) 13	(0) 5+nil=(0) 5	(0)17+ (0) 1= (0) 18
San Francisco	(0)18+ (0) 1= (0) 19	nil+ (0) 4= (0) 4	(0)18+ (0) 5= (0) 23
Association for Psycho-Anal. Medicine N.Y.C.	(0)28+nil=(0)28	(0) 6+ (0) 1= (0) 7	(0)34+ (0) 1= (0) 35
Topeka, Kansas	(0)16+nil=(0) 16	nil+ (0) 5= (0) 5	(0)16+ (0) 5= (0) 21
Washington, D.C.	(20)44+nil=(20) 44	(4) 0+ (1) 0= (5) 0	(24)44+ (1) 0=(25) 44
SOUTH AMERICA Argentina	(0) 7+nil= (0) 7	(0) 4+ (0) 3= (0) 7	(0)11+ (0) 3= (0) 14
Rio de Janeiro	(0) 3+nil= (0) 3	Nil	(0) 3+nil= (0) 3
Sao Paulo	(0) 4+ (0) 2= (0) 6	(0) 1+ (0) 1= (0) 2	(0) 5+ (0) 3= (0) 8
ASIA India	(5) 4+(10)11=(15) 15	(2) 7+(11)29=(13) 36	(7)11+(21)40=(28) 51
Israel	(0)16+ (0) 1= (0) 17	nil+ (0) 2= (0) 2	(0)16+ (0) 3= (0) 19

Note. The figures were taken from the printed lists of members published in the *International Journal of Psycho-Analysis*, 1933 and 1948.

Certain countries have been omitted because of political reasons or because the Societies or Institutes in those countries are not sufficiently established for their numbers to be comparable.

About fifty psycho-analysts reside in areas where there is now no organized society. The total number of psycho-analysts is therefore about 800.

XXI
METHODOLOGY AND RESEARCH IN
PSYCHO-PATHOLOGY[1]
(1951)

M R Chairman, Ladies and Gentlemen: while acknowledging the honour in being asked to open this Symposium on 'Methodology and Research in Psychiatry' I cannot conceal from myself, and therefore should not conceal from you, a certain feeling of whimsical humour in the situation, for I have never read a book on Methodology, so far as my memory serves me, nor extended by a hair's breadth man's horizon in the field of Psychiatry; the opener should at least have done one or other. But since Royal Commissions accept the testimony of non-experts in the topic they are considering perhaps the Medical Section may extend an equal clemency. However, if I have myself added nothing to Psychiatry I have been upon occasion a participant observer in the work of some of those who have, and though I do not pretend to express their august opinions I cannot deny my debt.

For convenience this short paper will be broken up into sections which may be given catchwords, viz. (a) *Number*, (b) *Pattern matching*, (c) '*No research without therapy, no therapy without research*', (d) *Summary*.

Number

The whole region of Psychology may be divided into areas of research according to the number of persons concerned. Thus we may speak of One-Body Psychology, Two-Body, Three-Body, Four-Body and Multi-Body Psychology.[2]

---

[1] Reprinted from the *British Journal of Medical Psychology* (1951), **24**, 1–7.
Contribution to a symposium given at a meeting of the Medical Section of the British Psychological Society, April 26, 1950. See author's appendix for note on sub-title.

[2] By the way, it has always puzzled me why some languages, e.g. Russian, start their grammatical plural at the number five. According to Statistical Grammar this is clearly an error; in respect to the

One-Body Psychology deals with the simpler neurological problems which used to fill the psychological journals: perception, memory, learning, reaction-times and the like. This has been called, not without unkindness, 'Rat Psychology' and 'Brass Instrument Psychology'.[1] *Two-Body Psychology* deals with the less simple neurology of Conditioned Reflexes, and in the clinical field with the derivations of two-person relationship, e.g. of mother and child. (I am aware that these two kinds of psychology are not usually brought so close together but such juxtapositions, if treated cautiously, are sometimes useful—one of the great differences between these two is that in reflexology there is a one-way, in the mother-and-child psychology there is a two-way traffic.)

In *Three-Body Psychology* we enter the area of the Oedipus complex, the two parents and the child, and the derivations of this in individual and cultural life. In *Four-Body Psychology* we deal with a new phase of complexity in that to the Oedipean situation there is added sibling rivalry. In *Multi-Body Psychology* we deal with more complicated group relationships.

One virtue of this way of looking at the whole field of psychology is that it provides one of the limits to each frame of reference which is employed in the different kinds of psychology, thus providing a useful (and, indeed, salutary) check on theorizing. Thus, for example, two-body psychology when applied to a multi-body situation has to bear in mind that its frame of reference is a different and perhaps less useful one than the psychologies based on study of three- and four-body situations.

Another advantage in dividing the region of psychology in this way is that it makes certain kinds of conceptualization somewhat easier. Thus, for example, a failure to effect 'closure' (in the Gestalt sense) to a two-body situation hinders the patient's freedom of movement in the three-body area of psychological space; to those who are familiar with genetic studies of child psychology this is an everyday observation.

When speaking thus of the number of bodies concerned in psychological study it should not be thought that satisfactory

Grammar of Social Relations there may be some sense in it, for when five or more bodies are involved there may be a (psychological) change of phase.

[1] Perhaps 'Push-Button Psychiatry' falls within the same frame of reference.

conclusions can be drawn from mere counting, but rather that the research worker has to discover and isolate and match against one another the patterns of behaviour with which he has to deal in his investigations. Thus it is sometimes found in a single analytical session that a patient behaves as if a third person were present, and this limits his freedom to speak (or he may think that the analyst's wife is in the next room and wants to hear what is said, which from this point of view is much the same thing), i.e. a three-body situation is being created out of what appears to be only a two-body situation. The patient may then go on to behave as if the only thing of importance was to get something from the analyst into himself, which is a characteristic of certain types of two-body situation. Then he may exhibit rage reactions of frustration which are similar to the unbalanced states of the epilepsies. This last touches on neurological problems concerned with one-body problems. Each of these areas of research (one-body, two-body, etc.) attract people who are best suited to work on them, but they are not the essential areas of the psychiatrist. His work is essentially a synthesis of them all in his diagnosis and therapeutic planning: herein lies the difference between him and the psychological research workers—he is faced with a responsibility to a person, he is not oriented to a particular discipline. (This brings us to the second section.)

Pattern matching

There are two kinds of mathematics I am led to understand; there is metrical mathematics and non-metrical. I believe that neither kind is of much use to psychiatrists at the present time. The former has acquired a great following but has produced nothing of much importance to psychiatrists; the latter (which some day may look hopeful)—I refer of course to topology—has not yet been developed to a point when it can cope with the fantastically complicated nature of the psychiatrist's daily work.

The metrical mathematicians select a part of a patient's behaviour and correlate it with other parts or with a diagnosis (using in the latter case categories which are daily proving of less and less value), and end up with a figure which apparently is of only momentary concern even to themselves. An exception to this generalization which occurs to me is the employment of intelligence tests when it is necessary to make a rapid grading of conscripts and other masses of people. There may be other exceptions—in view of the prodigious amount of time and energy spent on this sort of toil I sincerely hope there are. Statistical methods provide short cuts to psychiatric goals; I don't like short cuts.

A psychiatrist is a person who has to match patterns of behaviour with other patterns with which his experience has provided him. He is not just a psychologist with a psycho-pathological training, plus some genetics, plus neurology, plus some statistics, though some understanding of these things is a very great help—he is a person who at the moment of his most creative endeavour lets these disciplines sink into the background of his consciousness and senses the direction of a process of change and the degree of freedom of movement in psychological—or social—space in the patient who is seeking his advice. I am aware that in using these terms I am employing notions which have been developed in what are called the basic sciences (of which psychology is one), that is to say though the psychiatrist may use tools which others have devised, he is, in my view, under no obligation to regard as important the psychiatric conclusions which these same others draw from their researches when they handle psychiatric material.

The terms 'the direction of the process of change' and 'degree of freedom of movement' merit some attention in respect to our evening's topic. The work of those who employ the basic sciences is essentially a-historical. By that one means that the facts observed are events under immediate observation. But the pattern of an individual's development is not a thing which can be brought within the scope of an a-historical reckoning though the psychiatrist in the moment of his most creative endeavour by an act of intuitive synthesis does employ this a-historical method too—he is, in this synthesis, much influenced by a sense of *pattern changing in time*. Because the psychiatrist is a clinician he has to obtain a history of the patient (not only a history of the patient's complaint) and this is done in the psychiatric interview. In this interview the patient is allowed to give his life's story in his own way: anything may crop up, everything is relevant, though the connections may at first be obscure. In the course of the interview the physician has to tolerate the obscurity, the sense of frustration at the incompleteness of the data but, nevertheless, to go on listening. The endurance of incomplete conclusions is a very important part of the make-up of a good psychiatrist, and I think of the scientist too. (A scientist who is beginning to fail in his creative imagination gets more and more satisfaction from the clinching of easily verifiable hypotheses, and attaches more and more importance to the establishment of less and less significant events.)

This sense of pattern has been developed by the researches of the schools of psycho-analysis and psycho-biology, but was existent long before this century. It is exercised in common with every branch of clinical medicine and gives rise to such questions as 'How ill is this person?' The sense of pattern is transmitted from one generation of doctors to another by oral tradition and clinical demonstration, certainly not by books; the effective agency of this transmission, which is essential to a healthy school of psychiatry, is by a sort of empathy between teacher and pupil so that the latter identifies himself with the teacher and feels his way with the teacher's processes of thought. I am at a loss to reduce this process to methodological terms, but of one thing I am certain—psychiatry would be at a loss without it.

But what are these changing patterns which the psychiatrist strives to observe and to match? Again I am at a loss to define and must fall back on rather general descriptions. During the interview which covers, however inadequately, the patient's life-history the physician allows a picture to form in his mind of the patient in his social setting. The delineation of this picture is at first not precise, but the experience of listening, both to the unfolding chain of events and to the tone of the narration, allows of a spontaneous sharpening of the detail of that picture, so that it seems to move of its own accord. I might draw an analogy with the 'coming to life' in the reader's mind of the characters in a novel. The art of the interviewing physician is to allow that spontaneous coming to life to occur in his own mind, at first tentatively, later with an almost emphatic clarity, while listening to his patient's history of sufferings. This picture, this changing picture, must have the warmth of life, the chilling apathy of unchangeable despair, the venom of attack, the softness of cherishing affection—all of this differently mixed at different times, but all belonging to the picture, i.e. to the very person there in the chair opposite. Further, that picture, that person, must be felt to move back and forth through his life's experiences, through time and varying fortune, without flicker, without loss of smoothness of movement. Swift changes have to be perceived by a quickening of attention without blur, and slow almost immobile changes have to be observed without that loss of attention which boredom brings.

My ignorance of methodology prevents me from reducing this to scientific formulations, but it is at least a recognizable phenomenon on the rare occasions when it has happened to me. When it happens to me I feel that I am on the way to being a psychiatrist and that that is my job and for that moment is my complete justification for existence. Perhaps the same sort of satisfaction occurs within a factorial-analytical psychologist when he gets his sums to come out right. The difference, however, between the work of the psychiatrist and the mathematical psychologist lies in the degree of shared concern between the two parties to the undertaking—doctor and patient, or research worker and subject. The psychiatrist has a personal responsibility for his patient's well-being, and this must have top priority; the satisfactions of scientific curiosity must come second, or else that changing picture of the patient in the psychiatrist's mind will get jerky and mechanical, i.e. it will not move as once the patient moved and therefore the picture of his growth and ripening experience or his deterioration will get distorted. The aim of the psychiatrist vis-à-vis the patient is to take action but the active phase will only be of use to the patient if it is preceded by a phase of heightened and creative passivity on the part of the psychiatrist.

The initiators and especially the followers of research in the basic sciences have quite different priorities from those of the clinician, theirs are self-devised priorities where as the clinician has first to serve and then to learn and finally to weave theories. The research worker and the subjects of his research do not invest in the same undertaking, the psychiatrist and his patient do invest in the same undertaking—the therapy.

Returning to the pattern matching activity of the clinician, one feature, which has found but little expression in the literature, is the use that he makes of his own responses to his patient during the interview. The discourse of the interview is on two levels, there is the mass of data which a stenographer could take down and type out (this is the verbalized material) and there is the non-verbalized material, the tone of voice, the pauses and acceleration of speech, the gestures and those yet more eloquent moments of absence of mind or of movement. Clever thinking about psycho-pathology, neuro-psychiatry, endocrinology and the rest, is left in abeyance, and attention is given to the effect the patient is making by non-verbal means, chiefly emotional expression or its lack, upon the psychiatrist himself in the context of the unfolding life story.

Now then, once these all but fleeting and precious impressions are gained no pains are spared at a conscious rational level to think about the diagnosis, prognosis and therapeutic prospects by all the means at the psychiatrist's disposal. Here is where the basic sciences come in, and then and not till then is the psychiatrist grateful for them. But how to link these two phases? That at present defeats me. However, I undertake to give an adquate answer as soon as science explains art.

The service that the basic sciences can make to psychiatry is the provision of tools to work with or think with. Great learning in pharmacology does not qualify a man to use drugs with clinical discrimination, and so with the other basic sciences, not excluding psycho-pathology. This discussion is ostensibly about psychiatry, but every point that is put forward has equal validity in respect to ordinary clinical medicine.

'No research without therapy, no therapy without research'

There are broadly speaking, two kinds of research in the human sciences, that which gives full reckoning to the influence of mental pain on behaviour and that which does not. The implications of the former are considerable, if you are going to touch a person's sore spots you have to be able to assuage the pain or you will sooner or later lose contact with your research material.

A research worker can choose to have a limited field of investigation by avoiding painful areas of experience, or he can include these and lose his independence of choice in respect to the order, the timing and many of the conditions under which his data will appear. Pain is an experience with an arresting character, if the research worker is not to be detained by the pain when it appears he is not likely to discover the stages of change from the painful experience to its mental derivations in the one direction, or in the other from the painful event to its causes. The basic sciences, however basic, are of little use in dealing with mental pain unless the material and the theories of those basic sciences have been gained in the field of mental pain and its therapy.

Therapy calls for the same essential qualities as does research, toleration of frustration, endurance of utter failure and not over-joyousness at success, above all, humbleness of mind and patience. Much is written, I am told, about methodology, some may be about methodology in psychiatry, but if any of it involves techniques that put any barrier between doctor and patient it will not do much for psychiatry. I would like to ask the methodologists to tell us in what way methodology assists in the actual creative process of the psychiatrist; I am referring now to the processes I have tried to outline regarding the interview—the crucial doctor-patient relationship on which so much depends. I freely acknowledge the uses of methodology in the basic sciences on which the psychiatrist draws in the second, more conscious, phase of his activity.

I have from time to time amused myself with speculating on the course that psycho-analysis, one of psychiatry's basic psychological sciences, would have taken had Freud been a rheologist first and a neurologist second. In place of the concept of a reflex mechanism for maintaining a low and constant state of tensions he might have pictured mind as a plastic mass with certain measurable degrees of resilience and which under certain conditions, some analogues of temperature and pressure, suffered irreversible changes into rigidity.

In studies concerning the influence of already established ideas upon new ideas, the methodologist can no doubt help the psychiatrist to get out of routine ways of thinking, and help us to realize how readily we tend to accept the constructs of the basic sciences as if they were the bases of reality and not merely our seemingly most convenient ways of looking at Nature.

Summary

To summarize this paper in a few words should not be difficult for I have said very little in it.

Psychiatry is one of man's clinical activities; the sort of question that is basic to the psychiatrist is also basic to the clinician, viz. 'How ill is this patient?' By this the psychiatrist means how near is he to the point when he cannot cope with the situation in his inner and his outer worlds; in more psycho-dynamic terms:

how near is the process to irreversibility? The answer to this question involves an act of creative imagination and can only be made in a clinical examination in which the psychiatrist feels his way into the patient's state of mind and tries to get a sense of the changing pattern of the patient's life as a whole. This kind of creative activity of the psychiatrist is more like an art than a science, but without this activity psychiatry cannot develop, hence it is basic. But intuition, however profound, needs in the practical affairs of man to have its check, and this in the case of psychiatry is provided by its basic sciences; all of these should come into play, and he is a vain man who presumes to say which is the most important and a silly one who says that any of them can be neglected.

Since the boundaries between the basic sciences are artificial, being drawn by man—probably in conformity with some limiting factor in the personality of the scientists concerned—certainly not by Nature, another kind of artificial classification though not basic may be permitted. Psychiatry's basic sciences, then, may be viewed according to the number of persons directly concerned in the inquiry. Thus, for instance, a One-Body Psychiatry would include what exists at any moment within the skin of the patient, i.e. genetic factors, neurological questions (reaction time, memory and intelligence factors, electro-encephalography) and not least his bodily health. The Two-Body Psychiatry would include conditioned reflexology, the mother-child relationships, etc. The Three- and Four-Body Psychiatry would include the psycho-analytical contributions, and the Multi-Body Psychiatry (the importance of which we cannot yet begin to estimate) would include the interaction of the patient with his cultural environment. There is of course much overlapping, which it is not the purpose of this paper to discuss; but what is important is that in the checking process after the psychiatrist has made the 'discovery' of his patient, all of these frames of reference are used. That is to say, the relation of the basic sciences to psychiatry works in two stages, in the psychiatrist's education and later in his verification of his guesswork. Because so much of mental life is influenced by mental pain clinical research in psychiatry cannot be separated from therapy for the simple reason that the patient, until he can face his miseries, cannot get a comprehension of his potentialities, and this applies to his psychiatrist too. Psychiatric

Research (i.e. a deepening of our understanding of the whole person in his illness and of the ways of enabling him to achieve a better equilibrium) has a limiting factor in the research worker. He who cannot go with his patient in a sympathetic feeling into his suffering and show him just what is going on may add much to the theories of the basic sciences, but in my view will add but little to basic psychiatry which is a clinical activity.

Appendix

The paper to which this is an appendix endeavours to deal with the subject-matter of its title which was given me to write about, viz. Methodology and Research in Psychiatry. This done, the topic of the symposium was changed—that is apt to happen with symposia.

But if I had been asked to write on Methodology and Research in *Psycho-pathology* instead of Methodology and Research in *Psychiatry* I still think that the substance of the paper given above would have been relevant.

Before we discuss psycho-pathology let us consider ordinary medical pathology and the work of the pathologist. He is a technical man who is given bits of another doctor's patient and is asked to match these against a wide range of other bits from all sorts of other patients and normal people of all ages. He usually does not see the patient, certainly as a whole. By 'see' I mean not merely 'look at' but examine with a sense of responsibility for the whole person.

The pathologist works with the tools of metrical mathematics, his judgement is in the main statistical, though there are 'marginal cases' where the interpretation of his material is open to doubt, in which case he can only offer a 'hunch'; in such marginal cases, and guided or not by that hunch, the clinician must act. I know of only two situations in the field of psychological medicine that are comparable to the relation between clinician, pathologist and patient. The first of these is where a psychiatrist asks advice of a brother psychiatrist about a case (giving details of the interview—the bits of social behaviour of the patient) and where for some reason a consultation between the patient and the second psychiatrist is not practicable. The second case is where the student of psycho-analysis brings the data of his sessions with his patient to his supervising analyst, who has to act, among his other functions, as a psycho-pathologist.

In the work of pathologist and psycho-pathologist (in the analogous, perhaps narrow sense just stated) the process is frequently one of 'matching patterns'. In the case of the pathologist, especially in his histological functions, the pattern is fixed; in the case of the psycho-pathologist the pattern is changing, he watches a process of 'pattern changing in time'. This sort of matching process presents, I think, far greater problems than where the patterns are fixed, as in a stained section, and where they can be matched at greater leisure and by more than one person. As the technique of matching is more complex, so probably is the methodology in the case of psycho-pathology.

Coming now to the discussion of the three papers opening the symposium, I was told that I had 'dodged the column' since I had not discussed the techniques of methodology. In a measure this reproach was a just one, and is one I find hard to rebut. The more complex the data of a research process the more difficult it is to find a methodology adequate to that particular research process.

It is perhaps not irrelevant to note that an interest in methodology occurs in phases. When the Three-Body Psychology began to be a powerful force in the general field of human studies there was an increase in metrical mathematical methods in One- and Two-Body psychological studies; at the present time the Four- and Multi-Body Psychologies are rich growing points in the general field, and we find a new interest and at a higher conceptual level than in the case of the metrical mathematical phase, in the methods applicable to, or principally concerned with Three-Body Psychology. I am not sufficiently a methodologist or research worker to explain this curious fact, but I think it bears out, perhaps only in a vague and general way, the notion I put forward in this paper, that the basic sciences, even the basic philosophies, may follow—not precede—the creative phases which give meaning and satisfaction to work in the human sciences.

XXII
NUMBER AND THE HUMAN SCIENCES[1]
(1951)

An article for Géza Róheim's *Festschrift* should be about psycho-analysis and anthropology: as I have contributed nothing to either subject and he has contributed much to both it would be prudent to keep off both topics and talk about something else, let us say psychology.

Suppose one of those oft spoken of but seldom met travellers from Mars visited us to satisfy his naive curiosity about psychology; he would find a state of affairs which might at first seem somewhat puzzling. In the write-up of his field work he would report on one-person psychology, two-person psychology, three-person psychology, possibly a four-person psychology, and a multi-person psychology; what would strike him most would of course be the interrelation of these aspects of the subject.

'The breakup of the whole field of psychology into categories according to the minimum number of persons essential to the study of each branch of the subject is the first thing that strikes the visitor', he might write in his thesis, adding that distressing confusions sometimes occurred because these simple categories were thought to be irrelevant to the study of detail by the practitioners of each category and the implications so disconcerting that they were generally ignored.

One-Person Psychology concerns itself with what goes on inside one person taken in isolation. It studies the neurological aspect of the mind, sensation, reaction time, learning and forgetting, memory, imagery, hallucinations, introspection, etc.—a very varied field. It is true that in the study of some of these phenomena an experimenter or observer is usually present, but with the present richness of imagination and ingenuity now given to the construction of apparatus of all kinds it would be possible for most of the experiments in this branch of psychology to be carried out, not to be sure designed, by a robot. Where for reasons of economy or of scientific curiosity an observer is used

[1] Reprinted from *Psycho-Analysis and Culture* (1951), 150–55.

in place of a robot to carry out the routine of testing in the case of one-person psychology the relation between the observer and the person observed is reduced to a minimum. In situations where the responses of the subject of the experiment annoy the observer in one-person psychology the experimental situation is usually considered to be vitiated in some degree because only one person's responses are relevant to the problem being investigated. In the language of two- and three-person psychology the ego ideal of the observer in one-person psychology is a robot. The basis of the research is observations in the a-historical present, the 'here and now' of the laboratory. People with a gift for inventing harsh names would include much of what they call rat psychology and brass instrument psychology under the heading of what is here called one-person psychology.

In *Two-Person Psychology* we enter the psychological region of reciprocal relationships. In this it differs from one-person psychology but is linked with some if not all of the other psychologies. It studies the relation existing when two persons are in a more or less closed region and are tied to one another by simultaneously acting aims, tasks or needs. The example of two-body psychology which has proved of outstanding utility in both theory and practice is the psycho-analyst and his patient in the analytic transference situation, which is in one sense a closed region devoted largely but not exclusively to the study of a-historical events observed in the 'here and now'. The two psychologists who laid the foundations of this research are of course Freud and Ferenczi. (The transference phenomena seen in *statu nascendi* though originating in the past are noted by both analyst and patient in the present, and the counter transference phenomena are reckoned with by the observing analyst and frequently noted by the observant patient.) The analytic situation also gives insight into another occurrence of two-person psychology in the mother-child relationship, particularly in the stages of the nursing couple and the sphincter interests which they share and dispute.

Investigations in this seemingly closed two-person relationship, however, disclose that it is not in fact closed; though there are only two persons shut up in one room there is forced on the attention of both of them that some of the patient's behaviour can only be explained by the fact that he cannot consider himself alone with his analyst but is acting as if the analyst's wife (or husband) were in the closed region too. Thus a *Three-Person Psychology*, which goes by the name of the Oedipus complex, is forced on the observer under the conditions of the transference situation in analysis. A more direct observation of this kind of psychology, based however on the findings of analysis is recorded by Dr. Winnicott, when he makes his clinical examination of babies seated on the mother's lap. Doctors from time immemorial have interviewed two persons at once in clinical consultation, whether they be husband and wife or parent and child. What is striking about this fact is that in all this time these good observers have contributed almost nothing to the psychodynamics of the three-person relationship; perhaps we may return to this later.

Another derivation of the analysis of the transference situation is a study of sibling rivalry as a side issue in the examination of the Oedipus complex. This branch is not very clearly developed as yet but there is just enough to warrant the establishment of the *Four-Person Psychology*.

With *Multi-Person Psychology* we enter a quite different phase of research. Though in the analytic situation only the images of the other parent and/or sibling were present (i.e. they were not present in the flesh) they were really present in the sense that the effect on behaviour was comparable to that of their being present in the flesh, and on the definition of reality by Kurt Lewin (what is real is that which has effects) we can speak of a three- or four-person psychology in a two-person situation. With more than four we have group psychology, and where this is multi-structured we have as yet almost no clues. Freud has given us an outline of group psychology in relation to the analysis of the ego based on a three- and four-person psychology. He chose for study the groups with the simplest structure, the Army and the Church, where the individuals were all of one sex and related to one another through a father—ego ideal; neither of these are typical of groups generally. We are in fact without an adequate theoretical frame of reference for a group dynamics where there are more than four persons related to one another in more than one way. Our poverty of a well-ordered frame of reference in this field though embarrassing for progress should not surprise or shame us, for mathematicians tell us that the growth of complexity of the dynamics of ordinary particles (they despair to touch such complex things as human beings) increases enormously as the number increases, indeed only under certain limited conditions can they speak with certainty about the dynamics of three bodies considered simultaneously, with four, five or more the complexity is beyond their unravelling. There may be a further reason for our lack of theory, viz. that the subject is distasteful. When Freud described psychoanalysis as the third blow to man's narcissism (the other two being delivered by Galileo and Darwin) in that it showed him he was not master within his own house, there was left the hope—fostered, perhaps by a remaining shred of that same self-concern—that if he knew himself better he would attain that mastery of the forces within. But suppose a study of group dynamics shows us how we are more than children of our time and generation, are indeed its slaves, that we are in fact ruled from without by group forces of which we are unaware, then our narcissism would get another nasty knock and flinching before the scattering of another illusion we would pull round us the consoling blanket of incomprehension and keep our minds engaged within the cosy circle of the family and its simple social derivatives. A hint of this possibility is seen in some of the objections to field theory which are reminiscent of the more polite but vigorous repudiations of psycho-analysis after it delivered the third blow mentioned above, for though field theory does not halt at considerations of number, it is prepared to give full reckoning to the influence of the next higher phase of complexity being at least as important as the lower one on which there is general agreement.

Those who use this classification of the psychologies, assuming that it has any use at all, will choose one or other aspect of it for employment. One of the first things which has struck the present writer is the hint that it gives as to the limitations of prediction in the psychological field generally. Thus the strict student of one-person psychology is unable to predict much about what goes on in a two-person situation, for instance the unclinical psychology that is taught in the classrooms and laboratories, though useful in the highest degree (and for obtaining higher degrees, incidentally) in the academic psychology of introspection, sensation, perception, learning, memory, and the like, is nevertheless almost useless in a clinical situation, particularly the analytic situation. Of course if the student has heard of the theories and findings of the psycho-analysts and uses them in his thinking and in action he is not strictly speaking a one-person psychologist any more. Similarly a two-person psychologist who shut his mind to those transference manifestations which brought in the third party would not be able to make many useful predictions concerning three-person psychological situations. The range of accurate predictions is limited, it would seem, to social or psychological situations based on a comparable number of persons, or a comparable degree of complexity in the structure of the psycho-dynamic unit under consideration to that on which the basic research was done.

Assuming for the moment that the conclusion last mentioned is correct, an inference can be drawn on the relation between psycho-analysis and anthropology, viz. that psycho-analysis as we understand it today, however valuable its aid to anthropology may be, can *never* provide a framework of theory that will cover adequately the Multi-Person, Multi-Structured Psycho-dynamic Units with which anthropology is mainly and usually concerned. To say this is not in any way to belittle the amazing power and suggestiveness (indeed also the provocativeness) of the ideas which derive from, and could only be derived from, the work of psycho-analysts in their thorough studies of two-, three- and four-person psychologies in their encloistered consulting rooms.

Two features of psycho-analytic work are outstanding in importance for the human sciences. The first is its a-historical character: this gives it its power to resolve the complicated phenomena displayed into its component elements; the second is the fact that the problems of the subject under investigation have priority over the intellectual curiosity of the observer: the patient's associations settle the direction of the investigation, not the ingenious contrivance of the scientist's questionnaires. In the researches in multi-person psychology the same two features are found in the work of Bion and researches stemming from his study of groups. It is as yet too soon to appraise this work, and it may be many years before it will be applicable to anthropology, but it must be mentioned because the psycho-dynamic unit that is investigated consists of about eight persons.[1]

[1] It is incidentally interesting that the 'span' of the observer varies considerably, thus one observer can stretch his observations over only five persons in group discussion, beyond that number individual and group 'outlines' get confused, while another observer can en-

The matter of prediction is an important one for any science, even for the 'pattern sciences' (such as psycho-analysis, anthropology, aesthetics and the like) where it is less used than in the 'measuring sciences' such as physics. Géza Róheim predicted once that a tribe in Australia would be found (if not extinguished already) having such and such myths; and he was proved correct. This kind of prediction was not I think based directly on psycho-analytic researches but rather on a study of culture contact, e.g. on the pattern of totem animal relationships. But the verification of an hypothesis often comes at a later stage in the development of a science than is either psychoanalysis or anthropology at the present time. In the matter of following clues and co-ordinating them we have received much aid and stimulation from Géza Róheim's work.

If I knew a shred of the grammar and syntax of anthropology I could write in praise of his work perhaps with sense and understanding; not being so endowed I can only record my relief over twenty years ago to hear that an anthropologist was going into the field who had in the course of his dual training to face and uncover his own infantile amnesia—i.e. who had been analyzed. To see a strange culture clearly when the major defense against a perception of one's own mental processes had not been breached was, as Rivers pointed out to me just after the First World War, a thing anthropologists would not for long expect to do. His recommendation that every young psychiatrist and anthropologist should first be analyzed was not quickly followed. Géza Róheim was a pioneer and as such, however ignorant of his speciality we may be, we salute him.

compass seven or eight; one observer, whose work is known to the present writer, could easily span a dozen and with a little effort fifteen, but before he took up this occupation he was a sports journalist and had for years kept a lively eye for the personal characteristics of a scrimmaging mass of athletes in the usual ball games of his culture; number here relates to the range of the observer's power, not to the category of psychology considered.

XXIII
A SURVEY:
THE DEVELOPMENT OF THE PSYCHO-ANALYTICAL THEORY OF THE PSYCHOSES[1]. 1894–1926
(1926–1927)

1. Introduction

PART I

2. Defence Mechanisms, 1894
   Hallucinatory Confusion and Projection, 1894–6
   Mechanism in Hallucination, 1900
   Hysteria and Dementia Praecox compared, 1906
   Hysteria and Dementia Praecox contrasted, 1908
3. The Schreber Case, 1911
   The Mechanism of Paranoia, 1911
   The Mechanism of Repression, 1911
4. The Manic-Depressive Disorders, 1911
5. A Commentary on this Group of Papers

PART II

6. Narcissism
7. The Modification of the Feeling of Omnipotence
8. The Developmental Stages of the Libido
9. Melancholia
10. The Super-Ego (Ego-Ideal)
11. The Death Instincts

PART III

12. The Ego and the Id
    (a) Introduction. (b) The Id. (c) The Relation of the Ego to Consciousness. (d) The Oedipus Complex. (e) Changes in the Ego
13. The Sense of Reality
    (a) Introduction. (b) The Incorporation of Pleasant Experience with and the Expulsion of Unpleasant

---

[1] This paper is based on one read before the Medical Section of the British Psychological Society on December 17, 1924. See also p. 391.

Experience from the Ego (First Stage). (c) Negation of Unpleasant Ideas (Second Stage). (d) The Acceptance of Unpleasant Ideas (Third Stage). (e) Reviewing the Situation from another Aspect: Ego-Libidinal Polarity. (f) Utraquism. (g) Delusion and Dream

14. Anxiety
(a) Introduction. (b) Brief History: (α) Period of Shock Aetiology, (β) Period of Wish Aetiology, (γ) Narcissism, explains Libidinal Component of Traumatic Neurosis, (δ) Theory of Repetition Compulsion, (ε) The Threefold Division of the Psychic Apparatus. (c) The Danger Signal: (i) Fear and Anxiety, (ii) Neurotic Danger, (iii) Grief and Anxiety, (iv) Pain, (v) Defence: (α) Repression, (β) Isolating and Undoing, (γ) Reaction Formation, (δ) Regression. (d) Inhibitions and Symptoms: (α) 'Locus' of Inhibitions, (β) 'Locus' of Symptom-action, (γ) Ego-unity and Symptom-derivatives, (δ) Affective reproduction of past situations

15. Classification of the Neuroses, Psycho-Neuroses and Psychoses. With Tables

16. Miscellaneous
(a) On the Early Stages of Psychotic Conditions. (b) On Decomposition. (c) On Depersonalization. (d) On the Wish to get Well. (e) On Remissions. (f) On a Diagnostic Technique. (g) On Organ Speech and Restitution. (h) On Cerebral Pathoneuroses. (i) On Orgasm. (j) Some Brief Descriptions by way of approach to Definition. (k) Conclusion

17. Bibliography

1. Introduction

The contributions of psycho-analysts to psychiatry may be divided into three groups which fall roughly into three periods. The first period ranges from 1893 to 1914, the second from 1914 to 1923, the third from 1923 till the present. The first group is characterized by a simplicity not found in later work, and may be summarized by saying that the psychoses were viewed from the aspect of *libido development*; stress is laid on *fixation points*, on defence *mechanisms*, on the *aims* of the sexual instinct and on

H

object cathexis. The second group, while rejecting nothing in the work already done, makes additions which give rather a different orientation, the psychoses are viewed from the aspect of *ego development.* In the third group the *economic factor* is introduced, the *subdivision of the ego* into super-ego and real ego, *cathexis of the ego,* the *castration complex* and the *types of object-relationship* are brought to the foreground. These divisions into groups may serve for a brief exposition, but it must be confessed that they do violence to the chronological sequence of the contributions. There is no harm in this if the reader is aware of the fact that psycho-analytical psychiatry is only a part—and a small part— of psycho-analysis, and that he must add to his study of the part by an examination of the whole, preferably by a careful chronological study. The most that this paper can do is to give an account of selected contributions that will assist in the larger work of a systematic, chronological examination of the literature.

PART I

2. Defence Mechanisms, 1894

In his first psycho-analytical papers, published in the early nineties, Freud calls attention to the mechanism of psychosis.[1] He contrasts two cases with obsession in which the defence against an unbearable idea is effected by detachment of the affect (the idea itself remaining in consciousness, although weakened and isolated) with a case of 'hallucinatory confusion' in which a much more energetic and successful kind of defence exists; 'the ego rejects the unbearable idea together with its associated affect and behaves as if the idea had never occurred to the person at all. But, as soon as this process has been successfully carried through, the person in question will have developed a psychosis, and his state can only be described as one of "hallucinatory confusion".' The content of the symptoms consists in the accentuation of the very idea (*Vorstellung*) which was menaced by the experience which caused the outbreak of the illness. 'One is therefore justified in saying that the ego has averted the unbearable idea by a flight into psychosis, and the process by which this result is obtained again withdraws itself out of range of self-perception as well as of psychological-

[1] Freud, *Collected Papers,* **1**, Hogarth Press, London, p. 72.

clinical analysis. . . . The ego has broken away from the unbearable idea; but, the latter being inseparably bound up with a part of reality, in so far as the ego achieves this result, it has also cut itself loose from reality, totally or in part.' After thirty years Freud returned to this formulation,[1] in the meantime he had provided a number of working hypotheses to account for the outbreak and symptoms of hysteria, the obsessional neurosis, paranoia, dementia praecox, and melancholia. His first formulation now seems rather commonplace, but it bears repetition because it fits into a wider scheme of psychopathology.

Hallucinatory Confusion and Projection 1894-6

The next paper which concerns us, 'The Defence Neuropsychoses',[2] contains the analysis of a case of chronic paranoia. He found that this illness was a defence psychosis resulting from the repression of painful memories. Two important additions are now made to the theory, namely, that the *form* of the symptoms is determined by the content of the repressed memory, and that a special mechanism of repression, peculiar to paranoia, brings relief from the burden of the intolerable idea. Again making a contrast with the neuroses he saw that while in hysteria repression is effected by means of conversion into bodily innervation, and in obsessional neurosis by substitution, that is, by displacement of the affect along certain associated channels, in paranoia it is effected by *projection*. Here the patient erects his defences by directing his distrust against other people and thus becomes unable to recognize that he is himself the object of reproach; but while he thus guards against self-reproach he loses protection from the unbearable ideas which may come from without—they reappear in the delusions.

The symptoms are to be described as manifestations of a return of the repressed and bear traces of a compromise which allows of their entry into consciousness. The return from repression is not possible without a disguise, or censorship, and having attained to consciousness they exhibit another peculiarity—they absorb the thought processes of the ego until they finally come to

---

[1] Freud, *Collected Papers*, **2**, The Hogarth Press, London, p. 277.

[2] Freud, *Collected Papers*, **1**, The Hogarth Press, London, p. 169. In this paper the term 'psycho-analysis' is used for the first time and the term 'repression' is given its psycho-analytical significance.

be accepted without contradiction, that is to say, they alter the ego and by this means effect another or secondary stage of defence.

The repressed content in this case of paranoia, as well as that in the cases of hysteria and obsessional neurosis analyzed in the same paper, is a sexual experience in childhood.

This, the first case of paranoia to be analyzed, showed unmistakably that the defence was erected against intolerable homosexual ideas. The author does not comment on this point, but we note it now for later reference.

Mechanism in Hallucination 1900

For about ten years after this paper on 'The Defence Neuropsychoses' was written, psycho-analysis was concerned with the neuroses and psychical mechanisms in general. For instance, in *The Interpretation of Dreams*, the psychoses as such are not dealt with, and there are only sparing allusions to the formation of their symptoms. But we must note in passing one reference in it to the mechanism of hallucination. In the process of recollection the mind may follow a regressive path and allow the memory traces of past experiences to come up to consciousness in the form of visual images while the process of search for the desired experience is going on. The dream work employs this method when transforming latent thoughts into perceptual forms,—this representation of thought by visual images is called 'regression'. During the day this process may be voluntary as we have seen, but sometimes is involuntary, in which case the patient has an hallucination. Our interest is centred first on the factors which cause the mind to follow this regressive path and produce hallucinations, and secondly on the features which distinguish these from dreams. The theory to account for both states is that a high degree of cathexis must exist upon ideas which are separated from consciousness[1] by repression; it is as though there is an excitation in the central part of the (psychical) reflex arc which cannot pass off by the motor end of the apparatus and so by reflux as it were excites the perceptory end. This can happen easily in sleep because the perceptory end of the apparatus is not in a state of excitement from external stimuli, but in the waking state it is otherwise. The external world is supplying stimuli which normally excite the usual afferent—central—efferent

[1] Freud, *Traumdeutung*, 6th ed. pp. 406 and 407, *Ges. Schr.* Bd. 2, 465–6.

discharge, when there are hallucinations it seems as if the perceptory end of the apparatus is being stimulated from without
and from within (memory-images) and that to produce the
effect the latter have to be intense enough to overpower the
external stimuli. This helps to explain the fact that hallucinations appear more frequently in the dusk and in semi-silence in
those who are only slightly afflicted with hallucinatory symptoms.

Hysteria and Dementia Praecox compared 1906

Jung's paper on 'The Psychology of Dementia Praecox'[1] was
written in 1906. Under the influence of the Word-Association
tests he is dominated by the view that dementia praecox and
hysteria are due to complexes, that is to say, to groups of associated mental elements having become separated from consciousness and influencing the conscious psychical levels, so that
symptoms of various kinds are produced. He uses the term complex here to denote not only pathologically separated systems of
mental associations but also ideational masses which may even
function as parts or levels of the mind. For instance, 'The ego-
complex in the normal person is the highest psychical instance.
By it we understand the ideational mass of the ego which we
believe to be accompanied by the potent and ever-living feeling
tone of our own body. The feeling tone is an affective state which
is accompanied by bodily innervations. The ego is the psychological expression for the firmly associated union of all general
bodily sensations.'[2] He divides the effect of a complex into the
two familiar categories, acute and chronic. In the acute stage
the ego-complex is threatened by danger, and danger excites
fear; in the condition of fear bodily changes are produced which
alter the attention-tone of the ego, and it is compelled to give
way to the stronger sensations of the new complex, so that the
ego-complex is impoverished. If the danger passes rapidly the
disturbing complexes soon lose their attention-tone and the ego
resumes its normal characteristics, yet the affect continues to

---

[1] Jung, *Über die Psychologie der Dementia praecox.*
[2] Jung, *op. cit.* p. 38, authorized translation by Peterson and Brill.
But there is no reason to suppose that Jung is here referring to a part
of the ego being unconscious as Freud does in *Das Ich und das Es.*
[*The Ego and the Id*, The Hogarth Press, London.]

oscillate for a long time in its physical and hence in its psychical components. Thus strong affects (new complexes) leave behind extensive complexes, which may manifest themselves as disturbances of the bodily organs or of sleep, etc. The patient will for a long time be in a condition of 'complex-sensitiveness'. This leads him to the consideration of the chronic effects of the complex, which he summarized as either a prolongation of complex-sensitiveness, or else a state in which the affect is in a continuous state of provocation. The complex in these two cases is less at the disposal of the ego-complex, the affects are out of control, and he found the clinical conditions typical of both hysteria and dementia praecox.[1]

Jung draws several parallels between the two conditions; they are alike in that they show an affective state without adequate ideational content, and may show either the apparent indifference of catatonia or the *belle indifférence* of the hysteric, and in both conditions explosive affects are met with. 'The affects in dementia praecox are probably not extinguished but only peculiarly transposed and blocked, as we see on rare occasions when we obtain a complete catamnestic view of the disease. . . . If a catatonic is constantly occupied by hallucinatory scenes, which crowd themselves into his consciousness with elemental force and with a much stronger tone than the external reality, we can then without any further explanations readily understand that he is unable adequately to react to the questions of the physician. Furthermore, if the patient, as described by Schreber,[2] perceives other persons in his environment as fleeting shadows of men, we can again understand that he is unable to react adequately to the stimuli of reality, that is, he reacts adequately, but in his own way.'[3] Jung does not explain why persons are perceived as fleeting shadows or why the catatonic is constantly occupied with hallucinations—that had to wait for two or three years till further researches threw new light on the libidinal disturbances in the psychoses. He was concerned with the concept of ideational groupings and not so much with cathexis, the 'charge' of energy, which makes this or that group of presentations (*Vorstellungen*) significant.

[1] Jung, *op. cit.* pp. 39–49.
[2] The patient whose case will be referred to at length in a later paragraph.
[3] Jung, *op. cit.* pp. 72, 73.

Turning to the characterological aspects of the two disorders, he says that hysteria does not create a typical character but only exaggerates the already existing qualities; in dementia praecox, on the other hand, he found 'embellishments' of character, mannerisms, affection, etc. In this case the disease takes over the mechanism from hysteria. He instances the use of 'power-words' which elevate and garnish the personality: 'I grand duke Mephisto will have you treated with blood-revenge for Orang-Outang-representation.' Jung is here, of course, straining the boundary of hysteria too far, for such a sentence could not come from an hysteric and is not the exaggeration of an hysterical mechanism. He observed and stated with greater clearness than had been done before the similarities between dementia praecox and hysteria, but he let this emphasis on similarities obscure their essential difference, and this clouds his otherwise fine perception over and over again. He believed that the anomalies of consciousness, attention, orientation, hallucinations, stereotypies and even delusions of reference are common to both.

He summarizes the situation by saying, 'Hysteria contains in its innermost essence a complex which could never be totally overcome; in a measure the psyche is brought to a standstill since it is unable to rid itself of the complex. . . . In dementia praecox we find likewise one or more complexes which become tenaciously fixed. Here, too, we have complexes which can no longer be conquered. Whereas in hysteria there exists an unmistakable causal relation between the complex and the disease (a predisposition is presupposed), we are not at all clear about this in dementia praecox.'[1]

The last remark suggests that Jung was prepared to attribute this disease to a physical and not to a psychological cause, a view that receives some support from recent work (Mott), but he left the investigation of the psycho-genesis of the symptoms too early, and all we have from his pen on the psychoses that has any importance is given here in abstract.

1907

In 1907 Abraham made his first psycho-analytical contribution to the psychoses. In the paper 'On the significance of sexual dreams in youth to the symptomatology of Dementia Praecox'[2]

[1] Jung, *op. cit.* p. 97.
[2] Abraham, *Klin. Beitr. z. Ps.-a.*, p. 1.

he showed that in dementia praecox and in hysteria the symptoms were elaborations of sexual phantasies and these are of infantile character. The form that the sexual phantasies take is for the most part symbolic, a formation that is the more easily effected in dementia praecox because there is a concomitant and characteristic disturbance of attention.

Hysteria and Dementia Praecox contrasted 1908

In the following year Abraham published 'The psycho-sexual differences between hysteria and dementia praecox',[1] a paper that marks the beginning of the application of the libido theory to the psychoses. He starts with the following outline of the development of the libido which has a special interest for us in the light of his later work. The earliest sexual impulses of the child exist in connection with a single erotogenic zone—the mouth—the libidinal gratification being auto-erotic though obtained in many cases from the mother's nipple. The child at this stage has no sexual object other than itself, only later does object-love develop. In the stages which follow this mouth erotism other parts of the body acquire erotogenicity and a series of partial or component instincts are formed which normally unite to form the heterosexual impulse. The energies arising from those partial impulses which are withdrawn from application to their sexual object become deflected to important social aims and constitute the dynamic force of sublimation. Thus disgust arises from the sublimation of homosexual components, shame from infantile exhibitionism and peeping; horror, sympathy and similar feelings from the sublimation of sadistic and masochistic trends. Further, he adds that the social relations of mankind are based on a capacity for sublimated sexual transference; a positive or negative *rapport* develops when any persons are together for any length of time; graciousness or awkwardness showing a greater or less capacity for adaptation, that is, for transference. Man transfers his libido to the inanimate as well as to the animate and his subjective relation to objects in his environment springs from sexuality. Speech confirms this opinion in such expressions as 'the man is wedded to his

[1] *Op. cit.* p. 23; also in *Zentralblatt für Nervenheilkunde und Psychiatrie*, **31**, Jahrg. New Series, Bd. XIX. [A translation will be found in *Selected Papers* of K. Abraham, Hogarth Press, London.]

work'. A good example of this view is found in the case of collectors. The sexual relation of such a man to his collection is often clearly seen. He will make every sacrifice to obtain an object he desires, and will when obtained bestow on it the honour and affection that other men bestow on women. Such passions frequently undergo considerable change on marriage, or may even take the place of marriage in his emotional life. The sexual impulse of the neurotic, in contrast to the normal, is marked by the immoderate strength of these demands, so that he lacks the normal harmony, but whereas the normal person has co-ordinated the components of the sexual instinct to a common (genital) relation to objects, the neurotic is inhibited because the partial instincts are not co-ordinated and subordinated to heterosexual object-love, and are, indeed, in conflict with one another. From this conflict the patient takes refuge in neurosis, the symptoms being abnormal sexual activities. But apart from illness the neurotic libido manifests itself in exaggerated transferences, which overstep the limits of the patient's capacity for sublimation.

Having given this sketch (here much condensed) of normal and neurotic, Abraham goes on to contrast it with the condition in dementia praecox. In the typical case a patient far advanced in the disease appears to be quite cut off from the world, if he speaks it is only when he mutters to himself, indeed he may only gesticulate. He has no impulse to work, pays no heed to his surroundings, eats in a disgusting way, does not keep himself clean or even smears his excrements about and masturbates openly without shame. A lesser degree of the illness shows the same tendency but is not carried to the same extreme: his speech is peculiar, and, while complaining of his restrictions under certificate, he couches his appeals for liberty in a way showing inadequate affect. He may do work but only of a mechanical sort, and finds no satisfaction in it. He finds no pleasure in the company of his fellows, has no social needs, is without tact or fine feeling. Social *rapport* is impossible. Though he may have had intelligence, his productions are worthless, being either queer in concept or design, or lacking in aesthetic sense. The various forms and stages of the disease have this abnormality of emotional life in common. A light case may become a grave one, and a grave one may have remissions and appear to be a mild one, but whether mild or severe the essence of the disorder can be summarized in the formula that *dementia praecox destroys the capacity for sexual transference, for object-love*. This formula explains indifference to the outer world but does not explain the symptoms of the disease, and Abraham gives an explanation of two of these—the delusion of persecution and megalomania. In order to give his explanation the appropriate setting, he begins with an examination of the normal and neurotic child. The first unconscious sexual inclinations of a child are turned to its parents, particularly to that of the opposite sex, and there arises a feeling of insubordination to the parent of the same sex, which may amount to hate. This succumbs to repression under the influence of education and other factors. In the normal the relation to the parents is one of affection but in the neurotic this is frequently pathologically exaggerated, the insubordination to the parent of the same sex being correspondingly increased. In cases of dementia praecox as a rule the affection for relatives is lacking; we find indifference or even outspoken enmity. The process may go a stage further than this and an intense enmity may take the place of an unbounded affection. When in dementia praecox the libido has returned from an object upon which it was once lavished, its reflux to that object is impossible, or at least very rare. The patient who has withdrawn his libido from objects to himself has set up an antithesis between the outer world and himself; for the former he no longer has love (and his tendencies to hate go unchecked), for the latter alone is his love reserved. The situation is ripe for delusions of persecution and just those people who were formerly loved have now turned tormentors.

From the same source spring not only delusions of persecution but those of grandeur. In the case of the emotional tie between two normal persons who transfer their libido to one another the condition is of mutual 'over-estimation'—a condition that is most easily observed in the case when the two persons are in love. This over-valuation is discernible not only between two persons but, as we have seen, between a person and objects that he 'loves'. In general we may say that value radiates from the self to objects that are loved. And so it is in dementia praecox—only with the difference that there being no object-love there is no dispersion or attribution of value—only the self is loved, only the self is valued, and that to point of a boundless grandeur. This may be put in a formula: *The sexual over-estima-*

tion which has returned (reflexly or auto-erotically) to the ego is the source of the delusion of grandeur in dementia praecox. The grandiose ideas, which are a frequent manifestation of the general delusion of grandeur, may be traced to definite repressed wishes which give the *content* to the delusional ideas, the *size* of these ideas, so to speak, being swollen up to correspond with the megalomanic delusion of the greatness of the ego of the patient.

The auto-erotic separation from the outer world influences the patient's receptive as well as his reactive relation to objects. Shutting out the sensory experiences from the real world his unconscious supplies the lack by producing hallucinations, which correspond to repressed wishes—he boycotts the world and confers upon himself the monopoly of providing sensory impressions.

The patient who has lost interest in the outer world, who simply vegetates, whose lifeless expression looks utterly obtuse and intellectually and socially stupefied, is called a 'dement', and the facial expression justifies the term; but we speak of dementia in other conditions though they may be absolutely different from dementia praecox, e.g. epileptic, paretic and senile dementia. All these share one feature in common—the effect of these illnesses is to produce a lowering of capacity for intellectual activity. In G.P.I. or senile dementia intellectual capacity is destroyed fundamentally. In dementia praecox these capacities remain more or less undisturbed; the disorder lies in the sphere of the emotions. In some cases the patient may take in no new impressions for a time, may not react to the outer world at all, and yet may attain such a degree of remission that no one would suspect an intellectual defect. The epileptic never behaves with this indifference, he is either on the side of love or hate, but whichever way it is he is emotionally exuberant. He transfers his libido to an extraordinary degree upon persons and things, is pleased with work and holds on to his own property with tenacity. *In its auto-erotism dementia praecox stands in antithesis to hysteria; in the former we find return of the libido, in the latter over-much object cathexis; in the former loss of capacity to sublimate, in the latter increased sublimation.*

We can frequently observe the psycho-sexual peculiarities of hysteria in childhood though the outbreak of the grave symptoms may only come later, indeed some show manifest signs of illness in their early years. We therefore conclude that the psycho-sexual constitution of hysteria is innate. We are justified in drawing the same conclusion in dementia praecox. In the anamneses we frequently find that the patients at an early age were peculiar, dreamy, 'close'; long before the 'outbreak' of their illness they were unable to transfer their libido; scarcely a single case lacks this feature. Their marked tendency to onanism must also be mentioned, an infantile auto-erotism that has not been completely overcome. Their object-love has not fully developed. We can put this in a formula and say: *the psycho-sexual constitution of dementia praecox depends on an inhibition of development.*

The inhibition in the psycho-sexual development is found to consist not only in an incomplete overcoming of auto-erotism but also an abnormal persistence of the partial impulses. This last peculiarity is shared, to be sure, by the neuroses and simply indicates an inhibited development, but the neurotic lacks the auto-erotic tendencies. In dementia praecox the disturbance goes much deeper than in neurotics, the patients tend to slip back more and more into the auto-erotic stage of development. Abraham ends the paper with the hope that psycho-analytical research will help us to clear up the intellectual disturbances in the clinical picture of dementia praecox—a condition about which we know so little.

3. *The Schreber Case 1911*

The Schreber Case (dementia paranoides) has been referred to on page 230 in connection with Jung's contribution in *The Psychology of Dementia Praecox* (1906). Freud in 1911 carries the analysis much further.[1] He points out that paranoiacs have the peculiarity of betraying (in a distorted form) precisely those things which other neurotics keep hidden and it is therefore a disorder in which a written report can take the place of personal acquaintance with the patient. The source to which he goes for analytical data is Schreber's *Memoirs of a Neurotic* published in 1903. The patient was a Doctor of Law, President of the Court of Appeal in a part of Germany, and a man of superior mental gifts and endowed with an unusual keenness alike of intellect and of observation. At the age of 42 he had an

[1] Freud, 'Psycho-Analytical Notes upon an Autobiographical Account of a Case of Paranoia (Dementia Paranoides)', *Collected Papers*, Vol. 3, The Hogarth Press, London.

illness diagnosed as hypochondria, but he recovered after a few months sufficiently to continue his important legal work. In 1893, at the age of 51, his second illness began. He dreamed that his former illness had returned, and one morning in a state between sleeping and waking the idea occurred to him 'that after all it really must be very nice to be a woman submitting to the act of copulation'. The illness set in with a torturing bout of sleeplessness; he rapidly became worse, thinking he had softening of the brain, that he would soon be dead, that his body was decomposing; he had delusions and hallucinations, that he had the plague, that his body was handled in revolting ways; he sat rigid and motionless for hours, and several times attempted suicide. He thought he was living without a stomach, almost without lungs, that he swallowed his larynx with his food but that divine 'rays' restored the bodily organs which had been destroyed and thus saved him from a fatal outcome from injuries which would in other men prove mortal. Further, he thought his body was being transformed into that of a woman and the restored organs in female form would generate a new race of men by impregnation by God in his female body. The world was changed, trees and birds were only 'bemiracled' relics of former human souls. He was in direct communication with God and yet a plaything of devils; he thought his physician was a 'soul-murderer'—in a word his symptoms were those of a typical case of dementia paranoides. To complete the history: in 1902 his civil rights were restored after a deal of litigation and in 1903 he published his *Memoirs* describing the miracles that were performed on his body and the wonderful experiences he had with God. The medical reports stress two points, his delusions that he was a Redeemer and that he had been transformed into a woman.

In order to be able to follow the argument Freud puts forward to explain the case, it is necessary to read both his paper and the *Memoirs*, but for the moment a few additions to what has just been said must suffice. Schreber's relations to his physician were those of warm respect and gratitude for the cure effected in his first illness, and yet in the persecution mania which coloured the clinical picture of the second illness this person is represented as a 'soul-murderer', and Schreber fancied

---

[1] Freud, *Collected Papers*, **3**, The Hogarth Press, London, p. 424.

his body was being handed over to him for sexual abuses. The explanation offered[1] is that the person in whose hands all the threads of conspiracy converge is a person who played an equally important part in the patient's emotional life before the illness, or else an easily recognizable substitute for him. The intensity of the emotion is projected outwards in the shape of external power, while its quality is changed into the opposite. The person who is now hated and feared as a persecutor was at one time loved and honoured. The purpose of the delusional persecution is to serve as a justification for the change in emotional attitude.

Returning to the scanty information at his disposal to account for the outbreak of the second illness, Freud assumes that his dreams of the return of his first attack may be interpreted as a wish to see his first physician again. The fact that Schreber brings the dreams and the phantasy of its being nice to be a woman submitting to copulation into close association leads to the assumption that a recollection of his physician also roused in his mind a feminine attitude to him. The feminine phantasy at first was kept apart from his personality, he repudiated it, but later it carried everything before it. The exciting cause of the illness may be put down to an outburst of homosexual libido,[1] and his struggles against this produced a conflict which gave rise to the pathological phenomena.

The next piece of analytical work is the tracing of the effects of the conflict. The first step was the replacement of the physician by the superior figure of God, and though at first sight it looks like an aggravation it is seen really to be a preparatory

---

[1] For further case histories supporting this view, see: Freud, 1896, 'The Defence Neuro-psychoses', *Collected Papers*, **1**, The Hogarth Press, London, p. 169; Ferenczi, 1914, 'Some Clinical Observations on Paranoia and Paraphrenia', *Contributions to Psycho-Analysis*, The Hogarth Press, London, p. 238; Ferenczi, 1911, 'On the Part Played by Homosexuality in the Pathogenesis of Paranoia', *Jahrbuch für Psychoanalytische Forschungen*, **3**, pp. 101–19; Ferenczi, 1911, 'Reizung der analen erogenen Zonen als auslösende Ursache der Paranoia' (Beitrag zum Thema: Homosexualität und Paranoia), *Zentralblatt für Psychoanalyse*, **1**, p. 557; Maeder, 1910, 'Psychologische Untersuchungen an Dementia Praecox-Kranken', *Jahrbuch für Psychoanalytische Forschungen*, **2**, p. 185; Marischau-Beauchant, 1912, 'Homosexualität und Paranoia', *Zentralblatt für Psychoanalyse*, Band **2**. See also Bibliography 256, 490.

step to the solution of the conflict. It was impossible for Schreber to be reconciled to playing the part of a feminine prostitute to his physician, but the task of providing God himself with voluptuous sensations called up no such resistance on the part of his Ego. Emasculation was no longer a disgrace, it became 'consonant with the order of things' and was instrumental in regenerating the human race. His Ego found compensation in megalomania while his feminine wish phantasy gained the ascendancy and became acceptable. The patient's sense of reality, however, compelled him to postpone the solution of the conflict to the remote future.

The usual explanation of megalomania is that it develops out of persecution mania,[1] the patient being primarily the victim of the delusion that he is being persecuted by the most powerful influences; then, feeling the need to account for the persecution by so many and often such august persons, he hits upon the idea that he himself is a very exalted person and worthy of such attentions. This explanation of megalomania is clearly a 'rationalization', to use Ernest Jones's term.

But to return to Schreber: his persecutor is 'decomposed' into his physician and God, the former splitting up into two parts, 'an upper' and 'a middle', God dividing into 'an upper' and 'a lower'. This is characteristic of paranoia: 'Paranoia decomposes just as hysteria condenses. Or rather, paranoia resolves once more into their elements products of the condensations and identifications which take place in the unconscious.'[2] The decomposing process is adopted in order to mitigate the effect of too powerful transferences to any one person. In Schreber's case the two persons concerned appear to be his father (whose place in his delusional system was taken by God) and his brother (whose representative was his physician). The feminine phantasy thus traced to its root is directed towards his father and brother. The reference of his psychotic symptoms to his father is not a mere application of the Oedipus situation to an unanalyzed case without further consideration for details. A peculiar

---

[1] We may note in passing that this is one of the very rare instances where a psychical mechanism suggested by other clinicians is contradicted by psycho-analysts. In almost every instance psychoanalytic theories supplement the deductions made by trained observers in other fields of clinical work.

[2] Freud, *Collected Papers*, 3, The Hogarth Press, London, p. 434.

feature of his case is the subversion of God by his physician, indeed God became for him a person who could not deal with living men but only corpses. It happens that Schreber's father was a physician who devoted much energy to raising the standards of hygiene among youth in general and to physical culture in particular. The transition from a well-known and highly respected father to the Divine Person of God, though almost inconceivable to ordinary seeming, is by no means rare in history, even among such modern ancients as the Romans. Schreber's ambivalent feelings for his father found expression in translating him to the Deity on the one hand and on the other in the remark that God only understands corpses—a bitter satire on a physician, indeed. Further, a physician is sometimes, even to-day, credited with performing 'miracles' and restoring bodily organs. Looking again more closely at the remarkable *Memoirs*, it appears probable that the subdivisions of God into 'an upper' and 'a lower' are divisions made in accordance with the anterior aperture ('the forecourts of Heaven') as being a symbol for female and 'the posterior realms of God' as a symbol for what is male.

The case of Schreber is resolved into the familiar Father-complex, and the struggle with his physician becomes revealed as a conflict with his father. The details of this latter conflict are not given in the *Memoirs* and can only be inferred from the symptoms. As a rule the father appears as an interferer with auto-erotic gratifications or later with phantasies of a less inglorious kind. In Schreber's delusion the infantile sexual tendencies scored a glorious victory, for voluptuousness became God-fearing and God himself demanded incessant satisfaction. The most dreaded threat—castration—actually provided the material of his wish-phantasy, and he became transformed into a woman. The 'soul-murder' now becomes clearer, it is his emasculation and the fulfilment of his feminine wish-phantasy.

We have to consider another symptom—the enforced thinking. This is a frequent reaction to the threat or dread of losing one's reason as a result of indulging in sexual practices, especially onanism; indeed many of Schreber's hypochondriacal ideas coincide word for word with the fears of onanists.

Freud adds that he will not consider any theory of paranoia trustworthy unless it covers the hypochondriacal symptoms which almost invariably accompany the disease, and by way of suggestion adds: 'It seems to me that *hypochondria stands in the same relation to paranoia as anxiety neurosis does to hysteria.*' Concluding his summary he points out that the outbreak of the illness had a relation to a feminine wish-phantasy, and from knowledge of other patients it is known that the appearance of wish-phantasies can be brought into connection with some *frustration*, some privation in real life. In Schreber's case his childless marriage brought him no son to console him for the loss of his father and brother—to drain off his unsatisfied homosexual affections. His family line was threatened with extinction, but in his delusions he was going to re-people the world with a new race of men; the feminine attitude to his father in his infancy was manifested in regression only when the forward movement of his libido was frustrated.

With these *Memoirs* as illustration Freud proceeds to a consideration of the Mechanism of Paranoia.

The Mechanism of Paranoia 1911

The central position of the father complex and the wish-phantasy built upon it in Schreber's case is not characteristic of paranoia; the distinctive character of the disease lies in the peculiar form of the symptoms and in the mechanism by which they are produced or by which repression is brought about. An investigation showed that in the cases of paranoia examined by himself and some psycho-analytical colleagues a defence was set up against a homosexual wish-phantasy and that they all came to grief on attempting to master an unconsciously reinforced current of homosexuality. But in paranoia the sexual aetiology is by no means obvious; on the contrary social humiliations and slights appear as prominent features. This requires explanation, and the following is offered: where the individual is functioning normally it is impossible to see into the depths of his mental life and to see that his emotional relations with his neighbours have anything to do with sexuality, but the development of delusions never fails to unmask these relations and trace the social feelings to their roots in a brutally sensual erotic wish. While he was healthy Schreber had shown no signs of homosexuality in the ordinary sense of the word; that his delusions were full of it is equally obvious. We must turn for an explanation of this apparent contradiction to the development of the libido.

There appears to be a stage in the development of the libido on the way from auto-erotism to object-love which is called Narcissism. The individual at this stage unifies his sexual instincts (which have hitherto been engaged on auto-erotic activities) in order to obtain a love-object, and he begins by taking himself, his own body, as love-object, only subsequently proceeding from this to the choice of some other person. Some linger unusually long in this narcissistic stage and many of the features of this stage may be carried over to later stages of development. The point of central interest in the new love-object is sometimes the genitals and the path of development then leads to the choice of a person with similar genitals, i.e. to homosexual object-choice, and thence to heterosexuality. In the case of manifest homosexuals, it may be presumed, the fascination of the penis exerts a rigid influence on their object-choice, from which they cannot emancipate themselves. When the heterosexual stage is reached the homosexual tendencies are not done away with nor brought to a stop but are deflected from their aim and applied to fresh uses; they combine with portions of the ego-instincts and as anaclitic components help to constitute the social instincts, thus contributing an (aim-inhibited) erotic factor to friendship, *esprit de corps* and love of mankind in general.

The paranoiac has a fixation of his libido at the narcissistic level and is therefore in danger, when an unusually intense wave of libido arises that finds no other outlet, of having to undo the work of sublimation and to sexualize his social instincts. This state of affairs may come about by anything that causes a 'regression', whether from disappointment in regard to women or from the damming up effects of a mishap in his relations with other men (both 'frustrations') or from general intensification of the libido. Since paranoiacs endeavour to protect themselves against any such sexualization of their social instinctual cathexes we may take it that the weak point in their development—their fixation—lies between the stages of auto-erotism, narcissism and homosexuality.

The core of the conflict, then, in the case of a male is the homosexual wish-phantasy of *loving a man*—at any rate the supposition seems to be valid for one type of paranoia. It is, however, a remarkable fact that the most familiar forms of paranoia can all be represented as contradicting a single proposition: '*I* (a man) *love him* (a man).'

Persecution mania. In persecution mania the proposition is contradicted by the assertion, 'I do not love him.' But we remember that in the unconscious negative propositions do not exist, the only form possible is: 'I *hate* him,' but this, on the other hand, cannot become conscious to the paranoias in this form. The mechanism of symptom formation requires that internal perceptions or feelings should be replaced by external ones, consequently the formula is changed from 'I hate him' to 'He hates (persecutes) me, which will justify my hating him'. Observation leaves no room for doubt that the persecutor is someone who was once loved.

Erotomania. In persecution mania the verb is changed, in erotomania the object, thus: 'I do not love him' becomes changed to 'I love *her*', and by projection the proposition is changed into 'I notice that she loves me, and so I love her'. Observation supports this view because the subjects of erotomania may be distinguished from persons with heterosexual fixations by the fact that these infatuations invariably begin not with the internal perception of loving but with the external perception of being loved. In this form of the disease the stage 'I love *her*' can be conscious because it is not so contradictory as the antithesis between love and hate; it is possible to love both *her* and *him*.

Jealousy. Persecution is a change of verb, erotomania is a change in the object, jealousy changes the subject: not 'I love him' but 'It is not *I* who love the man—*she* loves him'. In the case of alcoholic jealousy the patient, not infrequently as a result of a disappointment over a woman, is 'driven to drink'; he resorts to the public-house and the company of men, getting there the emotional satisfaction he failed to get at home. He wards off the consciousness of the strong libidinal cathexis to men by distorting the formula as given above—and suspects the woman in relation to all the men he is himself tempted to love. There is no true projection in this case because with a change of subject the whole process is thrown outside the ego—he is not involved in the loving, whereas in the other cases he himself is involved. By an external perception he comes to the conclusion that *she* loves the men, not, be it noted, by an internal perception.[1]

[1] Freud, *Collected Papers*, **3**, The Hogarth Press, London, p. 450. This point is made clearer in his paper: 'Certain Neurotic Mechanisms in Jealousy, Paranoia and Homosexuality.'

A fourth kind of contradiction. In the given proposition of three terms it might be thought that there were only three contradictions, but another exists. It consists of a rejection of the whole set and runs: 'I don't love anything or anyone at all,' and since one's libido must be somewhere this can be resolved into '*I love only myself*,' and so gives the clue to megalomania, which, as was stated in the last section, is regarded as a sexual over-estimation of the ego.

Megalomania is essentially of an infantile nature and in the course of normal development is sacrificed to social considerations, but most of all it is sacrificed to love.

Though a repressed homosexual tendency is found to be a frequent if not constant factor in the aetiology of paranoia, it is not the distinguishing feature of the disease; Freud finds this in the mechanism by which the symptoms are formed and the way in which repression is brought about. That the two processes need not be identical will be shown.

In paranoia the most striking characteristic is the process of projection: an internal perception is suppressed, and instead of appearing in consciousness directly, its content, after undergoing a certain amount of distortion, enters consciousness in the form of an external perception. This is a modification of the theory put forward fifteen years before (see p. 227) but rather by addition to than subtraction from what was originally proposed. Projection, however, is not peculiar to paranoia nor does it play the same part in all forms of the disease. Indeed projection plays a regular part in our attitude to the external world. When we refer the causes of certain sensations to the external world, instead of looking for them (as we do in the case of others) inside ourselves, this 'normal' proceeding is projection.[1]

The Mechanism of Repression 1911

The mechanism of repression has been referred to and has been called in paranoia projection. But of the nature of repression in general little has been said. Freud divides it into three phases. The first consists of a precursory and necessary condition of *fixation* in which an instinct or instinctual component lags in the path of development and so remains in an infantile condition,

[1] For further papers on projection see Ferenczi, *Contributions to Psycho-Analysis*, ch. V and ch. XI.

behaving to later psychological structures as though it belonged to the system of the unconscious and was repressed. The instinctual fixations constitute the basis for the disposition to subsequent illness and particularly determine the outcome of the third phase of repression. The second phase is that of *repression proper*, emanating from the more highly developed systems of the ego and appearing as an active process in contrast to the passive lagging behind which characterizes fixation. It might be called the 'after-expulsion' of either the derivatives of the lagging instincts when these get reinforced and so come into conflict with ego-syntonic instincts or with the ego, or of psychical trends which have aroused strong aversion. Aversion alone does not lead to repression unless a connection is established between the unwelcome trends and those repressed already; when this occurs the *repulsion* of the conscious system and the *attraction* of the unconscious tend to the same end. The third phase is that of *irruption* or the *return of the repressed*. The irruption takes its start from the point of fixation and involves a regression of the libidinal development to that point. Just as there are various possible points of fixation so there may be various mechanisms of repression and it may be impossible to trace back all of these multiplicities to the developmental history of the libido alone.[1]

Turning to Schreber again it is noted that at the climax of his illness he had 'visions which were partly of a terrifying character and partly of an indescribable grandeur' (*Memoirs*, p. 73). He became convinced of the immanence of a great catastrophe—of the end of the world. He thought that the work of the past 14,000 years would be undone and at times that he was the only real man still surviving, the persons about him being only 'cursory contraptions'. In his delusion his ego was retained and the world was sacrificed. He thought the catastrophe was caused by the withdrawal of the sun, or by an earthquake in which he played a significant part, or his physician had wrecked the foundations of religion and spread neurotic states, general immorality and devastating pestilence abroad. This was the result, it can be surmised, of conflict between himself and his physician or himself and God. After his recovery, though he found no trace of the catastrophe in the outside world he felt that, in spite of everything appearing to the contrary, the world before him was a different one. In terms of the libido theory the

[1] This foreshadows some wide developments.

catastrophe may be explained as a withdrawal of cathexes from the persons and things of the environment, thus making it indifferent to him, and the explanation that persons are 'miracled up, cursory contraptions' has to be put down to a secondary rationalization. The end of the world is a projection of the internal catastrophe—his loss of love relationships. Perhaps with the loss of libidinal cathexes his interest in general (his egoistic cathexes) has vanished; but this question must be deferred. But he returns to the world, he rebuilds the world after the catastrophe, and this he does by *delusion formation which though usually taken to be a pathological product is really an attempt at recovery, a process of restitution.* Such reconstructions are never wholly successful, there is in Schreber's words a 'profound internal change' in the world, but the recaptured relation though often intense may now be hostile where formerly it was affectionate.

Repression, in this case, consists in a detachment of libido from persons and things that were previously loved. It happens silently; the reconstruction, however, which undoes the work of repression and brings the libido back to the people it abandoned, may be noisy. In paranoia the return of the libido on to the persons once loved is carried out by projection. It is not a perception which was suppressed internally that is projected outwards but rather what was abolished internally returns from without.

Detachment of libido, however, is not peculiar to paranoia, it occurs in grief after a death and in other ways too; what does appear to be characteristic of the disease is the application of the libido after it is set free by detachment. In the case of a person suffering a bereavement the libido thus released is kept in suspension in his mind, gives rise to states of tension and colours all his moods; in the course of time it is reapplied to a new love-object. In hysteria liberated libido becomes transformed into physical innervations or into anxiety, but in paranoia it becomes fixed on to the ego and produces megalomania. So we come back to a stage of narcissism in which a person's only sexual object is his own ego. Put into formulae: *the paranoiac fixation is at a stage of narcissism* and *the amount of regression characteristic of paranoia is the step back from sublimated homosexuality to narcissism.*

Detachment of libido may be only partial, a drawing back

from a single 'complex'; indeed this should be the commoner, and a general drawing back of libido a rarer event, since the influences of life usually provide a motive for only a partial withdrawal. In Schreber's case, for instance, the partial libidinal detachment was from the figure of his physician first of all; this was followed immediately by the delusion which brought back the libido to the physician again (with a negative sign—persecution instead of love) and thus annulled the work of repression. But the battle of repression broke out again involving more and more of the external world, till the conviction was gained that the world had come to an end and only the self had survived. The wealth of sublimations that were brought down in ruin by the catastrophe of the general detachment of his libido may be gauged by the details of his ingenious delusions: the hierarchy of God, the qualified souls, the forecourts of Heaven, the upper and lower God, and so on.

The next theoretical question that arises is whether general detachment of libido alone suffices to bring about the idea of 'the end of the world', or whether the egoistic cathexes which still remain in existence could not maintain *rapport*. If the former is true, then libidinal cathexes (that is, interest emanating from erotic sources) coincide with interest in general; if the latter, then we have to acknowledge that extensive disturbance in the distribution of the libido may bring about disturbance in the egoistic cathexes. This might be clearer if there was a well-founded theory of instinct, but none such exists. As a working hypothesis the psycho-analyst regards instinct as the frontier-line between the somatic and the mental, a mental representative of an organic force.

Returning to clinical considerations: 'we can no more discuss the possibility that disturbances of the libido may react upon the egoistic cathexes than we can overlook the converse possibility—namely, that a secondary or induced disturbance of the libidinal processes may result from abnormal changes in the ego. Indeed, it is possible that processes of this kind constitute the distinctive characteristic of psychoses.' But even at the height of the repressive process the paranoiac does not withdraw his interest so completely as a patient, for example, with some kinds of hallucinatory confusion. He perceives the external world and the effect it has on him stimulates him to invent explanatory theories (the 'cursory contraptions'), so the paranoiac's altered relation to the world is to be explained entirely or in the main by the loss of his libidinal interest.[1]

We next have to consider the bearing of these theories of paranoia on the psycho-analytical view of dementia praecox. Paranoia is clearly an independent clinical type, however frequently it may be complicated by the presence of schizophrenic features, and it resembles dementia praecox (from the standpoint of the libido theory) in that repression proper in both cases consists in detachment of the libido with regression on to the ego. It differs from dementia praecox by having its point of fixation differently located and by having a different mechanism for the return of the repressed (i.e. for the formation of symptoms). In dementia praecox the stage of agitated hallucinations is a struggle between repression and an attempt at recovery, that is, an attempt to bring the libido back to its objects. As Jung said, the deliria and motor stereotypies are relics of former object-cathexes clung to with convulsive energy. In dementia praecox the attempt at recovery (which some observers mistake for the disease itself) does not, as in paranoia, make use of projection, but employs an hallucinatory (hysterical) mechanism. The distinction between the two disorders can be drawn from another quarter: in dementia praecox the prognosis is more unfavourable than in paranoia, the victory lies with the forces of repression not with those of reconstruction, and most significant of all, repression travels back not merely to the stage of narcissism (manifesting itself in megalomania) but to the complete abandonment of object-love and a restoration to infantile auto-erotism. The dispositional point of fixation must be far back, at the beginning of the course of development from auto-erotism to object-love. Moreover, it is not at all likely that homosexual impulses, which play a so frequent, perhaps an invariable, part in paranoia fill the same rôle in the aetiology of dementia praecox.

The introduction of the libido theory with its emphasis on the points of fixation makes it easy to see that a case may begin with paranoid symptoms and yet develop into dementia praecox and that the symptoms of both disorders may be combined in any proportion. In Schreber's case the production of wish-phantasies and hallucinations shows paraphrenic traits, while its exciting cause, its use of projection and final issue exhibit a

[1] Freud, *Collected Papers*, **3**, The Hogarth Press, London, pp. 461–2.

paranoid character. At each fixation point there may be an irruption of the libido frustrated at a higher stage in the development, and as the illness develops earlier fixation points are reached that lie nearer the starting-point. In Schreber's case it would be interesting to know what factors favoured an approximation to recovery—perhaps because his father-complex was on the whole positively toned and in real life the later years of their relationship had been unclouded, he could reconcile himself to his homosexual phantasy—but his *Memoirs* do not give enough evidence to establish the point.

Freud ends this long case history with a statement of the two chief theses towards the establishment of which the libido theory of the neuroses and psychoses is advancing, namely, 'that the neuroses arise in the main from a conflict between the ego and the sexual instinct, and that the forms which the neuroses assume bear the imprint of the course of development followed by the libido—and by the ego.'[1]

4. *The Manic Depressive Disorders 1911*

We have now to deal with a paper delivered at the International Psycho-Analytical Congress at Weimar in 1911, which will turn our attention for the first, but by no means the last, time to the manic-depressive disorders.[2]

Abraham points out that the psycho-analytical literature while speaking much of anxiety has said but little about depression, although that symptom is as widespread among neuroses and psychoses as the other; indeed, they are frequently found in the same individual, an anxious patient is depressed, and a melancholic complains of anxiety. Anxiety arises from sexual repression and is thus aetiologically to be distinguished from fear, for in the former state the motives are unconscious and in the latter they are conscious. In the same way depression is to be distinguished from grief. Putting this into a formula, one can say: *As anxiety is to fear, so is depression to grief.* We fear a coming trouble, and grieve over an unexpected one. The neurotic falls into an anxiety if his impulses, striving for satisfaction, are thwarted by repression; depression sets in when he gives up his sexual aim unsatisfied, he then feels incapable of loving or of

---

[1] Freud, *Collected Papers*, **3**, The Hogarth Press, London, p. 466.
[2] Abraham, *Selected Papers*, Hogarth Press, London.

being loved, he casts doubts on both life and the future. This feeling is brought to an end by an actual change in the situation or by a psychical manipulation of the painful ideas, and by this manipulation neurotic depression tends to disavow life in a manner similar to that employed in the related condition of anxiety. The psychotic is different and we have to reckon with the changes from melancholia to mania and other complications.

In considering his clinical material, Abraham was struck in their very first analytical hour by the similarity of his depressed psychotics to the graver cases of obsessional neurosis in whom the libido displays the two tendencies of love and hate, the latter being so strong that the capacity for transferring love to objects in the outer world is diminished. Through repression of his hate, or, expressed in other terms, repression of the over-strong sadistic component of his libido, the obsessional neurotic is weak and lacking in energy, his incapacity to adjust his libido leads to general uncertainty and finally doubting mania, he can come to no conclusions, make no clear decisions, and feels in every situation incapable and helpless. This applies also to depressed psychotics.

Abraham gives case histories and draws the following conclusions from them: In cases of depression the outbreak of the illness followed a rupture in the patient's relation to the outer world, when he had to make a decision involving application of his libido to objects, that is, when he was about to fall in love. He notes a similar precipitating cause of illness in cases of obsessional neurosis. In depressed cases there is a feeling as if their capacity to love is paralyzed by feelings of hate, and this too is found in obsessionals. Of special significance is the uncertainty of their sexual rôle, there being a conflict between their masculine and feminine tendencies. In a later stage, however, the two types of illness begin to show divergences. In *obsessional neurosis* the patient takes up *substitutes* in place of the unattainable goals of his sexual impulses, whereas in the *depressed psychoses* the patient tries to overcome the obstacles originating in repression by the mechanism of *projection*. As he cannot love people he feels he must hate them (the deep-seated tendencies to hate exert their influence at this point), and this is changed by projection and subsequent 'rationalization' into the phrase, 'They hate me because I am cursed with inborn defects—so I am unhappy, I'm dejected.'

In utilizing the mechanism of projection to explain the symptoms in depression, Abraham is following the precedent of Freud's explanation of paranoia in the Schreber case, but it must be pointed out that there are objections to the application of the mechanism of projection to the depressive psychoses. In paranoia perceptions of events which are really internal are regarded as coming from without; the paranoiac will deny his own love-impulses and say that someone else is making love to him, whereas the depressive says, for example, that he is the only person in the world without capacity to love. The paranoiac has an ache of some kind and says it is the result of evil agencies; the depressive patient perceives someone else with an ache or misfortune and says it is his own doing—he is not the victim of crimes, but the doer of them, and he feels the guilt of his (supposed) misconduct. The paranoiac, however, feels blameless and aggrieved.

Abraham next takes up the fate of the repressed sadistic tendencies in depressed psychotics. These do not remain quietly repressed but return to consciousness as impulses to inflict injury on the environment, to revengeful and criminal acts. The acts, indeed, are seldom committed, one only learns of them indirectly in analysis; they represent attempts in phantasy to overcome the inborn afflictions from which the patient suffers. Like King Richard III, since he cannot prove a lover he resolves to be a villain, and when these hatreds or lusts for revenge are repressed they produce new symptoms—*ideas of guilt*. The more powerful the unconscious impulses to revenge the stronger are the delusions of guilt. Thus the patients think they are to blame for the sins of all men since the world began, and that they have engendered all the evil that exists; they become tortured by these feelings and develop the severest depressions. But all these depressions are none other than the fulfilment of wishes, *unconscious sadistic wishes which completely overpower the positive libidinal tendencies* of the sufferers. The melancholic shares with the obsessional neurotic an unconscious belief that his wishes are in fact equivalent to action, which only adds to his troubles, because he (unconsciously) believes that thinking of the death of someone may bring about that person's death. He believes that he has at hand a terrific weapon of destruction which he cannot control, consciously he is filled with anxiety at the consequences of its awful destructiveness, unconsciously he is gratified by the satisfaction of the sadistic impulses afforded by the gruesome phantasies.

As we have seen, depression, anxiety and self-reproach result from the repression of sadism, but something further may occur; masochism arises when the patient is barred from the *active* satisfaction of his passions—he turns them upon himself and draws pleasure from his own suffering.

Turning from a consideration of this particular mechanism to a more general view of the fate of the libido, Abraham calls attention to the frequency with which depressives just before their attack are found to have been active in their vocation. The libido has been sublimated (often under pressure, so to speak) so that they could deceive themselves that their conflict was over. But suddenly, when some situation involving extra application of libido has to be faced, the balance heretofore maintained is upset, the interests (sublimations) which before engrossed attention are abandoned, the patient's outlook on life contracts, he becomes depressed and may be completely obsessed with some one idea. Psychical inhibition is the character of the disease, *rapport* becomes impossible and there is no capacity for a positive application of libido. The lack of rapport corresponds to an auto-erotic disposition of libido gratification; the patient does not react to external stimuli, or does so only slightly, the condition resembles *stupor*—a symbolic death.

The details of the symptoms of depression are given closer examination. The patient complains that he and his family are poverty-stricken and will never be able to recover their fortune. He identifies libido with gold and sexual with pecuniary capacity. It is true for him in his depression that love has gone out of the world and everything of value has gone with it, he feels that he lacks capital because he lacks the power to love.

The apprehensiveness of the depressions of the involutionary period may be similarly explained. It appears in those whose love-life has not been satisfied; they have repressed their libidinal strivings and taken refuge in all sorts of compensations. Looking back at life from the climacteric they find it is too late to regain what they have lost; being too weak to banish the desire for satisfactions now denied them, they substitute apprehension of poverty for failure in love.

Abraham notes that mania, to outward appearance, is the reverse of depression; the patient appears cheerful and analysis shows the content of his delusions to be the reverse of those of the depressed psychotic. The same complexes are found in both, but the patient's attitude to them differs. Love and hate both surge up to consciousness without repression [according to later theory, because there is a change in the (repressing) ego]. The depressive is centred on death, the manic begins life at every moment anew, he returns to a state before repression began, before there ever was conflict in his life. His pleasure is similar to the pleasure of wit—the release of inhibition. *In depression inhibition is increased, in mania it is diminished.* But release of inhibition is not the only source of pleasure in mania, it makes all the infantile modes of gratification available as well: playing with words, deliverance from the bonds of logic and generally a replacement of infantile freedom. Ideas are pursued without regard to their relation to a goal; there is a flight of ideas, whereas in the depressive every movement of ideas is inhibited. In mania the flight of ideas appears to be influenced by similarities in the words rather than the ideas which the words represent, which recalls again the theory that wit is an economy in psychical activity, and serves to bring the characteristics of mania, wit and the infantile psyche still closer together.

In exalted mania the sadistic component may lead to violent action even though the external stimulus be only a small one, and in some cases of mania delusions of grandeur may be noted.

Of interest in connection with the nosogenesis of the first attack of mania at the age of 28 in a case of cyclothymia, Abraham mentions that at puberty there was a development of feminine tendencies, and when the instincts began to develo- he took more interest in women and less in auto-eroticism.

In regard to therapy, Abraham concludes his paper by expressing the conviction that psycho-analysis should be tried in selected cases of the manic-depressive psychoses.

5. Comment on this group of papers

A comment on the psycho-analytical contribution to psychiatry may best begin with a discussion of the 'mental mechanisms' which play such a large part in its development. The conception of the reflex arc which is borrowed from physiology is developed in psycho-analytical literature in some detail; usually in non-psycho-analytical writings authors are content to point out that in disease there is increased sensitiveness or increased reaction to stimuli from the environment, that the central organs of the reflex are hyper-excitable. But psycho-analysts distinguish two sources of stimulus, an external and an internal, the former consists of those impacts on the organism which are external and so can be avoided by alterations of environment, the latter are not impacts but continuous impulsions, which may be given the name of 'needs'.[1] They are of internal origin and cannot therefore be avoided by alterations of environment. The contrast is: external—internal, stimulus—instinct.

The conception of the reflex arc is applied to the working of the 'psychical apparatus' as a whole; this psychical apparatus is by hypothesis accorded a function similar to that of the majority of physiological reflexes, namely, to eliminate states of tension, in this case states of mental tension. The external stimuli of physical origin can be neglected for the most part in dealing with psychology because (a) they can be dealt with by flight from the source of disturbance, (b) they do not require mental adjustments of a prolonged and arduous kind (grave traumata excepted, see below), (c) owing probably to hereditary aptitudes of long acquirement the adjustment to physical conditions in the environment is relatively easy (again grave traumata excepted). The internal stimuli or 'needs' of instinctual origin, on the other hand, cannot be dealt with by flight, there is no way of removing the source of mental excitation except by changing the state at the source of the stimulus, e.g. satisfying hunger by providing the organism with the adequate material to eliminate the state of excitation; this process of satisfaction of need involves extensive mental adaptations of an individual kind, i.e. not by inherited reflex only, owing to the fact that in regard to instinct stimuli the technique for dealing with excitation has not become automatic, and individual effort (psychical work) is required which takes time and involves the expenditure of mental energy. Nevertheless it would be a mistake to assume that because the work involved in mastering instinctual stimuli is individual that it is either necessarily conscious or voluntary, rather we must be prepared for the contrary view that consciousness is a surface phenomenon only and that the greater part of the response of the psychical apparatus to internal stimuli is unconscious.

[1] See Freud, *Collected Papers*, **4**, The Hogarth Press, London, p. 62.

The psychical mechanisms are processes which occur in the mind in order to bring about relief of tension ('pain'), i.e. of mastering stimuli. None of these can be directly observed, they must be inferred, that is to say, the psychical mechanisms are all hypothetical. These hypotheses utilize a limited number of more or less definite concepts which occur over and over again in the literature. A certain amount of indulgence must be asked of the reader if no attempt at definition is made in regard to these elementary concepts; it is requisite that the notions should be discovered in their context and in this manner understood. Criticism is serviceable if it can show that a term is used one way in one place and another way in another; a general criticism of the vagueness of psycho-analysis is just only if similar stringency is employed in regard to the psychological concepts used in psychiatry and other mental sciences.

To return to our starting-point. Clinical observation immediately furnishes us with the final but not the initial excitations of the adaptive response. To take the case of *Projection*: a patient, *A* says he is persecuted by *B*, his remark is evidence of a relationship subsisting between him and *B*; but what sort of relationship? On the surface his words and conduct assert that *B* persecutes him, deeper down it appears that the relationship is that *A* loves *B*, but is not aware of his love. In order to keep the amount of excitation in the conscious levels of the psychical apparatus as low as possible *A* has had to employ an extraordinary device for protecting his conscious mind from his own inner feelings for *B*, no less, in fact, than changing his perceptions of both his inner and his outer experience. Viewed from the influence it exerts on consciousness, the mechanism is a defensive device; regarded from the unconscious of the patient the mechanism affords a gratification that would not otherwise be possible. From the double aspect (from within by empathy and from without by observation, i.e. analytically) the mechanism is seen to provide a working arrangement that suits both the patient's conscious and unconscious life, the adaptation in this case is not directed to outer but to inner necessity. Herein lies the difficulty for psychiatrists, to acquire a view of the inner necessities of the patient which shall appear to them equally valid (for the patient) with the outer ones. Projection is a defensive device—but defensive against what? Nothing external since the persecutor is usually a friendly person, e.g. Schreber's physician, but something internal: an impulse. In the case of paranoid projection the impulse is that of crude homosexual wishes that must be repressed in order to maintain the integrity of the ego. The projection of a positively toned emotional feeling (with 'change of sign') on to the outer world effects an economy in psychical expenditure in that the patient can employ the automatic defences of flight or fight against inner needs, the 'working through' of the emotionally toned ideas is accomplished more easily if the conscious-ego can co-operate in the process.

In *Hallucination* we are confronted with another mechanism for mastering stimuli. In one respect hallucination and projection have an element in common: something internal is not perceived as internal, but appears as external. But the mechanisms in the two cases are quite different. The one employed in paranoia serves to *defend the ego* against an internal instinctual impulse by *distortion* of the external world, whereas in hallucination the instinctual impulse finds *gratification* by an *addition* to the external world. Hallucination may be regarded as an hysterical mechanism because a certain amount of free-floating instinctual energy appears to be 'bound' in creating the hallucinatory image in much the same way that it is 'bound' in creating the paralyses, anaesthesias, etc., of hysterical conversion. In respect to the *mode of binding* psychical energy, then, it may be said that hallucination is an hysterical mechanism, but this does not explain the differences between it and the conversion symptoms of paralysis or spasticity, for instance. In both an affect-ladened idea is striving to find expression, in both the idea is unconscious, in both it is held in repression, in both the idea stirs up memory-traces attaching to it by association, but in hallucination they are turned back from the motor end of the psychical apparatus and stimulate the sensory end, i.e. the path of the excitation is backwards (regressive), in conversion, on the other hand, the motor end is stimulated, i.e. there is not a backward direction of the flow of energy in the reflex psychical system. Viewed as an adaptive response, hallucination is seen to be dealing with instinctual energy by a purely sensory means, in contrast to the purely psychical measures of projection. It is to be noted once more that in both projection and hallucination the emotionally toned ideas against which the patient seeks to protect himself are unconscious.

The concept of *Fixation* is not to be confused with that of mechanism, from which it may be distinguished by the following features: a fixation is an inhibition in the development of the libido, the mechanisms are concerned with changes in libidinal cathexis occurring at any given moment, i.e. they are not concerned with the fate of the libido as a whole but only with certain parts or quantities; a fixation determines the type of disorder, a mechanism explains how the changes in libido can bring about the change in clinical picture, i.e. the mechanism is a complicated hypothesis employed to explain the association of observed events which are otherwise inexplicable, a fixation is a phenomenon that is in the first remove from direct clinical observation.[1]

A fixation is an arrest in the development of the libido, it may occur at any point or there may be more than one. Representing the path of development by a line and the arrests by dots of

$$A \qquad B \qquad C \qquad D$$

varying size to show amounts of libido, we may depict full development as at *A*, where nearly all the libido has attained the goal of genital libido, *B*, where there is a considerable arrest at an early stage but some libido concentration at the genital stage, *C*, where there is a more scattered distribution, and *D*, where there is an almost complete arrest at an early stage. This crude diagrammatic representation only attempts to deal with the aims of the instinct, not the object.

There are three stages of object-libidinal relationship:

(1) auto-erotic, that is, objectless;

(2) narcissistic, in which the components of the instinct are unified but the instinct finds in the self its object and its source of gratification;

(3) allo-erotic, in which the libido is directed to objects other than the self; this is subdivisible into the homosexual stage, in which the external object is like the self (therefore not far removed from the narcissistic), and the hetero-sexual stage, which is the most complete form of allo-erotic object relationship.

Paranoia reveals a fixation as regards object-relationship somewhere between the narcissistic and homosexual, *dementia praecox*

---

[1] A mechanism is to be distinguished from a symptom; every symptom is produced by a combination of mechanisms.

at the auto-erotic stage of object-relation development. The mixed types, which are commonest, show fixation points between these two. In the case of *manic-depressive disease* the point of fixation for objects is not clearly established, it is probably at the narcissistic stage.

In respect to fixation on the changing path of sexual *aims* we find that the *manic-depressive* cases are clearly fixated at a sadistic stage [later to be defined as an oral-sadistic stage), *paranoiacs* at an anal, and the *precocious dements* at a pre-anal [later to be defined as oral] stage.

In regard to another feature of libido application, the *manic-depressives* show ambivalent love and hate reactions to a supreme degree while the *dementia praecox* withdraws his love from the outer world and places it upon himself, he has lost a capacity for transference to a greater or less degree. In *paranoia* there is usually a diminished capacity for positive transference but an increase of negative transference, i.e. the affect with which the patient meets the outer world is that of hate. *Dementia praecox* is pre-ambivalent, i.e. its fixation point is earlier than that at which ambivalence is manifest, *manic-depressive* disease is highly ambivalent, *paranoia* is a 'negative' (hate) disease.

So far *quantitative factors* have not been mentioned, these are of the greatest importance but very difficult to assess at all precisely. Thus in the case of dementia paranoides we find symptoms of paranoia on the one hand blending with dementia praecox symptoms on the other, and it seems as if this blending of symptoms reflects a fusion of impulses derived from two fixation points or that regression has proceeded to the two points of fixation in differing amounts. In practice no case is found that is a pure case of one or other, but in the intermediary or mixed cases we find apparently an inverse relationship between the two extreme types.

The quantitative factors cannot be neglected in the consideration of any psychical phenomenon. Thus in the case of an hallucination it is not the mere existence of an unconscious idea which gives rise to the reflex movement of excitations to the perceptory end of the psychical reflex system but the strength (i.e. the amount) of the libidinal charge or cathexis on the idea in question.

Repression is a method of dealing with mental stimuli (painful ideas) by thrusting them out of consciousness. The various disorders have each their own technique for doing this, in *hysteria* the idea is banished, in *obsessional neurosis* there is no amnesia but a detachment of affect from the idea so that the patient does not recognize the relevance of the pathological affect to the pathological idea. In *paranoia* the mechanism of projection is employed to avoid recognition of the painful idea, in *melancholia* the same process is at work that gives the special character to obsessional neurosis, which brings these two disorders close together in an aetiological system. A special feature of melancholic repression is found in the repression of the affect of hate, this results in depression, whereas the obsessional's detachment of affect results in doubt. In *dementia praecox* the same result is achieved by a withdrawal of libido from the outer world.

The return of the repressed is as important for a correct understanding and classification of the psycho-neuroses and psychoses as that of repression itself. In *anxiety hysteria* the libidinal excittation is attached not to the original object (the father, for instance) but to an associated object (an animal—hence, the animal phobias). In *toxic (confusional) states*, e.g. delirium tremens, the same mechanism is found, but the associated object is hallucinated (mice, rats, snakes, etc.).[1]

In *obsessional neuroses* the affects become attached to the associated ideas and require an endless effort of the peculiar obsessional repression. In *melancholia* there is a tendency to follow the path of displacement as in obsessional neurosis. In *dementia*

---

[1] A note on the hallucinations in delirium tremens: It is commonly said that as the patient deteriorates his hallucinatory objects grow smaller, they begin as bulls and elephants and end up as mice, snakes, and small crawling objects. The following suggestion is offered to explain this: in the first case the homosexual *object* is clearly a father-image; as regression proceeds the object decreases in importance, and the *phallic (later pre-phallic) aim* to an increasing extent determines the type of the visions, in other words, in the greater effort at repression required to keep the significance of the hallucinations from consciousness regression aids the work of repression. Sometimes these alcoholics, while manifesting the liveliest terror at their visions, cannot help expressing admiration for the beauty of the large creatures which they see; this feature I believe to be much rarer in the case of the small objects which are usually regarded with unmitigated horror and disgust; the deterioration is manifested not only in the regression of aim but also in the impoverishment of capacity to sublimate. [Cf. Rickman, 'Alcoholism and Psycho-Analysis', *Brit. Journ. of Inebriety*, Oct. 1925, **23**, No. 2.]

praecox the return of the repressed can occur by the hysterical pathway of hallucination, or as in the phobias or (in 'mixed' cases) as in obsessional neurosis.

Restitution symptoms. This concept is one of the few notions that is confined to psycho-analytical psychiatry; it denotes the process by which the patient who has withdrawn the cathexes from the external world shifts these cathexes from his ego to other pre-sentations again, i.e. to word-presentations or external object-presentations or even to his own organ-presentations. [The matter will be dealt with in a later section in more detail in relation to sublimation and to organ-speech, hypochondria (which, however, is not a restitution symptom) and narcissistic libido distribution.]

Miscellaneous. *Guilt* does not figure largely in the first period of analysis, its elucidation only came, or began to come, after the subdivision of the ego into super-ego and ego. *Secondary megalo-mania* is produced by the investment of the ego with cathexes withdrawn from external objects. This presupposes a primary megalomania in which the cathexis was originally wholly an ego-cathexis before its applicaion to external objects; the pre-supposition cannot be proved, but is certainly one of the most useful hypotheses which the psychiatrist utilizes since it affords a clue to the inverse relation of exaltation[1] to therapeutic accessibility: when the capacity for transference is greatest there is least exaltation and *vice versa*. The principal feature of the first period of psycho-analytical psychiatry is the establishment of the existence and the significance of transference, the principal feature of the second period is the existence and significance of narcissism.

[1] Note on exaltation: It must not be thought that the exaltation or megalomania here referred to is obtrusive, on the contrary, it may never be apparent without the aid of a delicate instrument to detect it. Such an instrument is found in the 'psycho-analytical situation'. This is in brief the affective relationship between analyst and analysand, and the analysis of this relationship affords the clearest insight into the types of and motives for affective relationships between individuals that clinical psychology has yet evolved. When, then, it is said that exaltation or megalomania is found in inverse proportion to therapeutic accessibility the less visible as well as the more obvious megalomania is referred to. [Later research showed that even the narcissistic disorders previously thought to be inaccessible to therapeutic influence could with care and in selected cases furnish therapeutic results.]

PART II

6. Narcissism[1]

In the detailed examination of the love-life, which was and to a great extent still is the main object of psycho-analytical study, one perversion among the numerous abnormalities observed stands out prominently by reason of its peculiarity—the patient is concerned only with himself, with his own beauty and charms. Rank[2] ascribed it to a special form of auto-erotism more commonly found among homosexuals, and thought it presented a stage in development prior to puberty when the sexual impulse was on its way from auto-erotism to object love. He also noted that it occurred in cases of disappointment in love (i.e. when frustrated by an external object, the love returned to the self) and that it subserved a 'rejuvenation tendency', or at least a wish always to stay at the same age. These superficial observations, however, did not affect analytical theory, for it was not until 1914 that Freud's 'On Narcissism: An Introduction' began the revolution in thought.

The attention of psycho-analysts was here turned to the phenomenon or phenomena of narcissism, not so much because of the perverse aspects of this disorder of love-life in overt form, but because in milder degree it appears so frequently in neurotics. In this connection it comes specially to prominence because it is a hindrance to progress in psycho-analytical work, that is in those cases where there is a preponderating amount of self-love or absorption in the self, it is observed that there is a diminished capacity for transference love to the physician. The theory that love can be shifted about from external objects to the ego and back again to objects had been put forward by Abraham in his papers on dementia praecox. If the charge of energy is directed to or upon the ego (the self) it is called ego-libido, if to objects in the outer world, object-libido; this does not imply a change in the essential character of the libido but

---

[1] Vide Bibliog. 4, 6, 7, 10, 13, 16, 21, 111, 115, 117, 119, 120, 142, 143, 151, 176, 200, 204, 226, 251, 293, 294, 295, 397, 400, 467, 481.

[2] The first psycho-analytical paper on this subject is by Rank, 'Ein Beitrag z. Narcissismus,' 1911, Jahrbuch, Bd. 3, 401. It is mentioned in the Schreber case, but not given special examination. The term was coined by Havelock Ellis, 1907. See Psychology of Sex, 1, p. 206, for cases illustrating this tendency, also Sadger, Jahrb. 6, 311.

only in its object. The reciprocity of ego- and object-libido is clearly seen not only in analysis but in the normal in cases of organic illness. In the condition of physical pain the patient relinquishes his interest in outside objects, his capacity for object-love diminishes and he becomes more selfish. Ferenczi[1] goes so far as to say that the flow of libidinal energy to the site of injury may play a regular part in the healing of organic wounds; by this he does not mean that the libidinal energy is a substance but a quantity of something in the psychical system which energizes the presentation of the bodily part, and that this produces physical effects useful in healing. It is, in Ferenczi's term,[2] if I understand him correctly, a genitalization of the wound, probably associated with an increased vascularization or tumescence and accompanied by peculiar sensations.

According to the theory of sexual development, at the final stage the libido is concentrated on the genital, which takes over the erotogenic functions of the other zones. Applying this notion to the case of organic illness we surmise that an explanation is now found for the 'desexualizing' influence of many bodily disorders, i.e. the libido has found a new distribution (within the self) and the sexual energy no longer clamours for genital expression (with an external object). It is no great step to include *hypochondria* in this scheme of libidinal distribution and to explain it as a concentration of the libido upon an internal organ, which thereupon becomes painful because of the impossibility or difficulty of erotic discharge (detumescence). If this be true we should find an inverse ratio between the liability to hypochondria and capacity for transference, i.e. we shall not find hypochondria prominently, if at all, in hysteria and obsessional neurosis (transference neuroses) but probably in prominence in dementia praecox, paranoia and manic-depressive disease, which are characterized by a diminished capacity for object-love.[3]

[1] 'Disease- or Patho-neuroses', translated in *Further Contributions to the Theory and Technique of Psycho-Analysis*, The Hogarth Press, London, and 'The Acceptance of Unpleasant Ideas', *idem*, p. 375.

[2] 'Disease- or Patho-neuroses', p. 85.

[3] This argument is worked out in detail in a paper by Ferenczi with the rather paradoxical title, 'The Psycho-Analysis of a Case of Hysterical Hypochondria,' *idem* chapter 10 and again in 'Disease- or Patho-neuroses'.

What is the relationship between the narcissism of sexual perversion on the one hand and the phenomena of hypochondria and the self-centredness of organic illness on the other? At the root of them all lies an erotic activity in relation to the self, to the patient's own body or mind or personality; but this erotic activity is not auto-erotic. The distinction at first appears to be a subtle one: in the earliest auto-erotic activities of childhood the zones of the body have an autonomous character, they have no sexual object, no abiding relation to any person, they are simply to be described as stimulation of erotogenic parts of the body, and the stimulation of one zone does not lead to stimulation of all. When unification of the sexual impulse occurs the infant takes its own body as the loved object; something has been added to auto-erotism to make narcissism, viz. unification of impulses and a love object. [It is possible that this unification is dependent on a certain degree of ego as distinct from libido development.]

The word 'love' is usually taken to imply a certain relationship to another person, though the use of the term self-love is a warning against a too narrow interpretation. In ordinary usage this self-love is generally assumed to be of a non-sensual character, a 'Platonic' attitude to self in which, in the Freudian terminology, only aim-inhibited impulses are experienced. The manifestations of auto-erotism have not escaped general observation but these have not been worked into the fabric of the individual love-life, in the first place because they have been (unwarrantably) assumed to be a phenomenon of adolescence and later life, and secondly, because they have been classed too much as wicked physical acts. Indeed the popular conception has erred—as it seems to the Freudian—in classing the phenomena of 'self-gratification' as physical, as reflex acts with no psychic participation, and those of self-love as psychical, ignoring the accompanying erotic element. In the perversion the erotic element in self-love is obvious for two reasons, first, there are physical manifestations of sexual activity, secondly, this form of gratification appears to take the place of erotic object-love. In normal persons there is often found not indeed this substitution of self-love for object-love but a mixture of the two; this is manifested in the choice of object taken as a lover.[1]

[1] A person may make a choice of love object:

To explain the psycho-analytical theory of narcissism it will be necessary to go into more detail than a survey would seem to warrant, but the importance of the hypothesis demands a full summary. The following account is a compilation from the literature, not taken from any one paper, but is a combination of many, but the writer believes it to represent a correct and coherent summary of widely held views.

The development of the adult libidinal organization can be traced far back by observation, though not quite to its beginnings; hypotheses are needed to bridge some gaps in the early stages. In making these there is no pretence that they are based on observation, they are assumptions made for the purpose of establishing certain starting points, and they will for brevity be put as dogmatic statements. In the womb the child has no object relationships, its ego-needs are provided, nourishment, warmth and an absence or minimum of stimulation, in a word, there is little for the psychical apparatus to do, for this apparatus only acts when stimulated. Libidinal impulses may exist, if they do, the probable outlet for discharge is by general muscular movements (the late Dr. Hug-Hellmuth, verbal communication). After birth there are definite and strong ego-needs, those of self-preservation. The assumption is that there is libidinal pleasure attaching to the act of self-preservation (sucking), and that this fusion of instincts is made possible by an erotogenic property of the mouth zone. The erotic property of any of the zones is comparable to an itching (a phenomenon of which practically nothing is known), and as with any other itch

(I) *According to the narcissistic type:*
    (a) What he is himself (actually himself) [e.g. a person of the same sex, occupation, race, etc.].
    (b) What he once was [e.g. a child, youth, an 'innocent', etc.].
    (c) What he would like to be [i.e. an ideal of himself, a leader hero, a person specially endowed with some outstanding attribute of strength, intellect, virtue, etc.].
    (d) Someone who was once part of himself [e.g. a child of his body—especially strong in the case of women].

(II) *According to the anaclitic type:*
    (a) The woman who tends [e.g. mothers, nurses, etc.].
    (b) The man who protects [e.g. father substitutes, princes, soldiers, etc.].

Table from Freud's 'On Narcissism: An Introduction', *Collected Papers*, 4, The Hogarth Press, London, p. 47. Notes in square brackets are added by the present writer.

appropriate stimulation relieves the 'tension'. Whether the 'itching' is a state of tumescence, or a state of excitability in the nerve endings, or something else, is not known, and for the present purpose is immaterial, but it is (*a*) localized, (*b*) periodical, (*c*) relieved by stimulation of an appropriate kind. The assumption is made that the persistence of the recurring excitability is due to the erotic part of instinctual life, i.e. it is a component of the sex-instinct, in this case centred in the mouth. In this way sucking may be regarded as a sexual activity but there is not at first a sexual partner, or rather the other person (mother, nurse) is not perceived as an object of erotic desire.[1] The sucking relieves the local erotic excitability without an accompanying love relation to the outer world, it is auto-erotic. But this is only for the first days or weeks of life. The stages to object-relationship are imagined to be as follows: At first the nipple is not conceived by the baby as an external object but as a part of the self;[2] when the itch-sensation or whatever it is occurs, it is relieved by stimulation from a solid object, the tongue, the thumb or the nipple, the last alone having the power to eliminate at the same time the craving of hunger which belongs to the self-preservative instincts. Smelling is probably at an early date related to the activity at the nipple, this is the prototype of all intellectual activity (Ferenczi)—in that an early discernment is made through it of what *will* be satisfying— nipple distinguished from 'comforter', etc. Visual perceptions play a part, too, but less than smell at first, perhaps because babies are often fed in the half dark and are usually muffled up. Thus there are three groups of sensory stimuli, buccal-tactile and taste, visual, and olfactory, associated with the presentations from the outer world, and two groups of presentations from within, the instinctual 'needs' of self-preservation and those of the libido. Just as the baby does not at first distinguish the nipple from itself, so it is quite possible it does not recognize

[1] The nipple is the nearest conceivable thing to an *object* to a child in the first days of life, its smell and tactile qualities doubtless exert an 'attraction' but for reasons to be given later it is not an external object in the psycho-analytical meaning of the term.

[2] Urine is an object external to the body to a physiologist but is consciously regarded by many adults as an internal object, part of themselves, till voided—it is necessary to gain, or regain, a *psychological* view of the elementary bodily processes in order to follow these theories.

12

the discomfort of hunger as belonging to itself. It builds up an elementary system of thought processes on the pattern of Pleasurable-Not-Pleasurable, and associates the pleasurable with those parts of itself which furnish the pleasure. It is possible on this line of argument that a sucked thumb may be at one time regarded as part of the Pleasure-Self series, when it temporarily satisfies libido, and at another time as part of the Not-pleasurable (not-self) series, when it fails to satisfy the hunger. This is, of course, a concept of the self as a body-self, a bodily attribute, not the socialized self-conscious part of the self which later comes into great prominence.

Other zones than the mouth are endowed with this kind of erotism, in each case the problem of the relation of zone to stimulating object is a special one; e.g. the anal zone (which includes the lower part of the rectum) is stimulated by the faeces, to which it reacts by peristaltic movements reflexly, the genitals are stimulated by friction in washing, etc. at an early date, later by friction of the hand. These zones are 'charged' or cathected with libido, and the 'itching' so produced leads to the organism's orienting itself to the outer world, in order, so to speak, that it may be scratched. Now one part of the body, now another, lays claim to the pathways of motility for this purpose; but the zones though autonomous have some intercommunication, i.e. the stimulation of one excites the erogenicity of the others.[1] The presentation of the self is distinguished from that of an outer object by three features, first, its continuity, second, the confluence of pleasurable experiences in different parts, and lastly, a certain *immediacy* in pleasurable experiences. The outer world includes what is the contrary of these, namely, what is impermanent, lacking in confluence of pleasurable experience, and immediate only in relation to painful experience (what is not pleasurable, is not a Me-part of experience).

While this process is going on in regard to immediate personal experiences the ego activities of self-preservation are testing the outer world in their fashion, sorting out the visual, auditory, olfactory, tactile memory images into those combinations which recur with pleasurable results and those which do not. Thus on both sides, the bodily or erotic and let us say the intellectual, the

[1] 'After being at the breast the infant generally empties its bladder: there are therefore connections.' Staercke, *Int. Journ. of Ps.-A.*, 2, p. 190.

inner and outer world is being tested by the touchstone of pleasure; just as the erotic impulses 'leaned on' the egoistic (the self-preservative) in the first place, so the egoistic were stimulated particularly by the erotic in the early days. What was pleasurable physically was memorable—a state of affairs from which no one entirely escapes. These two things have to be brought together and compared, first, the peculiar way in which erotic excitations pass or overflow from one zone to another, thus linking up the presentations of bodily erotism in different parts of the body by temporal association, and second, the character of the intellectual activity that combines presentations according to features which persist in spite of superficial complexities, e.g. the power of *recognizing* the whole from a part or number of parts. The former is a contribution from psychoanalysis, the latter is not in the field of psycho-analysis at all but of general psychology. So it comes about that there are in the early days of mental life two *Weltanschauungen*, a libidinal one almost wholly controlled by the pleasure-principle, and an egoistic one guided to some extent by pleasure yet also responsive to the dictates of the unchanging outer world. In the former case the criterion is that the object shall be a source of pleasure (in which case it is included in the category of pleasure objects and is introjected, forming a part of the Pleasure-ego), in the latter case that it shall have a constant set of features; in the former the pleasure-objects (owing to the overflow of excitations above mentioned) become more and more closely associated with the body as a whole.

Taking the former feature as a starting point of further speculation, it is apparent that the increasing experience of confluence of erotic excitation from the zones together with an increasing experience of the body from tactile stimulation must engender a conception of the bodily ego as a unified organism of firmer structure than presentations from the outer world, but the boundaries of this bodily ego are not necessarily the same as those drawn by the adult. Mention has already been made of the inclusion of the nipple in the self, but it was not made clear how the separation of nipple from the self could occur conceptually. It comes about through frustration and loss. If the nipple was always at hand to relieve hunger and still the erotic itch of the mouth, it would never be perceived as external, but it is an organ which is withdrawn and which finally is not provided at all. It does not obey the child's wish and appear when wanted, nor give all he asks. An association is formed between pleasure and frustration: what gives pleasure now cannot be relied on to give pleasure indefinitely, a deprivation follows pleasure. This association is of the greatest importance for the development of the mind, first, because it forces the boundaries of the self to be drawn on a reality-basis and not on a pleasure-basis, second, it causes the refractory object to become the centre of mental activity (testing and distinguishing the real from the phantasied), third, it may be a factor in producing a shifting of the chief seat of libidinal cathexis to another eroto-genic zone and thus giving a new (and so more varied) orien-tation of the ego to the outer world.[1]

So much for the mouth at the moment. The next zone of importance is the anus whose erotogenicity follows in time and often even exceeds it in importance. In certain aspects of their relationships the stool is to the anus what the nipple is to the mouth: (a) the nipple and stool represent solid stimulating bodies; (b) the child in each case changes its mode of behaviour, from a passive phase in which it experiences sensations and then leaves the rest to reflex action, sucking rhythm in the one case and defaecation in the other, to a later active phase of pre-dominantly muscular action, biting and anal-retention respec-tively; (c) in both cases the stimulating object (nipple, stool) is at first (and all the time in the unconscious) felt to be a part of the self. Now let us turn to the aspects wherein the anal and the mouth zone differ in the activities and object relationships; (i) in the mouth activity the mother or nurse is predominantly pas-sive, in the anal the child is coaxed and persuaded or even 'forced' to take the active rôle (to defaecate) and is rewarded with praise and love when it is obedient, i.e. the mother or nurse is definitely active; (ii) the child, being older when the education of the anal sphincter occurs, has already a more consolidated notion of the mother (nurse)- presentation than in the oral stage and has passed on to her part of the libidinal cathexis formerly

---

[1] Libidinal deprivation may explain the shifting of cathexis to a part of the psychical apparatus which hardly warrants the name 'zone' but which may by analogy be called one, viz. *the central nervous system as it is conceived by the unconscious*. The logical conclusion of this bold hypothesis is the concept of a polarity of narcissistic interest in the genital and the brain (intellect), with a reciprocity in the amounts of cathexis.

belonging to that part which had been once felt to be common to both, the nipple; (iii) more than in the mouth stage the anal stage is characterized by hate, for the child is forced to abandon a physical pleasure and to renounce the gratification at some stage of its crescendo, it has also to tolerate an interference with an activity that is to a high degree narcissistic; (iv) a conflict arises at the anal stage perhaps more sharply than at the oral between two different kinds of object relationships—love for a *part* of the self (faeces) and love or hostility for another person.[1]

This changing attitude to the outer world is a counterpart to a change in the ego, namely, an 'incorporating' stage in psychic activity, a phase of intense introjection, and later in the anal stage an ejecting (rejecting, hostile) phase, followed by a phase of retention and mastery of internal objects (faeces) and of external objects (toys, etc.). The last phase of infantile development (the phallic) occurs when the penis (clitoris) is the seat of the highest physical pleasure. By this time the child is able to comprehend the persons in the outer world as unified objects, having individual shape and emotional continuity and consistence to a far greater extent than in the previous stages. When the child now feels in an erotic mood in regard to a particular person it experiences a phallic (i.e. penis or clitoris) stimulation and may have an erection of the part, whereas in an earlier stage it would find physical outlet for intense erotic emotion by urination, defaecation or vomiting, i.e. the physical accompaniment of orgasm is at the earlier stages not ejection of sexual substance on crisis followed by detumescence, but ejection of the contents of the alimentary viscera. In earlier stages the important persons in the outer world were associated with the functions of mouth or anus, they now are related to the child's genital, the erotic contact with external objects is through the genital zone, which has absorbed to itself the 'object capacity of the other zones and by the unification has provided a more perfect instrument of erotic gratification, not least because *in exercising the erotic function the other organs are left to perform their physiological function undisturbed*' (Ferenczi).

[1] It is doubtful whether at this age, say about 9 months, the child attributes to the mother that unity of presentations which later experience affords. It is certain the small suckling does not; to him the mother is the background of a nipple and a mobile adjunct of a chamber-pot. The outlook on the world is dominated by physical needs.

The absorption of erogenicity into the genital and devolution of the same from the other organs gives the penis (clitoris) a special position in the bodily economy. By its erotic communication with other parts and its capacity for discharge of libidinal excitations it becomes identified with the body as a whole. The separation of the functions of pleasure and utility into the departments of genital and soma affords a new possibility for libidinal object relationships: the penis (or clitoris) may absorb all object cathexis or it may serve as the conduit of all object cathexes and thus perform an erotic service to the body by ridding it of libidinal tension. Whether by any of these means, or by a combination of them, or by some other process, the genitals acquire a power in the unconscious to represent the body as a whole, to represent the ego. An example of this is found in the unconscious attitude to death, which, to the unconscious part of the mind, is inconceivable in regard to one's own person; the nearest approach to it is the thought of castration. Castration, of all injuries and threats, exerts the profoundest effect on the mind, for in this loss there is an injury both to the egoistic and to the libidinal aspects of existence, the latter directly, the former by the identifications just mentioned between the body as a whole and the genital. But it should not be thought that the phenomenon of a devastating loss such as castration can occur only in connection with the genitals; a phenomenon of essentially similar nature can occur earlier in connection with the loss of the nipple and of the faeces. The castration element enters into these losses because the nipple and faeces are regarded as a part of the self, so that a part of the self is being removed when these are taken away,[1] they are valued (loved) because they are felt to be a part of the self. Such non-genital 'castrations' have been given various names, 'precastration narcissistic wounds or deprivations' is, though cumbersome, perhaps the best. The introduction of the word narcissistic is a reminder that no external object relationship is implied. The liability to strong castration-reactions does not occur at one sharply defined time but is an epoch in the development of the ego and the libido in which ego-instincts are united with sexual instincts to make *narcissistic* instincts. The normal individual outgrows the liability to castration shocks to a greater or less extent, the psychotic does not.

[1] And what is more they are taken away at the very moment when they are affording great erotic gratification.

Returning to Narcissism, let us discuss the course given to psychical development of the ego-libido, which, let me repeat, is libido attached to the ego, not arising from it. The first libidinal cathexes are directed to the ego, which as we have seen is not sharply limited to the bodily ego but includes other objects; later the libido is attached to two kinds of objects, the self and external objects, and becomes narcissistic libido and object libido respectively. The distinction, however, in this case as in the former one, must not be too sharply drawn on physical lines, because some persons are not loved *for their own sakes* so much as for their *likeness to the self.* At the stage when all or practically all libidinal cathexis is upon the self it is assumed that there is a concomitant over-estimation of the self. Put in other terms, we value what we love and we love what affords gratification, so when the self affords inordinate gratification it is inordinately loved. A child cannot go far along the path of life without finding that the gratification of its instincts and wishes leads to a conflict with its parents. It is assumed that the relinquishing of one type of gratification is not absolute and unconditioned but that there are compensations by a change in the type of gratification, or rather by a change in the 'organ-gratification' used in the widest sense. Just as the libidinal gratification of the mouth zone was not extinguished but transferred to a great extent to another zone, so in this case the organ-gratification is not entirely renounced under pressure of nursery education and nursery morality but transferred to the newly functioning unit —the self. There are two possible modes of gratification, the primitive way by direct organ-pleasure or the more indirect one by so comporting the body as a whole that it shall not come into conflict with the outer world (parents). The child forms an *ideal* of its behaviour from the parental injunctions and feels a psychical harmony and peace if it lives according to that ideal, and the gratification of this ideal absorbs the gratifications of the organ zones. The analogy of the genital zone's absorption of the other organ erotisms may be pointed out. This explains, in part at any rate, the development of the ego-ideal from the narcissistic libido and furnishes a clue to the infatuation with their own ideals which many persons demonstrate, i.e. the transference to *their* own *ego-ideal* of the primitive *over-estimation of the self*, unwilling to forego entirely the thought of the self being perfect, this perfection is attributed to the ideal which is retained as a part of the self and is seldom or never critized!

On an earlier page the theory was put forward that at one stage of development what was pleasant was part of the Me-world and what was unpleasant was part of the Not-Me-world; it may therefore seem to be puzzling that a child should accept so unpleasant a thing as a criticizing person into his psychical system at all. The solution of this problem is not difficult; it lies in the fact that the child has in the meantime developed an affection for its parents—the libidinal ties have been formed where the ego-needs (protection, nourishment, etc.) were strongest, so it comes about that it is primarily love for the parents and their surrogates which makes it well nigh impossible for the child to neglect their injunctions and it is at bottom the force of love which causes it to renounce its sensual pleasures—love and the *fear* of losing the protecting loved one. The nucleus of the ego-ideal is laid down by the influence of the parents upon the developing ego of the child but the process of ego-ideal formation does not stop with them but is carried on by parent substitutes, by school teachers, superiors in business relationships, civic affairs, and so on; the setting up of the ego-ideal is essentially a product of the parent-child relationship, whatever its later developments.

Putting these concepts into more technical terms, the parent is *introjected* into the ego for the particular purpose of restraining the instinctual impulses, the voice of the parents, which is of course external, becomes established as an internal admonishing influence, the vigilance which was once external is now internal. This helps to explain puzzling phenomena in the psychoses, viz. the delusion of being watched, the hearing of admonishing voices and the incessant criticism which some complain of. We can be reasonably certain, though our patients are not, that their self-reproaches for frightful crimes are in fact misplaced, as adults they have done no heinous wrong, but their ego-ideal (introjected parents) behaves relentlessly to the ego with the tyranny of a harsh parent, and the weak ego submits. Under internal duress the patient announces that he has done wrong, but cannot produce the necessary evidence; sometimes he trumps up trivial charges against himself but these are secondary not primary in importance, they are 'rationalizations' employed to fill a logical gap in consciousness.

It is always important when considering the application of the libido theory to psychical development or to psycho-pathology to consider it in regard to its distribution, for instance, in a perversion, a neurosis or an everyday action, to ask what amount of libido is gratified along primitive auto-erotic channels, what amount is devoted to object-relationships and what is absorbed and re-utilized in the form of ego-libido. The question should be asked even if it cannot be completely answered.

In the case of the ego-ideal we are confronted with exceptional difficulties, which are discussed at length in Jones's *The Origin and Structure of the Super-Ego*, but it may be said with a measure of confidence that the ego-ideal is a modification of a part of the ego or a modification of an ego function in which the individual can retain his self-love and at the same time keep the affection of his parents, the libido utilized in the ego-ideal activity is thus a combination of narcissistic-libido and object-libido (the latter being modified).

In briefest outline of the foregoing paragraphs we must distinguish two concepts, primary and secondary narcissism. The former is regarded as the state of complete self-satisfaction which does only and can only exist in the undisturbed intra-uterine state and after birth in dreamless sleep, which may be defined as a state in which there are no object-cathexes; the latter is again a term referring to distribution of libidinal cathexis and may be defined as a state in which object-cathexis is limited by a condition, namely, that the object cathected shall be the self; it belongs therefore to the stage of objectless libidinal distribution in respect to the absence of an external object but to the stage of object-libidinal distribution in that there is unity of *aim* of component impulses, and because the object (the self) has the capacity of absorbing libidinal cathexes in very varying amounts from the least to the greatest without making an alteration of the type of relationship. The ego-ideal is a device, so to speak, for maintaining narcissism which is in essentials inflexible in the face of a changing external environment that calls for modification of libidinal attachments, it is an adaptation of self-love to enable the self-lover to modify himself to his surroundings, it is a 'technique' for preserving a primitive impulse without the individual losing his capacity for survival; finally, it reveals the amazing capacity of the psychical apparatus to utilise as instruments of culture outgrown or primitive impulses which at first sight might be thought to be detrimental to developmental progress.

7. Modification of the Feeling of Omnipotence [1]

It is breaking the chronological order of the publications to leave this subject to Part II for discussion, for the first adumbrations appeared as early as 1900 in Freud's *Interpretation of Dreams*, and it was clearly set out by Ferenczi [2] in 1913. But these topics do not sift themselves out neatly and they must be ordered according to some plan, disturbing the chronological arrangement as little as possible.

'By means of a kind of empathy into the infantile mind,' Ferenczi arrived at the hypothesis that a child kept from pain would regard existence as a unity, the discrimination between 'good' and 'bad' coming only with the advent of pain. The mental state would be that of *unconditioned omnipotence*, and when pain and disappointments arrived the sense of omnipotence would be given up only by slow degrees. Defining omnipotence as the feeling that one has all that one wants and has nothing left to wish for, Ferenczi argues that the child in the foetal state has less to wish to change in its environment than any creature imaginable, and if we are justified in attributing to the foetus any mental processes at all we could in its case hardly call megalomania a delusion. Birth is a violent disturbance of this state of bliss, it interrupts physical composure and throws suddenly upon the baby a number of drastic physical needs which cannot but stir up its mental processes. A thoughtful nurse endeavours to give it as much of its earlier peace as possible, keeps it warm, softens the force of sound and light stimuli, puts it from time to time in a warm bath [3] and gives it regular food. The unconditioned omnipotence is broken into by wants. It is assumed that the first attempt at 'satisfying' these wants is by hallucination, i.e. the wish is represented as fulfilled—thus in this second

[1] *Vide* Bibliog. 111, 115, 135, 137, 139, 163, 166, 172, 302, 367.

[2] *Stages in the Development of a Sense of Reality.*

[3] Perhaps the warm bath treatment of manic crises may derive some of its effect from this re-establishment of the infantile and indeed pre-natal state. Stoddart [469] suggested that the reason the maniacal patients undress is because they feel their clothes an intolerable burden owing to a sensitive skin. I can see another reason—infantile exhibitionism—for their doing this, but if the maniac's skin is so sensitive the warm bath would be doubly soothing.

stage the only condition required for the fulfilment of wishes is to depict them as fulfilled; but this is unsatisfactory, the wants persist, the child cries. If when this happens the nurse arrives and supplies its needs (food, rearrangement of clothes or what not) it can but imagine that the cry or the gesture has produced the effect. This third is the stage of *magical gesture* by which the feeling of omnipotence is restored.

These three stages are represented in psycho-pathology: the first is the extreme withdrawal from all outer reality which is presumed to occur in some dementia praecox patients in the waking state, and in all of us when in dreamless sleep, the second is the state of dreaming, the third is the magical gestures, the 'power-movements' of the praecox patient, possibly of the ticqueur and of the obsessional who performs gestures and grimaces when doing such things as cursing, blessing, praying, etc. With the increase in the complexity of the wants there goes a necessary increase in the complexity of the *condition*, but the latter never 'catches up', an increasing number of wants always go unfulfilled. The early stage, during which all pleasant experiences are incorporated in the ego, Ferenczi calls the *Introjection Phase*; later, when the child recognizes that there are things which do not obey his will and that thoughts alone will not change the outer world, comes the *Projection Phase*; the latter is of course nearer to a perception of objective reality. The earlier phase is the prototype of *animism*, the perception in the outer world of the image of his own corporeality is the prototype of *symbolism*, the stage in which there is submission to the outer world is the *scientific* stage.

Speech gives the effect of exercising a greater influence on the outer world of persons and the conditioning of omnipotence by speech corresponds to the period in infancy of magical thoughts and magical words. This is found in clearest fashion in obsessional neurotics and also in the melancholic in remissions, and in the paraphrenics. Magical words appear in almost all mystical cults and lie at the bottom of belief in certain prayers and curses.

In science the omnipotence is dissolved into mere 'conditions', determinism rules, and the illusion of omnipotence is completely relinquished—or should be.

Thus far the egoistic impulses alone have been considered, but the feeling of omnipotence is experienced in the sexual sphere also. The analogies are close. The giving up of autoerotic activities that are objectless for a dependence on an object for satisfaction is a parallel development to that of the ego in its relation to the external world. Narcissism belongs to the auto-erotic-omnipotent stage, object-love is the counterpart to conditionalism.

8. *Developmental Stages of the Libido* [1]

The discussion of Narcissism has already made a serious inroad on this topic, it is now only necessary to bring out certain points more fully. As in the previous paragraphs the treatment will be explanatory rather than in the nature of a précis.

The first application to clinical conditions of the concept of *stages* in libidinal development is in Freud's paper in 1908 on Character and Anal Erotism. He found certain types of behaviour (ego activities) were to be associated with erotic gratification at zones of the body other than the genital, and these behaviour groupings can be more or less sharply separated from one another. These characteristics could be traced throughout the patient's life and the attitude to objects was found to be essentially the same as that to the proper stimulant to the zone in question. The matter might be put figuratively by saying that the individual orients himself to the world so that it shall give him gratification at the presenting zone in different ways at different times, according to the zone presented. First he presents his mouth to the world, later the anus, and by this is meant not that he turns his body about but that he turns his attention to the stimuli streaming in now from one, now from another zone. This turning of the attention is an ego function but guided by the libido, a psychical function that is possibly controlled by a physical factor. The persistence of one of these ego-orientations constitutes the ego-part of a fixation at the stage of libidinal development in question, or rather the tendency to persistence constitutes the fixation. It is found that a fixation does not prohibit development beyond its particular stage but that such

[1] Based primarily on Abraham's 'Versuch einer Entwicklungsgeschichte der Libido auf Grund der Psychoanalyse seelischer Störungen' (1), and abstracted with great lucidity by the late Dr. James Glover in the *British Journal of Medical Psychology*, 4, p. 326. Reference may also be made to 'Researches into the earliest pre-genital stage of development'. *Vide* Bibliog. 3, 4, 6, 9, 13, 14, 16, 212, 221, 223, 229, 247, 248, 252.

further development is unstable and on its being upset the relatively more stable condition at the fixation point gives the specific character to the behaviour. In a word, there is always a tendency to regress to the more stable from the unstable.

This much relates to the *aim* of the libidinal impulse, now a word about the *object*. A peculiarity of libidinal impulses is the capacity to change the object without altering the aim. An example at the anal stage will serve to illustrate this. There is one series of object-modifications relating to money[1] in which the child's desire to play with its dejecta is modified by substitution to an interest in games with mud and plasticine, then with sand (dehydration, deodorization, due to reaction-formation against the erotic enjoyment of moisture and smell), then with marbles, stones, later with coins and negotiable securities. The criterion observed by the ego in these cases appears to be an identity in particular qualities of the object, consistence, colour, etc., these qualities being taken *one or only a few at a time, the object is not treated as a whole nor in relation to its own environment*—not till the genital stage is reached.[2] This by way of preliminary to a consideration of the various modes of behaviour to objects in the different stages of development.

Abraham divides each of the three stages already considered (oral, anal and genital) into I an early, and II a late oral, III early, and IV late anal, V a phallic, and VI a genital. Oral and anal erotism display two opposed tendencies, 'positive' and 'negative'. In the 'positive' oral stage the tendency is for the object to be swallowed, to be retained, in the 'negative' stage the child wishes to disturb the object, to do something to it, by biting it destroys the object. In the 'negative' anal stage it desires to expel the object, to reject; in the 'positive' to do something to it, to master it, to exercise control. The 'positive' stages are seen in I and IV, the 'negative' in II and III. There is thus

[1] See in this connection Ferenczi, *The Ontogenesis of the Interest in Money*.

[2] It may be urged that there is no likeness in consistence between mud and negotiable securities. This is undeniable, but there is here a change in form and consistence by gradual replacement, the consistence being carried over from faeces to mud and plasticine, the odourlessness from the latter through stones to coins, etc., one particular quality serves for a time and gives place to another without an *integration* of the qualities. The *aim* does not change, it is in this case to possess, to manipulate, to store or hoard.

a period in which the child's attitude to objects is primarily 'negative', destructive, rejecting, interposed between an object-less stage which has elements of a 'positive' attitude in it, and the final stages (V and VI) when the attitude is increasingly and finally exclusively 'positive'.

One of the chief features of Abraham's paper is the inclusion of a new stage in the development of object-relationships. Before only the autoerotic, narcissistic and alloerotic had been discussed. He included between the last two a stage of part-love, i.e. the libidinal attachment was not to all the presentations of the object but only to one or a few of them. This theory had been forced on him from studies of hysteria, kleptomania, fetichism, paranoia and manic-depressive disease.

9. *Melancholia* [1]

(a) The relation of Grief to Melancholy
(b) The relation of Obsessional Neurosis to Melancholia
(c) The Narcissism of the Melancholic
(d) Melancholia and Mania
(e) The rôle of oral Libido in the Melancholic
(f) Efforts at Self-Cure
(g) The end of the attack

(a) *The relation of Grief to Melancholy. Grief* is a mental consequence of the loss of a loved object. This is usually a person but may be something inanimate such as a house or a mother-country or something abstract such as an ideal. The object lost is present to consciousness and the conscious orientation to the object is never abandoned, however deep the grief, furthermore there is no ambivalence, there are no self-reproaches, but only repining. The 'process' or 'mechanism' of grief lasts a variable but restricted time during which there is a greater or less degree of painful dejection, loss of interest in the outer world, a temporary loss of capacity to love and a variable amount of inhibition of life's activities.

Melancholia has some points of resemblance to grief but what are of special interest are the differences: the loss is not necessarily a 'real' loss, i.e. not a death or separation or loss of liberty or the like, the object lost is not present in consciousness, the 'process' is not necessarily temporary, there is a high degree of ambivalence, and, most important of all, in melancholia but not in grief there is a severe depreciation of the self-feelings.

[1] *Vide* Bibliog. 6, 10, 17, 190, 210, 303, 305, 348, 412, 413.

Persons suffering from grief do not revile themselves or entertain delusions of wickedness or of punishment, their world may for a time be empty but they do not feel that they have lost the capacity to love, and indeed they show that they still have this capacity by a returning interest in the world and a renewed bestowal of their love—on a new object. Once again we ask the question, where are the amounts of libido distributed when there is a loss of object cathexis? The psycho-analyst finds the differences between the distribution in grief and in melancholia to be the following: in grief the memories of the object are dealt with bit by bit, the libido after a painful struggle is detached,[1] temporarily shifts on to the ego and then returns to the outer world; in melancholia the libido is shifted to the ego but does not return to objects in the outer world. The increased cathexis of the ego thus brought about explains two features never absent[2] in melancholia—the megalomania, though this does not usually rise to the grandiloquent heights of that of the precocious dement, and the hypochondria. It also explains, or in part explains, the narcissistic element that is always present.

The person suffering from grief is not afflicted with self-reproaches, and though there is a temporary increase in libidinal cathexis of the ego there is no illness. In melancholia on the other hand the ego appears to have fallen into two pieces, one raging against the other. A close examination of the reproaches shows that they are not primarily directed against the self but against some other person and become only secondarily directed against the self through identification with the person reproached. Abraham makes a distinction between the cases in which the introjected love-object plays the part of the conscience (ego-ideal) and does the attacking and uttering the reproaches, and the cases where the patient's 'own' ego-ideal so to speak reproaches and criticizes the introjected person.

[1] In grief there is no disturbance of the relation of the ego to the outer world, therefore there is the pressingly real absence of the loved object to compel the detachment, the process takes times but is accomplished; in melancholia the ego-outer world relations are disturbed, the process may go on indefinitely.

[2] 'Never absent' is a strong phrase that may of course have to be withdrawn later; however, in criticizing it is not sufficient that these characteristics are not observable in an ordinary clinical interview, they may only appear when examination is made by a special diagnostic 'instrument'—the analytical situation.

It may be thought a contradiction in terms to assert that reproaches are heaped on a loved object (whether that object be introjected or not is immaterial for the moment) and it may be asked how it can come about that a loved object can be treated in that way. At the genital stage of development it is not possible but it is in the very essence of behaviour at the *anal sadistic* level.

(b) *The relation of Obsessional Neurosis to Melancholia*. In the preceding section of this paper the stages of development of the libido with the corresponding object relationships were discussed. Let us now apply this clinically. Anal erotism and sadism each have a positive and a negative tendency, to retain or to expel in the case of anal erotism, to master or to destroy in the case of sadism. One of the distinctions between the two diseases, obsessional neurosis and melancholia, in respect to instinct impulse, is to be found in the fact that in obsessional neurosis the object is retained (object cathexes are not relinquished) whereas in melancholia the object cathexes are 'given up' and there is a tendency for the object to be expelled from the libidinal system. Put in another way, the fixation point of obsessional neurosis lies in the late anal, of melancholia in the early anal or late oral stage. The dividing line between these two groups of stages, though sometimes difficult to draw in individual cases, is of the greatest importance theoretically and therapeutically, for the prognosis depends to a great measure on the amount of the libido which is represented in the fixation on one or other side of that line; it is important theoretically because it may later prove that the dividing line involves not only libidinal but concomitant ego changes of the greatest moment in the development of the individual.

This comparison between melancholia and obsessional neurosis throws light on several psychiatric problems of importance. A diagnostic doubt is liable to arise at a consultation when a severe obsessional first presents himself for an opinion and advice. The history is liable to be misleading because of the fluctuations in severity which frequently are a marked feature of the disease; furthermore, self-reproaches are met with in obsessionals, and obsessional ceremonials in melancholics. The difficulty can be overcome by undertaking not a therapeutic but diagnostic analysis which affords an insight into the capacity for transference; this, as has been said, is retained in obsessional neurosis but greatly diminished or absent in melancholia. The analysis shows in addition in particularly clear fashion the presence of hypochondriacal symptoms and usually these can be distinguished from hysterical manifestations without difficulty in analysis, true hypochondria being rare in obsessional neurosis. Most important of all, the analysis distinguishes the *self-punishing* tendency of the obsessional from the sadism directed against the introjected *object* in the melancholic.

Another problem of psychiatry is made clearer by the theoretical and descriptive comparison of the two diseases, namely, the mental condition of the melancholic during his remission. He is not really perfectly healthy but suffers from a condition which, if it is not obsessional neurosis itself, closely resembles it on superficial view, namely, the obsessional character. Put in another way, during the improvement in the melancholic his libidinal orientation undergoes an advance as regards aim from the oral stage through the late (positive) anal to the phallic; as regards his attitude to objects he loses most of his negatively toned ambivalence and can maintain a fairly satisfactory positive application of libido.

(c) *The Narcissism of the Melancholic.* A feature of melancholia which at once strikes a student who is familiar with psychoanalysis is the enormous rôle that narcissism plays in the disease. The self-love and self-centredness may take the common form of egotism and so be apparent, but it may also be disguised so that it needs special study to detect it. Thus one patient devoted nearly half an analytical hour to a description and discussion of a hair-cut. This on ordinary reckoning would be accounted simple egotism, but it was in fact particularly complicated. He had spent on that hair-cut nearly five times his usual sum. He justified it on the ground that he needed to bring himself up to his real standard. The barber looked foreign, he tried a little excellent French, to which the man modestly replied in the broken pronunciation of the English Tommy who had been in France. But he thought that by his fluency he would raise himself in the barber's eyes, and that one of the merits of education was that one could utilize occasions such as this. And the barber seemed to respect the shape of his head. He also broke out into a tirade at the amount of the bill which he had a few moments before considered not excessive for a man of his 'position'. It was an outrage, he couldn't afford it, his dependents would have to go without necessary things. Self-reproach now became apparent.

He was destroying them, it was necessary to have such things but his dependents were being undone by his needs, which of course had to come first. He was selfish, in fact the most selfish person in the world, but he couldn't help it. With the smell of the barber's oil still on him and the deference still in his mind his self-reproaches went no further. A day later (during the interval he had said nothing to anyone about the affair) and without mentioning the incident specifically he referred to his wicked extravagance. It was now so morally repulsive, only the foulest sort of person, for instance a masturbator, could do such a thing as to spend a large sum on personal adornment. It was in fact the masturbation coming out in another way and he was damned before all men. Everyone could see by his act [the expensive hair-cut] that he had done other things in secret. (This may also have referred to a homosexual incident in earlier life.) He was abhorrent to himself. The world could not contain such evil, there was nothing for it but suicide. God's punishment for masturbation would come hereafter, only it would not be heavy enough; he would have to suffer here for a bit too. . . . And much more in the same strain. He felt that in the magnitude of his self-reproach he was by ordinary accounts exaggerating, but said he had a special standard. He must be *perfect, absolutely* blameless. He asked if other people also masturbated and then at once went on to say that if they did it made no difference because they were by that fact proved imperfect and so no standard for him to judge himself by. All this is not the emptying of the ego of all its values and the heaping of them on a loved person—like a lover's humility. The real ego is regarded as poor and miserable, to be sure, but the love has not gone out to another ego or rather to another person's ego, but to his own, or a part of his own, to a tyrannical fantastic super-ego which knows nothing of clemency or proportion. At one moment he basks in an illiterate barber's flattery and sees in it a recognition of his due; at another he is no less a person than the World's Greatest Outcast.[1] The narcissistic nature of the Super-Ego has

[1] The incident also shows the infantile nature of libido gratification. He stroked his hair and then he sniffed his hands, this recalled a part of his lavatory ceremonial; the use of French was a part of his play with words which entered into his earliest phantasies; the fierce heat of his outburst at the amount of the bill (which was not excessive for what he had had done) revealed the sadism which later appeared in his self-accusations; the whole incident was also a

already been referred to in an earlier paragraph and will be mentioned again. It is the absorption of the libido in this part of the ego system which makes melancholics so difficult to handle in any form of psycho-therapy, particularly since the super-ego is mostly unconscious.

(d) *Melancholia and Mania.* Melancholia and Mania are associated in respect to the following points among others: (i) the same people may have both affections at different times in their lives, sometimes alternately, sometimes 'switching over' from one to the other with apparent suddenness;[2] (ii) in both the ego plays an outstanding part in the patient's libidinal distribution and often in his manifest symptoms, though in the one case he feels ill and weak, wicked and an outcast, while in the other he feels bursting with spirits, ready for anything, a good sort of fellow and the friend of all men; (iii) in both there is an incapacity to work and to love, in melancholia work is too hard, in mania 'too easy', in both love is a shallow thing, the former seeks it but can nowhere find it, the latter cannot stop to experience it.

To the psycho-analyst one of the most remarkable features of the change from melancholia to mania is the alteration in the functional activity of the super-ego, in the former state it makes a persistent relentless attack on the ego, in the latter state it seems to have disappeared altogether. This is a descriptive way

revenge and a compensation for a recent petty financial extravagance of his wife. Only an individual with an infantile fixation could have behaved in this way. The ego was behaving in infantile fashion to find compensation, for an academic setback in the mumblings of a barber, and for a domestic dispute in a hair-cut. His emphasis on the persistence of the fragrance of the barber's oil may throw some light on the manner in which the ego finds its compensations for a material loss in an aesthetic sensual gain. Since he was a person with considerable natural endowments and knowledge of the world before his illness, it is hard to see how, without taking into account the infantile libidinal element in his mind, he could have been so powerfully affected by an incident in a hairdresser's saloon in the Euston Road.

[2] The suddenness is more apparent to casual observation than to analytic investigation. The incident at the barber's showed evidences of transition, and in another case where I could trace no regular periodicity in the cycle of events I was usually able to tell from the transference three days beforehand when the manic phase was beginning, though the patient only knew a few hours beforehand that something was impending.

of stating the matter that needs correction. It would be better to say that in melancholia the cathexis is transferred to the super-ego and is withdrawn from the ego, which is weakened, while the super-ego exercises its sadistic vigilance over the ego; in mania the ego is released from its former rigid control, receives the entire amount of cathexis formerly investing the super-ego and proceeds with feverish activity to long prohibited infantile gratifications. This at least is one of the possible results of the transfer of cathexis, another is megalomania of quiet type, exaltation of spirit (euphoria) without the manifestation of interest in the outer world, which type results being determined presumably by the amount of object-cathexis existing at the time. The manic phase does not eliminate the hypochondria, and indeed on theoretical grounds one would not expect this to happen, but its expression is masked by the lack of subtlety in manner and phrase which frequently accompanies the disease.

The melancholic phase is characterized by mental pain of the acutest kind, which is borne by the ego; when the manic phase comes there is sudden release of strain and the patient appears to be joyous. The change may be put in terms of the difference in tension or hostility between the super-ego and ego. Probably the capacity of the ego to tolerate the super-ego is widely different in the two states. That the condition of the ego seems to be important is shown by a further fact, that mania is much more infantile in character, or rather that the manic's ego activities, as well as his libidinal, are more infantile. To give an illustration: in the depressed phase a patient had a prospect of a rise in the business world but feared that he was emotionally incapable of doing the extra work involved; he saw his career clearly, the present, past and future, and was aware of intellectual proficiency. Later in the manic phase he decided to cling to his present job, dwelt on its trivial pleasantnesses and behaved childlishly about the past in retrospect. As to the future: 'I don't give a damn what happens. I'll stick where I am till Hell freezes.' Comprehension of surroundings is of course in melancholia impaired in most cases to a greater or less degree, and overcast with uncertainty and portents of evil, but it retains its character of comprehending (bringing elements together) though the total range is restricted. In mania this is not so; here details, isolated elements or small combinations seem to function in the mind where larger combinations function in depression.

[I have not found this point mentioned in the literature and intend to refer to it in more detail in another paper.] It may be that the difference lies in the ego alone or in some non-ego change in the ego-super-ego relationship; at present it cannot be decided. Attention may therefore be directed to another aspect of the problem.

There is strong clinical evidence that in depression a person is being attacked; this person, whom the patient formerly loved, has been introjected (absorbed into the ego system) and in this new psychical position is the object of hostility. In hitting the object the patient hurts himself. The ambivalence to the object is transferred too; the adoration and the loathing. But what happens in the manic phase to the introjected object? Psychoanalysis is not yet ready for an answer to this, but it seems that sometimes the object cathexis is given up and the patient is in a measure objectless.

Perhaps the most striking characteristic difference is the immense sense of guilt in the depressed phase and the guilt-free state in the manic. Sin in the one case, surpassing the mercy of God to forgive, and utter indifference to moral values in the other. What is this sin?

(e) *The rôle of oral libido in the melancholic.* A patient came to me for consultation in a state of frightful agitation, on all sides his attention was directed to objects and situations which brought to his mind thoughts of blood. When he got on a bus the idea came to him, 'Suppose my children were in the roadway and got run over . . .' then he saw in his mind's eye gouts of blood on the bus wheels, rivers of blood in the road and mangled flesh. 'And worse thoughts than these . . . I can't eat . . . without thinking . . .' he stopped. I added, 'Of human flesh.' 'Yes, that's it, when I sit down to eat I keep on thinking that it's human flesh . . . my children's.' His family doctor (diagnosing this as neurasthenia) had ordered him for the sake of fresh air and exercise to dig in the garden. 'But,' he said to me, 'when I do I think as I turn over the sods with my spade, "It's all flesh. The entire earth must be by now made up of rotting corpses." And while I work I feel "It's everywhere, everywhere. Even the vegetables which grow in the soil are made of human flesh." '

This case has been given because it represents in a peculiarly condensed and forcible way the importance of the oral fixation in melancholia. Abraham drew attention to this first; what follows is based on his papers. The oral stage is sub-divided into a passive sucking stage and an active biting stage, the former is objectless, the latter is characterized by a peculiar relation to the object (the nipple) which is no longer regarded as a part of the self but is assuming (psychically speaking, of course) an external position and is felt to be in danger of being lost, a matter of importance because it is a source of pleasure. The nipple is seized on and devoured, it is drawn into the Self-system (the pleasure Me-system) to be retained. This happens at the time of weaning when the child's jaws are beginning to function (aided by teeth) in masticating food, no longer merely rhythmically pumping it into the upper end of the gut. The bite movements are not reflex peristaltic pulsations but voluntary efforts; the real ego, consciously controlling and modifying action to meet and master the outer world, is beginning to function in the bodily and psychic economy. Heretofore the world has come to the mouth, now the mouth goes to the world. This phase is accompanied by a psychical tension and excitement which finds relief in the act of gnawing and destruction. It is not to be supposed that the destructiveness is consciously felt as it is in the case of youths who revel in it on Guy Fawkes' Day and other celebrations, it is not a pleasure in seeing a complete and meaningful structure toppling to pieces or consumed in flames, it is rather the fierce pleasure in detaching pieces that attract and then mastering them with the means at the ego's control: jaws and claws.

This, the stage of oral sadism, gives place to the 'negative' anal stage, in which the attitude to the object (now faeces) is still aggressive but the desire is to expel the object with the intention of alienating it from the psychical system. But the impulse does not run its course unchecked, for in the earlier phase the tendency to passivity persists. The child cannot change its habit in a moment, old behaviour disturbs the acquirement of a new. The pleasure to be gained at first is not solely the thrill of passing but the steady sensation of pleasure when retaining; the muscular strain in and pleasure from the sphincter is balanced against the other pleasure to experience the sensory pleasure in the passing. The stool is after all a part of the self. Thus there is ambivalence at the anal stage as at the oral. This ambivalence is evidence of an unstable ego-object relationship which we must now consider more deeply.

In the preceding paragraphs we have considered two phases

of oral activity, one passive, objectless, and the other with an active destructive orientation to the object. This object was originally the nipple, which was the main thing in the suckling's world. The fixation at this stage of libido development means that there is a tendency to hark back to the infantile desire to suck and bite the nipple of the mother (the spontaneous utterances of melancholic patients show this tendency clearly enough in analysis) and that the behaviour of the patient throughout life is dominated in varying degree by those mental characteristics which belong to that phase: a sadistic attitude combined with an overstrong tendency to introjection; the object may be changed beyond recognition, the tendency is not.

The child cannot permanently satisfy its libido at the pregenital zones. It appears as if the libido must undergo a shifting of its concentration from one zone to another, oral, anal, genital, each being accompanied by a change in the ego, partly independent, partly dependent on the libido alterations. A little later the love-objects are no longer the self or parts of the self but those most important things in the environment—the parents. These are adored and feared, they have it in their power to give almost unconditioned happiness or to impose restrictions on pleasure to an unlimited degree. While they are loved the child is physically, mentally and morally wholly dependent on them; when they are hated, the child stands perilously alone. Obedience is rewarded by marks of their pleasure, of their love, disobedience by their displeasure, and their love is withdrawn. When this happens, the child is indeed helpless. Furthermore the parents require such extraordinary things, among others that the child shall acquire voluntary control over its 'autonomic' nervous system—at least in places, that it shall defaecate at 9 a.m. and not urinate while it sleeps, that at all times it shall be celibate in thought and deed and indulge in no 'smoking-room stories' ordinances which at least half the adult population would regard as ridiculous if applied to themselves (unless they had already inured themselves to obedience to them) are to be observed at the cost of parental displeasure—loss of love. It is not to be wondered at that there is a conflict in the child's mind between an inner longing for that love and an inner hatred of the people who act against its immediate self-interest (personal pleasure as it has hitherto experienced it). There are several possible outcomes, chief among which are the following: (i) the child's self-love may be gratified by a peculiar procedure—it identifies itself with its parents, takes their 'you must' (external) as 'I must' (internal) and so solves the external conflict by making it internal. The external injunction becomes now an internal one, and self-satisfaction (self-love) can be preserved so long as the orders are obeyed. The hostility to the interfering parent is transferred to the introjected parent (the Super-Ego) and is turned upon the self; this is where the Super-Ego gets its relentlessness, it is sadism reflected—and made less dangerous, at least to outer objects, to whom love feelings can now flow out, undisturbed by hate.[1] (ii) (a way leading to abnormality). The severity of the Super-Ego may be restricted to certain specific performances and not to all of those that the parent has prohibited, the introjection of prohibitions can be isolated from one another so that the individual has a conscience (super-ego function) that operates towards one type of instinctual gratification differently from that of another without developing unification of the 'moral character'.

From these two modes of Super-Ego formation result two different types of Super-Ego; in the one there is integration of the prohibiting tendencies, in the other there is not. The latter is for our present purpose specially important because it is correlated with unintegrated libidinal gratifications, i.e. those which have given rise to fixation and have (by repression) acquired to a certain extent an independent existence in the psychical economy. In the case of the future melancholic the process appears to be as follows: the individual being greatly desirous must check the strong libidinal tendency to get erotic gratification by sucking the loved object and devouring it. This is not a simple forward movement of love, he also hates it and wants sadistically to destroy it, but the sadism is turned against the self via the Super-Ego, so he punishes himself for the cruel lust by making painful the very source of his pleasure. His appetite is altered because he feels himself to be a cannibal-brute to the very objects he loves. He is right, of course, he has these desires, his Super-Ego with its usual precision blames him for his deepest ('most repressed') wish, and hauls it up before his eyes, as it

---

[1] Thus the impulse of sadism retains its sexuality when directed upon the self in melancholics, but is aim-inhibited when it is turned upon outer objects—another evidence of the auto-erotic feature of the disease.

were, as a perverted taint in his character. The ego of the patient, not comprehending the presence or the source of the desire, says, 'It's horrifying to me to have such thoughts, they are no part of me,' reckoning as Me only what is conscious. The Super-Ego, however, knows more of the instinctual desires than does the ego and sits in harsh judgement.

(*f*) *Efforts at Self-Cure.* It is necessary to know what has caused neurotic illness before we can estimate how far our efforts or the patient's are likely to alter his condition in the right direction. Among the causes of neurotic illness [1] *frustration* holds the most prominent place. This is an external factor and occurs when, after deprivation of an object of gratification, there is no substitute. The effect of frustration is to dam up the libido so that it creates a state of uneasiness; this is relieved either by a transposition into energy directed to the outer world which is made finally to give the actual satisfaction required, or else the libidinal satisfaction is deflected from its erotic goal and sublimated. The danger in either case is that the person will turn from reality and use the psychical energy whose external outlet is blocked in re-animating old phantasies and regressive aims.

Two other causes are the *inability to adapt to reality*, which may precipitate neurosis at any age, and *inhibition in development*, for the action of which a certain stage of development is required.[2] In the more pronounced cases, the latter of these two causes is due to the former.

The fourth type of nosogenesis deals with the capacity to tolerate only certain *amounts of libido*, if these are exceeded the patient falls ill because his ego cannot cope with the task of repression.

With this outline in mind, let us approach the question, what makes the melancholic fall ill? In some cases the attack begins after a real loss, in others no such external cause can be found, and presumably an illness of an organic nature predisposes to the melancholia only because it weakens the ego's capacity to tolerate a certain *amount* of libidinal tension.

Let us turn to the events of childhood, in particular the pecul-

---

[1] Freud, 'Types of Neurotic Nosogenesis', *Collected Papers*, **2**, The Hogarth Press, London, pp. 113–21.

[2] This is to be distinguished from a stationary infantilism by the fact that there appears to be an effort to overcome the infantile fixations.

iar melancholic Oedipus situation. Like all children, these patients in this stage of development desire as an expression of the love of their parents to have a child from or by them. All children are of course frustrated in this, but the melancholics-to-be treat this as a *narcissistic* blow, as a castration, and being weak in their genital organization regress to earlier levels. If they had more capacity for object-relationship they would be able to divert their libido to other objects, but theirs is a narcissistic character and they cannot do this. *What object-capacity they do possess also takes a regressive turn* and they strive to keep the object by the means which their fixation ordains, viz. by *oral incorporation*. This serves a twofold purpose, it preserves the object from the effects of overt sadism (since it is within the self, psychologically speaking) and at the same time it combines the little object-capacity that does remain with a narcissistic gratification, for the self has now grown greater by the incorporation and the object is there. The Super-Ego knows well the sadistic nature of the manœuvre and brings punishment down on the ego for the act—food is made loathsome, the organs of digestion are perverted, the world (which the melancholic retains by an oral bond only) is turned to filth and excrement, all flesh is human flesh, all soil is rotting corpses and 'even vegetables are made of human flesh', as my patient said. The melancholic self-reproach is now somewhat clearer, it is directed against the self because of the cannibalistic impulse which disturbed the child at, and prior to, and after the Oedipus stage.

Viewed in this way, the most striking symptoms of the disease are efforts at self-cure. By the violence of the self-punishments the ego hopes to be rid of the sense of guilt, by the oral incorporation of the object (the cannibalism) that object is in fact preserved from external violence, by the regression the genital integrity of the mother is preserved, and by the fantastic strictness of the Super-Ego the patient deflects his hostility away from his father. The disease symptoms show that they are even biologically adaptive!

What then causes melancholia? We can now give a fairly complete aetiological formula: (i) Constitutional increase of oral erotism. (ii) Special fixation of libido at the oral stage of libido organization. (iii) Severe injury to the child's narcissism (weaning is often traumatic—psychically—in these cases) so that they suffer from a sense of desertion. (iv) Imperfect attainment of the phallic stage of libido organization with a distortion of the Oedipus situation, disappointment at this stage causing a regression to the oral sadistic stage, hence a permanent association of love-relationships and destructive-oral impulses. These factors lie dormant until in later life there comes (v) A frustration in object-relationships (in so far as these have formed) or wound to narcissism, or anything which by weakening the ego incapacitates it in its permanent task of repression. Between attacks melancholics do not attain full object-love; though the tendency to incorporate the object and destroy it is in abeyance, ambivalence and a measure of hostility remains.

(g) *The end of the melancholic attack* is for our inquiries as interesting as its initiation. It is thought (Abraham) that the melancholic can give up the oral-introjection when the violence of the sadistic phase ends, when, that is to say, the object is no longer endangered by the patient's hostility.

It is a curious notion that the illness is a device—among other things—for protecting *another* person from harm, and particularly curious in such narcissistic subjects as fall ill of melancholia, but we must remember that the phase of oral introjection serves also a primitive erotic impulse as well and that the object is preserved for egoistic reasons and not for 'pure love'.

This picture of melancholia shows it to be a cycle of changes, no pretence is made that every phase is clearly understood or firmly established [1] but the psycho-analytical theories at least open up avenues of research which seem profitable to examine.

10. *Super-Ego (Ego-Ideal)* [2]

(*a*) Introductory
(*b*) What the Super-Ego is not
(*c*) Stages in its Development
(*d*) The Decline of the Super-Ego and Return of the Ego
(*e*) Disorders of the Super-Ego

[1] For instance, changes in the ego last for such strangely variable times, without our being able at present exactly to determine some of the factors which cause the duration.

[2] The reader is particularly referred to Dr. Ernest Jones's 'The Origin and Structure of the Super-Ego' (Bibl. 293) and to Dr. Sylvia M. Payne's 'Observations on the Formation and Function of the Super-Ego (conscience) in Normal and Abnormal Pathological States' (*Int. Jnl. of Psycho-anal.* VII) and to Bibl. 1, 3, 4, 109, 115, 170, 178, 182, 190, 192, 204, 216, 224, 249, 295, 339 *a*, 348, 395, 402.

(a) *Introductory*. There has been an inevitable overlapping of detail in the preceding paragraphs, so that readers will have begun to form some impression of the group of mental functions subsumed under this title.

The Super-Ego as well as everything else in psycho-analysis has its own course of development which is bound up with that of the libido, the acquirement of object relationships and ego development. Super-Ego activity is a technique for maintaining object relationships while at the same time affording an outlet for instinctual energies that often tend to destroy these relationships. Its function is adaptive, it is slowly acquired, integrated with other psychical functions and liable to disorders.

(b) *What the Super-Ego is not*. It will prove a saving of time to say at the beginning what the Super-Ego (Ego-Ideal) is *not*, and to clear away some mistaken notions frequently met with.

First, it is sometimes regarded as being a final criterion in conduct acting after the manner of a divine voice speaking within the mind; this is derived from theological beliefs and clearly shows the working of an infantile narcissism which projects omnipotence on to the Father (God) and later endows the introjected parental injunctions with the omnipotence of childhood again.

The *second* error is to assume that the Super-Ego is derived from Society at large, that it is a manifestation of an ill-defined 'herd instinct' and as such takes rank in regard to power, though not antiquity, with the instincts of hunger and love. This contains a grain of truth in a bushel of chaff. It does appear that the capacity to introject parental images is variable in different people and it may well be that there are familial and racial differences in respect to ability to form the working arrangements included under the term Super-Ego, but this is not the same as saying that its function is analogous to one of the primitive instincts. As for its derivation from Society at large, the matter is really the other way about; the opinions of Society are derived from processes of identification which are also operative in forming the individual's Super-Ego.

The *third* mistake is to assume that it is qualitatively identical in everyone and only quantitatively different. This is probably a disguised form of the theological error mentioned above, which tacitly assumes an absolute standard but allows for differences of perception due to mortal weakness.

The *fourth* assumes that it is synonymous with conscious aims and visions of the self as one ought to be. The worst form of this error is to identify the Super-Ego with systems of law; it assumes that the law is a product of the father alone[1] and that conscience is identified with conscious repressive processes. The old term Ego-Ideal may be partly responsible for this confusion. I should like to reserve the term Ego-Ideal for these conscious views of what the self ought to be and Super-Ego for the unconscious processes that give rise to them and give them strength. *The Super-Ego is an unconscious mental function*, the effects of its actio may be at times conscious.

The *fifth* point is related to the last: it is assumed that the Super-Ego or conscience begins to operate when the child becomes conscious of moral sanctions: the matter is otherwise, it begins to operate before the child has established full object relationships—certainly before the beginning of the third year.

(*c*) *Stages in its development.* With this much said by way of clearing the ground of misconceptions, we can now discuss the development of the Super-Ego as it appears to the psycho-analysts, but some departure from chronological order must be permitted once more. The psycho-analyst operates a limited number of mechanisms which he finds adequate when properly combined to produce formulations for the different diseases and mental attributes with which he has to deal.

Those relating to the Super-Ego are: (i) the Fechner-Freud pleasure-principle (being the fundamental principle of psychical activity), (ii) the development of the libido, (iii) the development of reactive impulses in the ego, (iv) the element of deprivation through external causes (parents), (v) changes in object relationships, (vi) the mechanism of identification. I am aware that these mechanisms are themselves complicated and that some of them can and perhaps some day all of them will be reduced to fewer and simpler components.

One function of the Ego is to act as an intermediary between the instinct impulses, which are internal, and stimuli from the outer world. It follows that if there is a change in the character or the distribution of the instincts there will be a change in the

[1] See present writer's review (*International Journal of Psycho-Analysis*, 1925, **6**, p. 92) of Goitein's *Primitive Ordeal and Modern Law*, in which legal theories are discussed in terms of the Oedipus Complex.

behaviour of the Ego (assuming for the moment that there is no change in the outer world); we shall therefore be justified from our knowledge of the changes from pre-phallic to phallic and from phallic to genital stages in the libido to expect modifications in the Ego in the course of its development. Another function of the Ego is to keep the amount of excitement in the psychical apparatus as low and as constant as possible; it is the regulator of discharge, and is influenced as was said above by internal and external events. The Super-Ego is a *part* of this regulating mechanism which slowly develops in early childhood as a specially functioning part of the Ego-System to act as an Indicator when a certain kind of internal tension increases above a certain limit. It issues a warning signal to the Ego, so to speak, that there is danger to the Ego from the instincts, but the Super-Ego does not itself take part in the act of control (repression) which is a function of the Ego. It is not an instinct, it has no 'psychical energy' of its own at its disposal, but it makes use of such energy as it has acquired from the ego in the course of development. Finally it belongs to the systems in the mind that do not operate in the conscious levels. These metapsychological generalizations may be of service as an introduction to the study of the development of the Super-Ego in that they indicate a mechanistic attitude of the psycho-analysts rather than a mystical or anagogic one to the phenomena which are called by lay persons 'conscience'.

Three stages may be distinguished in Super-Ego development: pre-phallic, phallic and post-phallic. They are not sharply defined, and, following as they do libido development are open to the objections that changes of object relationship are at least as important as libidinal aims, and that this classification gives no prominent place to the reactive impulses of the ego.

I. *Pre-phallic Stage of Super-Ego Development.* In this stage the sphincter activities are endowed with large amounts of erotic excitement which are prized by the child and lead him under the influence of reactive ego impulses to rivalry with his parents (to eat as much as they do, to make flatus like them, to defaecate at his own time and not at theirs, to urinate strongly or at 'inappropriate' times, etc.). This pleasure in 'zone' or sphincter play is deprecated by parents and they show their disapproval by display of superior strength, physical and mental, so that the child can enjoy its own sphincter pleasures only at the cost of actual chastisement (physical) or at the cost of isolation from the parents (mental); in both cases the child is reduced to a condition of helplessness in the presence of parental strength. The alternative course is to adopt the parental injunction and renounce the sphincter pleasure; this can only come about by a process of identification with the parents. But why does the ego change its mode of regulating discharge? It does so from dire necessity: the ego is in contact with outer reality and is capable of recognizing danger, it is the organ which operates with memory-images and can recollect past discomforts (which the unconscious mind being opportunist does not, the ego on the other hand can take a longer view); when faced with superior strength and the danger of being left by the parents (i.e. scolded, cut off from the warm response of their love) the ego submits to the deprivation of immediate gratification, and furthermore to a sort of pre-castration, i.e. it allows a *part* of the self to be removed (faeces, urine), or a pleasurable libidinal activity to be ignored (gorging with food, playing with the jet of urine, erection even) without complaint because it can compensate the loss of a part with the gain by introjection of another part-object, viz. the parental interest in the activity in question.[1] The danger is not a direct threat to the ego as a whole but to the part or to the activity which offends the parents, it is a non-genital danger, it therefore evokes 'pre-castration' reactions. Object relations in the early part of this stage are a blend of narcissistic and autoerotic, in the later period of the same stage are part-object relationships. The greater the cathexis of the zone in question, the more it has absorbed erotogenicity from other zones and become a centre of ego-identifications, the more will parental interference with the gratification at that zone approximate to castration.[2] At the same time as this development in libidinal aim there is a change in object-relationship.

We can sum up this stage of Ego or more correctly of pre-

[1] The parent is not a unified figure but a conglomeration of presentations having less cohesion into a unified presentation than intense discrete presentations concerned with relatively isolated activities.

[2] Castration is an injury to ego and libidinal interests simultaneously, indeed that may be taken as its definition for the purposes of psycho-analysis. A 'castration-period' may be defined as a stage of development in which there is concentration of libido on, accompanied by considerable ego-identification with, a particular zone.

Super-Ego development by giving a number of technical terms more or less endowed with exact meaning: it is a *pre-conscience* stage operating at a *pre-Oedipus* phase of *object-* and at a *pre-phallic libidinal*-phase of development, it is set in motion by the danger of *helplessness* in the face of superior parental strength (which danger does not however involve the unified ego-*i*dentifications = genital), the sacrifice to be faced is *loss of a part of the self* in return for continued parental part-gratification, the whole process is under the dominion of the *pleasure-pain principle*. The *reactive ego-impulses* are simple reflex responses of hatred at being interfered with.

II. *The Phallic Stage of Super-Ego Development* emerges from the pre-phallic. As a result of the concentration of erotogenic excitability in the genitals and increase of ego-identification with them the libidinal and ego impulses undergo a change which introduces for the first time a sexual conflict in the narrower or popular meaning of the term; that is to say, the stimulation of a part of the body (genitals) now evokes a loving attitude to one parent and a hostile attitude to the other. The Oedipus Complex is in full force at the beginning of this stage, indeed the Super-Ego may be defined as the mechanism for solving the conflict set up by Oedipus wishes (to kill the father and lie with the mother in the case of the normal male).

In the previous stage the boy's attitude to his father has been an admixture of love and hate which have flowed together to form the anal-sadistic organization, i.e. the love bond is maintained because hate has acquired an erotic character. The Oedipus stage inherits, so to speak, an already established fusion of ego and libidinal impulses toward each parent; we are now concerned with the utilization of the legacy. In the Oedipus stage the boy experiences erotic genital desire for his mother; this cannot come to expression because of the interference of the father, he cannot put up a fight owing to three factors, (1) his affectionate feelings for his father, (2) physical weakness, (3) fear that any expression of erotic desire for his mother would endanger his genitals (castration fear affecting ego and libido). The conflict has to be solved in such a way that the ego may undergo as little danger as possible and yet afford the libido as much gratification as possible. The way out of the difficulty involves alterations in object relationship to father and mother and in libido organization; these must be considered in turn.

The love for the mother forces the boy to a hostile attitude to his father, but this person was already loved, or rather was regarded ambivalently. If the hatred is strong the unmodified love relation to the father is dissolved, part of the erotic impulse regresses to the anal-sadistic stage and turns to sadism, another part is preserved on the direct alloerotic genital level but is inhibited in its aim, it maintains the attitude of affection which children have for their parents. The boy does not work out the sadism directly upon the father for reasons of fear, he 'short circuits' his antagonism by a mechanism which has been discussed already under 'Narcissism'. He set up the father-imago within himself, object-love giving place to identification, and thus provides within his own ego-system a replica of the conflicting elements in his life; by this introjection some object-libido is passed over to the ego (a narcissistic advantage) so that the ego now can operate a larger amount of libido than formerly; part of it is robbed of its sexual aim, i.e. it is desexualized or sublimated, part, as has been said already, is turned to.sadism. By the process of identification the character of the ego is changed (it is thought that this change utilizes some of the ego-libido above mentioned) so that the ego has now some of the attributes of the introjected person. He was not silent before and is not now. He issued injunctions and claimed prerogatives so that his *imago* after introjection treats the ego as he did. The hostility to the father becomes through the introjection now directed to the ego which is plied with imperative orders, the fusion of erotic feeling and hostility affords an outlet for libido gratification in sadism—only the victim is the self. Other libidinal component impulses act through the super-ego in the same way, so that the ego is forced to be orderly, dutiful, is watched and punished.

The relation to the mother suffers only one change, viz. the renunciation of the genital aim; this is not the same as complete deflection of the libido because some gratification is possible through 'aim-inhibited' relationships, so far as the genital aim is concerned there is liberty given but it must be exogamous.

This may be called, in contradistinction to the earlier stage, a *Conscience Stage* of development because the ego (under duress, to be sure) has acquired an internal mentor telling it not only what it is not allowed to do but also what it must do (wherein this stage differs from the former). It comes into prominence at

K2

the *phallic stage* of libido- and at the *Oedipus stage* of object-development because only here is the conflict between the sexes unavoidable, it is set in motion as formerly by the helplessness of the ego in face of the next greatest *danger* to death itself, viz. castration, neglect of the danger involves a *loss* not of a part of the self but of the unified ego- and libidinal-impulses, and isolation from parental love. Here again the ego shows its subjection to the *pleasure principle*, and the *reactive-impulses* of hate and fear are seen clearly at every stage of the development.

III. *The Post-Phallic Stage of Super-Ego development.* The 'stages' are artificial and should not be classed with the pre-genital stages of libido development, for the latter relate to distributions of libido and are easily demonstrable, whereas these super-ego 'stages' describe types of response to complicated internal and external stimuli. It would have been possible to call the first the 'pre-castration', the second the 'castration' and this, the third, the 'loss of love' stage, which nomenclature would follow the consequences in the erotic life resulting from disregard of the super-ego's interference. Another alternative classification would have called the first the stage of 'helplessness', the second the 'danger', the third the 'boycott' stages, directing attention to the type of danger experienced by the ego. On taking another aspect of the individual's development, namely, the relation to the parents, it would be possible to talk of pre-Oedipus, Oedipus, and post-Oedipus stages. Perhaps the reason why these terms have not been employed in the psycho-analytical literature is that they are if not inaccurate at least likely to be misleading, and this not merely because sharp dividing lines cannot be drawn but because in so many cases where there is fixation at say the anal level the child not only plays out a great deal of its Oedipus complex in terms of anal rather than genital relationships, but also finds strong ego-identifications with the anal zone and the anal products and so may be said by all but purists to suffer from a castration complex at that stage.

In the paragraphs on the Oedipus-phallic-castration-danger-stage (call it what you will) stress was laid on the rivalry between father and son for the mother in which the original hostility between son and father was replaced by a friendly object-love which in turn was replaced by identification. This manipulation of cathexes produces the profoundest change in the individual, or more correctly, ushers in the change, for from this moment the child is a social being. From now on he deals with his fellows on the pattern of his mastering the Oedipus complex. With the inhibition of the aim of the sexual impulse towards the mother there occurs an inevitable increase in libido accumulation requiring outlet; the new direction of libido outlet is thus forced on the child from internal and external causes and the ground is prepared for aim-inhibited gratification. This change is accompanied by a corresponding increase in the capacity to form the identifications following friendly object relations with potential rivals, viz. other persons of the same sex. It was not only through fear of the father that the ego took on his attributes by instituting the super-ego but also through love of him, so in this later or post-Oedipus stage it is not only fear of public opinion but love for fellow beings which maintains the function of conscience. The fear of chastisement becomes the sense of guilt. Thus the two factors at work in bringing an individual into society and keeping him aware of its demands spring from the primal relationships to his parents, love for companions and compatriots being derived from the homosexual component of the libido and sensitiveness to social opinion being a derivative of the hostile impulses.

(d) *The Decline of the Super-Ego and Return of the Ego.* The formation of the Super-Ego begins in the nursery to meet the requirements of the nursery code; it changes from a sort of 'Sphincter Morality' to a 'Genital Morality' which latter is designed to prevent incest; furthermore the sphincter- and genital-moralities work unconsciously, for the most part. Viewed in this way it is not difficult to see that the super-ego or conscience is at these stages ill designed to meet the needs of adult life, for in its second stage the prohibition covers not only incest but all genital activity, and in general its mode of action by repression, inhibition and enforcing regression is archaic, and not like conscious reactions finely graduated to suit the circumstances (the stimuli) of the moment. The super-ego, under the influence of social opinion, gradually in the third stage loses its rigid character in respect to certain actions (for instance, genital prohibition relaxes in respect to exogamous unions) but is preserved more or less strongly in others (for instance 'habits' such as the passing of wind).[1] The mechanism of this relaxation was

[1] It is difficult—apart from the libido theory—to find a biologi-

discussed in the third stage; it is substitution of other persons for the father, a series of introjections provided by everyday life. Hostility which originally led to identification with the father, later leads the individual to turn his libido away from the domestic circle to the outer world, there to find mother- and father-*imagines* and objects to which he can respond without mental strain and fear. The further the displacement from the parents the more is the ego likely to be stimulated without reference to father-hate and mother-desire. By experiencing exogamous sexual relationships the ego discovers that the sexual act is not accompanied by death, castration or boycott; the unconscious force of the super-ego is weakened at the expense of the conscious regulation of mental excitation and discharge which the ego exercises; while the regulation of the psychical apparatus is relegated to the archaic unconscious, the mechanism of conscious adaptation is, if not impossible, at any rate difficult.[1]

The assumption of control by the ego does not mean un-

cally adequate reason for such prohibitions or probably for those against incest for that matter; so far as we can observe them, animals are not shocked at actions which put nursemaids in consternation; yet we find the human adult for no obvious reason taking more notice of pre-genital activities than the sub-human groups. The explanation probably lies in the fact that culture rests on the unstable basis of partially modified impulses, if man took too much manifest erotic delight in these pre-genital activities he would lose interest in the refined evolutionary products of these activities; if he had no inclination to them at all, if his life was a simple rut and non-rut (the latter being only a filling of the belly till the next rut) he would not trouble to—could not trouble to—labour over these aim-inhibited activities. By the interference of the latency period man's sexual life is divided into a stage of relatively uninhibited sexual gratification, a stage of sublimation and the final stage of relatively uninhibited sexual gratification; the gratifications allowed by culture ease the work of repression of the pre-genital erotic needs, some repression is needed to safeguard the genital.

[1] The super-ego of woman appears to be more infantile in character than that of man. This may be explained in part by the character of persons she identifies herself with being more infantile (i.e. mothers hand on their infantile egos to their daughters as super-egos, thus perpetuating the sexual differences within the ego-system), and in part because the opportunity in the social and economic world for working off the super-ego in a succession of *imagines* of widely different type is more restricted than in the case of the male—at least this may have been so till the recent changes in the life of woman have made the sexual differences less marked.

bridled licence and violence; unlike the super-ego it is in touch with reality and can adjust its mode of response to the external as well as to the internal stimulus. The adult's attitude to his fellow men is one of attention to their modes of response coloured with a kindly feeling, not blind subjection to codes of behaviour, which is the nursery way. The ego should supplant the super-ego as a regulator and leave it only the duty of signalling the unconscious infantile instinctual demands. This supplanting of the super-ego by no means always occurs; if it does not we may suspect disease of the function in question, which will now occupy our attention.

(e) *Disorders of the Super-Ego.* Where there is normally development there will be found in some individuals arrests in that development producing disorders of growth. We have found this to be the case in regard to the libido and the sense of omnipotence, and some day we may have a series of ego diseases to classify in the same way. The super-ego is no exception to this general rule; little is known of its intrinsic disorders, more is known of its anomalies due to concomitant disturbance of libido-cathexis and object-relationships.

We may start a consideration of the disorders of the super-ego with a re-examination of *melancholia.* Here we find that there is fixation at the anal-sadistic stage and that the individual tries to master the accumulated libidinal tension (which has a sadistic aim) by turning this upon himself; he acts not actively nor passively but reflexively. This theory is not intelligible without the inclusion of the super-ego, which is seen to be the introjection of the father-imago at the individual's sadistic stage of development. The self-punishments are acts of hostility made harmless externally at the expense of the ego. The greater the hostility to the external object the greater the danger to the self.

In the *obsessional neurosis* the ego forms extensive reactive formations to evade the sense of guilt caused by the hostile impulses, e.g. washing ceremonials, penances, etc. The ego is not aware of the reason for these acts but responds to the promptings of the super-ego (which is unconscious) and so reacts as if it were guilty. These peculiar behaviours are ascribed to (i) precocious ego development, and (ii) to the formation of the super-ego at the anal-sadistic stage, i.e. the child works out its Oedipus complex at the anal-sadistic not at the phallic stage.

Confession is an attempt to ease the need for punishment (for impulses of which the subject is not aware) by replacing the inner condemning factor in the mind (conscience, super-ego) with an external person. It is a step to social life in the sense that there is a move away from dependence on the early parental injunction to a substitute in the current life of the subject, but the technique is bound to be unhelpful in the long run because (i) the confessor substitutes the father without at the same time detaching the patient from his early fixations, (ii) confession cannot penetrate to and deal with unconscious tendencies, and (iii) punishment is not the means to *alter* instinct impulses, seeing that it gratifies them. It is useless for a reformer to preach total abstinence after he has made his hearer drunk. In the same way punishment by gratifying the sadism re-enforces the pre-genital fixation, it does not lead the subject to a more adult synthesis of libidinal aims.

Self-criticism—a useful super-ego function that persists under the regime of the re-established ego—may be exaggerated, as in melancholia. This exaggeration is due as before mentioned to increase of sadism directed to the self combined with a scoptophilic impulse carried over into the super-ego.

The criminal is a person who has a super-ego defective in the capacity for self-criticism. It appears that the super-ego is cut off in some way from access to the outer world, so that the working-over process is prevented. In addition there has been a defective development of the super-ego in the earliest stage, the component impulses acted in isolation or rather produced isolated reaction formations. Guilt if present is connected with symptoms not with conscious acts.

Bad up-bringing, i.e. cases where the parents' conduct obviously falls below the standard set up by the super-ego, exerts a traumatic effect on the parental identifications, impairing the ease with which the original hostile impulse is changed to affectionate object-choice and later identification. The end result of this state of affairs is that the child cannot enter the third stage, i.e. transfer to society the parental complex and satisfactorily work it through.

The super-ego arises as a compromise between the desire to love and to be loved, it is maintained for a time as a mechanism for incorporating into the infantile ego a standard of conduct to which it will have to conform now and in the future (while the home influence is important to it), it provides an outlet for aggressive libidinal impulses without disturbing external relationships, and finally by duress it urges the ego to change its character and assume control of instinct impulse not according to its (the ego's) standards but those of the outer world. When it breaks up, the anal-sadistic element of it is changed into an impulse to mastery of external objects, which is taken over by the ego, and a vigilant element (derived from a blend of sadism and scoptophilia) which now acts as an agent of the ego in co-ordinating internal and external impulses.

11. *Death Instincts*

Some years ago Freud gave rein to his speculative inclinations regarding the nature of instinct and evolved a theory which will be given in brief in this paragraph. He said of it himself that he does not know how much credence to give these theories which differ from the other psycho-analytical theories he has put forward in being speculations rather than close or relatively close deductions from observation.[1]

Analysis of cases of traumatic neurosis showed that the symptoms were due not only to a libidinal wish—to a desire for erotic gratification, however distorted in expression in the symptoms —but to a compulsion to repeat in the mental life of phantasy, dream and symptom the original situation of trauma, and master the great amount of psychical excitation which it evoked by a mental means. The repetition gave an opportunity to take the trauma in 'divided doses' and so deal with it more easily than would be possible if the shock had to be mastered at a stroke.[2] From these observations, from a similar tendency to repetition in the phenomena of transference in the analysis of neurotics

[1] Vide *Beyond the Pleasure Principle*, The Hogarth Press, London.

[2] This explains the phenomenon of 'battle-dreams' being repeated long after the outer danger is over. The course of battle-dreams is usually (*a*) 'pure' battle-dream with intense anxiety, (*b*) mixed battle- and 'civilian'-dreams (i.e. dreams of civil life) with a decreasing amount of anxiety, (*c*) a stage in which the war element is absent on most occasions but is revived whenever the patient is in a state of emotional excitement which may have no direct connection with the war. It looks as if the excitations due to extreme physical danger could be more easily mastered if they were mixed with libidinal excitations, and that the 'mixed battle-dream' was indicative of an economic (psychical) process at work in effecting a cure, or at least some relief.

and from the play of young children Freud surmised that '*an instinct would be a tendency innate in living organic matter impelling it towards the re-instatement of an earlier condition,*' i.e. a manifestation of inertia in organic life. But this, as he hastens to point out, does not explain certain features of the sexual instincts which appear to follow a different path in that they seem ever to strive to create new individuals. This may be more apparent than real: with the division of gonads and soma the body may be divided into organs which strive to create earlier conditions of living protoplasm—unicellular germ cells—and those which serve no such direct tendency; the former are the physical source of the life-instincts, the latter of the death-instincts, the interplay of these two accounting for the almost infinite variety of physical and psychical manifestation of organic life. 'The one group of instincts presses forward to reach the final goal of life as quickly as possible, the other flies back at a certain point on the way only to traverse the same stretch once more from a given spot and thus to prolong the duration of the journey. Although sexuality and the distinction of the sexes certainly did not exist at the dawn of life, nevertheless it remains possible that the instincts which are later described as sexual were active from the very beginning and took up the part of opposition to the rôle of the "ego-instincts" then, and not only at some later time.'

Every cell is on this hypothesis assumed to possess these two instincts; when the organism becomes multicellular the sexual impulses of the somatic cells take the other cells as 'objects' but the gonad cells remain 'narcissistic'. This division into a sexual and non-sexual function allows the concentration of sexual energies in the sexual cells to go forward unchecked (and thus the sexual cathexis is conserved for their enormous constructive activity) while the non-sexual cells utilize their sexual energies in 'neutralizing' their own and each other's death-instincts. This ingenious hypothesis has one application at least in psychiatry, viz. in suicide. Normally the death-instinct is turned outwards to the world and either combines with the sexual to form sadistic impulses or acts in isolation as the impulse of aggression. When turned outwards death-instincts are innocuous to their possessor, they only injure the external object; if, however, the object is introjected, this instinct is no longer innocuous to the possessor and the danger to the self may be so great that self-destruction results. Whether readers will share Freud's own 'tepid feeling of indulgence' to these views or will reject them is no great matter, since psycho-analytical psychiatry can get on very well without them at present.

Postscript to Part II

The reader is reminded that this part of the Survey only covers about a decade and does not bring the theories up to date. It opens with the concept of Narcissism which effected a revolution in thought; looking back at the literature before this (1893–1914) one cannot help reflecting on the relative poverty of the analytical instruments then employed for dealing with the problems of the psychoses. At the conclusion of the Survey of the third period (1923–1926) a like reflection in regard to the second will arise. The subdivision of the psychical apparatus into three parts, Ego, Super-Ego and Id, and the new views on Anxiety, transform the picture once more; here again the greater part of the work is done by Freud.

PART III

12. *The Ego and the Id*[1]

(a) Introduction
(b) The Id
(c) The Relation of the Ego to Consciousness
(d) The Oedipus Complex
(e) Changes in the Ego

(a) *Introduction.* Freud's paper on narcissism had changed the psycho-analytical theory by introducing a new 'partner' in every love relationship, the self; his brochure on *The Ego and the Id* introduces no new concept but restates so many old ones and shows up their relationships so clearly that it may be used as a boundary post in this survey to separate the second or narcissism period from the third period, which deals chiefly with the functions of the ego. For our present purpose, of the views contained in *The Ego and the Id* only those which immediately concern these ego processes will be summarized.

(b) *The Id.* The psychical apparatus has been described as an organ whose duty is to keep the amount of excitation within the

---

[1] Bibliographical references: 178, 182, 184, 196, 198, 200, 244, 246, 251, 263, 293, 295, 395. [*The Ego and the Id*, The Hogarth Press, London, is a short book—81 pages—which should on no account be left unread.]

organism as low and as constant as possible. Excitation proceeds from two sources, external and internal, the former being in the nature of impacts (stimuli), the latter (instinct impulses) exciting a continuous influence (though varying in intensity). The latter concept presupposes a source continually creating a state of tension; this has been thought to be the erotic element in life which throws the psychical apparatus into a state of unrest. The view now put forward is that this source is an undifferentiated part of the apparatus called the 'id', it is a reservoir of libidinal 'tensions' which have to find outlet in gratification. Another part of the psychical apparatus is specially modified to bring unity or coherence into the various modes of discharge. This modified part furthermore is subject to influences from without, so that it is a correlating organ of internal and external stimuli, is in short an adapting mechanism which is influenced by both and can in turn modify both. In popular language the id is the function of passion; the modified part, which we can now call the 'ego', corresponds to the function of reason and sanity.

The tension created by the id is libidinal in nature, it becomes effective in producing a change in the orientation of the organism when attached to presentations, but it is characteristic of id-cathexes that they can be shifted from one presentation to another without apparently altering them to any great extent. The ego as the regulating mechanism for discharge of tension has to deal with these cathexes, it can do so without difficulty if the external obstacles are not strong; if they are it must either employ some device for shifting the cathexes to an object which will allow of discharge without interference from without or else by damming the outflow of discharge endure the tension which results. In practice it does both, *the cathexis is shifted on to the ego itself* (becoming ego-libido), the libido is desexualized and is used up or partly used up in the process of making a change in the character of the ego itself; put in another way the ego substitutes itself for the libidinal object of the id, which it is able to do by behaving as the object behaves, i.e. by identifying itself with the object. This affords an explanation of secondary narcissism in which one part of the psychical system can take another part as a love object, a concept that is unintelligible without the additional hypothesis that the latter alone is in perceptual contact with and can adapt itself to the outer world.

Enough has been said already about the first object-identifications which result in the formation of the super-ego to make the task of giving the details of the process again unnecessary, but it may be pointed out how much more intelligible becomes the concept of the super-ego with the addition of the concept of the id, for it was in the process of mastering id impulses that the ego was forced to modify itself to the extent of forming this specialized portion.

(c) *The Relation of the Ego to Consciousness*. We now have four elements to deal with in examining mental life, (1) *the external world*, (2) *the ego* (these two are able to influence each other), (3) *the id* (which is not in direct contact with the external world), and (4) *the super-ego* (which is not in direct contact with the external world but does appear to be in very close connection with the id). The question now presents itself: What is the relation of the three elements of the mind (ego, id, super-ego) to consciousness? The psycho-analyst defines four states of consciousness, which *do not* correspond to the four elements above mentioned; this point cannot be made too emphatic.

The term *conscious* is descriptive of the state of an idea; but we are not conscious of our ideas for long, most of the time they are latent, when they may be called *preconscious*; they may become conscious in the psycho-analytical sense when they receive an increase of cathexis and affect that part of the psychical apparatus which registers perceptions, the *perceptual consciousness*. But there are ideas which can affect behaviour without being conscious; these are *unconscious* in the sense that they cannot by mere increase of cathexis become conscious. An idea which before was unconscious becomes conscious by a coupling of it to a word-presentation, it then becomes preconscious and from being that takes the next step and stirs the system perceptual-consciousness, which is commonly called 'consciousness'. Word-presentations originate in the outer world so that it follows that there is no consciousness of anything except through the mediation of memory images. Analysis may be defined as the work of attaching word-presentations to ideas which were formerly incapable of making the union owing to 'resistance' (which is an ego function); put in another way analysis aims at increasing the power of the ego so that it shall not set up these resistances (which are due to fear) and ultimately that the field of consciousness shall be extended.

In analysis a patient is asked to say all that comes to his mind; in the course of a longer or shorter time he falls into silence and does not know why; he feels the presence of something in his mind; his behaviour, restlessness, nervous apprehension or what not, betray the fact that his mind is troubled but he can give no satisfactory explanation. What is the cause of this? His ego— 'the coherent organization of mental processes'—which controls the outlet of excitations presumably is inhibiting the passage of a thought to the preconscious and so to the perceptual consciousness systems: this is nothing else than saying that a part of the ego is unconscious, indeed that part which puts up the inhibition or resistance. That the part of the ego which is unconscious is an important and powerful part is shown by the fact that it can inhibit powerful and important ideas.[1] The unconscious then does not coincide with the repressed, e.g. the unconscious part of the ego is not preconscious, for if it were there would be little or no difficulty in making it perceptually conscious. An important part of the unconscious part of the ego is the super-ego, which, as has been said before, corresponds very roughly with what is called the conscience, so that not only the 'lowest' in the mind, the repressed impulses, but the 'highest', the conscience, are alike unconscious.

(d) *The Oedipus Complex.* In the simplified case of the male the child develops an object-cathexis of his mother and an identification with his father. When the father is perceived to be an obstacle the full Oedipus complex is developed. This is dissolved by the object-cathexis of the mother becoming changed to an intensified identification with the father and so consolidating the heterosexual attitude or to an identification with the mother (leading to a homosexual attitude). The outcome of the Oedipus situation is determined by the relative strength of the masculine and feminine dispositions, i.e. whether the energies of the abandoned object-cathexis shall accentuate a father or a mother identification. Analysis, however, shows that this simple state of affairs rarely exists. The bisexual constitution manifests itself in a double Oedipus complex, that is, the boy while being

[1] It follows therefore that to ascribe neuroses to a conflict between conscious and unconscious parts of the mind is inaccurate, rather the conflict is between the organized ego and what is repressed and dissociated from it. [*The Ego and the Id*, The Hogarth Press, London, p. 17.]

ambivalent to his father and affectionate to his mother also behaves like a girl and displays an affectionate feminine attitude to his father and a corresponding hostility and jealousy to his mother. Thus a series can be formed with the normal or positive Oedipus complex at one end and the negative or inverted Oedipus complex at the other. The outcome of the Oedipus phase of development is the formation of an alteration in a part of the ego system, which as has been shown in a previous paragraph is separate from the rest and is the superego.

(e) *Changes in the Ego.* In connection with melancholia it was said that the abandoned object was set up in the ego, in the case we were just discussing the relinquishing of an object-cathexis effects a change in the ego, or rather in a part of it; more correctly still, modifies some of the ego functions, but not in the same way as happens in melancholia. We may draw up a series in respect to the ego modifications subsequent to object-abandonment: (a) withdrawal of cathexis from the object and distribution of it upon the ego (leading to megalomania, e.g. in dementia praecox); (b) withdrawal of cathexis from the external object with re-establishment of the object plus its cathexis within the ego system (melancholia); (c) partial withdrawal of object-cathexis, the 'energies' so 'released' being 'used up' in effecting a change in ego function to form the super-ego (a normal process); (d) partial withdrawal of object-cathexis joining with repressed autoerotic activity to form character-alterations, e.g. anal, urethral, oral (and ?genital) character-traits, which if not too strongly marked may be accounted normal. We now see that the process of withdrawal of cathexis is not necessarily pathological, the determining factor whether the outcome shall be pathological or not depending on (i) the amount withdrawn, (ii) the maintenance of object-relationship, (iii) the subsequent utilization of the withdrawn cathexis by the ego. It may be surmized, and rightly, that the important thing is the amount of cathexis that is withdrawn and re-utilized; if this is very great a condition of psychosis or something analogous to a psychosis may result whether the re-application be in conjunction with repressed impulses (in character-anomalies) or not, for whatever the subsequent fate of the withdrawn cathexis there will be disturbance of the balance of internal (or ego) and external cathexis.

13. *The Sense of Reality* [1]

(a) Introduction
(b) The Incorporation of Pleasant Experience with and the Expulsion of Unpleasant Experience from the Ego. (First Stage)
(c) Negation of Unpleasant Ideas. (Second Stage)
(d) The Acceptance of Unpleasant Ideas. (Third Stage)
(e) Reviewing the Situation from another Aspect : Ego-Libidinal Polarity
(f) Utraquism
(g) Delusion and Dream

(a) *Introduction.* The psycho-analyst is not concerned with philosophical questions as to the nature of reality but solely with the mechanism and disorders of the function of reality testing apparent in clinical experience (to be explained later); his sources are not confined to psychotic delusions or hallucinations but to neurotic manifestations which disturb the patient's objective relation to the outer and inner world. For convenience the subject will once again be treated in the first place ontogenetically (subsections (b), (c) and (d)) which might be called *Stages in the development of capacity for objectivity*; then leaving the ontogenetic it will be examined from the aspect contained in this formula: There is a polarity in the psychical apparatus, ego—libido (neither can be disturbed without affecting the other), the former contributing the intellectual component of the sense of reality, the latter the libidinal. The hypothesis will be put forward that capacity for complete objectivity is not possible if the genital stage of libido development is not reached; in other words, if the pleasure requirements of the id do not find outlet on the genital level it is not possible for thought processes to occur without distortion; or, put the other way about, if thought processes are disturbed by the pleasure principle it is evidence that libidinal gratification is finding other outlets than on the genital level.

(b) *The Incorporation of Pleasant Experience with and the Expulsion of Unpleasant Experience from the Ego* characterizes the first stage in the development of the capacity for objectivity; that is to say, at the beginning there is no capacity for objectivity at all. Just after birth the child, having recently undergone a severe blow

[1] Cf. Bibl. 1, 26, 39, 90, 91, 92, 93, 111, 113, 115, 121, 127, 135, 137, 139, 148, 151, 156, 157, 158, 161, 164, 166, 172, 174, 178, 180, 196, 198, 204, 205, 214, 243, 246, 251, 260, 265, 294, 323, 350, 352, 353, 360, 367, 395, 467, 477, 479, 481.

to its peace of mind in the change from an undisturbed state to one of cataclysmic sensations, cannot but feel the outer world to be for the most part repulsive; more correctly it responds to most stimuli with an impulse to repel them. Certain objects or experiences are, however, attractive, chief among these being the nipple. The ego, the controller of action, is induced to a favouring attitude to the nipple because it affords egoistic and libidinal gratification, it incorporates into itself what is pleasant and turns away from or thrusts away the unpleasant. It *identifies* itself in a measure with the pleasant as if to say, 'That is a Me-part,' and of other things, 'That is not a Me-part of what I experience around me.' The ego at this stage is called the Pleasure-Ego, because it is dominated by the need for *immediate* satisfaction. It takes cognizance only of those things it can with pleasure incorporate into its own pleasure system, so that the world is divisible into what is Inside-Me (good) and Outside-Me (bad).

(*c*) In the next stage, that of the *Negation of Unpleasant Ideas*, the ego has undergone a considerable modification. It would seem that it acquires a capacity to tolerate the painful tension of id excitations in some degree, or at least is not so much disturbed by them, so that the insistence of the id loses its immediate compelling power. Meanwhile the ego has developed its capacity for combining presentations and is, in a way, a better instrument for directing id discharge. It recollects where objects in the external world are when wanted. A new task now arises, the ego must be able to distinguish a memory image from a perception; in the earlier stage this was not necessary because the type of ego response was simply one of attraction or repulsion, it is now one of *consideration*. The point to be decided is again one of internal or external, whether the origin of the presentation is in the perceptual-conscious part of the ego system or in the part dealing with memory traces. In the case of hallucinations the function of testing this question of internal and external is suspended in respect to particular presentations, and these are found on close examination to be ones that are highly charged with affect and related to past situations in which there had been a failure of adaptation; that is to say, in a past situation the ego had been unable to tolerate the instinctual excitement and had avoided a situation of helplessness by repressing the presentation. This first act of repression constitutes the first break with reality, the second occurs when the cathexis of the idea increases, but the outlet instead of passing to the motor end of the psychical reflex arc flows back to the sensory end and places in the outer world a presentation that is not there, the perceptual system being excited from within. Put in other words: if the cathexis is mainly on presentations of external origin the ego will react passively to them as regards the sensory end but actively as regards the motor end of the arc, if the cathexis is almost wholly on internal presentations the ego will react actively to them as regards the sensory end and will act passively as regards the motor end of the arc. One of the stages in the testing of reality, then, is a self-perception, more precisely a perception of the movement of excitation in the psychical reflex arc.

(d) In the Acceptance of Unpleasant Ideas the final stage is reached in the Sense of Reality. It is not a single step but several, fused to a greater or less extent in normal life, divisible in certain pathological conditions into recognizable elements.

When an unpleasant presentation cannot be abolished by negative hallucination (ignored) it may be admitted to consciousness coupled to another presentation that more or less abolishes the pain, such as '. . . but it is not true', or '. . . but Dr. So-and-so (who is so pleasant) says it is so'. In the latter case obviously some pleasure is needed before the pain can be accepted; put in another way, the non-acceptance of the painful idea would bring in its train other pains that would be worse. It looks, then, as if an unpleasant idea can be accepted if it is given a negative sign or is introduced by another idea of outshining attractiveness; when the latter process occurs there is 'Compensation as a Means of Discounting Repression' (Bibliog. 477). It is necessary to assume this compensation in every acceptance of painful ideas, or else we shall be driven to renounce the universality of the search for pleasure as the fundamental psychical trend. It is unthinkable that a creature that has every want immediately satisfied can have concrete ideas, because they would be regarded as part of his subjective-ego, satisfaction would not be related to objects but entirely to the self. If, however, there were painful intervals between desire and relief, then the objects which brought gratification would be capable of being objectified, i.e. loved; but in that interval would they be loved? Not entirely, they would be treated ambivalently, loved as potential satisfactions, hated because of immediate dissatisfaction. During the ambivalent stage things acquire an objective existence but of only temporary duration, they get abolished by the hate and drawn into the ego by the love impulses, they are by turns in the Outside (nowhere) and the Inside (Me) realms; the lack of satisfaction has led to a de-fusion of the love and hate impulses which rule our attitude to the world. Only when a new instinct fusion occurs can the object be set up in the outer world on anything like a permanent basis. The fusion occurs when the impulses are *inhibited* in their action, when both love and hate recombine to prevent the abolition from or absorption of the object into the ego-system. Judgement, contemplation, the capacity for objective action depend on the impulses neutralizing one another.

(*e*) In psycho-analysis we are accustomed to regard the genital as the main conduit for the discharge of libidinal tensions; I wish to add a hypothesis to explain the discharge of the hate tensions when action is inhibited to the degree requisite for thinking, namely, a 'thinking-apparatus'. This is concerned to carry out what are in essence destructive acts (psychically speaking) on the object, turning attention to the elements of which it is composed, comparing the elements with others of like features, counting them, etc. If this view is correct there is a polarity in the psychical apparatus into genital and the thought-apparatus, which function quite differently; the former finds adhesive attachments to objects one at a time and for as long as gratification is needed, the latter has no such positive 'bond' but passes rapidly over characteristics, splitting up the presentations into elements, indifferent to their number and nature. The whole system is upset if the genital quality (one at a time) is transferred to the opposite pole, so that counting is disturbed, or contrariwise if the counting, splitting-up mechanism is transferred to the genital pole when one-at-a-time love relationships are in progress.

(*f*) For the psychical apparatus to work efficiently in accordance with reality, it is necessary that the two opposite processes should either be given different fields to work in or should work alternately; the former is a *sine qua non* for the individual, the latter probably for science;[1] Ferenczi calls the latter 'Utraquism'.

[1] This may be seen with special clearness in the case of the biological sciences, in which there are distinguishable periods: one (the introjection phase) being characterized by an intense interest in and

Now to come back to the Acceptance of Unpleasant Ideas—it is obvious that this can only be done at the expense of the self-feeling of the ego, i.e. the ego must experience a loss every time it occurs. There are two solutions, either that the ego harbours a belief that all such losses will be compensated for in a glorious but distant future, or else there is some mechanism which is at work that we have not yet touched on to compel the ego to accept the renunciation however disagreeable. I refer to traumatism of the ego being compensated for by repetition-compulsion, the ego being driven to endlessly repeated shocks to overcome some grave injury to its being. It is probable both processes are at work.

(g) When there is a long course in the physical and psychical development of an individual, we may expect arrests or failures to group themselves at special points in the pathway; it is therefore incumbent on me to relate the previous paragraphs to different clinical entities. The stage of incorporation of pleasant with, and expulsion of unpleasant experiences from, the ego characterizes the advanced stages of dementia praecox; the stage of the negation of unpleasant experiences characterizes negativism when it is almost universal and repression when it concerns only particular ideas, and this may fade off into 'normal prejudices' and 'dislikes' leaving us with the third stage which is characteristic of pure science.

Dreams are hallucinatory mechanisms characteristic of the earliest period of waking life to which we can regress when asleep, because external perceptions are weaker than internal stimuli.

In delusions the 'thinking-apparatus' functions perfectly well except as regards some pathogenic presentation, there is usually no universal loss of a sense of reality but loss of reality regarding one thing at a time.

love for the objects studied ('natural history'), the other being al-most completely ruled by the discipline of the physical sciences (measuring and weighing the animals in any given species, their organs, their number, their physiological peculiarities, etc.). There is a corresponding division in the 'human sciences', on the one hand we have psychology, ethnology, etc., on the other anthropometry, experimental psychology, psycho-galvanic-reflex studies and the like.

14. *Anxiety*

(*a*) Introduction

(*b*) Brief History: (α) Period of Shock Aetiology, (β) Period of Wish Aetiology, (γ) Narcissism explains Libidinal Component of Traumatic Neurosis, (δ) Theory of Repetition-Compulsion, (ε) The Threefold Division of the Psychic Apparatus

(*c*) The Danger Signal: (i) Fear and Anxiety, (ii) Neurotic Danger, (iii) Grief and Anxiety, (iv) Pain, (v) Defence: (α) Repression, (β) Isolating and Undoing, (γ) Reaction Formation, (δ) Regression

(*d*) Inhibitions and Symptoms: (α) The 'locus' of Inhibitions, (β) The 'locus' of Symptom-action, (γ) Ego-unity and Symptom-derivation, (δ) The Affective Reproduction of Past Situations

(*a*) *Introduction*

Many criticisms have been made of the psycho-analysts but only one has occasioned them much inward concern, viz. that their work is not co-ordinated to the biological outlook common to the related sciences as it should be. Freudians have resisted— or rather Freud has resisted—any premature attempt to link his theories to the current views regarding fear-instincts, for the simple reason that these are extraordinarily difficult to 'place' in the structure of psycho-analytical theory; he has preferred to let the theory expand by its own natural growth till it included them, instead of transplanting them from the outside. In *Hemmung, Symptom und Angst (Inhibitions, Symptoms and Anxiety,* 1926) he goes further than in any other work to satisfy those who desire to see the reaction to danger included as an integral part of psycho-pathology. He made this inclusion for the reason that something in psycho-analysis, not something in someone else's theory, required it. Psycho-analytical psychiatry had to wait thirty years for this important link with biological theory, but a premature attempt to graft a reactive ego response to danger on to the theories of the mechanisms of repression and regression, the libido theory, the grades in the ego, etc., might have resulted in the same failure that has dogged the steps of those well-meaning persons who try to combine psycho-analysis with the other sciences without long preliminary experience of analytical practice.

It is not so much a matter of interest to discover what held psycho-analytical theory back from participating in theories regarding the influence of response to danger in the neuroses as what enabled these to be included in the elaborate design. It was the discovery of *differentiating grades in the ego*.

(b) Brief History of the Anxiety Theories in Psycho-Analysis

True to a habit which becomes second nature to psycho-analysts, this topic will be treated historically and for convenience broken up into periods. Certain of these periods, it may be added, correspond roughly with the three periods of psycho-analytical psychiatry into which this Survey falls.

(α) *The Period of the 'Shock' Aetiology* (1893–1905).[1] The earliest papers on psycho-analytical psychiatry deal with the disturbances caused by 'unbearable ideas'. It is as if the ego is too weak to deal with some external influence and 'takes flight'. Among the causes of the unbearable ideas are psychic traumata of childhood, usually of a sexual nature. The ego *defends* itself against these ideas by various mechanisms, repression, displacement of affect, hallucinatory confusion, etc., presumably under the compulsion of a need for self-protection. There was, however, another theory developing at the same time based on observation of neurotics whose chief symptom was anxiety. It was found that unlike hysteria or a traumatic neurosis there was no single shock[2] to account for the anxiety state but that there was a disturbance of the *vita sexualis* in every case, viz. an accumulation of libido due to deflection of sexual excitation from the psychical field. It was thought that the psyche developed the affect of anxiety when it felt iself incapable of dealing by an adequate reaction with a task (danger) approaching it externally, and developed the neurosis of anxiety when it felt itself unequal to the task of mastering (sexual) excitation arising internally, that is to say, it reacts as if it had projected this excitation into the outer world. The affect and the neurosis corresponding to it stand in a close relation to each other; the first is the reaction to an exogenous, the second to an analogous, endogenous, excitation. The affect is a state which passes rapidly, whereas the neurosis is a chronic state, because an exogenous excitation acts like a single impact, an endogenous one like a constant pressure. The nervous system reacts to an internal source of excitation

---

[1] The reader is warned that the dates given are not taken as anything more than approximations, and that the titles given to these periods are indicative of landmarks selected for contrast.

[2] Written in 1894 under the influence of the Shock Theory.

with a neurosis, just as it reacts to an external one with the corresponding affect. (Freud's *Coll. Papers*, I, 101–2.)

(β) *Period of the 'Wish' Aetiology (beginning in* 1905).[1] In 'My views on the part played by Sexuality in the Aetiology of the Neuroses' (*Coll. Papers*, I, 272–83) Freud puts forward a new aetiological view, viz. that the early sexual phantasies of children proved on analysis to be defences against memory of their own sexual activities and that these phantasies, and not only actual seductions, were capable of acting traumatically on the patient's psycho-sexual life. This momentous change in outlook (explained by the strength of the child's impulses which are relatively greater than his power of control) throws new light on the rôle of anxiety in neurosis: symptoms are endeavours to avoid the state of anxiety, thus anxiety is of the utmost importance in the genesis of neurotic disorders.

(γ) *Narcissism explains Libidinal Component of Traumatic Neurosis (theory started between* 1911 *and* 1914).[2] Psycho-analysts explain the impotence which is such a characteristic feature of shell-shock cases by the assumption that there is a disturbance of libido in the direction of increased narcissism. The shock or threat to life acts as a castration threat (unconsciously, of course) and mobilizes the libido to an increased concentration on the self with diminished object capacity. (Compare the narcissistic cathexis of wounds and the loss of object cathexis in physical illness.) The bearing of this on anxiety may not be obvious, because it is not contended that increase of narcissism necessarily produces illness in adults.[3] The explanation is as follows: the trauma breaks through defensive barriers in the ego and produces a concentration of libidinal cathexis about the memory-presentation of the event, so that not only similar events but any situation which calls for expenditure of libido leaves the ego in a state of helplessness with no resources. Dangers to life or to parts of the body with which there is a strong ego identification can produce these traumatic effects on ego and libido, and those who have not attained maturity in object-relationship with corre-

[1] See footnote to (α).   [2] See footnote to (α), p. 316.

[3] [It may be, however, that there is a point beyond which narcissistic cathexis cannot go without causing anxiety, but this seems only likely to apply to the earliest days of development; after birth, the psychic traumatism to narcissistic cathexis inevitable in life's experiences may insure against this 'primary narcissistic anxiety'. This is very much a matter of speculation at present.]

sponding genital organization are liable to traumatism from lesser shocks than more developed persons.

It follows from what has been said that in these traumatic cases any increase of instinctual impulses is reacted to as to an external danger (cf. mechanism of anxiety neurosis given above).

(δ) *The Theory of Repetition-Compulsion.* Analysis of traumatic neuroses has shown that the symptoms cannot be explained as wish-fulfilments but as expressions of an impulsion to experience again and again psychically the type of event which started the trouble, each time, it may be, with modifications of details. What purpose is served by repeating something painful, unwished for? How can this be reconciled with the doctrine of the pleasure-principle so often enunciated? The answer to these questions involves a modification of views: the traumatic experience acts as if it were a foreign body which must be 'mastered', so that the patient is forced to experience repetitions of the painful affect till the process of mastering of excitation is accomplished. It is probable that this compulsion to repeat is never absent in neurotic symptoms though in most cases it is present only to a slight extent.

(ε) *The Threefold Division of the Psychic Apparatus* (*theory began* 1911–14 *and culminated in* 1921 *as regards Super-Ego; in* 1923 *as regards the Id; and elucidated fully*—'*Ego and Id*'—*in* 1923.) [1] The division of the mind into id, ego and super-ego presents a new question in the anxiety problem, viz. in which part of the psychical apparatus is anxiety felt and what part reacts defensively to this emotion? The question has only to be put in this form to be answered without difficulty: the ego is the portion responding to anxiety whether it take the form of external danger (leading to fear) or increase of internal (i.e. instinctual) excitation (leading to *Angst*). We can put the problem now in a new way and ask what parts of the three levels of consciousness are affected by anxiety: but reflection shows that this is a vain question for affects are never preconscious, they are either conscious or unconscious. Since a part of the ego—a very important part—is unconscious, it is easy to see that the anxiety problem is not one that can possibly be approached from the side of consciousness alone; since some of the executive functions of the

[1] See footnote to (α).

mind (ego) are not conscious it is not necessary for the affect to appear in consciousness for the ego to initiate defensive action.

(c) *The Danger Signal* (1926)[1]
(i) General Remarks on Fear and Anxiety, (ii) Neurotic Danger, (iii) Grief and Anxiety, (iv) Pain, (v) Defence : (α) Repression, (β) Isolating and Undoing, (γ) Reaction Formation, (δ) Regression

(i) *General Remarks on Fear and Anxiety.* It is important to distinguish between fear and *Angst*, a German word which will be used henceforth in this paper for neurotic fear; the former is occasioned by a real object, the latter is characterized by an indefinite feeling of expectation *about* something but lacks an object. In real danger we experience fear for elements in the situation which are known, in 'neurotic danger' the elements in the situation which excites the affect are unknown because it is an instinct. In real danger we develop two reactions, first the affect of fear, then the protective handling of the situation. In neurotic danger there is an affective state of preparedness (which often is excessive) and the handling of the situation is frequently ill-directed, first because the object is not perceived, and second because action is often paralyzed by excess of affect. When real and neurotic dangers are mixed we find the danger is perceived but the affect is more pronounced than it should be. Neurotic danger is not entirely different from real danger, it shares one important character: the condition of helplessness which the individual feels to be immanent. This indeed is the only occasion for apprehension at any time, in real danger it is a matter of physical helplessness, in neurotic danger of psychical helplessness in the face of instinct impulse. Psychologically we can distinguish trauma from realization of danger by assuming the former to be characterized by helplessness, the latter to be characterized by the *recognition* of a situation which preceded helplessness; in *anticipating* trauma we become prepared—to be forewarned is to be forearmed. The situation which conditions the anticipation is the danger situation which gives, so to speak, the 'Anxiety Signal' of impending helplessness. The anxiety is on

[1] Freud's *Inhibitions, Symptoms and Anxiety*, The Hogarth Press, London, should be studied in this connection. It is one of his most revolutionary writings. It not only says what he himself has said in a new way, but, besides adding enormously to psycho-analysis, it also throws a flood of light on general biological concepts.

the one hand an expectation of the trauma, on the other a repetition of a small dose of it. In other words the danger-stage is the known, remembered, expected situation of helplessness, the apprehension (Angst) is the original reaction to helplessness in the trauma; the apprehension is reproduced subsequently as a Signal of Danger. The ego which was passive during the original trauma is now active in the stage of expectation (reproduction of the small dose of trauma in memory) and can lay plans of action to avert catastrophe. The demands of instinct in many cases may, though internal and in themselves harmless, be a source of danger because their gratification would lead to external danger, the inner danger thus may represent an external one.

(ii) We can now come closer to the heart of the problem of *Neurotic Danger*, by employing the well-tried chronological method. The process of birth is a danger for the child, but it does not realize this. What it does realize probably is a feeling of complete helplessness accompanied by violent disturbance of respiratory, circulatory, and other systems—manifest only as violent sensations, which stand of course in strong contrast to the preceding state of serenity. Little is known of the psychological effects of birth, but it may be surmized that later Angst is a revival of a small portion of that earliest trauma. Other anxiety situations (being alone, darkness, presence of strangers) are more intelligible, they have one thing in common: the absence of a loved person, the mother or nurse, who provides comfort and security. Probably in the cases above mentioned (being alone, etc.) the child first tries to hallucinate the presence of the loved one; this being a failure it tastes the first stage of helplessness and reacts with anxiety (if it cries quite often the danger of helplessness is averted by the arrival of the mother—hence omnipotence of gestures, which are regarded as a method of warding off danger). But the child only wants its mother for gratification of its needs (physical and libidinal) so that the development of instinctual tension precipitates the child into the danger situation. Thus from the first Angst is inevitable if instinct needs are not gratified. Passing over a number of years we come to the stage in which the libidinal excitations are concentrated on one zone—in the phallic phase. Here the penis is the organ which enables the individual to return to the womb, castration accordingly means psychically the impossibility of effecting this gratification, it means a permanent damming up of libido which can never find outlet. In the further development of the child castration Angst changes, as we have seen in a previous paragraph, to conscience-anxiety, to dread of society's disapprobation. This can be put into a series of formulations: separation from the womb—separation from the source of gratification—separation from the crowd, corresponding to physical, libidinal and social stages of development. Expanding the last point, the social-Angst, we can say that the ego reacts to the anger, to the punishments, and to the loss of love of the super-ego, with the danger signal of anxiety.

(iii) *Grief and Anxiety.* Since we know of old that grief is caused by a loss of object and since we now learn that anxiety may also be due to a loss of object, the new question arises, What brings about the one and not the other? The answer is that in the earliest experiences of life the two are not to be separated, only when the child learns that though the object is present it is not necessarily loved by it (i.e. if the mother or nurse is angry with it) is the condition established for *loss of love* which *is a precondition of grief.* Later when ego-development has advanced to the point of being able to test reality and the child finds that the object is lost beyond recall, the painful frustration of the loss of love compels it to withdraw the object cathexis from situations in which there had been before so much gratification.

(iv) *Pain* occurs when a stimulus breaks through the defensive barriers or when it acts continuously like an instinct impulse. Pain which is physical has little apparent similarity to loss of object; but there is reason to use the term pain, for both in physical pain and in loss of object the ego is emptied of its cathexes, in the one case by hypercathexis of the painful part of the body, in the other by hypercathexis of the object-presentation at the expense of narcissism; both by reason of their continuity and the difficulty in preventing their action these processes of cathexis produce the same condition of psychical helplessness.

(v) *Defence.* Various mechanisms are employed to deal with the situation produced by increase of instinct impulse when this reaches a point regarded by the ego as dangerous. (α) *Repression* is the technique of flight applied to stimuli of instinctual origin and is of two kinds: actual repression (Nachdrängung) and primal repression (Urverdrängung). The latter, which is necessary before the former can exist, is caused by a response of the

L

ego to the breaking of an overstrong excitation through the defensive barriers (compare the mechanism of anxiety neurosis), the former is occasioned by the signal of danger set going by the super-ego. By this technique the ego itself is but little changed, it exerts itself to keep the disturbing idea from consciousness. Repression is typified in hysterical amnesia. (β) Another mechanism is found which serves the same purpose of preventing recognition of the significance of an idea, namely, *Isolating* it from its emotional context; this is characteristic of obsessional neurosis. Here we find no amnesia but in its place a memory of the event with a detachment of affect from it, so that the event seems trivial and meaningless. Another obsessional technique is found in '*Undoing*'; here we find negative magic being employed to undo the harm 'done' by the omnipotent thoughts—as the neurotic views the situation. In both of these there is a more extensive alteration in the ego function itself. But in (γ) *Reaction Formation* the process of ego-modification is carried further still; it appears that certain repressed impulses have exerted a profound influence on the ego, so that it behaves in regard to all activities as if they were related to the repressed, e.g. scrupulous avoidance of inflicting pain on any persons or animals is characteristic of obsessional neurosis in contrast to excessive tenderness to one particular person as in the case of hysteria.

(δ) The three preceding mechanisms are predominantly of ego character, but among the possible modes of defence there is an alteration in the nature of libidinal attitudes to objects, viz. a *Regression* from the genital to the anal-sadistic or other pregenital stage. If in the reader's mind the question arises how it can be that a regression to an anal-sadistic attitude can be advantageous as a defence, it indicates that the psychological nature of these defences has not been sufficiently clearly put forward in this Survey. A regression from the phallic stage—the stage in which there is a high degree of ego identification with the genital together with a concentration of libidinal cathexis on that part—may occur when that part is endangered; with a scattering of cathexes and a dispersion of the ego-identifications there is, to use a homely phrase, a distribution of eggs in several baskets in place of their all being carried in one. The defence would not be needed at all if the instinct-impulse did not involve conflict with the external world in the person of the father (or mother); by avoiding a genital conflict, the greatest danger to the ego and libido combined, viz. castration, is to a large extent eliminated. Though the premium on the actuarial risk of castration by the parents may be so small as not to be worth quoting, the psychological premium paid by countless thousands of sufferers in the form of neurotic symptoms is enormous. The explanation has already been given in the paragraphs on Libido Development, Narcissism, and in other places in this Survey: the ego, which pays the premium, is not stimulated thereto by probability, for *in the unconscious the concept of probability does not exist*, but by the following facts: (*a*) there has already been experience of disconcerting deprivations following gratification, weaning, stool, etc.; (*b*) the excitation in the genital excites the combative impulse against rivals as well as erotic desire for a mate; (*c*) (this is important) in the development of the power of curbing instinct impulse, the individual employs the technique of turning the impulse against the self, especially in the case of the aggressive impulse, so that attention is directed towards the persons's own penis when the aggressive attitude is taken up against another person; (*d*) the rival is at the same time a love object as well, and as such is protected from the expression of pure hostility, accordingly the reflexive technique is specially useful in aggression against the father; (*e*) under the influence of phallic predominance and 'part-love' (a preliminary stage to full object-love) it is the *organ* rather than the *person* which receives the hostile attack, whether that attack is directed outwards or reflexively directed back on the self;[1] only when the genital stage is reached is the object dealt with as a whole and in full relation to its environment. This by way of explanation of the fact that in the phallic stage there is a dread of castration viewed from the *unconscious* aspect.

What have these defence mechanisms to do with anxiety? What, for instance, has the negative-magic in the 'undoing' of the obsessional patient to do with the diminution of nervous dread? The answer to this question calls for an examination of Symptoms and Inhibitions.

(*d*) *Inhibitions and Symptoms*
(α) The 'locus' of Inhibitions, (β) The 'locus' of Symptom-action, (γ) Ego-unity and Symptom-derivation, (δ) The affective reproduction of past situations.

---

[1] This throws a light on what might be called 'psychical autotomy'.

(α) *The 'locus' of Inhibitions.* Inhibitions are reductions in function. To give two examples, the disturbances of sexual function occur at different points in the sexual act (the deflection of libido from the initiation of the act—absence of psychical pleasure, the absence of physical preparation—absence of erection, abbreviation of the act—ejaculatio praecox, suspension of the final reflex—absence of ejaculation, absence of psychical element—absence of pleasure in orgasm). These disturbances, however, occur because there would be anxiety if the act were completed, *the inhibition saves the patient from an outbreak of Angst.* In the case of locomotor anxiety the locomotor function is abandoned entirely or in part (phobias of certain places: open places, closed places, heights, etc. when ego function is limited by special psychical conditions, if these places are avoided the Angst does not occur). Put in another way, *the ego renounces a function wholly or in part in order to avoid a conflict with the (id) instinctual impulses.* In cases where the super-ego strongly condemns an activity, we can add to the above formulation—*or with the super-ego.* There are other limitations of function, viz. when the ego is emptied of cathexes by grief or great pain, these have the special feature of being general or more or less uniform inhibitions of all functions, not of some only.

(β) *The 'locus' of Symptom-action.* The whole business of inhibition lies in the ego itself, it is otherwise with symptoms. 'The symptom is an indication and a substitute for an instinctual gratification which has not been carried out on account of the process of repression.' To take an example: if Angst is aroused when a patient goes to a high place he has only to limit his ego function to the extent of avoiding heights, to insure against an attack of anxiety; but if a person is afraid of being in the presence of a horse the fear of the horse is a symptom because the affect is not primarily attached to the animal but is displaced from the father. The anxiety roused by the high place results from the mechanism of anxiety neurosis, it is not a psycho-neurosis but an 'actual neurosis'; it is of course a symptom but is not a psycho-neurotic symptom. In the other case the symptom is psycho-neurotic in character; it is to be noted that it does not always abolish anxiety but conditions the psychical functioning in such a way that the ego has to exert itself defensively against something external to the immediate situation which rouses the affect, the exteriorization being produced by the psychical mechanism of substitution. There is of course ego-limitation in this as in all symptoms, but respecting an external object and its associated ideas, not internal presentations (impulses) and their associated ideas. The conflict has now shifted from the ego-versus-impulse battle-ground to that of ego-versus-symptom, to the relief of the patient's need for repression.

(γ) *Ego-unity and Symptom-derivatives.* It is now fairly easy to see the connection of this extension of the anxiety theory with symptom formation, at least in regard to phobias. The process of substitution enables the patient to exchange a conflict with the parent for an ego-limitation of the order of the anxiety neuroses; this is a psychical economy and leads to the substitution (e.g. of a horse for the father) becoming part of the defensive devices of the ego against anxiety, but since this substitution is a symptom it means that the symptom is incorporated into the ego system. That is to say there are two stages in the process of psycho-neurotic symptom formation which can be distinguished, in the first the substitution occurs, in the second it becomes attached to the ego but is the subject of conflict again; the outcome of this second conflict (which is the only one apparent to the patient or the physician before analytical treatment has uncovered the resistances) is of course a compromise between the forces tending to expel the symptom and those utilizing it. The symptom is difficult to eliminate (not to change, which is a very different matter) in the later stages because the ego has undergone an alteration, an adaptation, not indeed to external reality but to this inner situation. A certain type of analytical resistance arises from this ego change particularly in obsessional and paranoid types, partly from the fact of the ego change itself, partly from the secondary epinosic gains.

(δ) *The affective reproduction of past situations.* It is possible to imagine a path of development so smooth that every response was adapted to meet the circumstances of the stimulus (whether internal or external), every event or tendency in the past having contributed its influence, of course, but in harmony with all other events and tendencies. The condition of such a finely acting automaton would differ from the condition found in patients in that the adjustments would be all proportionate. It is with the aberrations in adjustment that the psychiatrist is naturally concerned, and for the most part he confines himself to an examination of the current event. Psycho-analysts are forced by an unwitting tendency in their patients to view things chronologically, and they have brought forward observations and hypotheses which, while inadequate to explain all of the phenomena, at least indicate precise points for consideration.

The development of the libido (oral, anal, genital stages) presents to the developing ego a succession of tasks in adaptation. Mention has been made of the change over from the rhythmical pump to the spasmodic bite method of obtaining nourishment involving a casting off of one type of ego action for another; the example is however not a purely ego one but includes a libidinal activity as well, that is to say, the baby has to renounce an erotic pleasure easily obtained for another which involves acquirement of a new technique. It has been suggested[1] that such acquirements are brought about by a change of libidinal cathexis, the ego becoming temporarily overcharged to facilitate the new procedure; the acquirement of a new technique, then, requires (a) a mobility of libido, (b) that the ego should be able to carry the extra charge *temporarily*. So far this is a restatement of much that has been said in Parts I and II of this Survey, but we are now faced with a new problem, that of the ego's potential or actual anxiety in the transition periods.

The situation which evokes anxiety is that in which the ego is helpless, a state which may arise if external circumstances are overpowering or if internal (instinctual) stimuli cannot be mastered. There are crises in the course of development when new stimuli leave the child in a condition of helplessness just because adequate pathways for discharge of excitation have not been opened, such, for example, as the change over from sucking to biting already mentioned. When there is weakness in the development of the ego[2] the new 'steps' are particularly difficult, or if there is a stimulation of or strong satisfaction from one zone constitutionally determined (the effect is the same as a weakness of the ego), the result in such cases is a *fixation*. A fixation is a tendency to revert to or to keep to an archaic mode of gratification. In the early days the occasions of anxiety, i.e. the times when the ego was liable to be helpless as a result of libido tension, were the developments of activity at a fresh zone, *the disturbance coming from adjustment to something new*; but

[1] Kapp, 'Sensation and Narcissism', *Int. Jnl. of Ps.A.*, 1925, **6**, 292–9.
[2] The development of the ego has not been worked out in any detail yet by psycho-analysts.

this is not the only possibility, there can be anxiety from a fail-ure on the part of the ego *to renounce an old gratification at the behest of the super-ego.* These two occasions of anxiety are not entirely separable since in respect to this mechanism of adap-tation the super-ego may be regarded as having an influence like a sort of new zone in the psychical life.[1] Thus there are two sources of helplessness: an instinctual mode of reaction which has not been mastered may throw a strain on the ego on the one hand, while on the other the ego may revert to an older mode of gratification; the former corresponds to anxiety of id-origin (id versus ego), the latter to one resulting from a conflict (ego versus super-ego).

The introduction of the super-ego into this argument reminds us that in this sub-section of the history of anxiety theories we have been dealing with libidinal aims and have neglected libidinal objects, and yet the object, if a parent, is very closely bound up with libidinal aims, e.g. nursing, discipline of the stool, castration, etc. If for any reason there is a lack of plasticity in the ego, a need for alteration of libidinal relation to the parents will reduce the ego to a condition of helplessness in the face of instinct excitation. The thought of castration stands pre-eminent as a source of anxiety, so much so that in many cases it seems to absorb the fear from all other situations into itself. We can now review the situation from the new aspect provided by the Danger-Signal Theory. The excitation produced by instinct impulse is hardly to be regarded as a danger in itself but it may be regarded by the ego as a danger (*a*) if the ego is weak and cannot master the impulse (anxiety neurosis), (*b*) if the gratifi-cation of the impulse would bring about conflict with the super-ego (transference neuroses), (*c*) if the attempt to master the impulse leads to extensive alterations of ego-function (psychoses).[2]

[1] Having *no* bodily locality, I hasten to add. [The identification of the super-ego with the phallus in certain cults (Roheim) is another matter which lies more within the compass of anthropology than of psychiatry.]

[2] This may sound obscure at first reading. By way of explanation: an attempt to change the outlet of instinct impulse leads to a hyper-cathexis of the ego; if the desexualized libido employed by the ego in its own functioning does not suffice for this purpose there is a with-drawal of libidinal cathexis from objects in the external world, which then becomes to a greater or less extent meaningless and without capacity for affording gratification; the economic advantages of this procedure are (i) to reduce the significance of the real object (father

In the cases where the ego is responsive to instinct impulse in this inflexible way defensive devices are employed before ever the state of helplessness has set in, and according to its capacity to tolerate either the increase of instinct tension on the one hand, or the risks attendant on hypercathexis of itself, will its responses be normal or pathological.

No one probably is *alarmed* by an experience merely because it is new; it is comprehended as alarming because it arouses old situations which were alarming, in other words, what excites Angst is a *re*-discovery of helplessness, impending or actual. The ego responds to a relatively small quantity of affect as if it were the full devastating experience itself, it uses the anxiety as an alarm signal to rouse up the defences. The danger is real and important for the ego so long as it has no strength to master the situation; treatment consists in consolidating the ego's capacity to tolerate the danger ahead. This is done by the arousing of past situations with appropriate affect and so affording the ego a chance to re-experience consciously and to master consciously reactions that had before been dealt with reflexly and unconsciously. The fixations are undone by the ego gaining more courage to face the primitive modes of instinct gratification (modification of super-ego—ego relationship) and acquiring more capacity to tolerate instinct impulse (ego—id relationship).

15. *Classification of the Neuroses, Psycho-Neuroses and Psychoses. With tables*

Kraepelin's masterly classification was based on two kinds of data, the symptoms apparent to a clinician walking the wards on any given day and the end-results of the disease on the

and mother in Oedipus situation, and their *imagines*) and so reducing the pressure from without and narrowing the zone of danger, (ii) to constrict the field of id gratification to the self (compensation for dangers consequent on separation from alloerotic objects), (iii) to release the ego from the necessity for reality testing in regard to its own activity, hence delusional objects which can be varied replace immutable real objects which require adaptations of the ego.

If the relations to the outer world are not disturbed to any great extent there will be a character-change; if however the relations to the outer world are changed, and as has been said already little is known of ego-development and purely ego-pathology, there will be psychosis.

patient. His main divisions are not contested by psycho-analysts, the lesser ones are subject less to a revision than a revaluation.

Psycho-analytical observation is carried out in a sort of laboratory where special precautions are taken to enable a minute examination of the capacity of the patient to experience love-attachments to objects, and accordingly the first division of mental disorders is into cases in which the capacity to transfer love from the self to external objects is strong and those in which it is weak, the former being called transference neuroses, the latter narcissistic neuroses.

Applying Bain's rule of classification—'Place together in classes the things that possess in common the greatest number of attributes'—we naturally inquire whether the class of transference neuroses contains more than this one attribute of transference, and an examination of the larger subjoined table will show that it does. Of first importance is the fact that all the transference neuroses have libidinal fixation points later than the early anal, that is to say, the dividing line between transference neuroses and narcissistic neuroses is not only in respect to capacity for transference but in respect to the aim of the libido as well, or, expressed in other words, during and after the late anal stage there is a permanent bond forged between the ego and the outer world, and there is no strong tendency to annihilate it (late oral) in or to expel it (early anal) from the psychical system. There is a further attribute which unites the transference neuroses together and separates them from the narcissistic neuroses, viz. the relative strength of the ego or its capacity to deal with id impulses. (In this connection the fact that the character of the super-ego in transference neuroses is different from that in the narcissistic neuroses is of little classificatory importance since it is a derivative of forces whose attributes have already been used in the classification.)

The sub-divisions of the two classes already mentioned are a continuation in detail of the analysis of the general attributes in question; the stages in the march of the libido give the divisions roughly between dementia praecox, manic-depressive disease, and paranoia on the one hand, and obsessional neurosis and hysteria on the other; and as regards object love we can detect an increasing scale in the order named.

This general corroboration of Kraepelin's list must be a gratification to both psychiatrist and psycho-analyst; but a further examination raises difficult questions for the latter. It is not apparent why, for example, a strong tendency to autoplastic modifications should be formed in such remotely separated disorders as hysteria and dementia praecox, or why there should be such strong correspondences between manic-depressive disease and obsessional neurosis in regard to ambivalence, magical gestures, and importance of the rôle of the super-ego, while their fixation points are late oral and late anal respectively, i.e. separated by the early anal. Such 'difficulties' remind us that the diseases in question result from an interplay of aetiological factors and therefore cannot be sorted into sequences which increase with uniform smoothness in whatever particular syntactic attribute is chosen.

The inherent difficulties in any logical classification led me to put down in tabular form a number of diseases and their principal mechanisms opposite them (Table facing p. 330). It is far from complete. The 'difficulties' warn us against expending much energy in classification at the moment but rather to keep to investigation.

Prominence has just been given to the difference between transference and narcissistic neuroses (which are the disorders with which the psycho-analyst has chiefly to do) because it is of great practical as well as theoretical importance, but it throws a one-sided light on the classification. We may try a hazard with a bifurcate division. (See p. 331.)

It may be said of such a table that though it has a certain intellectual elegance it avoids almost every difficulty; for instance, traumatic neuroses which involve an increase of narcissism and decrease of object-capacity find no place, and the patho-neurotic group appears in the wrong place, for they are in fact linked to the 'object-group' as much as to its fellow on the opposite side. Tiqueurs are narcissistic yet maintain a large degree of object-capacity. The omission of Fetichism will warn readers against taking such tabulations too seriously, for it is necessary to include the links between perversion and neurosis, the former being the negative of the latter, as Freud said in one of his earliest papers.

Turning to the large table, some brief explanations will be required:

Type of social feeling is a loose term for the affective element in the neurosis with which the patient meets the claims of his fel-

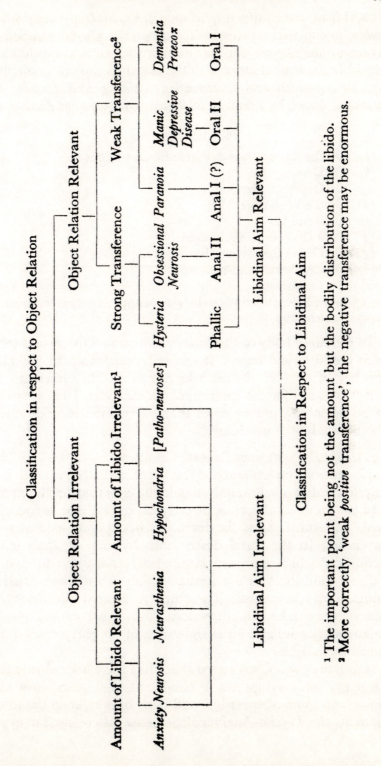

Classification in respect to Object Relation

Object Relation Irrelevant — Object Relation Relevant

Amount of Libido Relevant — Amount of Libido Irrelevant[1]

Strong Transference — Weak Transference[2]

Anxiety Neurosis *Neurasthenia* *Hypochondria* [Patho-neuroses] *Hysteria* *Obsessional Neurosis* *Paranoia* *Manic Depressive Disease* *Dementia Praecox*

Phallic Anal II Anal I (?) Oral II Oral I

Libidinal Aim Irrelevant — Libidinal Aim Relevant

Classification in Respect to Libidinal Aim

[1] The important point being not the amount but the bodily distribution of the libido.
[2] More correctly 'weak *positive* transference', the negative transference may be enormous.

lows, it is of descriptive importance only. *Mode of repression* and *mode of dealing with the return of the repressed* might be grouped together under *Defence* but for the fact that certain mechanisms should be associated more with the one than the other function, e.g. *Decomposition* and *Condensation*. *Isolating* and *Undoing* are terms employed by Freud in *Inhibitions, Symptoms and Anxiety, q.v.*

16. *Miscellaneous*

(*a*) On the Early Stages of Psychotic Conditions
(*b*) On Decomposition
(*c*) On Depersonalization
(*d*) On the Wish to get Well
(*e*) On Remissions
(*f*) On a Diagnostic Technique
(*g*) On Organ Speech and Restitution
(*h*) On Cerebral Patho-neuroses
(*i*) On Orgasm
(*j*) Some Brief Descriptions by way of approach to Definition
(*k*) Conclusion

In the main body of this Survey, which mainly treated topics from the historical aspect, it was not practicable to include a number of smaller themes which present themselves to the curiosity if not for the solution of the analysts. They are rather to be taken as random notes than as systematic additions to psycho-analytical psychiatry.

(a) On the Early Stages of Psychotic Conditions
No reader who has reached this point in this Survey will be in any doubt that psycho-analysts hold the view that developmental and environmental factors in early childhood play a conspicuously important part in the development of psycho-neuroses and psychoses. In the 'brief descriptions by way of approach to definition' which end this paragraph I endeavour to give the earliest time limit to the formation of each disease, this is of course only theoretical; if we turn to clinical experience our observations take two directions, the direct examination of infant psychotics and an examination of the early years during an adult analysis.

From my own observations of adults I have been able to trace clear psychotic symptoms in childhood (5–8 years) in a paranoiac and manic-depressive, and need only refer to the discussions in the Psycho-Analytical Societies where similar experi-

ences are reported. We therefore have to interpret the term
'Early Stages' as meaning not the first signs of alienation from
reason or 'normal' conduct (which is what most psychiatrists
usually mean) but stages of the disease that bear unmistakable
psychotic features in the early years of life. There are children
who project their unconscious homosexual passion and cover up
the projection from themselves by delusional systems, and yet
maybe appear to their parents and elders only as somewhat
queer and reserved; and children who introject one or other
parent into the ego system and treat themselves (and the introjected image) with sadistic severity, alternating perhaps with a
phase in which the ego—super-ego barrier vanishes—these are
cases of Early Stages of Psychotic Conditions which in a few
cases presumably do not require a psycho-analysis to disclose
them. Such cases have at present little theoretical interest, they
are comparable to carcinomatous conditions in the young—
unusual but not inexplicable.

Another aspect of the subject is more difficult to elucidate,
namely, whether an individual can become psychotic without
having characteristic defects in respect to ego and libido development, so that at twenty, say, he could without doubt be
diagnosed as a case of obsessional neurosis and at thirty as a
case of manic-depressive disease, assuming of course that the
analytic diagnostic technique was employed in the best possible
way on both occasions.

It is commonly believed that by treating psycho-neurotics it is
possible to do sound prophylactic work in reducing the number
of psychotics; psycho-analysts do not share this belief, not because it is in itself incredible but simply that it requires proof or
at least some explanation. The first question that has to be decided is whether the mere presence of a mechanism that is
found in psychotics is to be regarded as a sufficient justification
for thinking of the case as potentially psychotic. The answer is
in the negative for two reasons, first because a mechanism is a
device for reducing painful tension in the mind, it is not even a
pathological process but is sometimes brought into action on
account of one; and secondly because to lay stress on this or that
mechanism obscures the importance of quantitative elements.
For example, smoking is an autoerotic activity, but it is not true
that smokers are incapable of object-relationships; projection is
the mechanism used more than others by paranoiacs, but it is

not true that he who sees his own faults in another is necessarily paranoiac.

The matter is complicated by the fact that character formation is on the one hand linked to psychosis in that it implies a restriction of ego-adaptation to the outer world, and on the other is linked to object-love which is certainly not a psychotic characteristic. So we are left in a position of being unable exactly to say what is a pre-psychotic condition and must turn on those who profess to deal prophylactically with a condition they have not defined and ask them for their evidence.

It is not uncommon in the lax·phraseology of a Mental O.P. Department to hear of a case in which a psycho-neurosis 'masks' a psychosis; I have used the term myself, but with inward misgiving. There should be no talk of masks if a case is fully understood, and certainly not if the case has not received a tireless examination—except, of course, as a brief descriptive term comparable to 'shut-in' .or 'apprehensive', which carry our understanding of the case no further.

So far, as it seems to me, we have not been putting our questions properly, for we have not considered the matter in the light of our knowledge of nosogenesis. Some people fall ill when the external world fails to provide them with the satisfaction they need, others having a different constitution fall ill because their inner requirements prohibit gratification, and thirdly there are people who can only tolerate a certain *amount* of frustration. The question arises whether it is possible to say of any person that he or she will fall ill of a psychosis if the amount of libido tension increases for any reason beyond its accustomed degree. Such an opinion would be justified: (*a*) if sublimation capacities were known, (*b*) if the degree of character-change were already established, and (*c*) if the amount of libido gratification were already known in respect to the different channels of outlet. A further examination of 'normal' people will probably furnish the clue to the Early Stages of Psychotic Conditions because the failures of adaptation in the so-called healthy person are usually more connected with ego than with libido development.

(*b*) *On Decomposition*

The term is borrowed from literature. A dramatist wishes to portray a situation existing, for example, between father and son, in the brief time of a play and within the limitations of his technique he cannot show all that he wishes to develop before and after the climax, so he introduces subsidiary characters who bear the same general relation to one another and carries out 'developments' in these minor parts not only as illustrative setting but to increase and decrease the 'tension' of his main action. A similar process is often to be observed in organized delusions. A patient thought himself to be a 'high official' at the Courts of Rameses, Julius Caesar, the Empress of China and others, and that he received secret information from another high official who practised a special surgery on Royal Personages (sewing the spinal column with gold and silver wire); indeed he was a sort of liaison officer for all Courts and high officials; his emissaries and their activities were legion; they were rôles which he played by proxy, as it seemed to me, and I interpret his delusion as a desire to officiate in the secret life of his own home; this wish was both so strong and at the same time so strongly forbidden that he had, even in phantasy, to multiply the officers and the offices manifold to get relief or outlet for it. Another type of decomposition concerns not the self (which relatively speaking is unchanged) but some particular person.

A patient had in the same ward about a dozen 'ancestors'[1] including myself; he played with the pedigree like a professional genealogist, adding 'query-ancestors' and 'reputed-ancestors' from time to time. The mechanism of displacement is similar to that found in the Schreber case (§ 3 above) in that the affective attitude to the father is shifted, not to the one and awe-inspiring figure of God but to many fellow-patients and physicians. We may presume that he needed an interplay of his phantasy and real persons but with a mitigation of the direct relation to his own father; if he had made one person his 'ancestor' his phantasy would have been too intense and love and hostility would have forced themselves into action; he chose the method of substitution and then decomposition. Again to revert to literary terminology, the 'tension' is made more manageable when this decomposition takes place. We can however dispense with literary alliances and carry on the discussion in terms of clinical experience: a war-shock patient with battle-dreams modifies his traumatic neurosis by coupling elements of the painful scene to harmless civilian events; he couples the bangs of the war scene to

[1] Like those of the Arunta mythology they were remote or distant ancestors—alcheringa.

the explosions in motor-car 'silencers' and finally to the tapping on the door when he is called in the morning; he is taking divided doses of the traumatism and 'binding' it with associative links to events that he can master. In like fashion, as I understand the matter, the psychotic or neurotic takes father-features and 'binds' them by associative connection to relatively harmless or relatively non-exciting persons in his environment. We recognize two kinds of decomposition, the transient and the permanent, the former is explained by the success of the manœuvre, the latter by the supposition that the father-conflict has become too strong for the defence mechanism in question and it in turn has been employed to serve as a pleasure-outlet by coupling the libidinal conflicts of yesterday with the libidinal satisfactions of to-day, i.e. it has become stabilized as a symptom.

(c) *On Depersonalization*[1]

We meet cases who have gone through or are in a stage in which they feel estranged from themselves or from their surroundings. There are the familiar objects and the familiar faces but they themselves are different; or contrariwise, they feel that the objects, though recognized as old acquaintances, are nevertheless altered in some way; there are of course great degrees of variation in this peculiar feeling.

In the paragraph on the Sense of Reality it was remarked that the sense of Inner and Outer was not sharply defined in the dawn of our psychical life, neither is it ever absolute. We therefore are led to suspect that the feeling of 'alteration' may have something to do with a return to the stage when the distinctions were still less sharp than they later became. The clearest cases are those which, like Schreber, suffered a World Catastrophe in which external things became mere phantoms, men 'cursory contraptions' and birds and trees 'bemiracled' relics of former souls. In that case as in others it appears that the 'depersonalization' occurred after a partial withdrawal of libidinal cathexis from the objects in question. Nunberg holds that this state is a kind of narcissistic illness of longer or shorter duration and is to be distinguished from the partial withdrawal of cathexis in cases of other psycho-neurotic illness, in that in the latter there is partial libido gratification in the symptoms,

[1] Nunberg, 'Ueber Depersonalisationszustände im Lichte der Libidotheorie,' *Zeit. f. Psychoanalyse*, 1924, **10**, 17–33.

whereas in the depersonalization there is a more or less prolonged state of lack of libido satisfaction. The paraphrenic (paranoiac and schizophrenic) experiences delusions of grandeur or hypochondria when the libido surges back on the ego; the patient with depersonalization on the other hand feels a loss of accustomed sensibility, but without total loss of object-cathexis. A disparity is thus produced which distorts the perception of the antithesis Inner-Outer and therefore (since there is also regression) of what is real. Put in other words, since libidinal gratification is cut off, there is no basis for the conviction of external reality and so the patient goes back to internal reality as in the days when what was good was a Me-part of experience, i.e. before the limitations of the self were clearly realized. The patient however, since there is some object-cathexis left, feels that he himself is at fault for not obtaining the gratification, so we come to the paradox that an infantile regression is accompanied by a sense that a part of the ego is lost—to him, of course, it seems to be lost—because a part is attached to the object. Now the perception of objects and their reality is usually strengthened by cathexis; how comes it then that there is a feeling of loss of reality in these cases? The answer is of course that the objects are unconscious presentations—unconscious phantasies. So for depersonalization to occur there must be (i) partial withdrawal of object and ego cathexis, (ii) a pathological condition of the ego which responds to loss of cathexis as to a narcissistic injury, (iii) a relative hyper-cathexis of unconscious phantasies.

(d) *On the Wish to get Well*[1]

No one wishes in the depths of his mind to get rid of his symptoms, for these are not his trouble but defences raised to ward off trouble. They are deceived by appearances who think that their patients really wish to be rid of the defences. The symptom is erected in place of a conflict, what *the patient desires is to get rid of the helpless feeling which he is beginning to experience owing to the failure of the symptoms to function properly*; but he does not know this, he asks to be rid of an obsessing thought or a phobia and yet manifests the greatest reluctance to part with it. Some requests for cure sound reasonable but they carry no weight when put to the test. A patient came for treatment because he had made some silly mistakes and felt it desirable to get rid of a 'complex' (un-

[1] Bibl. 350.

defined) that disturbed his work when he was excited by any strain. In free association of ideas it became apparent that he really wished analysis in a few months to make him—Prime Minister! The contrast between conscious and unconscious motives is here clearly seen; he could and did acknowledge the former, the latter surprised him when first expressed but he came to realize that it was a real deep-seated infantile wish. The analysis was a long struggle in adaptation to reality; in the process it was necessary to go over not only this but many other infantile desires, egoistic to some extent but chiefly erotic. The wish for improvement expressed on rational lines masked a number of unconscious gratifications, many of them out of touch with reality. This throws fresh light on the question of insight; if by this term is meant only that the patient feels he is ill, then in the writer's experience all psycho-neurotics and nearly all psychotics have insight; in paranoia and dementia praecox the 'unwellness' that they feel is often a hypochondriacal depression and may not be divulged for a long time on account of suspiciousness, but it is there and can be elicited—granted that the patient will address himself to his physician, of course, i.e. that there is some capacity for (need for) transference.

We have then to distinguish between insight into the fact of suffering and insight into its cause, and, since so-called normal persons are moved by unconscious instinctual impulses and unconscious super-ego reactions to these, we needs must be careful where we draw the line when we say that absence of insight is pathognomonic.

Some patients assert that they know they are ill but have no desire to take steps to change their condition. It is as great a mistake to take this at its face value as the opposite condition, a 'reasonable' wish for cure. In the former case the patient is apprehensive of the pressure of id impulses being increased, in the latter lest ego defences be weakened. They can be reduced to a common formula in both cases: the patient is apprehensive lest his ego be burdened to master an instinct impulse relatively too strong for it.

To return to the question of the wish to get well, which at first sounded so simple but is really complicated: we have to decide whether the more important factors in the aetiology of the neuroses and psychoses are conscious or unconscious, for this determines the direction of therapeutic endeavour. Those who hold that conscious factors produce disease must find themselves in a quandary when trying to explain their slowness or 'difficulty' in curing their patients, e.g. by Dubois' persuasion or its equivalents.

(e) On Remissions

Every professional man approaches this matter with his own criteria ready made; the lawyer thinks of legal responsibility and testamentary capacity, the asylum committee of social responsibility, the almoner of earning capacity, the psychiatrist of all together, the psycho-analyst on top of all adds his complicated psycho-pathology.

A remission in psycho-pathology consists in a reversion to a previous ego-adaptation to external and internal stimuli, i.e. one that affords sufficient libido gratification with not too much reaction formation. A remission is a return to a former level of ego and libido development. Thus for example the manic-depressive in respect to libidinal aim advances in his remission from a late oral through the early anal to a late anal and early phallic phase (the change can be noted in the construction and content of the free associations); in his treatment of the object we can observe a diminution of the violent ambivalence and a high degree of narcissism to a part-love and later to tolerance of object-love; in respect to the modification of the feeling of omnipotence the remission is marked by a weakening of the omnipotence of gesture and word and an increasing submission to the reality-principle. To the psycho-analyst these criteria are an advance to orderly thinking even though they lack precise boundaries, to the clinician about to make a prognosis they are invaluable as an aid when he checks the details of the progress made and therefore the chances of relapse. By the employment of such criteria the teaching of psychiatry is made easier because more intelligible, but this does not lessen the need for and value of what might be called pure clinical intuition. No matter how exact the criteria, the translation of the patient's state in terms of the standards has still to be made and in nothing is this more difficult than in judging remission.

The wish to get well resolves itself into a wish for infantile gratification plus a freedom from the paralysing feeling of helplessness. Not infrequently the patient gets a sense of the freedom and appears for the moment happier, more capable, more at ease, than he really is. He passes out of the physician's care and owing to increase of some contributory aetiological factor he may for example experience again a burst of guilt feeling for his infantile sexual wishes, and, if a manic-depressive, may kill himself. The test of the remission is the diminution of the proportionate strength of unconscious impulses; to gauge these it is necessary to employ a special technique for exploring the unconscious or trust to intuition based on an ordinary clinical interview. By setting up detailed criteria for remission and cure the psychoanalyst is employing psychological concepts which are as proper to the treatment of his material as are measure and scales to the physiologist's. We ask of the latter when he comes to our wards definite answers in terms of number or chemical structure and should ask of the psycho-pathologist definite answers in terms of psychological mechanisms; unlike physiology, psycho-pathology is in the hands of physicians who are also clinicians.

(f) On a Diagnostic Technique

Recent advances in psychiatric diagnostic technique may be divided into two classes, those which employ the apparatus of the physical sciences—the measure and scales in all their forms —and those which rely on a modification of introspection in the observer, viz. a special psychological 'instrument' for detecting small psychological changes (chiefly affective) in another person.[1] The two methods should not be confused; the one works by employing probabilities (e.g. the blood constituents in hebephrenics are usually so and so, the blood constituents in this patient are thus and thus, therefore the probability that this patient is hebephrenic is x), the other by recognizing certain characteristic mechanisms in action (e.g. projection, hallucination, delusion) and assessing their importance. In regard to the latter method, the psychiatrist relies on an interview which is largely an interrogation, the psycho-analyst employs a special device, which is profoundly different.

In the case of an analysis for diagnosis the physician strives to obtain a view of the patient in certain psychical situations rather than relying on a report of these from the patient and his relations. The question arises at once, what situations are diagnostically important? The answer is *not* such as those with which

[1] I read a paper on this topic before the British Psychological Society, Medical, Section in May, 1926.

the patient has to cope in everyday life or a psychiatric consultation, to which he can adapt himself by falling back on automatic mechanisms he acquired before he fell ill, but such as result from the removal of the patient from an everyday environment in order to uncover his deeper unconscious mental processes, i.e. to take away his usual techniques for dealing with persons and things and let him be observed in unfamiliar circumstances so that his groping may the more clearly display the movements of his object-relationships, his libido-attachments, their kind, their strength and their aim. We know that in the psychiatric interview with its pointed interrogations the patient is stimulated to defence, but we do not see the defence at work, we only recognize the end-effect; we also know that the physician has to manœuvre his patient often with the patient knowing full well what is going on; but the greatest disadvantage of all is that we cannot see clearly the beginning and end of the libidinal attachments which develop (even under interrogation) in the patient to his physician.

In the psycho-analytic diagnostic technique the patient is asked at an early stage in the interview to recline on the couch and say all that comes to his mind. To introduce such a queer novelty into a psychiatric consulting room may appear to physicians strange, but patients do not take unkindly to it if the analyst does not. By this method it is possible to watch in a clearer way than otherwise the degree of interaction between unconscious, pre-conscious and conscious levels of functions of the mind and those of ego, super-ego and id, and so of course the types of defence against painful ideas; further the physician does not have to manœuvre his patient to anything like the same extent as in interrogation, often not at all, and he can observe the beginning and the end of the libidinal relationship. By this last is meant not the beginning and end of a treatment but of an interview or series of interviews. To make the characteristic points intelligible it would be necessary to go into details of psycho-analytic technique in general, but a word may be said by way of illustration of the phenomena of the end of the interview: some patients, when told to come at such and such an hour on the morrow, will reply with a narration of the difficulties of fitting in a time (though just before they have asserted that they have no engagements); others will instantly grow suspicious that a trap will be laid for them (the psychiatrist's interest usually is satisfied at the fact of the suspicion of a trap, the psycho-analyst's interest, however, is beginning to be warmed up for more details—what kind of a trap, how the trap selected fits into the patient's past experience and present desires for libidinal gratification, etc.); others will see in this a coldness on the part of the analyst because he does not go on and on to-day with the consultation, whilst others will see in the next appointment a sign of his further interest in them; some will question the analyst exactly how much he has discovered, others will tell him there is yet more to say. The psychiatrist may guess some of these things, but without familiarity with the technique of free association he will not be able to make them pathways to deeper research into the patient's mental mechanisms.

There is no doubt in the writer's mind that the technique under discussion gives better opportunities for studying the case than the interview; it remains for him to say what can be made of the opportunities. The process reveals the patient's behaviour in a special way in that a separation into component mechanisms is far easier than by ordinary clinical observation; for instance, it is possible to tell a delusional projection from a statement of fact about another persons's conduct by the setting of the statement in the stream of associations; this sometimes furnishes a further clue not only to the genesis of the delusion but to its importance in the daily life of the patient. In other cases it is possible to distinguish obsessional neurosis from manic-depressive disease in remissions apart from the history, and hysterical conditions from conversion symptoms in dementia praecox during the long spells of 'recovery'. The discovery of such mechanisms is of course of the greatest service in making a prognosis.

The dangers of such a diagnostic technique are those of analysis itself, it should never be employed by those who are not trained in it.

(g) On Organ Speech and Restitution

In the unconscious, ideas exist that are not attached to word-presentations. If they are attached to visual images and if they receive sufficient cathexis they appear at the sensory end of the psychical apparatus and are perceived as hypnogogic visions; the alternative path to consciousness is by union with a word-image. This latter kind of union takes place in the preconscious, and is of importance in affording great flexibility to though processes and is also of social importance in communicating ideas from one person to another; it is in addition one of the minimal acts which afford an outlet for libidinal excitation. It is as if ordinary speech were an intermediary stage between mastery of the object or union with it physically and a manipulation of it psychically. When listening to or giving utterance to speech we normally pass over the word and pay attention to the thing, but in schizophrenia we find the object-cathexis is abandoned to a greater or less extent; where does it go? If not to the ego (producing megalomania and more or less complete indifference to the outer world) it may pass to the word-presentation. The word now stands for the object as a source of libidinal satisfaction. This throws light on one of the most peculiar activities of these patients—their play with words; it appears that they substitute play with words for action with things. An example from Jung (see p. 231): one of his patients says, 'I grand duke Mephisto will have you treated with blood-revenge for Orang-Outang representation.'[1] Here the patient appears to be treating words as dream images are treated to make dream thoughts, by condensation and displacement of cathexis from one idea (or word in this case) to another.

While the relation between external object and the corresponding word-presentation becomes more remote in the schizophrenic, that existing between the word-presentation and the patient's own organs becomes more intimate. I recall a patient whose capacity to express his ideas in terms of his own organs seemed almost unlimited, he contrived the weirdest puns apparently without effort. His financial affairs were not in a bad way in spite of his disease—or because of it—as he made his living as a cabaret contortionist, who alternated in his turns between the writhings of his body and the organ-punning, to the delight of his audience; but he was a fully developed schizophrenic, having practically no love or hate feelings to anyone; everything was equally meaningless or equally a joke. There were three at the consultation; he pointed at my colleague and then at his nose while looking at me. I asked what he was saying by that; he replied, 'He knows.' I remarked on this in the medical vernacular; he stroked his forehead upwards—'Highbrow'—so I translated what I had said into plain English, remarking that he used organs other than those of speech to ex-

[1] Jung regarded this as hysterical, it is of course schizophrenic.

press his thoughts, whereupon he pointed to his own and our boots and then to another part of himself, and said by way of interpretation, 'Our-soles!' He desired treatment because the strain of censoring his own remarks on the stage sometimes got too much for him and the management received complaints. Beneath many of his remarks lay the crudest sexual ideas, some of them disguised in the most transparent symbolism; but whether thinly or thickly veiled he could always interpret them himself. It looked then as if the cathexis of external objects had been passed over to the word-presentation, but that the latter was not repressed. In hysteria and obsessional neurosis exactly the opposite is the case, the patients lose none of their object cathexis, and the act of repression is directed to separating the thing from its word-presentation. This patient knew all of his thoughts—his most erotic ones too—in regard to external objects, and endeavoured to regain his hold on the outer world, but since the cathexis had remained on the word, not the thing, he could only make puns about, not make love to what lay outside himself.

If this position is established, then, we gain insight into another phenomenon, namely, the Restitution process of paraphrenia in the attempt at self-cure. The illness (for purposes of description only) can be broken up theoretically into two stages, that of detachment of cathexis from the object, and that of absorption of the cathexis by the ego. It seems as if the latter process is hindered by two things, first a tendency for cathexis to return to objects, second, a tendency of the ego to unburden itself of the accumulation of cathexis.[1] The process of self-cure is designed to mitigate the pain of the second by increasing the pleasure in the first; but there are hindrances: first the objects were the occasions of conflict, so a restoration of full object cathexis would bring on the ego a burden of troubles it once sought to avoid; second the ego is not able fully to permit the discharge of tension by means of potentially dangerous objects for the reason just given, it is itself suffering from a weakness in control of or in checking strong discharges of tension; and third (dependent on the above) it can find pleasure in an intermediate step in activity with objects, i.e. in a special kind of phantasy.

[1] In pure megalomania (if it exists) there is an unlimited capacity of the ego to tolerate its cathexis; the degrees of megalomania, then, would correspond to the degree of this ego tolerance.

This special kind of phantasy takes its character from the mechanism employed, in one case it is a union of organ cathexis and word-cathexis to form organ speech, in another it is more simply a manipulation of word-cathexes to form neologisms, in others where there is more of the original object-cathexis remaining there is an interest in the outer world but only of a weakly affective kind (this favours the delusional state), in others the mechanism is hysterical and there are hallucinations. Sometimes the affective life is almost purely narcissistic but led by traces of object-cathexis (which defensively is uniformly spread, so to speak); not objects but the relationships and properties of objects are the subject of manipulation and so of libidinal gratification; this occurs in the schizophrenic mathematician.

To return for a moment to organ speech: we observed that it served as a means of expressing a thought comparable to dreams, sometimes of conveying thought, e.g. 'He knows,' 'Highbrow'; but at the same time it serves an autoerotic function in that the cathexis does not 'leave' the ego. In some cases the narcissistic element appears with great clearness, not to say blatancy. Some years ago I saw in the Prater (Vienna) a woman displaying her tattooing;[1] she began her harangue in this way: 'Ladies and gentlemen, I carry on my body the creative genius of the whole world, on my breast you may see the famous Goethe, here on my right forearm Napoleon, here Beethoven, here we have Shakespeare, and on my leg Julius Caesar . . .' etc. It is hard to resist the idea that she substituted an object-relation to these great ones and their works by bringing them into connection with her own organs. Normal people behave in the opposite way; through loving admiration of the poet and enjoyment of his works they produce his plays, go to Weimar or Stratford-on-Avon to strengthen their phantasy and bring themselves yet nearer to him, they mould their behaviour in the way that lovers do to obtain a deeper union with their beloved, they think of him and let him take the centre of their lives for the time being, and they 'take up' one such person at a time; or they may regress from an object-love to identification and adopt one of his characteristics in order to be by that much the *same* as

[1] The proportion of tattooed among dementia praecox patients, it is said, is higher than among other asylum inmates, bearing witness to the relation of this form of organ speech to their disorder.

their adored. This tattooed woman took all great persons equally and simultaneously upon herself, and moulded only patches of her skin. When looking at her one felt she was really no whit nearer to Goethe for having Goethe pricked out on her dermis, but for her it was an object-relationship or rather as much of it as her defective ego and libido could manage; it showed traces of more object-attitude than the megalomaniac who sits alone and thinks himself to *be* the universe itself; she had avenues to the outer world open, but they were traversed only by—names!—words for the thing, not love for the thing.

(h) On Cerebral Pathoneuroses

Ferenczi made an avowedly speculative excursion into the psycho-pathology of the symptoms of megalomania, hypochondria, delusional formations and the like in G.P.I. His book (with Hollós) was abstracted once by the present writer at great length,[1] and that will not be repeated here; but this question arises, whether the psychical symptomatology of the abiotrophic and arteriosclerotic patients should not be re-examined in the light of his Cerebral Patho-neurotic suggestions.

(i) On Orgasm[2]

(i) The doctrine that in genital orgasm the organism finds the maximum of discharge for accumulated sexual tension has a corollary, viz. that without it the organism cannot function free from the strain and inefficiency of repression.

(ii) Potency has a psycho-physical quality that does not allow of separation of the elements to an unlimited extent, but it is necessary to distinguish between orgastic potency and erective power in the male and between orgastic potency and pleasurable genital sensations in the female.

(iii) The function of thought should proceed undisturbed by pleasure and the sexual act proceed unchecked by processes of thought.

These three analytical dicta have led to an important deduction, that in assessing the extent of cure and the safeguards of the patient against relapse the genital's capacity to act as a free and open conduit of sexual tension must be studied minutely.

[1] *Brit. Journal of Medical Psychology* 5, p. 120.
[2] *Vide* Bibl. 121 and 391–397.

The criteria that may be applied have been suggested by Reich.[1]

(i) The acts of forepleasure should not be too prolonged; this weakens orgasm.

(ii) Fatigue or sleepiness and a strong desire for sleep should follow the act.

(iii) Among women with full orgastic potency there is often a tendency to cry out at the acme.

(iv) A light clouding of consciousness is the rule in complete orgastic potency, unless the act is done too often.

(v) Disgust, aversion or weakening of tender impulses to the partner after the act argues against intact orgastic potency, and indicates that conflict and inhibition were present during the act.

(vi) The anxiety of many women during the act that the penis will relax too soon before they are 'ready' also speaks against this orgastic potency.

(vii) Disregard on the part of the man for the woman's gratification bespeaks a lack of tenderness in the bonds between them.

(viii) The postures should be studied: incapability to perform rhythmic movements hinders orgasm and wide opening of the legs and a firm rest for the back is indispensable for the woman.

A direct interrogation is of course useless in this as in nearly every type of psychological investigation, but the information is often forthcoming if an analysis is in progress; not that it may not be obtained without it, but the fine points which tell so much, the antecedent and following free associations, reveal more than bare statements can ever do, for they show the emotional context in the unconscious mind.

Such criteria as these have merit in being definite and such standards of cure as they imply deserve the close attention of psychiatrists. If more is known of aetiology in the psychoneuroses and psychoses there will be less said of 'inexplicable' relapses; whatever may be said of psycho-analysis, let no one say it shirks detailed investigation and explanation, and let no

[1] Wilhelm Reich, 'Further Remarks on the Therapeutic Significance of Genital-Libido,' *Brit. Jnl. of Med. Psych.* 1925, **5**, 238–40. (An abstract by the present writer from a paper in the *Int. Zeit. f. Psychoanalyse.*)

one think that it does not demand detailed refutation or detailed modification and criticism.

(*j*) *Some Brief Descriptions by way of approach to Definition*

Anxiety Neurosis

Group: actual neuroses.

Mechanism: due to accumulation of libido, the accumulation being caused by deflection of sexual excitation from somatic to psychical.

Aetiology: (i) *Constitutional* factor: probably weak ego tolerance of increase of erotic tension.

(ii) *Specific:* deflection of libido from somatic to psychical: rude awakening to sexual problems, impotence of partner, coitus interruptus, voluntary abstinence, climacteric increase of libido, frustrated sexual excitement.

(iii) *Predisposing:* any aetiological factor which lowers the ego powers of resistance: infection, intoxications, over-strain, etc.

(iv) *Precipitating:* any shock having the effect of (iii) or of increasing (ii).

Age Incidence: earliest, in infancy; *commonly,* at the crises of vita sexualis, i.e. puberty, late adolescence, climacteric.

Course: in recent cases a change in vita sexualis gives opportunity for recuperation of ego-tolerance; if noxae are prolonged and disease runs a chronic course there is very extensive deflection of libido from the physical sphere.

Symptoms: general irritability, anxious expectation, anxiety attacks and larval forms of the same (palpitation, pseudo-angina, nervous dyspnoea, sweating often nocturnal, tremors, ravenous hunger, diarrhoeas, vertigo, vasomotor neuroses, paraesthesias, pavor nocturnus).

Differential Diagnosis: from *anxiety hysteria* (often difficult) by the fact that the libido in anxiety hysteria is finding outlet in more infantile forms in symptoms which are also of psychological significance; from *obsessional neurosis* by absence in the former of obsessional thoughts, regression to anal-sadistic stage, ambivalence; from the anxiety of *melancholia* by presence in melancholia of self-reproaches, symptoms of obsessional neurosis, anal-sadistic regression and character traits; from anxiety of *paranoia* by presence in the latter of projective mechanisms; from *G.P.I.* (in addition to physical and serological signs) by presence in

G.P.I. of peculiar libido distribution—strong organ cathexes, especially cerebral pathoneuroses, i.e. disturbance of ego (*C.N.S.*) —genital psychical polarity (note fluctuating potency in G.P.I. varying with euphoria followed by hypochondria and impotence; masking of anxiety by grandiose ideas).

Neurasthenia

Group: actual neuroses.

Mechanism: due to diminution in the amount of sexual tension, the decrease of tension being felt by the ego to be painful; it is an 'ego-hypochondria' (Ferenczi).

Aetiology: (i) *Constitutional* factor: probably weak ego tolerance of decrease of erotic tension.

(ii) *Specific:* masturbation, overt or larval.

(iii) *Predisposing:* any aetiological factor which lowers the ego's powers of enduring psychical pain.

(iv) *Precipitating:* any situation calling for increase of ego or libidinal activity.

Age Incidence: earliest, in infancy; *commonly,* in adolescence and at crises involving increase of ego or libidinal activity.

Types: one day neurasthenia, due to a single act of masturbation or of onanism *in vaginam*; *chronic neurasthenia,* usually due to masturbation.

Course: the ego adapts its surroundings to its diminished capacities by flight from strenuous situations; a balance is thus reached.

Differential Diagnosis: from *mental exhaustion* by the fact that holidays do not recuperate the neurasthenic, and the neurasthenic usually feels better towards evening; from *G.P.I.* (see anxiety neurosis).

Note: cases of pure neurasthenia must be very rare. An adult does not masturbate unless there are neurotic complications in his case; infantile neurasthenia from infantile masturbation is not unknown.

Hypochondria

Group: actual neuroses.

Mechanism: due to physical sensations which usually are subliminal, being received in consciousness from internal organs. Causes of the sensations being perceived: (*a*) the patient directs attention to them; (*b*) increase in strength of afferent impulses, due to (i) increase of 'residual' cathexis (owing to imperfect or incomplete concentration of libido in the genital), (ii) reflux of cathexis after a genital primacy has been reached and lost (genitalization of non-genital organs without concomitant object relationship).

Aetiology: (i) *Constitutional:* weakness of genital organization.

(ii) *Specific:* Fixation or reflection of libido to organs.

(iii) *Predisposing:* painful diseases may predispose.

(iv) *Precipitating:* general systemic illnesses.

Age Incidence: earliest, in infancy theoretically (but very rarely); *commonly,* in climacteric, when retrogression of libido is occurring.

Course: narcissistic regression with masochistic compensation.

Symptoms: see text-books.[1]

Differential Diagnosis: from *melancholia* by absence of guilt, obsessional symptoms and sadistic regression and character traits; from *paranoid symptoms* by absence of projection.

Note: cases of pure hypochondria must be very rare; the libido changes are so bound up as a rule with object-relationships that psycho-neurotic or psychotic alterations seem theoretically to be inevitable.

Conversion Hysteria

Group: psycho-neurosis or transference-neurosis.

Mechanism: defence against over-strong libidinal excitation by a mysterious conversion of the psychical excitation into physical innervation; the innervation is not haphazard but represents a genitalization of the bodily part in relation to an unconscious love object.

Aetiology: (i) *Constitutional:* impaired psycho-sexual development.

(ii) *Specific:* fixation at the phallic stage of libido development; tendency to autoplastic modifications.

[1] Psycho-analysts have nothing new to say except to point out how remarkably similar are the complaints of hypochondria to those of neurasthenics in regard to vague pains in the body. Is there then anything in the act of masturbation to cause the reflux of libido to parts of the body erotically unprepared for it? For example, the lips become turgid in the normal sexual congress and pass some of their excitement to the genitals; in the libidinal explosion of orgasm there is a recoil to organs but recently active and ready for the discharge; in masturbation the other zones are not prepared and so cannot deal with the reflux, hence organ-libido accumulation and pain.

(iii) *Contributory:* frustration in external life with strong unconscious phantasies.

Age Incidence: earliest, at phallic stage; *commonly,* after the latent period at any time.

Incidence in the Population: one of the most widespread of all illnesses, aetiologically important in the majority of cases of constipation, gastric neuroses, nausea and vomiting of pregnancy, many eye symptoms, headache, etc.

Differential Diagnosis: from *organic disease*: diagnosis of hysteria can be made and should be made on positive evidence, not by exclusion; conversely, there is a characteristic libido distribution in organic disease which can often be used as a positive sign in detecting non-psychological changes; from *dementia praecox*: in dementia praecox there is often an appearance of conversion hysteria in the symptomatology but having a different aetiological origin and 'meaning' (see section on Organ Speech).

Anxiety Hysteria

Group: psycho-neuroses or transference-neuroses.

Mechanism: (*a*) a reaction of fear caused by a paralysing conflict in the ego due to an increase of sexual excitation attached to an unconscious object.

(*b*) The fear is avoided by displacing the conflict to an object or situation outside the ego system.

Aetiology: (i) *Constitutional:* (*a*) impaired psycho-sexual development; (*b*) tendency to anxiety reaction.

(ii) *Specific:* fixation at phallic stage and frustration.

(iii) *Contributory:* any factor weakening ego.

(iv) *Precipitating:* anything increasing libidinal excitement.

Age Incidence: earliest, earlier than conversion hysteria; *commonly,* after latency period and at crises of *vita sexualis*.

Incidence in Population: nearly as common as conversion hysteria, accounts for most of the ill-defined 'nervousness' of which patients and their relations complain.

Differential Diagnosis: from the anxiety states in *melancholia* (cases not infrequently come to Mental O.P. with diagnosis of anxiety states that really are mild melancholics) association in melancholia of anxiety (and depression) with obsessional symptoms, particularly the sadism of the super-ego.

Obsessional Neurosis

Group: psycho-neuroses or transference-neuroses.

Mechanisms: (a) separation of affect from the presentation (Undoing, Isolating); (b) regression to anal-sadistic level; (c) turning of the impulse against the self; (d) omnipotence of thought.

Aetiology: (i) *Constitutional:* impairment of ego and libido development.

(ii) *Specific:* fixation of libido at anal-sadistic stage and ego at stage of omnipotent thoughts.

(iii) *Contributory:* any frustration of post-anal-sadistic libidinal aim or any factor weakening ego.

(iv) *Precipitating:* any situation leading to increased gratification of anal-sadistic impulse may excite reflexive response and lead to outbreak.

Age Incidence: earliest, in early childhood before latency; not uncommon in latency period, at puberty usually patients are less affected, in post puberty and adolescence it is common.

Differential Diagnosis: from melancholia by presence in obsessional neuroses of strong transference, no tendency to introject object, weaker oral element, super-ego less vindictive.

Paranoia

Group: psychoses.

Mechanisms: (a) repression of homosexual impulses; (b) return of repressed dealt with by projection; (c) regression from sublimated homosexuality to narcissism; (d) decomposition assisting repression.

Aetiology: (i) *Constitutional.*

(ii) *Specific:* fixation at a pregenital stage of libido development and at an early stage of ego development (and some important but unknown relation between these two fixations).

(iii) *Contributing:* (a) frustration in object relationships, (b) overstrong libidinal excitations that cannot be mastered (e.g. resulting from operations on erotogenic zones), (c) anything that weakens the ego's power to deal with psychical stimuli.

Age Incidence: earliest, at any time after the Oedipus situation has been resolved by adopting an unstable homosexual attitude; *commonly,* at the crises in the *vita sexualis.*

Types: dependent on the re-distribution of the libido: (a) *megalomaniac,* in which the libido returns to the ego; (b) *perse-*

cutory, in which object relationship is maintained, a once loved person being now a persecutor; (*c*) *erotomania*, in which the sex of the person loved is changed; (*d*) *jealousy*, in which there is no true projection but an altered external perception.

Course: (*a*) complete absorption of libido into ego, i.e. a change in ego making this possible, or a weakening of object bonds; (*b*) *restitution*, more or less complete modification of ego to repressed id tendencies so that it reacts to these, later acquiring by secondary modifications a working compromise between these and the demands of the outer world; (*c*) *compensation*, more or less complete modification of id tendencies which is done at expense of the ego's freedom in libidinal but not intellectual outlet.

Differential Diagnosis: from *hysteria* in cases of erotomania by the fact that in hysteria perception of the love relationship is first endopsychic, in paranoia is by projection; from *dementia praecox* the distinction is in many cases exceedingly difficult, since in dementia praecox there is regression and decomposition, but in paranoia the regression is not so complete, the schizophrenic symptoms are less important (e.g. organ speech negativism); from *G.P.I.*, persecutory type: the hated person was not necessarily once loved, erotomanic type: compensatory for impotence; jealous type: not necessarily due to homosexual love; from *patho-neuroses:* in paranoia the cathexis from the outer world is drawn on to the ego as a whole, not on to organs as in patho-neuroses.

Manic-Depressive Disease

Group: narcissistic neuroses.

Mechanisms: (*a*) ambivalent conflict between tendency to (anal) expulsion of object from ego system and (oral) incorporation into it while conflict lasts; (*b*) pathological separation of ego and super-ego (melancholia) or fusion (mania); (*c*) recovery by (anal) mastery resulting in temporary or permanent obsessional neurosis or obsessional character.

Aetiology: (i) *Constitutional:* strengthening of oral libido.

(ii) *Specific:* fixation in oral stage of libido, introjection of parent-imago before a strong positive transference has been established.

(iii) *Contributory:* any blows to narcissistic libido, especially Oedipus disappointments.

M

(iv) *Precipitating:* frustration in object love accompanied by narcissistic shock.

Age Incidence: earliest just after failure to overcome Oedipus situation; *commonly*, after failure in the early post pubertal attempts to establish a new object love.[1]

Types: according to the relation of ego to super-ego; if there is pathological separation of function there will be melancholia, or if fusion, mania.

Dementia Praecox

Group: psychoses.

Mechanism: (a) withdrawal of libido from outer world, absorption of libido into the ego (megalomania), (b) return of libido to outer world in delusional systems, organ speech, negativism, etc., (c) ego compensation.

Aetiology: (i) *Constitutional:* impaired ego and libido development.

(ii) *Specific:* fixation at the early oral stage.

(iii) *Contributory:* anything which frustrates libido gratification or weakens ego resiliency (e.g. increase in the demands in love-life, or in work, or illnesses).

(iv) *Precipitating:* sudden increase of (iii).

Age Incidence: earliest, in early infancy; *commonly*, in adolescence (this last statement is based on a few observations only. It is necessary to examine the love-life with great care. *Most* of the attacks which are first observed in the twenties are recurrences after remissions).

Course: marked by remissions, that is to say, to a re-cathexis of objects on a more advanced stage of libido development; if the patient is seen in a remission it may be difficult to detect the

[1] I refer to the beginnings of the disease which are too frequently overlooked because in taking the anamnesis the psychiatrist does not distinguish clearly enough between alterations which appear of a non-manic-depressive nature but which really are curative attempts (obsessional character) revealing (on analysis) an underlying manic-depressive attack. It may be said once more that the psycho-analyst has to deal with mechanisms that influence the patient's life more than symptoms which the relations may notice; accordingly he dates the onset of disorders unduly early on ordinary psychiatrical reckoning, the difference being the outlook of a psycho-pathologist on the one hand and on the other of an observer only concerned with outward signs or conscious mental processes.

presence of the disease, but marked compensation mechanisms should make one suspect dementia praecox.

Differential Diagnosis: from the *normal* (if the case is in remission) by the decrease of character developments and overemphasis of compensations.

Pathoneuroses

Group: narcissistic neuroses (Ferenczi calls them disease-neuroses).

Mechanism: hypercathexis of organs affected by injury or disease with libido withdrawal from outer world.

Aetiology: (i) *Constitutional:* weakness of genital capacity and increased capacity of organs to absorb libido.

(ii) *Specific:* injury or illness affecting organs.

(iii) *Contributory:* frustration in libido gratification and factors weakening object attachment.

Age Incidence: earliest—very early, the fixation of early spasms as quasi-tics is thought to be pathoneurotic; not uncommon in latent period; it is a more widespread disease than is commonly realized.

Differential Diagnosis: from *hypochondria* by absence in hypochondria of illness or injury while in pathoneuroses organic changes are invariable.

Traumatic Neurosis

Group: traumatic neurosis.

Mechanism: owing to a shock that breaks through the ego defences a large *amount* of libido is required in order to master the excitation; the libido thus mobilised is withdrawn from that normally applied to external objects and from the ego itself; this produces diminished ego-capacity and sense of weakness.

Aetiology: (i) *Constitutional:* weakness in ego defence mechanism.

(ii) *Specific:* shock threatening life or appearing to.

(iii) *Contributory:* any factor which weakens ego resiliency, toxic conditions, exhaustion, etc.

Age Incidence: rare in very early life because of the protective effect of the child's narcissism, relatively rare in latent period owing presumably to lability of libido, commonest in middle life, not merely because at this time there are more shocks but because the ego's powers are weakening (impending age looms as a castration threat and predisposes).

Differential Diagnosis: from *pathoneurosis* usually more by history than anything else, except on analysis when the traumatic neurosis reveals a self-curative linking of traumata with libidinal excitations; from *dementia praecox* by complete absence in traumatic neurosis of negativism, organ speech, and other signs of early libido fixation.

(k) Conclusion

Mendel achieved his results by respecting the individuality of every seed; he treated each one separately and studied its peculiarities both manifest and potential. The Mendelian theory is based on close examination of individual idiosyncrasies. In similar fashion Freud studied the separate elements in his patients' symptoms, dreams, slips of the tongue and gestures; by the method of free association he related each of these elements to its presentational setting and elaborated a number of theories which bear the name psycho-analysis. The difference in method between Mendel and the scientific horticulturist lies in the method of approach. Mendel took them one at a time, the horticulturist in large quantities; the former discovered certain mechanisms inherent in the particular, the latter properties shared by the general; the former was concerned with endoplasmic processes, the latter predominantly with exoplasmic processes, relation to soil, light, etc. It is much the same in respect to the psycho-analyst and the psychiatrist; the former is almost wholly concerned with endopsychic processes, the latter—if the literature and the discussions in Societies are a guide—with exopsychic processes, biochemistry, histology, dietetics, pharmacology, etc. I do not know what the scientific horticulturist has to contribute to the pure discipline of genetics, but what the 'Mendelians' have to contribute to horticulture is well enough known. In the same way, I do not know what the psychiatrists have to add to psycho-analysis (unless they adopt the technique of investigation); I have tried to outline here some of the things the Freudians have to offer to psychiatry.

The tendency of psychiatry up to the present time has been to turn for help to the methods of the physical sciences, which resolve themselves to number, measure and scales. This direction follows a mental tendency which employs the 'reckoning apparatus' and is based on egoistic or, if one prefers, intellectual impulses (I am using both terms in rather a special way); psycho-analysis now has to offer another method, which does not enumerate, measure or weigh; it deals only with presentations in the mind and tries to find by its technique how they are *arranged*, how they *interact*, and how they take *effect* in behaviour. A proper combination of the two methods is the inevitable destiny of psychiatry; at present there seems to be no way of fusing the two, so the clinician is obliged to use the two alternately, viewing now the psychical, now the chemical, regarding the patient at one moment ontogenetically, at the next as a subject of statistical research.

This Survey has been bare of acknowledgements to other workers than psycho-analysts; it may be that others have done the same work, but they have not to any appreciable extent influenced the Freudian school, which stands as self-contained and independent as chemistry did fifty years ago. The reader will have noticed that psycho-analysis, while not uncourageous in making observations or forming hypotheses, or in withstanding opposition, has had occasion to upset only one psychiatric hypothesis and that a trivial one.[1] The work of Kraepelin is neither the starting point nor the target of psycho-analytical work; as has been hinted above his methods and those of Freud are complementary, and only by approaching its problems from both ends will psychiatry make its proper advance.

Postscript

This Survey was in proof before the tenth International Psycho-Analytical Congress, at which Ernest Jones read a paper on 'The Early Development of Female Sexuality'. This paper throws a new light on the mechanisms and functions of anxiety, guilt, castration, deprivation, and frustration, and of homosexuality. It will certainly produce a great change in psychoanalytical opinion, comparable to that produced by Freud's 'Inhibition, Symptom and Anxiety', and so ushers in the *fourth period* of this Survey.

[1] See § 3, p. 239, footnote 1.

17. A BIBLIOGRAPHY OF PSYCHO-ANALYTICAL PSYCHIATRY

1893–1926

The 500 papers here referred to represent the principal papers on psychiatry and closely related topics so far as the present writer's reading goes; he has omitted many, of course, but has included many almost against his better judgement. If a paper is on a psychiatric subject, though scientifically valueless, it has been included for the sake of completeness; if it is not of direct and obvious psychiatric importance its inclusion is evidence of its significance (at least in the present writer's view of the subject) to the general topic of this paper. The more important papers are indicated by a bibliographical number in thick type.

Abbreviations employed in this Bibliography:

J. = International Journal of Psycho-Analysis. (Institute of Psycho-Analysis, London.)

Z. = Zeitschrift für Psychoanalyse. (Int. Psychoanalytischer Verlag, Wien. Early vols. out of print.)

I. = Imago (Wien, Int. Psa. Verlag. Early vols. out of print).

Y. = Jahrbuch für Psychoanalyse. (Nearly out of print. Deuticke, Wien.)

C. = Zentralblatt für Psychoanalyse. (Out of print. Bergmann, Wiesbaden.)

M. = British Journal of Medical Psychology. (Cambridge University Press.)

R. = Psychoanalytic Review. (Nervous and Mental Disease Pub. Co., Albany, New York, and Washington, D.C.)

S. = Sammlung kleiner Schriften zur Neurosenlehre [Freud]. (Wien, Int. Psa. Verlag.)

G.S. = Gesammelte Schriften zur Neurosenlehre [Freud]. (Wien, Int. Psa. Verlag.)

C.P. = Collected Papers [Freud]. (Institute of Psycho-Analysis, London.)

The other abbreviations employed are those in general use.

1. 1927. ABRAHAM, KARL. *Selected Papers*. (London: Institute of Psycho-Analysis and Hogarth Press.)

2. 1925. —— Psychoanalytische Studien zur Charakterbildung. (Intern. Psa. Bibliothek, Nr. xvi.)

3. 1924. —— Versuch einer Entwicklungsgeschichte der Libido auf Grund der Psychoanalyse seelischer Störungen. (Neue Arbeiten zur ärztlichen Psychoanalyse, Nr. ii, Int. Psa. Verlag.)

4. 1924. —— *Character Formation on the Genital Level of Libido-Development.* (Chap. 3 of 'Psychoanalytische Studien zur Charakterbildung.') **J.** VII, 214–222.

5. 1924. —— Beiträge der Oralerotik zur Charakterbildung. (Vortrag, VIII. Int. Psa. Kongress, Salzburg, 1924. Chap. 2 of 'Psychoanalytische Studien zur Charakterbildung'.)

6. 1924. —— *The Influence of Oral Erotism on Character Formation.* **J.** VI, 247–258.

7. 1921. —— Klinische Beiträge zur Psychoanalyse. (Int. Psa. Bibliothek, Nr. 10, S. 301.)

8. 1921. —— (mit J. HARNIK). Spezielle Pathologie und Therapie der Neurosen und Psychosen. (Bericht u. d. Fortschritte der Psychoanalyse, 1914–1919, S. 141–163.)

9. 1921. —— Tic-Diskussion. (Report.) **Z.** VII, 393.

10. 1921. —— *Discussion of Tic.* (Report.) **J.** II, 477–480.

11. 1921. —— Zwei Fehlhandlungen einer Hebephrenen. **Z.** VII, 208.

12. 1921. —— Ergänzungen zur Lehre vom Analcharakter. (Berlin Psa. Soc., Jan. 1921.) (Chap. 1, 'Psychoanalytische Studien zur Charakterbildung.') **Z.** IX, 27–47.

13. 1921. —— *Contributions to the Theory of the Anal Character.* **J.** IV, 400–418.

14. 1920. —— Zur narzisstischen Bewertung der Exkretionsvorgänge in Traum und Neurose. **Z.** VI, 64–67.

15. 1919. —— (with S. FERENCZI, ERNST SIMMEL, ERNEST JONES). *Psycho-Analysis of the War Neuroses.* (Int. Psa. Lib. Nr. 2.)

16. 1916–17. ——Untersuchungen über die früheste prägenitale Entwicklungsstufe der Libido. **Z.** IV, 71–97.

17. 1911. —— Die psychosexuelle Grundlage der Depressions- und Exaltations-zustände. Publiziert unter dem Titel: Ansätze zur psychoanalytischen Erforschungen und Behandlung des manisch-depressiven Irreseins und verwandter Zustände. **C.** II, 302–315.

18. 1910. —— Ueber hysterische Traumzustände. **Y.** II, 1–32.

19. 1908. —— Die psychologischen Beziehungen zwischen Sexualität und Alkoholismus. (Ztschr. f. Sexualwissenschaft, Nr. 8, 449–458.)

20. 1908. —— *The Psychological Relations between Sexuality and Alcoholism.* (Translated.) **J.** VII, 2–10.

21. 1908. —— Die psychosexuellen Differenzen der Hysterie und der Dementia praecox. (Zentralblatt f. Nervenheilkunde u. Psychiatrie, XIX, 521–533.)

22. 1907. —— Ueber die Bedeutung sexueller Jugendträumen für die Symptomatologie der Dementia praecox. (Deut-

scher Verein für Psychiatrie, Frankfurt, April 27. Zentralblatt f. Nervenh. u. Psych. xviii, 409–415.)

23. 1925. BARKAS, MARY. *The Treatment of Psychotic Patients in Institutions in/ the light of Psycho-Analysis.* (British Psa. Soc. Feb. 18; publ. in Jnl. of Neurology and Psycho-pathology, 1925.)

24. 1919. BAUER (und P. SCHILDER). Ueber einige psycho-physische Mechanismen funkt. Neurosen.

25. 1912. BEAUCHANT, MORICHAU. Homosexualität und Paranoia. C. ii, 174–176.

26. 1922. BERKELEY-HILL, O. A .R. *A Case of Paranoid Dissociation.* R. ix, 1–27.

27. 1921. —— *The Anal Complex, and its Relation to Delusions of Persecution.* (Indian Med. Gaz. lvi.)

28. 1911. BERTSCHINGER, H. Illustrierte Halluzinationen. Y. iii, 69–100.

29. 1911. —— Heilungsvorgänge bei Schizophrenen. (All. Zeit. f. Psychiatrie u. psych.-gerichtliche Medizin, lxviii.)

30. 1920. BIANCHINI, M. LEVI. Negativisimo mnesico e negativismo fasico. Contributo allo studio psicoanalitico della 'conversione nelle demenze endogene (primitive).' (Arch. Gen. di Neurologia e Psichiatria, i, fasc. 2.)

31. 1921. BINSWANGER, LUDWIG. Psychoanalyse und klinische Psychiatrie. Z. vii, 137–165.

32. 1914. —— Psychologische Tagesfragen innerhalb der klinischen Psychiatrie. (Ztschr. f. d. ges. Neur. u. Psych. xxvi, H. 5.)

33. 1914. —— Klinischer Beitrag zur Lehre vom Verhältnisblödsinn (Bleuler). (Ztschr. f. Psychiatrie, lxxi. Unter dem Pseudonym Lothar Buchner erschienen.)

34. 1924–5. BIRNBAUM. Die Psychoanalyse vom Standpunkt der klinischen Psychiatrie. (Deutsch. Med. Wochenschr., Nr. 51, 52, 1–24.)

35. 1911. BJERRE, POUL. Zur Radikalbehandlung der chronischen Paranoia. Y. iii, 795–847.

36. 1919. BLEULER, EUGEN. Das autistisch-undisziplinierte Denken in der Medizin und seine Ueberwindung. (Julius Springer, Berlin.)

37. 1918. —— (und MAIER), Kas. Beitrag zum psychol. Inhalt schizophrener Symptome. (Jahrbuch f. d. ges. Neurol. xliii, 1918.)

38. 1912. —— Das autistische Denken. Y. iv, 1–39.

39. 1911. —— *The Theory of Schizophrenic Negativism.* (Nervous and Mental Disease Monograph Series, No. 11.)

40. 1911. —— Dementia Praecox oder Gruppe der Schizophrenien. (Aschaffenburg's Handbuch der Psychiatrie, 1911.)

41. 1908. —— (und C. G. Jung). Komplexe und Krankheits-ursache bei Dementia praecox. (Zentralblatt f. Nerven-heilk. u. Psych. xxxi. Jg., S. 220.)

42. 1906. —— Affektivität, Suggestibilität, Paranoia. (Halle: Carl Marhold.)

43. 1906. —— Freudsche Mechanismen in der Symptomatologie von Psychosen. (Psychiatrisch-Neurol. Wochenschr.)

44. 1914. Bork, F. Tierkreisforschungen. (Anthropos, 1914, H. 12.)

45. 1893. Breuer, Josef. *The Psychic Mechanism of Hysterical Phenomena.* (Nervous and Mental Disease Monograph Series, No. 4: 'Freud: Selected Papers on Hysteria,' re-translated in Freud's 'Collected Papers,' i, Chap. 2, p. 24.)

46. 1911. Brill, A. A. *Psychological Mechanism of Paranoia.* (New York Med. Jnl., Dec. 16, 1911.)

47. 1911. —— *A Case of Periodic Depression of Psychogenic Origin.*

48. 1909. —— *A Case of Schizophrenia (Dementia praecox).* (Amer. Jnl. of Insanity, July 1909, p. 53.)

49. 1908. —— *Psychological Factors in Dementia praecox, an analysis.* (Jnl. of Abnormal Psychology, Oct. 1908, p. 219.)

50. 1916. Burr, C. B. *Art in the Insane.* R. iii, 361–385.

51. 1925. Bychowski, Gustav. Psychoanalytisches aus der psychiatrischen Abteilung. Z. xi, 350–352.

52. 1925. Campbell, C. Macfie. *On the Mechanism of some Cases of Manic-Depressive Excitement.* (Nervous and Mental Disease Monograph Series, No. 41, Studies in Psychiatry, ii.)

53. 1925. —— *On the Mechanism of Convulsive Phenomena and Allied Symptoms.* (Nervous and Mental Disease Monograph Series, No. 41, Studies in Psychiatry, ii.)

54. 1915. —— *The Application of Psycho-analysis to Insanity.* (Cornell University Med. Bull. Studies from the Dept. of Psychopathology, v, No. 1.)

55. 1915. —— *The Form and Content of the Psychoses. The Rôle of Psycho-Analysis in Psychiatry.* (Cornell Univ. Med. Bull. Studies from the Dept. of Psychopathology, v, No. 1.)

56. 1909. —— *A Modern Conception of Dementia praecox, with five illustrative cases.* Rev. of Neur. and Psychiatry, Oct. 1909, p. 623.)

57. 1924. Caravedo, Baltazar. Actitudes regresivas en los esquizofrenicos. (Revista de Psiquiatria, v, No. 2, Lima.)

58. 1921. Carver, Alfred. *Epilepsy from the Psychological Standpoint.* (British Medical Journal.)

59. 1921. —— *Notes on the Analysis of a Case of Melancholia.* (Jnl. of Neur. and Psych. i, p. 320.)

60. 1925. Cassity, John Holland. *Comments on Schizophrenia.* (Jnl. of Nervous and Mental Disease, LXII, No. 2, 477–484.)

61. 1919. van der Chijs, A. Ueber Halluzinationen und Psychoanalyse. **Z.** v, 274–284.

62. 1925. Clark, L. Pierce. *The Phantasy Method of Analyzing Narcissistic Neuroses.*

63. 1925. —— *Psychopathic Children.* (Nervous and Mental Disease Monograph Series, No. 41, Studies in Psychiatry, II.)

64. 1925. —— *Some Therapeutic Considerations of Periodic Mental Depressions.* (Nervous and Mental Disease Monograph Series, No. 41, Studies in Psychiatry, II.)

65. 1923. —— *Manic-Depressive Psychoses: Contribution to a Symposium.* (Jnl. of Nervous and Mental Disease, Feb. 1923, p. 161.)

66. 1922. —— *A Study of the Unconscious Motivations in Suicides.* (New York Med. Jnl., Sept. 26, 1922, pp. 254–263.)

67. 1921. —— *Some Emotional Reactions in Epileptics.* (New York Med. Jnl., June 1, 1921; p. 785.)

68. 1921. —— *Remarks upon Consciousness in the Epileptic Fit.* (Boston Med. Jnl. CLXXXV.)

69. 1920. —— *A Clinical Study of Some Mental Contents in Epileptic Attacks.* **R.** VII, 366–375.

70. 1919. —— *Some Practical Remarks upon the use of Modified Psychoanalysis in the Treatment of Borderland Neuroses and Psychoses.* **R.** VI, 306–308.

71. 1919. —— *A Psychological Study of Some Alcoholics.* **R.** VI, 268–295.

72. 1918. —— *The True Epileptic.* (New York Med. Jnl., May 4, p. 817.)

73. 1918–19. ——*The Psychologic Treatment of Retarded Depressions.* (Amer. Jnl. of Insanity, LXXV, No. 3, p. 407.)

74. 1917. —— *The Psychological and Therapeutic Value of Studying Mental Content during and following Epileptic Attacks.* (New York Med. Jnl. CVI, No. 15.)

75. 1917. —— *A Further Study of Mental Content in Epilepsy.* (Psychiatry Bulletin, Oct. 1917.)

76. 1917. —— *Clinical Studies in Epilepsy.* (Psych. Bull., Jan. 1916, April 1916, Jan. 1917.)

77. 1916. —— *Some Therapeutic Suggestions Derived from the Newer Psychological Studies upon the Nature of Essential Epilepsy.* (Med. Rec. LXXX, No. 10, March 4, 1916.)

78. 1915. —— *Study of Certain Aspects of Epilepsy compared with the Emotional Life and Impulsive Movement of the Infant.* (Interstate Med. Jnl. XXII, No. 10.)

79. 1914. —— *Remarks upon Mental Infantilism.* (Med. Rec., March 28, 1914.)

80. 1914. —— *A Personality Study of the Epileptic Constitution.* (Amer. Jnl. of Ment. Sci. CXLVIII, p. 729.)

81. 1914. —— *Some of the Newer Methods of Treatment in Nervous and Mental Diseases.* (New York State Jnl. of Med., June 1914.)

82. 1914. —— *The Mechanisms of Periodic Mental Depressions as shown in two cases, and the therapeutic advantages of such studies.* (Rev. of Neur. and Psych. XII, No. 10.)

83. 1914. —— *The Nature and Pathogenesis of Epilepsy.* (New York Neurological Society, Dec. 1, 1914. New York Med. Jnl., Feb. and March, 1915.)

84. 1917. CORIAT, ISADOR H. *The Treatment of Dementia Praecox by Psychoanalysis.* (Jnl. of Abnormal Psychology, XII, No. 5, p. 326.)

85. 1923. COTTON, HENRY A. *Manic-Depressive Psychoses: Contribution to a Symposium.* (Jnl. of Nerv. and Ment. Dis., Feb. 1923, p. 161.)

86. 1923. DELGADO, HONORIO F. (with H. VALDIZAN). Factores psicológicos de la demencia praecoz. (Revista de Psiquiatria, No. 4, 1923.)

87. 1922. —— El dibujo de los psicopatas. (Lima.)

88. 1918. —— La psiquiatria psicologica. (Revista de Psiquiatria.)

89. 1925. DEUTSCH, HELENE. Zur Psychogenese eines Ticfalles. **Z.** XI, 325–332.

90. 1922. —— Ueber die pathologische Lüge. (Pseudologia phantastica.) **Z.** VIII, 153–167.

91. 1923. DEVINE, HENRY. *The 'Reality-Feeling' in Phantasies of the Insane.* **M.** III, 81–94.

92. 1921. —— *A Study of Hallucinations in a Case of Schizophrenia.* (Jnl. of Ment. Sci. LXVII, 172–186.)

93. 1916. —— *The Biological Significance of Delusions.* (Jnl. of Ment. Sci., Jan. 1916.)

94. 1921. DOOLEY, LUCILLE. *A Psychoanalytic Study of Manic Depressive Psychoses.* **R.** VIII, 38–72, 144–167.

95. 1918. —— *Analysis of a Case of Manic-Depressive Psychosis showing well-marked Regressive Stages.* **R.** V, 1–46.

96. 1914. DROSNÉS, L. M. Die biopsychologische Grundlage der Wahnideen von Geisteskranken. (Therapeut. Rundschau-russ.-Odessa, 1914, Nr. 4.)

97. 1920. DUKES, GEZA. Kriminológia és pszichoanalizis. (Jogtudományi közlöny, Nr. 4, 1920.)

98. 1917. EDER, M. D. *War Shock. The Psychoneuroses in War.* (London: Wm. Heinemann, pp. 154.)

99. 1916. —— *The Psychopathology of the War Neuroses.* (Lancet, Aug. 12, 1916.)

100. 1921. EISLER, MICHAEL JOSEF. Der Ausbruch einer manischen Erregung. **Z.** VII, 198–203.
101. 1921. —— Ueber Schlaflust und gestörte Schlaffähigkeit. **Z.** VII, 166–178.
102. 1924. ENDTZ, A. Ueber Träume von Schizophrenen. **Z.** x, 292–295.
103. 1916. EVARTS, ARRAH B. *The Ontogenetic against the Phylogenetic Elements in the Psychoses of the Colored Race.* **R.** III, 272–287.
104. 1914. —— *Dementia Praecox in the Colored Race.* **R.** I, 388–403.
105. 1922. FARNELL, F. J. *The Influence of the Psycho-Analytical Movement on American Psychiatry.*
106. 1923. FEDERN, PAUL. Die Geschichte einer Melancholie. **Z.** IX, 201–206.
107. 1921. FELDMANN, S. Ueber Erkrankungsanlässe bei Psychosen. **Z.** VII, 203–207.
108. 1910. FELZMANN, O. B. (On the Problem of Suicide.) Psychotherapia, Nr. 6. (In Russian.)
109. 1926. FERENCZI, SANDOR. *Further Contributions to the Theory and Technique of Psycho-Analysis.* (London: Institute of Psycho-Analysis and Hogarth Press.)
110. 1926. —— Das Problem der Unlustbejahung. **Z.** XII, 241–252.
111. 1926. —— *The Problem of the Acceptance of Unpleasant Ideas: Advances in the Knowledge of the Sense of Reality.* **J.** VII, 312–323. (Included in No. 109.)
112. 1923. —— Lampenfieber und narzisstische Selbstbeobachtung. **Z.** IX, 69.
113. 1926. —— *Stage-fright and Narcissistic Self-observation.* (Included in No. 109.)
114. 1922. —— (und S. HOLLÓS). Zur Psychoanalyse der paralytischen Geistesstörung. (Beihefte der Int. Ztschr. f. Psa. No. 5.)
115. 1925. ——*Psychoanalysis and the Psychic Disorder of General Paresis.* Trans. by G. M. Barnes and G. Kiel. **R.** XII, 88–107, 205–233. Nervous and Mental Disease Pub. Co., New York, 1925. Reviewed in **M.** v, 120–126.
116. 1921. —— Tic-Diskussion. (Reply to Criticisms.) **Z.** VII, 395.
117. 1921. —— *Discussion on Tic: Report.* **J.** II, 481.
118. 1921. —— Psychoanalytische Betrachtungen über den Tic. **Z.** VII, 33–62.
119. 1921. —— *Psycho-Analytical Observations on Tic.* **J.** II, 1–30. (Included in No. 109.)
120. 1919. —— Hysterie und Pathoneuroses. (Int. Psa. Bibliothek, Nr. 2, also pub. in Hungarian, Verlag Mano Dick.)

Enthält: (1) Ueber Pathoneurosen. (2) Hysterische Materialisationsphänomene. (3) Erklärungsversuch einiger hysterischer Stigmata. (4) Technische Schwierigkeiten einer Hysterieanalyse. (5) Die Psychoanalyse eines Falles von hysterischer Hypochondrie. (6) Ueber zwei Typen der Kriegshysterie.

121. 1926. —— *Hysteria and Pathoneuroses:* [*Containing 6 papers, translations of which are included in No.* 109, *under the titles:* (1) *Disease- or Patho-Neuroses.* (2) *The Phenomena of Hysterical Materialisation.* (3) *An attempted Explanation of some Hysterical Stigmata.* (4) *Technical Difficulties in the Analysis of a case of Hysteria.* (5) *The Psycho-Analysis of a Case of Hysterical Hypochondria.* (6) *Two Types of War Neuroses.*]

122. 1919. —— Sonntagsneurosen. **Z.** v, 46–48. *Sunday Neuroses* (in No. 109).

123. 1919. —— Technische Schwierigkeiten einer Hysteriean lyse. **Z.** v, 34–40.

124. 1916–17. —— Von Krankheits- oder Pathoneurosen. **Z.** iv, 219–228.

125. 1916–17. —— Mischgebilde von erotischen und Charakterzügen. **Z.** iv, 146.

126. 1916–17. —— Ueber zwei Typen der Kriegsneurose. **Z.** iv, 131–245.

127. 1916. —— *Contributions to Psycho-Analysis.* Authorised Translation by Ernest Jones. (Boston: Richard Badger and Co., pp. 288.)

128. 1915. —— Psychogene Anomalien der Stimmlage. **Z.** iii, 25–28.

129. 1926. —— *Psychogenic Anomalies of Voice Production.* (Translation included in No. 109.)

130. 1914. —— Allegemeine Neurosenlehre. **Y.** vi, 317–328. (Gyógyászat, 1916.)

131. 1914. —— Schwindelempfindung nach Schluss der Analysenstunde. **Z.** ii, 272–274. (Translated in No. 109.)

132. 1914. —— Zur Nosologie der männlichen Homosexualität (Homoërotik). **Z.** ii, 131–142.

133. 1914. ——Einige klinische Beobachtungen bei der Paranoia und Paraphrenie. **Z.** ii, 11–17. (Translation in No. 127.)

134. 1913. —— Glaube, Unglaube und Ueberzeugung. 'Populäre Vorträge über Psychoanalyse,' 1922. Wien, Int. Psa. Verlag. (Trans. in No. 109.)

135. 1926. —— *Belief, Disbelief and Conviction.* (Included in No. 109.)

136. 1913. —— Zur Ontogenese der Symbole. **Z.** i, 436–438.

137. 1916. —— *The Ontogenesis of Symbols*. (Translation included in No. 127.)

138. 1913. —— Entwicklungsstufen des Wirklichkeitssinnes. **Z.** I, 124–138.

139. 1916. —— *Stages in the Development of the Sense of Reality*. (Translation included in No. 127.)

140. 1912. —— *The Psychoanalysis of Suggestion and Hypnosis*. Transactions of the Psycho-Medical Society, London, 1912, III, Part 4.

141. 1912. —— Ueber Onanie. Wiener psychoanalytische Vereinigung, 1912. Verlag J. F. Bergmann, Wiesbaden, 1912.

142. 1916. —— *On Onanism*. (Translation included in No. 127.)

143. 1912. —— Zur Begriffsbestimmung der Introjektion. **C.** II, 198–200.

144. 1911. —— Ueber die Rolle der Homosexualität in der Pathogenese der Paranoia. (Gyógyászat, 1911.) **Y.** III, 101–119.

145. 1916. —— *On the Part Played by Homosexuality in the Pathogenesis of Paranoia*. (Translation included in No. 127.)

146. 1911. —— Reizung der analen erogenen Zone als auslösende Ursache der Paranoia. **C.** I, 557–559.

147. 1911. —— Ueber obszöne Worte. **C.** I, 390–399.

148. 1916. —— *Obscene Words*. (Translation included in No. 127.)

149. 1911. —— Alkohol und Neurosen. Antwort auf die Kritik von Herrn Prof. Dr E. Bleuler. **Y.** III, 853–857.

150. 1909. —— Introjektion und Uebertragung. **Y.** I, 422–457.

151. 1916. —— *Introjection and Transference*. (Translation included in No. 127.)

152. 1908. —— Zur analytischen Auffassung der Psychoneurosen. (In 'Populäre Vorträge über Psychoanalyse,' 1922.)

153. 1908. —— A mániás-depressiv elmezavar suggestiv világításban. [Manic-depressive disease in subjective elucidation.] Gyógyászat, 1908.

154. 1908. —— Ueber Aktual- und Psycho-Neurosen im Sinne Freuds. (Wien. Klin. Rundschau, Nr. 48–51.)

155. 1926. —— *On Actual- and Psycho-Neuroses in Freud's Meaning of the terms*. (Translation included in No. 109.)

156. 1921. FORSYTH, DAVID. *The Infantile Psyche, with special reference to Visual Projection*. Brit. Jnl. of Psychology, XI, p. 263.

157. 1921. —— *The Rudiments of Character. A Study of Infant Behaviour*. **R.** VIII, 117–143.

158. 1919. —— *Psycho-Analysis of a Case of Early Paranoid Dementia*. Proc. Royal Society of Medicine. XIII, 3, 1919–20. Sect. Psychiatry, pp. 65–81.

159. 1923. FREUD, ANNA. Ein hysterisches Symptom bei einem zweieinvierteljährigen Kinde. I. IX, 264–265.

160. 1926. —— An Hysterical Symptom in a Child of Two Years and Three Months Old. J. VII, 227–229.

161. 1926. FREUD, SIGM. Hemmung, Symptom und Angst. (Wien, Int. Psa. Verlag.)

162. 1925. —— Einige psychische Folgen des anatomischen Geschlechtsunterschieds. Z. XI, 401–410. Translation in J.

163. 1925. —— Die Verneinung. I. XI, 217–221.

164. 1925. —— Negation. J. VI, 367–371.

165. 1924. —— Der Realitätsverlust bei Neurose und Psychose. Z. x, 374–379. G.S. VI

166. 1924. —— The Loss of Reality in Neurosis and Psychosis. C.P. II.

167. 1924. —— Das ökonomische Problem des Masochismus. Z. x, 121–133. G.S. V.

168. 1924. The Economic Problem in Masochism. C.P. II.

169. 1924. —— Der Untergang des Oedipuskomplexes. Z. x, 245–252. G.S. V.

170. 1924. —— The Passing of the Oedipus Complex. C.P. II. J. V, 419–423.

171. 1924. —— Neurose und Psychose. Z. x, 1–5. G.S. V.

172. 1924. —— Neurosis and Psychosis. C.P. II.

173. 1923. —— Eine Teufelsneurose im Siebzehnten Jahrhundert. I. X, 1–34. G.S. x. Selbständig in Buchform, Int. Psa. Verlag, 1924.

174. 1925. —— A Neurosis of Demoniacal Possession in the Seventeenth Century. C.P. IV.

175. 1923. —— Die infantile Genitalorganisation. Eine Einschaltung in die Sexual-theorie. Z. IX, 168–171. G.S. V.

176. 1924. —— The Infantile Genital Organisation of the Libido. J. V, 125–129. C.P. II.

177. 1923. —— Das Ich und das Es. (Wien, Int. Psa. Verlag.) Pp. 77. G.S. VI, 353–405.

178. 1926. —— The Ego and the Id. (London: Institute of Psycho-Analysis and Hogarth Press.)

179. 1922. —— Ueber einige neurotische Mechanismen bei Eifersucht, Paranoia, und Homosexualität. Z. VIII, 249–258. G.S. V.

180. 1923. —— Certain Neurotic Mechanisms in Jealousy, Paranoia and Homosexuality. J. IV, 1–10. C.P. II.

181. 1921. —— Massenpsychologie und Ich-Analyse. (Wien, Int. Psa. Verlag.) 2te Aufl. 1924. G.S. VI

182. 1922. —— Group Psychology and the Analysis of the Ego. (London: Inst. of Ps.-A. and the Hogarth Press.)

183. 1920. —— Jenseits des Lustprinzips. (Wien, Int. Psa. Verlag.) 2te Aufl. 1921; 3te, 1924. **G.S.** vi.
184. 1922. —— *Beyond the Pleasure Principle.* (London: Inst. of Ps.-A.)
185. 1919. —— 'Ein Kind wird geschlagen.' Beitrag zur Kenntnis der Entstehung sexueller Perversionen. **Z.** v, 151–172. **S.** v. **G.S.** v.
186. 1920. —— *'A Child is being beaten.' A Contribution to the Study of the Origin of Sexual Perversions.* **J.** i, 371–395. **C.P.** ii.
187. 1918. —— Aus der Geschichte einer infantilen Neurose. **S.** iv. in selbständiger Buchform. (Wien, Int. Psa. Verlag, 1924.) **G.S.** viii, 439–567.
188. 1924. —— *From the History of an Infantile Neurosis.* **C.P.** iii.
189. 1916–17. —— Trauer und Melancholie. **Z.** iv, 288–301. **S.** iv. **G.S.** v.
190. 1924. —— *Mourning and Melancholia.* **C.P.** iv.
191. 1916–17. —— Vorlesungen zur Einführung in die Psycho-analyse, 1916–17 separat: I. Teil, Einleitung, Fehlleistung, 1916; II. Teil, Traum, und III. Teil, Allgemeine Neurosenlehre, 1917. 2te Aufl. (bereits in einem Band), 1918. Wien, Int. Psa. Verlag. **G.S.** vi, 1–482.
192. 1920. —— *Introductory Lectures to Psycho-Analysis.* Trans. by Joan Riviere. (London: Geo. Allen and Unwin and Inst. of Psa. 1922.)
193. 1916. —— Ueber Triebumsetzungen insbesondere der Analerotik. **Z.** iv, 125–130. **S.** iv. **G.S.** v.
194. 1924. —— *On the Transformation of Instincts with especial Reference to Anal Erotism.* **C.P.** ii.
195. 1915. —— Das Unbewusste. **Z.** iii, 189–203, 257–269. **S.** iv. **G.S.** v.
196. 1925. —— *The Unconscious.* **C.P.** iv.
197. 1915. —— Die Verdrängung. **Z.** iii, 129–138. **S.** iv. **G.S.** v.
198. 1925. —— *Repression.* **C.P.** iv.
199. 1915. —— Triebe und Triebschicksale. **Z.** iii, 84–100. **S.** iv. **G.S.** v.
200. 1925. —— *Instincts and their Vicissitudes.* **C.P.** iv.
201. 1915. —— Mitteilung eines der psychoanalytischen Theorie widersprechenden Falles von Paranoia. **Z.** iii, 321–329. **S.** iv. **G.S.** v.
202. 1924. —— *A Case of Paranoia running counter to the Psycho-Analytical Theory of the Disease.* **C.P.** ii.
203. 1914. —— Zur Einführung des Narzissmus. **Y.** vi, 1–24. **S.** iv. **G.S.** vi.
204. 1925. —— *On Narcissism: An Introduction.* **C.P.** iv.
205. 1913. —— Zwei Kinderlügen. **Z.** i, 359–362. **S.** iv. **G.S.** v.

206. 1912. ——*A Note on the Unconscious in Psycho-Analysis. Written (in English) at the request of the Soc. for Psychical Research, and first published in a special Medical Supplement of their Proceedings.* Part LXVI, vol. XXVI, 1912. **C.P.** IV.

207. 1913. —— Ueber fausse reconnaissance ('déjà raconté') während der psychoanalytischen Arbeit. **Z.** II, 1–5. **S.** IV. **G.S.** VI.

208. 1924. —— *Fausse Reconnaissance (déjà raconté) in psycho-analytic Treatment.* **C.P.** II.

209. 1913. —— Die Disposition zur Zwangsneurose. Ein Beitrag zum Problem der Neurosenwahl. **Z.** I, 525–532. **S.** IV. **G.S.** V.

210. 1924. —— *The Predisposition to Obsessional Neurosis.* **C.P.** II.

211. 1912. —— Ueber neurotische Erkrankungstypen. **C.** II, 297–302. **S.** III. **G.S.** V.

212. 1924. —— *Types of Neurotic Nosogenesis.* **C.P.** II.

213. 1911. —— Formulierungen über die zwei Prinzipien des psychischen Geschehens. **Y.** III, 1–8. **G.S.** V. **S.** III.

214. 1925. —— *Formulations regarding the two Principles in Mental Functioning.* **C.P.** IV.

215. 1911. —— Psychoanalytische Bemerkungen über einen autobiographisch beschriebenen Fall von Paranoia (Dementia Paranoides). **Y.** III, 9–68. **S.** III. **G.S.** VIII.

216. 1925. —— *Psycho-Analytic Notes upon an autobiographical Account of a Case of Paranoia (Dementia Paranoides).* **C.P.** III, 387–466.

217. 1911. —— Nachtrag zu dem autobiographisch beschriebenen Fall von Paranoia (Dementia Paranoides). **Y.** III, 588–590. **S.** III. **G.S.** VIII.

218. 1925. —— *Postscript to Psycho-Analytic Notes upon an autobiographical Account of a Case of Paranoia (Dementia Paranoides).* **C.P.** III, 467–470.

219. 1910. —— Einleitung und Schlusswort zur Selbstmorddiskussion der Wiener Psa. Vereinigung in 'Ueber den Selbstmord, insbes. d. Schülerselbstmord.' (Verlag Bergmann, Wiesbaden.) **G.S.** III, 321–323.

220. 1908. —— Charakter und Analerotik. Psych.-Neur. Wochenschr. IX, Nr. 52. **S.** II. **G.S.** V.

221. 1924. —— *Character and Anal Erotism.* **C.P.** II.

222. 1905. —— Drei Abhandlungen zur Sexualtheorie. (Wien: F. Deuticke.) 2te Aufl. 1910; 3te, 1915; 4te, 1920 (Vorwort hierzu auch abgedr. in **Z.** VI, 1920); 5te, 1922. **G.S.** V, 1–119.

223. 1910. —— *Three Contributions to the Theory of Sexuality.* Trans. by A. A. Brill. New York.

224. 1904. —— Zur Psychopathologie des Alltagslebens. Monatschr. f. Psychiatrie u. Neurologie, x. Berlin. 10 Aufl. 1924. Wien, Int. Psa. Verlag. **G.S.** iv, 1–310.

225. 1914. —— *On the Psychopathology of Everyday Life.* Trans. by A. A. Brill. (London: Fisher Unwin.)

226. 1900. —— Die Traumdeutung. (Leipzig u. Wien: F. Deuticke.) 2te Aufl. 1909; 3te, 1911; 4te, 1914; 5te, 1919; 6te, 1921; 7te, 1922 (4te–7te Aufl. mit zwei Beiträgen von Otto Rank.) **G.S.** ii u. iii.

227. 1913. —— *The Meaning of Dreams.* Trans. by A. A. Brill. (London, 1913.)

228. 1898. —— Die Sexualität in der Aetiologie der Neurosen. (First published in the Wiener kl. Rundschau, 1898, Nr. 2, 4, 5, 7.) **S.** i. **G.S.** i, 439–464.

229. 1924. —— *Sexuality in the Aetiology of the Neuroses.* **C.P.** i.

230. 1896. —— L'Hérédité et l'Étiologie des Névroses. (First published in the Revue Neurologique, iv.) **S.** i. **G.S.** i, 387–403.

231. 1924. —— *Heredity and the Aetiology of the Neuroses.* **C.P.** 1.

232. 1896. —— Weitere Bemerkungen über die Abwehr-Neuropsychosen. (First published in the Neurologischen Zentralblatt, 1896, Nr. 10.) **G.S.** i, 363–387. **S.** i.

233. 1909. —— *Further Observations on the Defence-Neuro-Psychoses.* 'Freud: Selected Papers on Hysteria.' Nerv. and Ment. Dis. Monograph Series, No. 4; also re-translated in **C.P.** i.

234. 1895. —— Obsessions et Phobies. Leur mécanisme psychique et leur étiologie. (Revue Neurologique, iii, 1895.) **S.** i. **G.S.** i, 334–342.

235. 1924. —— *Obsessions and Phobias: Their Psychical Mechanisms and their Aetiology.* **C.P.** i.

236. 1895. —— (mit Josef Breuer). Studien über Hysterie. (Leipzig und Wien: F. Deuticke.) **G.S.** i, 1–238.

237. 1895. —— Ueber die Berechtigung, von der Neurasthenie einen bestimmten Symptomkomplex als 'Angstneurose' abzutrennen. (Neurolog. Ztbt. 1895, Nr. 2.) **S.** i, **G.S.** i, 306–333.

238. 1909. —— *On the Right to separate from Neurasthenia a definite Symptom-Complex as 'Anxiety Neurosis.'* 'Freud: Selected Papers on Hysteria., Nerv. and Ment. Dis. Mon. Ser. No. 4; also re-translated in **C.P.** i.

239. 1894. —— Die Abwehr-Neuropsychosen. Versuch einer psychologischen Theorie der akquirierten Hysterie, vieler Phobien und Zwangsvorstellungen und gewisser halluzinatorischer Psychosen. (Neurolog. Ztbt. 1894, Nr.

10 u. 11.) **G.S.** I, 290–305. **S.** I, and in 'Studien über Hysterie.'

240. 1909. —— *The Defence-Neuro-Psychoses.* 'Freud: Selected Papers on Hysteria.' Nerv. and Ment. Dis. Mon. Ser. No. 4; re-translated in **C.P.** I.

241. 1893. —— (mit JOSEF BREUER). Ueber den psychischen Mechanismus hysterischer Phänomene. Vorläufige Mitteilung. (Neurol. Ztbt., Nr. 1 u. 2, 1893.) 'Studien über Hysterie.' **S.** I. **G.S.** I, 1–24.

242. 1909. —— *The Psychic Mechanism of Hysterical Phenomena.* 'Freud: Sel. Papers on Hysteria.' Nerv. and Ment. Dis. Mon. Ser. No. 4; re-translated in **C.P.** I.

243. 1926. FRINK, H. W. *The Significance of a Delusion.* **R.** XIII, 16–31.

244. 1926. GLOVER, EDWARD. *A 'Technical' Form of Resistance.* **J.** VII, 377–380.

245. 1926. —— Einige Probleme der psychoanalytischen Charakterologie. **Z.** XII, 326–333.

246. 1926. —— *The Neurotic Character.* **J.** VII, 11–30.

247. 1925. —— *Notes on Oral Character Formation.* **J.** VI, 131–154.

248. 1924. —— *The Significance of the Mouth in Psycho-Analysis.* **M.** IV, 134–155.

249. 1924. —— *'Active Therapy' and Psycho-Analysis.* **J.** V, 269–311.

250. 1926. GLOVER, JAMES. Der Begriff des Ichs. **Z.** XII, 286–291.

251. 1926. —— *The Conception of the Ego.* **J.** VII, 414–419.

252. 1925. —— *The Conception of Sexuality.* Contribution to a Discussion. **M.** V, 175–188, 196–207.

253. 1917. GLÜCK, BERNARD. *Studies in Forensic Psychiatry.* (Boston: Little, Brown and Co., pp. 269.)

254. 1920. GOJA, HERMANN. Halluzinationen eines Sterbenden. **Z.** VI, 357–359.

255. 1917. GORDON, A. *Obsessive Hallucinations and Psychoanalysis.* (Jnl. of Abnormal Psychology, XII, 423.)

256. 1912. GREBELSKAJA, SCH. Psychologische Analyse eines Paranoiden. **Y.** IV, 116–140.

257. 1918. GREENACRE, P. *Content of the Schizophrenic Characteristics occurring in affective disorders.* (Amer. Jnl. of Insanity, LXXV, No. 2.)

258. 1924. GRUSZECKA, ANNA. *Transitivism, the loss of the Limits of the Personality and the Primitive Mental Attitude in Schizophrenia.* (Schweiz. Archiv f. Neurol. u. Psych. XV, 64.)

259. 1912. HART, BERNARD. *The Psychology of Insanity.* (Cambridge Univ. Press, 1912.)

260. 1911. —— *The Psychological Conception of Insanity.* (Arch. of Neur. and Psych. V, 90.)

372 SELECTED CONTRIBUTIONS TO PSYCHO-ANALYSIS

261. 1915. HASSALL, JAMES C. *The Rôle of the Sexual Complex in Dementia Praecox.* **R.** II, 260–276.
262. 1917. HENNING, H. Versuche über die Rezifiven. (Ztschr. f. Psychol. LXXVIII, H. 3–4.)
263. 1926. HERMANN, IMRE. Das System Bw. **I.** XII, 203–210.
264. 1925. —— Regressionen der Ich-Orientierung.
265. 1923. —— Organlibido und Begabung. **Z.** IX, 297–310.
266. 1923. —— Die Randbevorzugung als Primärvorgang. **Z.** IX, 137–167.
267. 1919. HERSCHMANN, H. (und PAUL SCHILDER). Träume der Melancholiker, etc. (Ztschr. f. d. ges. Nerv. u. Psych. LIII.)
268. 1914. HITSCHMANN, E. Ueber Nerven- und Geisteskrankheiten bei katholischen Geistlichen und Nonnen. **Z.** II, 270–272.
269. 1913. —— Paranoia, Homosexualität und Analerotik. **Z.** I, 251–254.
270. 1913. —— Swedenborgs Paranoia. **C.** I, 32–36.
271. 1922. HOCH, AUGUST. *Benign Stupors. A Study of a new manic-depressive reaction type.* (Camb. Univ. Press. New York: Macmillan Co.)
272. 1914. —— *Precipitating Mental Causes in Dementia Praecox.* (Amer. Jnl. of Insanity, Jan. 1914.)
273. 1908. —— *A Study of the Mental Make-up in the Functional Psychoses.* (New York Psych. Soc., Nov. 4, 1908. Jnl. of Nerv. and Ment. Dis., April 1909, p. 230. Disc.)
274. 1907. —— *The Psychogenic Factors in the Development of Psychoses.* (Psych. Bull., June 1907, p. 161.)
275. 1907. —— *The Psychogenic Factors in some Paranoic Conditions, with suggestions for Prophylaxis and Treatment.* (New York Psych. Soc., Mar. 6, 1907. Jnl. Nerv. and Ment. Dis., Oct., 0. 668. Disc.)
276. 1925. HOLLÓS, ISTVÁN. Der Sinn des Geisteskrankheitens.
277. 1914. —— Psychoanalytische Beleuchtung eines Falles von Dementia Praecox. **Z.** II, 367–375.
278. 1923. HOLLÓS, S. Aus der psychiatrischen Anstaltpraxis. **Z.** IX, 71–75.
279. 1923. —— Psychoanalytische Spuren in der Vor-Freudschen Psychiatrie. **Z.** IX, 48–57.
280. 1922. —— (und S. FERENCZI). Zur Psychoanalyse der paralytischen Geistesstörung. (Beihefte der Int. Ztschr. f. Psa., No. 5.) **Z.** VIII, 354–358.
281. 1925. —— *Psychoanalysis and the Psychic Disorder of General*

Paresis. **R.** xii, 88–107, 205–233. (New York: Nerv. and Ment. Dis. Co., 1925.)

282. 1919. ——Die Phasen des Selbstbewusstseinsaktes. **Z.** v, 93–101.
283. 1924. van der Hoop, J. H. Een geval van Schizophrenie-psychopathologische Studie. (Dissertation: H. J. Paris, Amsterdam.)
284. 1924. —— Ueber die Projektion und ihre Inhalte. **Z.** x, 276–288.
285. 1920. Isham, Mary K. *A Case of Mixed Neurosis with some Paraphrenic Features.* (Med. Record, June 12, 1920.)
286. 1920. —— *Some Mechanisms of Paraphrenia.* (Amer. Jnl. of Insanity, July 1920.)
287. 1920. —— *The Paraphrenic's Inaccessibility.* **R.** vii, 246–256.
288. 1913. Itten, W. Beiträge zur Psychologie der Dementia Praecox. **Y.** v, 1–54.
289. 1926. Jelgersma, G. Die Projektion. **Z.** xii, 292–297.
290. 1926. —— *Projection.* **J.** vii, 353–358.
291. 1923. Jelliffe, S. E. *Manic-Depressive Psychoses: Contribution to a Symposium.* (Jnl. of Nerv. and Ment. Dis., Feb. 1923, p. 161.)
292. 1926. Jones, Ernest. Der Ursprung und Aufbau des Ueber-Ichs. **Z.** xii, 253–262.
293. 1926. —— *The Origin and Structure of the Super-Ego.* **J.** vii, 303–311.
294. 1924. —— *The Classification of the Instincts.* (Brit. Jnl. of Psych. xiv, 256.)
295. 1923. —— *The Nature of Auto-Suggestion.* **J.** iv, 293–312. **M.** iii, 194–212.
296. 1922. —— *Some Problems of Adolescence.* (Brit. Jnl. of Psych. xiii.)
297. 1920. —— *Treatment of the Neuroses.* (New York: Wm. Wood and Co., pp. 233.)
298. 1920. —— *Recent Advances in Psycho-Analysis.* **J.** i, 161–185. **M.** i, 49–71.
299. 1919. —— *Anal-Erotic Character Traits.* (Jnl. of Abnormal Psychology, xiii, p. 261.)
300. 1913. —— *Papers on Psycho-Analysis.* (New York: Wm. Wood and Co., pp. 731. London: Baillière, Tindall and Cox.) (2nd ed. 1918; 3rd, 1923.)
301. 1918. —— *War Shock and Freud's Theory of the Neuroses.* (Proc. R.S.M., vol. xi.)
302. 1916. —— *The Theory of Symbolism.* (Brit. Jnl. of Psych. ix.)
303. 1913. —— *Hate and Anal Erotism in the Obsessional Neurosis.* Chap. 30 of 'Papers on Psycho-Analysis'.

304. 1913. —— *Analytic Study of a Case of Obsessional Neurosis.* Chap. 29 of 'Papers on Psycho-Analysis.'
305. 1909. —— *Psycho-Analytic Notes on a Case of Hypomania.* (Amer. Jnl. of Insanity, Oct. 1909, p. 203.)
306. 1909. —— *Remarks on a Case of Complete Autopsychic Amnesia.* (Jnl. of Abnormal Psych. IV.) Chap. 24 of 'Papers on Psycho-Analysis.'
307. 1919. JUNG, C. G. *Studies in Word Association.* Trans. by M. D. Eder. (New York: Moffat, Yard and Co., pp. 575. London: Heinemann.)
308. 1917. —— *Psychology of the Unconscious: a Study of the Transformations and Symbolisms of the Libido. A Contribution to the History of the Evolution of Thought.* Trans. by B. M. Hinkle. (New York: Moffat, Yard and Co., pp. 449.)
309. 1908. —— (und E. BLEULER). Komplexe und Krankheitsursache bei Dementia praecox. (Ztbt. f. Nerv. u. Psych. XXXI, 220.)
310. 1908. —— Der Inhalt der Psychose. (Freuds Schr. z. angew. Seelenk., H. 3.) 2te Aufl. 1914.
311. 1907. —— Ueber die Psychologie der Dementia praecox. (Verlag Carl Marhold, Halle.)
312. 1909. —— *The Psychology of Dementia praecox.* (Nerv. and Ment. Dis. Mon. Ser. No. 3. Auth. trans. by Frederick Peterson and A. A. Brill.)
313. 1921. KEMPF, EDWARD J. *Psychopathology.* (C. V. Mosby and Co., St Louis, Mo. London: Kimpton, 1921, pp. 762.)
314. 1926. KIELHOLZ, A. Analyseversuch bei Delirium tremens. **Z.** XII. 478–492.
315. 1925. —— Trunksucht und Psychoanalyse. (Schweiz. Archiv f. Neur. u. Psych.)
316. 1922. —— Von schizophrenen Erfindern, zweiter Teil. Autoref. **Z.** IX, 125.
317. 1922. KLÄSI, J. Ueber die Bedeutung und Entstehung der Stereotypien. (Berlin: S. Karger.)
318. 1925. KLEIN, MELANIE. Zur Genese des Tics. **Z.** XI, 332–349.
319. 1912. KOVACS, S. Introjektion, Projektion und Einfühlung. **C.** II, 253–263, 316–327.
320. 1925. KOVACS, VILMA. Analyse eines Falles von 'Tic convulsif'. **Z.** XI, 318–325.
321. 1926. LAFORGUE, RENÉ. Ueber Skotomisation in der Schizophrenie. **Z.** XII, 451–456.
322. 1926. —— Verdrängung und Skotomisation. **Z.** XII, 54–65.
323. 1925. LANDAUER, K. Automatismen, Zwangsneurose und Paranoia. Autoref. **Z.** XI, 507.
324. 1914. —— Spontanheilung einer Katatonie. **Z.** II, 441–459.

325. 1914. LANG, J. B. Eine Hypothese zur psychologischen Bedeutung der Verfolgungsidee. (Psychol. Abhandl. von Jung, I, 35–55.)

326. 1913. —— Ueber Assoziationsversuche bei Schizophrenen und den Mitgliedern ihrer Familien. Y. v, 705–755.

327. 1922. LEHRMAN, P. R. A Study of Paranoid Trends in Hysteria. (New York State Jnl. of Medicine, June 1922.)

328. 1917. LUGARO, E. La psichiatria tedesca nella storia e attualità. Studio critico. VI. I Secessionisti. (Rivista di Patologià Firenze.)

329. 1920. MARKUSZEWICZ, ROMAN. Beitrag zum autistischen Denken bei Kindern. Z. VI, 248–252.

330. 1908. MEYER, ADOLF. The Rôle of the Mental Factors in Psychiatry. (Amer. Jnl. of Insanity, July 1908, p. 39. Disc.)

331. 1908. —— Fundamental Conceptions of Dementia praecox. (B.M.J., Sept. 29, 1906, p. 757.) (New York Neur. Soc., Oct. 2, 1906. Jnl. of Nerv. and Ment. Dis., May 1907, p. 331. Disc.)

332. 1906. —— The Relation of Psychogenic Disorders to Deterioration. Boston Soc. of Psychiatry, Nov. 15, 1906. (Jnl. of Nerv. and Ment. Dis., June 1907, p. 401. Disc.)

333. 1921. MITCHELL, T. W. The Psychology of Medicine. (London: Methuen and Co.)

334. 1915. MODENA, G. La psicoanalisi in neuropatologia e in psichiatria. (Quaderna di Psichiatria, Rivista mensile teorica e pratica sotto la direzione del Prof. Enrico Morselli, II, 1915.)

335. 1921. MOORE, THOMAS VERNER. The Parataxes: a Study and Analysis of Certain Borderline Mental States. R. VIII, 252–283.

336. 1921. MÜLLER, F. P. Eine Spermatozoenphantasie eines Epileptikers. Z. VII, 457–460.

337. 1922. —— A Spermatozoa Phantasy of an Epileptic. J. III, 50–54.

338. 1920. —— De insufficientie theorie der dementia praecox getoetst aan een geval dier ziekte. (Psych. en Neur. Bladen.)

339. 1925. MÜLLER-BRAUNSCHWEIG, CARL. Beiträge zur Metapsychologie: Ueber Desexualisierung, Identifizierung und den Gesichtspunkt der Richtung. I. XII, 1–22.

339 a. 1926. —— The Genesis of the Feminine Super-Ego. J. VII, 359–362.

340. 1918. MACCURDY, J. T. Epileptic Dementia. (Cornell Univ. Med. Bull. VII, No. 4.)

341. 1917. —— War Neuroses. (Psych. Bull. July 1917, 243–254.)

342. 1916. —— A Clinical Study of Epileptic Deterioration. (Cornell Univ. Med. Bull. VII, No. 4. Also Psych. Bull. April 1916.)

343. 1915. —— (with W. L. TREADWAY). *Constructive Delusions*. (Jnl. of Abn. Psych. x, 153.)

344. 1914. —— *The Productions in a Manic-like State illustrating Freudian Mechanisms*. (Jnl. of Abn. Psych. VIII.)

345. 1914. —— *A Psychological Feature of the Precipitating Causes in the Psychoses and its Relation to Art*. (Jnl. of Abn. Psych. IX.)

346. 1912. NELKEN, JAN. Analytische Beobachtungen über Phantasien eines Schizophrenen. **Y.** IV, 504–562.

347. 1926. NUNBERG, H. Schuldgefühl und Strafbedürfnis. **Z.** XII, 348–359.

348. 1926. —— *The Sense of Guilt and the Need for Punishment*. **J.** VII, 420–433.

349. 1925. —— Ueber den Genesungswunch. **Z.** XI, 179–193.

350. 1925. —— *The Will to Recovery*. **J.** VII, 64–78.

351. 1924. —— Ueber Depersonalisationszustände im Lichte der Libidotheorie. **Z.** x, 17–33.

352. 1921. —— Der Verlauf des Libidokonfliktes in einem Falle von Schizophrenie. **Z.** VII, 301–345.

353. 1920. —— Ueber den katatonischen Anfall. **Z.** VI, 25–49.

354. 1917. OBERNDORF, C. P. *Cases Allied to Manic-Depressive Insanity*. (New York State Hosp. Bull. v, 3.)

354 *a*. 1916. —— *Simple tic mechanisms*. (Jnl. Amer. Med. Assn. LXVII, July 8, 1916.)

354 *b*. 1915. —— *Analysis of a Claustrophobia*. (Med. Record, Aug. 28.)

354 *c*. 1916. —— *An analysis of certain neurotic mechanisms*. (N.Y. Med. Jnl. CIV, No. 4, July.)

354 *d*. 1917. —— *Traumatic Hysteria*. (N.Y. Med. Jnl. CVI, No. 19, Nov. 10, 1917.)

354 *e*. 1914. —— *Substitution Reactions*. (N.Y. Med. Jnl. pp. 715–718.)

355. 1923. O'MALLEY, MARY. *Transference and some of its Problems in Psychoses*. **R.** x, 1–25.

356. 1921. VAN OPHUIJSEN, J. H. W. Tic-Diskussion. **Z.** VII, 395.

357. 1921. —— *Discussion of Tic. Report*. **J.** II, 480.

358. 1920. —— De inhoud van den vervolgingswaan. (Sitzungsbericht. Ned. Tyd. v. Geneesk. 1921, I, 900.)

359. 1920. —— Ueber die Quelle der Empfindung des Verfolgtwerdens. **Z.** VI, 68–72.

360. 1920. —— *On the Origin of the Feeling of Persecution*. **J.** I, 236–239.

361. 1912. OPPENHEIM, HANS. Zur Frage der Genese des Eifersuchtswahnes. **C.** II, 67–77.

362. 1918. OSNATO, M. *A Critical Review of the Pathogenesis of Dementia praecox, with a Discussion of the Relation of Psychoanalytical Principles*. (Amer. Jnl. of Insanity, LXXV, No. 3.)

363. 1913. Ossipow, N. 'Aufzeichnungen eines Geisteskranken.' Unvollendetes Werk von L. N. Tolstoi. (Zur Frage der Angstemotion.) (Psychotherapia—in Russian—1913, Nr. 3.)

364. 1912. —— Gedanken und Zweifel anlässlich eines Falles von degenerativer Psychopathie. (Psychotherapia—in Russian—1912, Nr. 6.)

365. 1912. —— Gedanken und Bedenken über einen Fall von degenerativer Psychopathie. (Psychopathie—in Russian—III, H. 4, 5 u. 6.)

366. 1914. Payne, Charles R. Some Freudian Contributions to the Paranoia Problem. R. I, 76–93, 187–202, 308–321, 445–451; II, 93–101, 200–202.

367. 1926. Penrose, Lionel S. Psycho-Analytic Notes on Negation. (Author's abstract in J. VII, 533.)

368. 1911. Pfenninger, W. Untersuchungen über die Konstanz und den Wechsel der psychologischen Konstellation bei Normalen und Frühdementen (Schizophrenen). Y. III, 481–524.

369. 1919. Pfister, Oskar. Die Bedeutung der Psychoanalyse für die öffentlichen Irrenanstalten. Z. V, 306.

370. 1913. —— Kryptolalie, Kryptographie und unbewusstes Vexierbild bei Normalen. Y. V, 117–156.

371. 1911. —— Die psychologische Enträtselung der religiösen Glossolalie und der automatischen Kryptographie. Y. III, 427–466, 730–794.

372. 1910 —— Die Frömmigkeit des Grafen Ludwig von Zinzendorf. (Freuds Schr. z. angew. Seelenk. 8, 1910.) 2te Aufl. 1925.

373. 1909. —— Wahnvorstellung und Schülerselbstmord. (Schweiz. Blätter f. Schulgesundheitspflege, Orell Fussli, Zürich, Nr. 1.)

374. 1921. Prideaux, E. Criminal Responsibility and Insanity. (Psyche, II, 29.)

375. 1919. —— Stammering in the War Psychoneuroses. (Lancet, CXCVI, Feb. 8, 1919, p. 217.)

376. 1921. Prinzhorn, H. On Drawings by the Mentally Deranged and by Primitive Peoples.

377. 1919. Rähmi, L. Die Dauer der Anstaltbehandlung bei Schizophrenen. (Zürich.)

378. 1922. Rank, Otto. Perversion und Neurose. Z. VIII, 397–420.

379. 1922. —— Perversion and Neurosis. J. IV, 270–292.

380. 1920. Read, C. Stanford. The Psychopathology of Alcoholism and some so-called Alcoholic Psychoses. (Jnl. of Mental Science, LXVI, pp. 233–244.)

381. 1920. —— *The Pathogenesis of Epilepsy.* **M.** i, 72–83.

382. 1919. —— *War Psychiatry.* Proc. R.S.M. xii, No. 8, p. 35.

383. 1919. —— *Military Psychiatry in Peace and War.* (London: H. K. Lewis and Co.) Second Edition under title *Abnormal Mental Strain.*

384. 1918. —— *A Case of Pseudologia Phantastica.* (Rev. of Neur. and Psychiatry, xvi, Nos. 7 and 8.)

385. 1918. —— *A Survey of War Neuro-Psychiatry.* (Mental Hygiene, ii, No. 3, pp. 357–387.)

386. 1916. REED, RALPH. *A Manic-Depressive Attack presenting a Reversion to Infantilism.* (Jnl. of Abnormal Psychology, xi, No. 6, p. 359.)

387. 1916. —— *An Analysis of an Obsessive Doubt with a Paranoid Trend.* Amer. Psa. Soc., May 10.

388. 1915. —— *A Manic-Depressive Episode presenting a frank Wish-Realisation Construction.* **R.** ii, 166–176.

389. 1922. REEDE, EDWARD H. *Conversion Epilepsy.* **R.** ix, 50–59.

390. 1914. REGIS (et A. HESNARD). La Psychoanalyse des Névroses des Psychoses. (1 vol., 384 pp. Paris: Alcan.)

391. 1926. REICH, WILHELM. Ueber die chronische hypochondrische Neurasthenie mit genitaler Asthenie. **Z.** xii, 25–39.

392. 1925. —— Weitere Bemerkungen über die therapeutische Bedeutung der Genitallibido. **Z.** xi, 297–317.

393. 1925. —— Eine hysterische Psychose in statu nascendi. **Z.** xi, 211–222.

394. 1925. —— Zur Struktur und Genese der 'hypochondrischen Neurasthenie.' Ref. **Z.** xi, 511.

395. 1925. —— Der triebhafte Charakter. (Neue Arbeiten z. ärztl. Psa., No. 4. Int. Psa. Verlag.)

396. 1925. —— Der psychogene Tic als Onanieäquivalent. Ztschr. f. Sexual-wissenschaft, xi, 302–313.

397. 1924. —— Ueber Genitalität. **Z.** x, 164–179.

398. 1920. REIK, THEODOR. Infantile Wortbehandlung. **Z.** vi, 163.

399. 1920. —— Ueber kollektives Vergessen. **Z.** vi, 202–215.

400. 1915. —— Zur Psychoanalyse des Narzissmus im Liebesleben der Gesunden. (Ztschr. f. Sexualwissenschaft, ii, 41–49.)

401. 1915. —— Einige Bemerkungen zur Lehre vom Widerstande. **Z.** iii, 12–24.

402. 1924. —— *Some Remarks on the Study of Resistance.* **J.** v, 141–154.

403. 1925. RICKMAN, JOHN. *Alcoholism and Psychö-Analysis.* (Brit. Jnl. of Inebriety, Oct. 1925, xxiii, No. 2, pp. 66–74.)

404. 1923. RIGGALL, R. M. *Dual Personality.* (Lancet, i, 1155.)

405. 1923. ——*Homosexuality and Alcoholism.* **R.** x, 157–169.
406. 1905. RIKLIN, F. Ueber Versetzungsbesserungen. (Psych.-Neurol. Wochensch. Jg. 1905, Nr. 16–18.)
407. 1924. RIVERS, W. H. R. *Medicine, Magic and Religion.* (London: Kegan Paul, pp. viii + 147.)
408. 1923. —— *Conflict and Dream.* (New York: Harcourt, Brace and Co., pp. 195. London: Kegan Paul.)
409. 1921. —— *Affect in the Dream.* (Brit. Jnl. of Psych. xii, 0. 113.)
410. 1920. —— *Instinct and the Unconscious. A Contribution to a Biological Theory of the Psycho-Neuroses.* (Cambridge Univ. Press, pp. 252.) 2nd ed. 1922, pp. viii + 277.
411. 1917. —— *A Case of Claustrophobia.* (Lancet, Aug. 18, p. 237.)
412. 1923. RÓHEIM, GÉZA. Nach dem Tode des Urvaters. **I.** ix, 83–121.
413. 1921. —— Das Selbst. **I.** vii, 1–39, 142–179, 310–348, 453–504.
414. 1921. —— *Primitive Man and Environment.* **J.** ii, 157–178.
415. 1917. —— Spiegelzauner. **I.** v, 63–120. (Int. Psa. Bibl. Nr. 6.)
416. 1923. ROSS, T. A. *The Common Neuroses—their Treatment in Psychotherapy.* (London: Edward Arnold and Co., pp. xi + 256.)
417. 1922. ROWS, R. G. *Modern Methods in the Treatment of the Psychoses.* (Lancet, i, p. 522.)
418. 1925. SACHS, HANS. Metapsychologische Gesichtspunkte zur Wechselbeziehung zwischen Theorie und Technik in der Psychoanalyse. **Z.** xi, 150–156.
419. 1925. —— *Metapsychological Points of View in Technique and Theory.* **J.** vi, 5–12.
420. 1923. —— Zur Benese der Perversionen. **Z.** ix, 172–182.
421. 1920. —— Gemeinsame Tagträume. Autoref. **Z.** vi, 395. Also in book form.
422. 1921. SADGER, J. Die Lehre von den Geschlechtsverirrungen (Psychopathia sexualis) auf psychoanalytischer Grundlage. (Leipzig und Wien: Deuticke.)
423. 1919. —— Deutung und Heilung paranoider Zustände bei einem Fall von traumatischer Neurose. (Neue ärztl. Zentralztg., April 1919.)
424. 1915. —— Neue Forschungen zur Homosexualität. (Berliner Klinik, Feb. 1915, H. 315.)
425. 1911. —— 'Ist das Asthma bronchiale eine Sexualneurose?' **C.** i, 200–213.
426. 1911. —— Haut-, Schleimhaut- und Muskelerotik. **Y.** iii, 525–556.
427. 1910. —— Ein Fall von multipler Perversion mit hysterischen Absenzen. **Y.** ii, 59–133.

428. 1910. —— Ueber Schülerselbstmord. (Wiener Diskussionen, H. 1.)

429. 1924. DE SAUVAGE-NOLTING, W. J. J. Ueber den Verfolgungswahn beim Weibe. **Z.** x, 300–302.

430. 1925. SCHILDER, PAUL. Zur Psychologie der progressiven Paralyse. (Ztschr. f. d. ges. Neur. u. Psych. xcv.)

431. 1925. —— Entwurf zu einer Psychiatrie auf psychoanalytischer Grundlage. (Int. Psa. Bibl. Nr. 17, pp. 208.)

432. 1924. —— Zur Psychologie epileptischer Ausnahmszustände (mit bes. Berücksichtigung des Gedächtnisses). (Allg. Ztschr. f. Psychiatrie, LXXX.)

433. 1924. —— Medizinische Psychologie für Aerzte und Psychologen. (Berlin: Verlag J. Springer.)

434. 1924. —— Zur Lehre von der Hypochondrie. (Monatschr. f. Psych. u. Neur. LVI.)

435. 1923. —— Seele und Leben. Grundsätzliches zur Psychologie der Schizophrenie und Paraphrenie, zur Psychoanalyse und zur Psychologie überhaupt. (Heft 35 der Monogr. a. d. Gesamtgeb. d. Neur. u. Psych. Berlin: J. Springer.)

436. 1923. —— Zur Psychologie epileptischer Ausnahmszustände. (Ztschr. f. d. ges. Neur. u. Psych. LXXXI, 174–180.)

437. 1922. —— Ueber elementare Halluzinationen des Bewegungssehens. (Ztschr. f. d. ges. Neur. u. Psych. LXXX, 424–431.)

438. 1922. —— Ueber eine Psychose nach Staroperation. **Z.** VIII, 35–44.

439. 1921. —— Vorstudien einer Psychologie der Manie. (Ztschr. f. d. ges. Neur. u. Psych., Orig. Bd. LXVIII, S. 90.)

440. 1921. —— Zur Theorie der Entfremdung der Wahrnehmungswelt. (Allg. Ztschr. f. Psych. LXXVI, H. 5–6.)

441. 1920. —— Ueber Identifizierung auf Grund der Analyse eines Falles von Homosexualität. (Ein Beitrag zur Frage des Aufbaues der Persönlichkeit.) (Ztschr. f. d. ges. Neur. u. Psych., Orig. Bd. LIX.)

442. 1920. —— Ueber Halluzinationen. (Ztschr. f. d. ges. Neur. u. Psych. LIII, H. 3–4.)

443. 1919. —— Selbstbewusstein und Persönlichkeitsbewusstsein. (Berlin.)

444. 1919. —— (und H. HERSCHMANN). Träume der Melancholiker etc. (Ztschr. f. d. ges. Neur. u. Psych. LIII.)

445. 1919. —— Psychogene Parästhesien. (Deutsche Ztschr. f. Nervenheilkunde, LXIV, H. 5–6.)

446. 1918. —— Wahn und Erkenntnis. (15 Heft d. Monogr. aus d. Gesamtgeb. d. Neurol. u. Psych.)

447. 1916. —— Bemerkungen über die Psychologie des paralytischen Grössenwahnes. (Ztschr. f. d. ges. Neur. u. Psych. LXXIV, H. 1–3.)

448. 1914. —— (und HERMANN WEIDNER). Zur Kenntnis symbolähnlicher Bildungen im Rahmen der Schizophrenie. (Ztschr. f. d. ges. Neur. u. Psych. XXVI, H. 2, 1914.)

449. 103. SCHREBER, DANIEL PAUL. (Senatspräsident beim Kgl. Oberlandsgericht Dresden a. D.) Denkwürdigkeiten eines Nervenkranken nebst Nachtragen und einem Anhang über die Frage: 'Unter welchen Voraussetzungen darf eine für geisteskrank erachtete Person gegen ihren erklärten Willen in einer Heilanstalt festgehalten werden?' (Oswald Mutze, Leipzig, 1903.) [Though Dr. Schreber can hardly be counted among the psycho-analysts, his book has proved such a valuable clinical document that it seemed worth while to include it for the sake of the publisher's reference.]

450. 1914. SHOCKLEY, FRANCIS M. *The Rôle of Homosexuality in the Genesis of Paranoid Conditions.* **R.** I, 431–438.

451. 1909. SILBERER, HERBERT. Bericht über eine Methode, gewisse symbolische Halluzinations-Erscheinungen hervorzurufen und zu beobachten. **Y.** I, 513–255.

452. 1920. SILK, S. A. *Compensatory Mechanism of Delusions and Hallucinations.* (Amer. Jnl. of Insanity, LXXVII, p. 253.)

453. 1925. SIMMEL, ERNST. Eine Deckerinnerung in statu nascendi. **Z.** XI, 77–80.

454. 1919. —— (mit S. FERENCZI, K. ABRAHAM, E. JONES). Zur Psychoanalyse der Kriegsneurosen. (Int. Psa. Lib. Nr. 2.) See No. 15.

455. 1918. —— Kriegsneurosen und psychische Trauma. Ihre gegenseitigen Beziehungen, dargestellt auf Grund psychoanalytischer, hypnotischer Studien. (München und Leipzig, 1918.)

456. 1925. SMITH, M. HAMBLIN. *The Psychopathic Personality.* (Jnl. of Mental Science.)

457. 1925. —— (with ANNE FAIRWEATHER). *The Case of Richard Loeb and Nathan Leopold.* (Jnl. of Mental Science.)

458. 1924. —— *The Mental Conditions found in certain Sexual Offenders.* (Lancet.)

459. 1923. —— (with G. W. PAILTHORPE). *The Application of Mental Tests to Offenders.* (Lancet.)

460. 1922. —— *The Psychology of the Criminal.* (London: Methuen and Co., pp. 182.)

461. 1923. STÄRCKE, AUGUST. Ein noch nicht beschriebenes Symptom bei Depressionszuständen. (Ned. Tyd. v. Geneesk. I, 414.)

462. 1921. —— Psychoanalyse und Psychiatrie. (Beihefte der Int. Ztschr. f. Psa., Nr. 4.)

463. 1921. —— *Psycho-Analysis and Psychiatry.* **J.** II, 361–415.

464. 1920–21. —— Demonstration von 40 Zeichnungen u. Plastiken eines leicht hebephrenen Bildhauers. (Ned. Tyd. v. Geneesk. 1920, ii, 103; 1921, i, 897.)

465. 1920. —— Die Beziehungen zwischen Neurosen und Psychosen. Autoref. **Z.** VI, 399.

466. 1920. —— Der Kastrationskomplex. **Z.** VII, 9–32.

467. 1921. —— *The Castration Complex.* **J.** II, 179–201.

468. 1919. —— Die Umkehrung des Libidovorzeichens beim Verfolgungswahn. **Z.** V, 285–287.

469. 1926. STODDART, W. H. B. *Mind and its Disorders. A Text-Book for Students and Practitioners of Medicine.* 5th ed., with 87 illustrations, including 11 plates (6 coloured). Demy 8vo. (Philadelphia: P. Blakiston's Son and Co. London: H. K. Lewis and Co.)

470. 1915. —— *The New Psychiatry. Being the Morison Lectures for 1915 delivered before the Royal College of Physicians of Edinburgh.* (Rev. of Neur. and Psych., May, June and July, 1915. London: Ballière, Tindall and Cox, 8vo, pp. 67. Also pub. by Medical Press and Circular.)

471. 1911. STORFER, A. J. Zur Sonderstellung des Vatermordes. Eine rechtsgeschichtliche und völkerpsychologische Studie. (Schr. z. angew. Seelenkunde, H. 12. Leipzig und Wien, F. Deuticke.)

472. 1920. TANSLEY, A. G. *The New Psychology and its relation to Life.* (London: Geo. Allen and Unwin. Pp. 283. New York: Dodd, Mead and Co. Revised and enlarged edition, 1922, pp. 316.)

473. 1919. TAUSK, VIKTOR. Ueber die Entstehung des 'Beeinflussungsapparates' in der Schizophrenia. **Z.** V, 1–33.

474. 1916. —— Diagnostische Erörterungen auf Grund der Zustandsbilder der sog. Kriegspsychosen. (Wiener Med. Wochenschr., Nr. 37 und 38, 1916.)

475. 1915. —— Zur Psychologie des alkoholischen Beschäftigungsdelirs. **Z.** III, 204–226.

476. 1913. —— Entwertung des Verdrängungsmotivs durch Rekompense. **Z.** I, 230–239.

477. 1924. —— *Compensation as a Means of Discounting the Motive of Repression.* **J.** V, 130–140.

478. 1926. WÄLDER, ROBERT. Ueber schizophrenes und schöpferisches Denken. **Z.** XII, 298–308.

479. 1926. *Schizophrenic and Creative Thinking.* **J.** VII, 366–376.
480. 1924. —— Ueber Mechanismen und Beeinflussungsmöglich-keiten der Psychosen. **Z.** X, 393–414.
481. 1925. WÄLDER, ROBERT. *The Psychoses: their Mechanisms and Accessibility to Influence.* **J.** VI, 259–281.
482. 1926. WEISS, EDOARDO. Der Vergiftungswahn im Lichte der Introjektions- und Projektionsvorgänge. **Z.** XII, 466–477.
483. 1925. WHITE, WILLIAM A. *Essays in Psychopathology.* (Nervous and Ment. Dis. Pub. Co., New York, pp. 140.)
484. 1925. —— *Outlines of Psychiatry.* Tenth Revised Edition. (Nervous and Ment. Dis. Co., New York.)
485. 1921. —— *Foundations of Psychiatry.* (Nervous and Ment. Dis. Co., New York, pp. 136.)
486. 1921. —— *Some Considerations bearing on the Diagnosis and Treatment of Dementia Praecox.* **R.** VIII, 417–422.
487. 1915. —— (with S. E. JELLIFFE). *Diseases of the Nervous System. A Text-Book of Neurology and Psychiatry.* (Philadelphia: Lea and Ferbiger, pp. 796. 4th ed., revised and enlarged, 1923, pp. 1088 + xlii.)
488. 1917. WHOLEY, C. C. *Revelations of the Unconscious in a Toxic (Alcoholic) Psychosis.* (Amer. Jnl. of Insanity, LXXIV, No. 3, 437–444.)
489. 1916. —— *A Psychosis presenting Schizophrenic and Freudian Mechanisms with Scientific Clearness.* (Amer. Jnl. of Insanity, LXXIII, No. 4, 583–595.)
490. 1913. WULFF, M. Zur Psychogenität des Asthma bronchiale. **C.** III, 202–205.
491. 1912. —— Die Lüge in der Psychoanalyse. **C.** II, 130–133.

Addenda.

492. 1926. 'A PARANOIAC.' *Paranoia from the subjective Point of View.* **R.** XIII, 200–209.
493. 1916–17. K... M... Der Beginn eines Verfolgungswahnes. **Z.** IV, 330.
494. 1925. KAPP, R. O. *Sensation and Narcissism.* **J.** VI, 292–299.
495. 1927. JONES, ERNEST. *The Early Development of Female Sexuality.* **J.** VIII, 459–472.

APPENDIX I
NEED FOR BELIEF IN GOD[1]
(1938)

1. *Introduction*

FREUD's classical work *Totem and Taboo* brought religion within the framework of the Oedipus complex and made clear the hitherto inexplicable connection between the totem feast and exogamy on the one hand and the human conscience on the other, but it does not explain several later developments of human custom, e.g. the *endogamy* which is almost obligatory in many religious communities; the obligation to marry someone who eats the same God in the same way, i.e. people who are joined in the Eucharist.

The psycho-analytical contribution to the study of religion falls into three confluent streams; these may be roughly classed as centring on

(*a*) the activities of the (Primal) Father.

(*b*) the influence of the Mother's activity in the child's conception of the primal scene; and

(*c*) the activity of the child's own psychical processes particularly in respect to early direct relationships.

Theories are mainly associated with the work of (*a*) Freud, (*b*) Róheim-Ferenczi and (*c*) Klein, respectively. I shall deal almost entirely with the last.

The theories of the primal horde deal with the father's interference with the sexual activity of the adolescent sons, their cannibalistic destruction of him and his return as a ghost in the pricks of conscience if the orphaned horde sought satisfaction from the females of the horde. The main figure in this primal drama is a 'whole object' and is external; when introjected as conscience or super-ego it behaves more or less as did the father figure in real life.

The typical punishment is castration, the typical method of avoiding trouble is to avoid the father's women-folk. The Oedipus situation has sharp outlines because the objects are separ-

[1] Read at the Fifteenth International Psycho-Analytical Congress, Paris, 1938.

ated, external people; the primal sons kill one corner of the eternal triangle, so to speak, and then turn to the other—or avoid it.

The researches of the child analysts on early object-relationships disclose the fact that the mechanisms of projection and introjection play a far larger part than was formerly thought, and that these processes are very strong even before the establishment of 'whole object' relationships. The early oedipean triangle cannot be dealt with one corner at a time because man's sexual activity is not based on a tropistic orientation, now to the hated father, now to the desired mother, but is based on a 'primal scene' in which the parent figures are united in coitus, and the onlooker is identified in differing degree with each one of the two partners. Religion is a means of dealing with the tension caused by what may be called the triune relationship and it employs two interrelated means for this purpose: (a) the modification of the conception of parent-god figures and their relationship to one another and (b) restriction of sexual activity and enjoyments of the individual together with an injunction to perform socially useful activities. The first of these is inferred from the religious beliefs and ritual. The second is seen in the ethical code accepted by the believers.

If we restrict the primal scene to the simple elements employed in the theory of the primal horde we not only narrow our conception of religion but tend to lose sight of the part it has played in the building up of our civilization. On the other hand if we enlarge our definition to include what the child phantasies about the relation of the parents to one another, we obtain a picture which not only approximates more to what the ordinary man means when he talks about the civilizing influence of religion, but we are dealing with a concept which is easier to link up with our clinical experience.

2. Quaker Beliefs

We are accustomed to find religion concerning itself with a Holy Family consisting of Father, Mother and Son, with Saints (or demons), with festivals, holy places, and ritual, with a creed and with priests; it will test, if not tax, our theories if we apply them to a sect which has none of these, yet has endured with and without persecution for three centuries; the Quakers provide the challenge.

N

Belief centres on what they call 'The Inner Light', an 'indwelling of God in man'. It is called 'God's Power', 'the Sustainer', the 'element of the divine in every man', the 'life-giver'. It enables the individual to become confluent with 'the ocean of divine love' which fills the Universe; it guides its possessor into paths of righteousness. It lifts him above the morass of loneliness and lovelessness, of misery and degradation into which he would otherwise sink, and offers him 'a sure foundation' and the possibility of 'complete fulfilment' in this life on earth.

Thus guided the Quaker can dispense with a permanent priesthood and since God dwells within there is no need for ritual. Worship consists in 'waiting upon God'. It is not thought proper to control the movements of the Divine Being by magical observances and the initiative is to be taken by the God. The worshipper's duty is to prepare himself for the reception of the Divine Essence.

Having reached this point, our investigations can take two directions, either we may consider the Inner Light as a symbol for the Divine penis or semen, or we may consider the influence it exerts on the Quaker outlook on the world. The latter has the merit of showing it in action.

The Quakers have two peculiar 'Testimonies' or Regulations of Conduct; they will not take a civil oath, and they will not fight. They do not object to force absolutely; for instance it is thought right to restrain lunatics and criminals (incidentally they were pioneers in the humane treatment of lunatics and in penal reform). I believe the objection to the Oath to be the unconscious dread lest the oath binds the God sworn by no less than the person taking the oath. The second rule of conduct concerns war. It appears that the main objection to killing is not the attack on the man but the aggression against the 'God in man', the Inner Light. In other words both rules of conduct are directed ultimately to the avoidance of aggression against an object which lies within the personality.

In the first place it is the degree of emphasis on intrapsychic events which makes Quakerism such an important field for the study of religion, and in the second its central beliefs relate to an earlier organization of the ego-object relationship than do those of other sects or religions. To put it another way, the regressive defence in the case of Quakerism is more thorough.

3. *Early Object Relationships*

The light thrown by the child analysts on early object relationships will assist us to clarify some of the problems of Quaker belief that are not so readily explained by psycho-analytical concepts based on later mental development. I think we should begin with a consideration of the period of great emotional instability (reflected in object relationships) when the child is overwhelmed by the belief that its destructive wishes are omnipotent and there is no simple solution of its difficulty. Driven by desire to obtain control over what is felt to be good, it uses the apparatus of incorporation, which is also that of destruction; and, since its need for good objects is accentuated by fear that it has also absorbed bad objects, and also that it needs good objects to counteract its own destructiveness, its orientation in action to the outer and to the inner world is troubled and fervid. Further, in respect to the intra-psychic orientation, what has been incorporated remains in a measure *sui generis* and is felt to be still autonomous, not completely a part of the Me, not completely foreign. These 'internal objects' are on the narrowest interpretation the precursors of the super-ego, and have qualities that are in the main *attributed to* rather than inferred from observation of the external world. Psychical orientation is thus duplicated; hopes and fears are felt in respect to the objects within no less than for those without. (If we regard these internalized objects only as functional appendages of the ego we lose sight of their position as objects.) When we speak of the child dreading its destructive wishes we have to consider whether the object to be attacked lies in the external world or within the personality, similarly with the dread of persecutors; and when we speak of rescue phantasies we must reckon with those in which good objects are saved from bad ones though both may lie within the self.

4. *Application to Quaker Beliefs*

Religious sects are of two kinds, those which originate by fission of a Mother Church and those that are formed by the agglutination of individuals who have left the Mother Church because they did not find there the satisfaction their spirit required.

Quakerism was of the second or agglutinative kind and the

writings of its first members throw much light on their state of mind. They desired a relationship with God which would save them from utter loneliness of spirit, from wickedness and degradation and loss of capacity for love; they recognized a terrific need for God and furthermore a God that would live in them and make them independent of all outside aid—Churches, priests and ceremonial observances.

We may ask ourselves what conditions of early ego development and object relationship satisfy the condition that they can be regarded as focal points (starting points or regressive goals) for the Quaker beliefs.

We are struck by two facts: the overwhelming sense of inner desolation caused by the ego's own destructiveness and the need for an omnipotent good object both to take away the feeling of chaos and to put things to rights again; this corresponds closely with the depressive position which Mrs. Klein postulates as the turning point in psychical development. In this phase the child is appalled by the effect in its phantasies of its wishes and employs every means at its disposal to avert a catastrophe.

Let us take, for example, the matter of this need for God; the ordinary Christian has only a *periodic* need for religious observances, whereas the Quaker in theory 'makes of every meal a sacrament'. In his view God is within him always and in an equal state of activity; the Quaker's spiritual struggles are directed to removing his own evil and inhibiting control of the God within.

I would direct your attention to the great importance in these beliefs in the *internalness* of the good object (or God) and of the preoccupation with the control of aggression whether against an external or internal object. If this was all there was to tell of Quakerism we could sum it up as a regressive flight to a psychotic condition, or in Dr. Schmideberg's phrase 'a flight to a good internal object'. But we have to take account of the constructive or restitutive phantasies as well, for in the stage of early object relationship these play an equally important part. The conception of the mother as the victim of a sadistic coitus is offset by the wish to make her whole and well and happy again by a 'good' coitus, in which the penis is to play the part of an invigorating, strengthening and withal pleasure-giving thing. Now I venture to think that the discovery of this early phantasy throws some light on the nature of the incest-impulse. We do not ascribe incest to animals because they satisfy their sexual needs on the nearest and most tropistically powerful (i.e. attractive) object. We speak of incest when the sexual impulse is *bound*. It is a special case of fixation of impulse to a particular object. Incest may have several roots. It may be ascribed to a conditioned reflex in which the sexual drive is attached to a mother figure through early experience, e.g. a dependence on her through feeding (compare Pavlov's dogs); but important as such factors are, it is in my view to be ascribed *in part* to an unconscious compulsion to make good the damage to the mother which the individual himself has done in his sadistic phantasies (or by his alliance with a phantasied sadistic penis-father).

The early phantasies have further ramifications, for in incest the penis taken in jealousy from the father (and incorporated) is given back to the mother (where it belongs so to speak). And I believe this phantasy plays an important part in the endogamous tendency which is found in so many religions and sects, including the Quakers.

In endogamy, the penis 'bleibt in der Familie'. There may be another motive, viz. an over-estimation of the mother and depreciation of others so that the penis is thought of as too good to be thrown away on outsiders. I believe the Jews hold similar sentiments—and it has often surprised me that psycho-analysts, many of whom are not unacquainted with Jewish custom, should have paid so little attention to endogamy.

Returning to the Quakers: they are a most puritanical sect and enjoin on *all* of their members the degree of chastity which most sects only demand of their priests. When we remember that the Quakers have no priesthood and that any one of them can function as a preacher if 'moved by the Holy Spirit', we can see that the endogamous impulse is attended by *inner* (as well as the obvious outer) restrictions. In other words, when the sexual function is over much yoked to reparative needs in the unconscious phantasy its pleasure function is greatly diminished. We must recollect that the Quaker has no Father-Mother-Son God, no Holy Family, the reason (already given) being that the sexual function is as far as possible *denied*.

When studying Quakerism we must not forget that it is kept going by the accession of individuals who are unable to get satisfaction elsewhere; their chief complaint is loneliness of spirit. I would say that it is a religion of defence against this sense of desolation. It is a religion which more than any other emphasizes quietism and avoidance of aggression against its Good Objects. The Quaker's emphasis on chastity and the desexualizing of the god (there are no gods or goddesses but just this 'Inner Light') shows us another thing which disturbs their inner peace, i.e. the desolation is associated with phantasies of parental coitus which is conceived of as of a sadistic nature.

Their worship is peculiar—'a silent waiting upon God'—and the satisfaction they derive from the 'secret stirring of God within' discloses to us both the feminine and the *secret* nature of their relation to the god. Further in the unconscious phantasy the god is believed to be nearly moribund, any sign of his inner stirring is therefore a great secret joy. Quakerism is a religion which strives to achieve conviction that God is not dead, that the Good Object, which has been introjected, is not destroyed by the subject's own sadism.

Time does not allow me to disentangle this theme from the rather simple conception of the death of the Father of the Primal Horde, but let it be sufficient for our present purposes for me to point out that this sect which is joined so to say as a last resort because of godlessness or better of 'good objectlessness', i.e. as a last resort from utter despair, focuses its attention on the good object that is permanently within, and guides its believers to the doing of good works. It achieves its therapeutic success through the same means by which the earliest depressions of our infancy are overcome, namely, by restitution for damage done in sadistic phantasy, but unlike the process in the normal person, the Quaker's restitutive process is very much restricted—the genital is not wholly good. Though full of good deeds he tends to be harsh with himself and towards others. Following the paper given by Dr. Jones yesterday, his character type is moral rather than loving.

Quakerism at first sight with its absence of creeds, priests, Holy Family or set observances seems to be an exception to our formulations of religion and for this very reason it must be studied. If the later organization of the super-ego does not explain it we must employ the discovery of the early object relationship and of internal objects. Then, perhaps, we shall find that so far from being an exception, Quakerism gives a clue to man's great need for God, viz. a means to overcome his inner, and to a large extent, unconscious despair.

APPENDIX II

LIST OF PUBLICATIONS BY JOHN RICKMAN

1919. Six articles in the *Manchester Guardian*, reprinted in pamphlet form entitled: 'Eye Witness from Russia'.

1919. Common Sense and our Russian Policy. U. D. C. Memoranda on a Democratic Peace. Pamphlet No. 35a.

1919. The Need of Russia—Schools. *Cambridge Magazine*, 15.2.19, p. 404.

1919. What is Bolshevism? *Cambridge Magazine*, 9, 29.11.19. (Debate with Sir Bernard Pares.)

1921. An Unanalysed Case. Anal Erotism, Occupation and Illness. *Int. J. Psycho-Anal.*, 2, 424.

1924. Photography as a pseudo-perversion. Abstract in *Int. J. Psycho-Anal.*, 6, 238.

1925. Alcoholism and Psycho-Analysis. *Brit. J. Inebriety*, 23, ii, 66–74.

1926. Ein Psychologischer Faktor in der Aetiologie von Descensus Uteri, Dammbruch und Vaginismus. *Int. Z. f. Psychoanalyse*, 12, iii.

1926. A Psychological Factor in the Aetiology of Descensus Uteri, Laceration of the Perineum and Vaginismus. *Int. J. Psycho-Anal.*, 7, 363.

1926–27. A Survey: The Development of the Psycho-Analytical Theory of the Psychoses, 1894–1926. *Brit. J. Med. Ps.*, 6, iv, 270–94; 7, 94–124, 321–74.

1927. Discussion on Lay-Analysis. *Int. J. Psycho-Anal.*, 8, i, 207–212.

1927. Discussion: T. S. Good's Paper, 'An Attempt to Investigate and to treat Psycho-neuroses and Psychoses at an Outpatient Clinic.' *Brit. J. Med. Ps.*, 7, 65.

1928. On Some Standpoints of Freud and Jung. *Brit. J. Med. Ps.* 8, i, 44–8.

1928. *Index Psycho-Analyticus*, 1893–1926. London, Hogarth Press and Int. Psycho-Analytical Press.

1928. *The Development of the Psycho-Analytical Theory of the Psychoses*, 1893–1926. London, Baillière, Tindall and Cox.

1928. Lecture Notes on the Psycho-Analytical Contribution to Psychiatry. Cyclostyled Brochure, January–March.

1929. Reflections on the Problem of Discipline. *New Era*, 1929, 147.

1929. On the Aetiology of the Prolapse of the Uterus. *J. of Obstetrics and Gynaecology of the British Empire*, 36, i, 3–15.

1929. On Quotations. *Int. J. Psycho-Anal.*, 10, ii/iii, 242.

1932. The Psychology of Crime. *Brit. J. Med. Ps.*, 12, iii, 264.

1934. Discussion: 'A Symposium on the Psychology of Peace and War.' Glover and Ginsburg. *Brit. J. Med. Ps.*, **14**, 288.

1935. Anonymous: 'The Cathartic Function of General Elections.' *The Lancet*, 16.11.35.

1935. Annotation: 'The Ministry of Women'. *The Lancet*, 14.12.35.

1935. Review: *Dictionary of Psychology.* Edited by H. C. Warren. London, Allen & Unwin, 1935. *Brit. J. Med. Ps.*, **15**, 242.

1935. Review: *Emotions and Bodily Change,* by H. F. Dunbar. Columbia University Press, 1935. *Brit. J. Med. Ps.*, **15**.

1935. Review: *The Ministry of Women.* Report of Archbishop's Commission, London. The Press and Publications Department of the Church Assembly, Westminster, 1935. *Brit. J. Med. Ps.*, **15**, 338.

1935. Critical Review: *Psychology and Modern Problems:* A Series of Lectures organized by the Institute of Medical Psychology, edited by Dr. Hadfield, London. University of London Press, 1935. *Brit. J. Med. Ps.*, **16**, 78.

1935. Critical Notice: *Psychology and Religion:* A Study by a Medical Psychologist, by David Forsyth. London, Watts and Co. *Brit. J. Med. Ps.*, **15**, 321.

1935. Collective Review: 'Seven Books on Sex'. *Brit. J. Med. Ps.*

1936. Review: *The Dangers of Being Human,* by Edward Glover. London, Allen & Unwin, 1936. *Int. J. Psycho-Anal.*, **17**, 521.

1936. Anonymous: 'On Feeling Secure'. *The Lancet*, 21.3.36.

1936. Review: Roots of Crime: Psycho-Analytical Studies. *Life and Letters.* London, 2.6.36.

1936. Anonymous: 'Co-Education'. *The Lancet*, 4.1.36.

1936. Anonymous: 'Speech'. *The Speech J. of the Brit. Soc. of Speech Therapists*, **2**, i,

1936. Edited: *On the Bringing up of Children,* by five Psycho-Analysts. London, Kegan Paul.

1937. A Discursive Review. *Brit. J. Med. Ps.* **17**, 361

1937. On 'Unbearable' Ideas and Impulses. *American. J. of Ps. November*, 1937, 248–53. Cornell University.

1937. Anonymous: 'On Crowning the King'. *The Lancet*, 8.5.37.

1937. Annotation: 'Reflections on the Marriage Bill'. *The Lancet*, 24.7.37.

1937. Review: *Psycho-Analysis and Social Psychology,* by Prof. W. McDougall. Methuen & Co., 1936. *Nature*, 16.1.37.

1937. Review: *Accidents and Their Prevention,* by H. M. Vernon. Cambridge University Press, 1937. *Life and Letters To-Day,* Spring, 1937.

1937. Anonymous: 'The Russian Trials'. *The Lancet*, 6.2.37.

1937. *Psycho-Analytical Epitomes,* edited by John Rickman. London, Hogarth Press and the Institute of Psycho-Analysis:

(1) A General Selection from the Works of Sigmund Freud.
(2) Love, Hate and Reparation. Two Lectures by Melanie Klein and Joan Riviere.

1938. (3) Superstition and Society, by R. E. Money-Kyrle.
(4) Civilization, War and Death. Selections from three works by Sigmund Freud.

1938. Review: *Psychology Down the Ages*, by C. Spearman. Macmillan, 1937. *Man*, August, 1938.

1938. Anonymous: 'After the Strain'. *The Lancet*, 8.10.38.

1938. Annotation: 'The Psychology of A.R.P.' *The Lancet*, 9.7.38.

1938. Review: *Psychology Down the Ages*, by C. Spearman. Macmillan. 1937. *Life and Letters To-day*, Spring, 1938.

1938. Review: *Psychology for Everyone*, by W. J. H. Sprott, Longman. *Life and Letters To-day*, Spring, 1938.

1938. Review: *Popular Psychological Fallacies*, by J. G. Taylor. London, Watts & Co., 1938. *Brit. J. Med. Ps.*, 6.7.38.

1938. Articles on The Russian Peasant signed 'Vratch', *The Lancet*.

1938. Panic and Air-Raid Precautions. *The Lancet*, 1291, 4.6.38.

1938. The Medical Section of the British Psychological Society. *The Medical Press and Circular*, Sept. 7, 1938.

1938. Mental Rest and Mental Pain. *The Nursing Mirror and Midwives Journal*.

1938. A Discursive Review: *Air Raid: The Technique of Silent Approach, High Explosive, Panic*, by John Langdon-Davies. *Brit. J. Med. Ps.*, **17**, iii/iv.

1939. War Wounds and Air-Raid Casualties: The Mental Aspects of A.R.P. *Brit. Med. Journal*, 457, 26.8.39. Published also in book: *War Wounds and Air-Raid Casualties*. London, H. K. Lewis & Co. Ltd., 1939.

1939. Letter: 'Sigmund Freud: A Personal Impression'. *The Lancet*, 7.10.39, 813.

1939. Anonymous: A Peace of Understanding. *The Lancet*, 2.9.39.

1939. Anonymous: The Search for Truth (manuscript headed 'Science and Peace'). *The Lancet*, 21.10.39.

1939. Letter to *The Times:* 'Government and A.R.P.', 6.1.39.

1939. Letter to *The Times:* 'Evacuation and the Child's Mind', 2.5.39.

1939. Annotation: 'Conscription', *The Lancet*, 8.4.39.

1939. Sexual Behaviour and Abnormalities. *Brit. Encyclopaedia of Medical Practice*, **2**, 110–25.

1939. The General Practitioner and Psycho-Analysis'. *The Practitioner*, **143**, 192–8, August, 1939.

1940. Anonymous: 'Two Ways'. *The Lancet*, 1.6.40.

1940. Foreword: Special—March. 'On Evacuation of Under Fives'. *The New Era in Home and School*.

1940. On the Nature of Ugliness and the Creative Impulse. *Int. J. Psycho-Anal.*, **21**, iii, 294–313.

1941. Letter: 'Medical Planning', *The Lancet*, 8.3.41.

1941. A Case of Hysteria: Theory and Practice in the Two Wars. *The Lancet*, 785, 21.6.41.

1941. Sigmund Freud, 1856–1939: An Appreciation. *Brit. J. Med. Ps.*, **19**, 1–8.

1943. A Story-Completion Test Suitable for Adults. *Brit. J. Med. Ps.*, **19**, 454.

1943. Interim Report of the Committee on Psychological Medicine of the Royal College of Physicians of London on Undergraduate Education in Psychiatry. October. (Member of the Committee.)

1943. Intra-Group Tensions in Therapy: Their Study as a Task of the Group, by W. R. Bion and John Rickman. *The Lancet*, 678, 27.11.43.

1945. Anonymous: 'The First Fruits of Peace'. *The Lancet*, 5.5.45.

1945. Obituary: Dr. Thomas Walker Mitchell. *Brit. J. Med. Ps.*, **20**, iii, 204–5, 1945.

1946. Anonymous: 'Nuremberg'. *The Lancet*, 12.10.46.

1947. Psychology in Medical Education. *Brit. Med. Journal*, Sept., **2**, 363.

1947. A Few Notes on Psycho-Analysis. Tavistock Institute of Human Relations. *The Student's Notebook*.

1947. Second of the two Third Programme Talks on Psycho-Analysis. Tavistock Institute of Human Relations. March 25. *The Student's Notebook*.

1948. Anonymous: 'A Symbol Reborn'. *The Lancet*, 20.11.48.

1948. The Application of Psycho-Analytical Principles to Hospital In-patients. *Journal of Mental Science*, **94**, No. 397, October, 1948.

1948. Obituary: Dr. Adrian Stephen. *Int. J. Psycho-Anal.*, **29**, i, 4–6. (Anonymous.)

1948. Guilt and the Dynamics of Psychological Disorder in the Individual. *Proceedings of the International Conference on Mental Health*, 3, p. 41. London, H. K. Lewis & Co. Ltd.

1949. Editorial. *Brit. J. Med. Ps.*, **22**, 1.

1949. *The Peoples of Great Russia*, by Geoffrey Gorer and John Rickman. London, Cresset Press.

1949. A Report on Tensions Meeting. *U.N.E.S.C.O. Courier*, July, 1949, I, No. 6, p. 3.

1950. How the Idea of God Arises. *The Listener*, **44**, No. 1137, p. 742, Dec. 14, 1950.

1950. Broadcast Talk on Psycho-Analysis. 'Cairo Calling', 28. iv, 50.
1950. Psycho-Dynamic Notes. *Tensions that Cause War*, edited by Hadley Cantril. University of Illinois Press, Urbana
1950. On the Criteria for the Termination of an Analysis. *Int. J. Psycho-Anal.*, **31**, iii, 200.
1950. The Role and Future of Psycho-therapy within Psychiatry. *Journal of Mental Science*, **96**, No. 402, January, 181–9.
1950. The Development of Psychological Medicine. *Brit. Med. Journal*, January 7, **1**, 30.
1950. The Factor of Number in Individual and Group Dynamics. *Journal of Mental Science*, **96**, No. 404, 770–3, July.
1950. Obituary: Claud Dangar Daly. *Int. J. Psycho-Anal.*, **31**, v, 290.
1950. Obituary: Susan Sutherland Isaacs. *Int. J. Psycho-Anal.*, **31**, iv, 279.
1950. Obituary: Wulf Sachs. *Int. J. Psycho-Anal.*, **31**, iv, 288.
1950. Obituary: William Henry Butter Stoddart. *Int. J. Psycho-Anal.*, **31**, iv, 286.
1951. Reflections on the Functions and Organization of a Psycho-Analytical Society. *Int. J. Psycho-Anal.*, **32**, iii, 218.
1951. Methodology and Research in Psychopathology. *Brit. J. Med. Ps.*, **24**, i, 1–7.
1951. Number and the Human Sciences: In *Psycho-Analysis and Culture*. New York, International Universities Press.
1951. The Development of the Moral Function. *The Yearbook of Education*. London, Evans Bros.
1953. *Psycho-Analytical Epitomes*, edited by John Rickman. London: Hogarth Press and the Institute of Psycho-Analysis.
     Civilization, War and Death. Selections from three works by Sigmund Freud. New enlarged edition.

y of lly	Type of 'social feeling'	Ego resiliency to external shocks or frustrations	Super-ego in relation to ego	Signs of improvement characterized by
	No inhibition of impulses	'Cannot stand being born'	Complete resorption into ego, with resulting megalomania	Increase of psycho-neurotic symptoms
	Anxiety and guilt	Separation from anaclitic love object may precipitate regression (weaning, cleansing, bereavement, etc.)	Melancholic phase: introjection of father-imago *before* strong positive libidinal transference, therefore sadistic super-ego. Manic phase: fusion of super-ego into ego	Increase of obsessional symptoms (Obsessional character)
	Anxiety	Sensitive to anal regulation; later wounds to social self feeling badly borne	Super-ego appears to be weaker than in preceding or following stages	Modification of restitution symptoms. Diminution of negative reactions. Introjection
ent-	Guilt. Sympathy. Shame	Owing to loss of support of early super-ego, ego overreacts to social influences. Sphincter morality too strong. Castration sensitiveness	Introjection of father-imago *after* strong positive libidinal transference, therefore less sadistic super-ego	Decrease of ambivalence. Return to phallic and genital phases (Sometimes phobias reappear)
	Modesty (guilt and anxiety less marked)	Castration anxiety in purest form	Super-ego *versus* id dominates ego function	Decrease of castration anxiety
	Social feeling (love)	Ego's adaptability unimpaired, i.e. no strong tendency to character formation, and castration anxiety easily tolerated	Ego takes over super-ego function	—
s.	Has no relation to social life as such	The frustration in question is in regard to disjunction of psychical and somatic libido gratification	Super-ego not a mechanism operating in symptoms	Tolerance of abstinence
	Has no relation to social life as such	The frustration in question is insufficient psychical preparation for the explosive orgastic discharge	Super-ego not a mechanism operating in symptoms	Tolerance of sexual discharge
	Has no relation to social life as such	External shock is more than ego can master at one time. Any frustration may cause reflux over cathexis and return of symptoms	Super-ego not a mechanism operating in symptoms	Tolerance of frustration. Tolerance of traumatism. Decrease of traumatophilia
	Guilt, later no inhibition of impulses	Shocks which once would not be pathogenic become so owing to incipient patho-neurosis. Frustrations, particularly homosexual, badly borne	Super-ego 'degeneration' (? toxic patho-neurosis)	Return of sublimated, homosexual and heterosexual object-love
	Guilt and modesty	Castration anxiety	Peculiar super-ego tolerance modifies ego gratifications	Tolerance of castration anxiety
s	Has no relation to social life as such	React strongly to injuries to organs with which there is strong ego-identification	Super-ego, not a mechanism operating in symptoms	Increase of psycho-neurotic symptoms
ing.'	Guilt	React strongly to irritation in organs with which there is strong ego-identification	Peculiar super-ego tolerance modifies ego gratifications	Increase of libido discharge along transference-neurotic paths

INDEX

Abdication, progressive, *see* Officers

Abnormality, and mental suffering, 53

Abraham, Karl, 161, 231–3, 249 –253, 261, 276n., 277–8, 279, 285

Absolute, of Creativeness and Beauty, 87

Absolutism, psycho-analysis and, 188

Accident-proneness, 124

Addition, to external world, 256

Adler, Alfred, 49, 160

Aesthetics, 68 ff.; and psychoanalysis, 69, 72

Affects, in dementia praecox, 230

Agenda, written and unwritten, 194

Aggression, *see* Aggressiveness

Aggressiveness, 157; and crime, 45 ff.; denial of, 124; and guilt, 123, 160; Quakers and, 386, 388; and repression, 51, 124; toleration of, 128; and work, 49

A-historicity of psychotherapy, 177, 133, 139, 210, 222

Aims, sexual, and fixation points, 258

Alcheringa, 335 n.

Allo-erotism, 257

Alteration, feeling of, 336

Ambivalence, 70, 73–4, 81, 123, 151, 312; in anal stage, 286; in children, 126, 157–8; in psychoses, 258; religion and, 125; towards father, 122

Amnesia, 62, 66, 168; hysterical, 322; infantile, Freud and, 98; removal of, 128

Anal erotism: case of, in labourer, 19–21; positive and negative tendencies, 280

Anality, infantile, 153

Anal sadistic level, reproach of loved object at, 280

Anal-sadistic organization, 296

Anal stage, 268–70, 276–7, 286

Analysis: and aesthetics, 69, 72; goal of, 35, 115; mechanistic, in medical education, 106; and non-analytic therapy, 116 –117; purpose of technique, 36; termination, criteria for, 127 –130; *see also* Psycho-analysis

Analyst(s); aim of education of, 26, 28–9; and legal privilege, 29; numbers, 183, 206; obligations of, 29 n., 30; and patient, non-interference, 35; – relation, 26, 33; – transference relation, 63; professional rules, 30; sociology of, 182 ff; training of, 64; wish to cling to, 128; world distribution of, 206; *see also* Psychiatrist

Analyst, lay: fees of, 31; how classified, 30; status, 182

Angst, 319; *see also* Anxiety

Animal phobias, 259

Animals, Man and, compared, 152

Animism, 275

Anomaly, sexual, 124

Anthropology, and psychoanalysis, 222

Anticathexis, 29 n.

Antique-fetishism, 75

Anxiety, 315 ff.; causes of, 65; and depression, 249; and fear, 319; Freud on, 55; and guilt, 120; as inhibiting aesthetic enjoyment, 76; primary narcissistic, 317 n.; where felt, 318; *see also* Castration anxiety; Conscience anxiety

Anxiety hysteria, 259; description and differential diagnosis, 351

Anxiety neurosis, 327; description and differential diagnosis, 348–9

Anxiety theories in psychoanalysis, history, 316 ff.

Apparatus, psychical, 254; threefold division, 318

Apprenticeship, medical, 105–6

Art: in children's phantasies, 80; consolidating and revolutionary, 193; and destructiveness, 69; 'Escape', 80; impulse to produce, in young, 74; satisfying element in, 79 ff.; social function of, 193; see also Aesthetics

Artist: and ego-ideal, 156; unbearable ideas and, 58

Association, free, 97, 133, 135, 146 ff.

Austria, analysts, 184

Auto-erotism, 236, 257; and narcissism, 263

Autosuggestion, 157

Autotomy, psychical, 323 n.

Aversion, and repression, 245

Bacon, Francis, quoted, 205

Bain, James, 329

Bath, warm, treatment, 274 n.

Battle-dress, 303 n., 335

Baynes, H. G., 32–6

Beauchamp, Sally, 47, 50

Beauty: and deathlessness, 85; origin of need for, 88

Behaviour; definition, 57; ego and, 159; in transference situation, 173

Belle indifférence, 230

Bereavement, 246

Binding of energy, 256

Biological theory, and psychoanalysis, 315

Bion, W. R., 134, 166, 222

Birth, as disturbance of bliss, 274

Bisexuality, 156

Biting, 286

Body-ego, boundaries of, 267

Body-self, 266

Breast, child's attitude to, 158; see also Nipple

Breuer, Josef, 61–2, 147–8

Case reports, preparation, 192

Cases: woman dressed in black, 83–4; soldier with hysterical paralysis, 90–3; woman who disclosed only eyebrow, 142 n.; Breuer's, of girl with neurosis after nursing father, 148; Schreber, 236 ff.; melancholic who discussed his haircut, 281–2; maniac who feared deficiency for job, 284; melancholic obsessed with thought of blood, 285; delusions of sewing spinal column of royal personages, 335; patient with numerous 'ancestors' in ward, 335; punning contortionist, 343

Cassel Hospital, 179

Castration, 323; definition, 295 n.; excessive use of concept, 43 n.; non-genital, 270; and primal horde, 384

Castration anxiety, 48, 270, 296, 327

Castration complex, 23, 226, 298

Castration-period, 295 n.

Catatonia, 230

Catharsis, mental, 62, 148

Cathexis, 230; definition, 154–5; of ego and objects, 226; id and, 306; libidinal, and interest, 247; transfer of, in mania and melancholia, 284; withdrawal of, 309

Cells, and instincts, 304

Censorship, 227

Change, direction of, 210

Character formation, 334

Character traits, origin of, 50

Chastity, Quakerism and, 389–390

Childbirth, see Parturition

Children: effects of study of, 98; guilt feelings in, 126

Classification, of neuroses and psychoses, 328 ff.

Clergy, and guilt, 133

Clitoris, 270

Collective unconscious, 34, 36, 161

Collectors, 232–3

Combinations, mental, in manic-depressives, 284

Committees, functioning, 194

Communication: as discounting repression, 312; oral, 202 ff.; in psycho-analytic society, 192, 197, 199–201

Compensation, in paranoia, 353

Compilations, 41

Complex, Jung's use of term, 229

Complex-sensitiveness, 230

Compromise formation, 124

Compulsiveness: in crime and neurosis, 45; and guilt feelings, 124

'Concern' for patient, doctor's, 107

Conference, research, 196–7

Confession, 301–2

Conflict(s): internal, in criminal, 45–6; solution of, in art, 80–2; uncovering, in interview, 140

Conformity, social, 123, 124

Confusion, hallucinatory, 226

Conscience: and parental injunctions, 120; psycho-analytical attitude to, 294; and super-ego, 122; unconscious, 308

Conscience-anxiety, 321

Conscience stage, 297

Consciousness, 52; ego and, 307–308; four states of, 307; perceptual, 307; and response to stimuli, 254

Consideration, 311

Constructiveness, 57–8

Contiguity of ideas, 91–2, 94

Contradiction, in dreams, 150

Conversation, and psychiatric interview, compared, 139

Conversion hysteria, description and differential diagnosis, 350–1

Conversion symptoms, 256

Co-operation: of analyst and other doctors, 117–18; of organizations, 177–8

Countertransference, 172, 219

Creative impulse, 58, 69

Creativeness: and father figure, 81; in psycho-therapy, 134; reinforced by guilt-reaction, 124, 160

Crime: aetiology of, 47–8, 49–51; aggressiveness and, 45 ff.

Criminality: as character-trait, 50; as neurosis, 49–50; super-ego and, 302

Culture preferences, and phantasy, 75

Cyclothymia, 253

Daly, Major, 39 n.

Danger: neurotic, 320–1; reaction to, 315; real and neurotic, 319; signal of, 319–320

Day-dreams, in common, 78; see also Phantasies

Death: art and, 83; Freud's attitude to, 99–100; unconscious attitude to, 270

Death instincts, 303–5

Decomposition, 334–6

Defence, 321; manic, 124; unconscious, 115

Defence mechanisms, 225, 256, 321 ff.

Deformity, attitude to, 73

Degenitalization, 22

Delay, anal origin, 50

Delirium tremens, 259; hallucinations in, 259 n.

Delusion formation, 246

Delusions, 314

Dementia, 235

Dementia paranoides, 236 ff., 258

Dementia praecox, 229 ff., 257–258, 314; Abraham on, 233; affects in, 230; characterology in, 231; description and differ-

Dementia—(*continued*)
ential diagnosis, 233, 354–5;
paranoia and, 248; and quotations, 40; repression in, 259;
return of repressed in, 259–60;
withdrawal and power-movements in, 275
Denial, limits of, 88
Depersonalization, 336–7
Depression: and guilt, 121, 126;
person attacked in, 285; in
psycho-analytical literature,
249; *see also* Manic-depressive
disorders
Depressive position, 388
Descensus uteri, 22–4
Desexualization, in organic illness, 262
Destructiveness, 49, 57; and art,
69
Determinism, 32
Diagnosis, and therapy, distinction, 30
Discharge of instinct, direct and
indirect, 47
Discussion groups, 201–2
Discussions, in psycho-analytical
society, 173; preparation for,
197
Displacement, 335; from parents,
300
Disputatio, 195–6
Disruptiveness, defences against,
134
Dissociation, 50, 90–1
Distortion, 256
Distribution, of analysts, 184,
206
Don-Juanism, 124
Dreams, 21, 314; classification,
78; Freud and, 97, 150–1;
latent and manifest content,
150; and quotations, comparison, 38; and racial history, 29;
see also Battle dreams
Dream-work; and art, 77–9; displacement of emotion in, 150;
regression in, 228
Dualism, in religion, 125

Dupe, compulsive, 47
Dynamics, of particles, 220–1

Economic factor, in psychoses,
226
Education: of analyst, 26–8;
individual and statistical, 105;
medical, aim of, 28–9;
– methods of, 105; pre-analytical, relative advantages of
disciplines, 28
Ego: in analysis, 308; assumption of control by, 300–1; as
boundary phenomenon, 158–
159; changes in, 309; and consciousness, 307–8; development of, 155–6; development,
and multi-body dynamics,
180; function of sanity, 306;
and id, 34, 197, 305 ff.; as
intermediary between instinct
impulses and external stimuli,
293; as regulator of discharge,
294; return of, 299; sensitivity
of, 51; subdivision, 226; and
super-ego, 294; – tension in
mania, 284; traumatism of, 51
Ego cathexis, 226
Ego-complex, 229–30
Ego development, psychosis and,
226
Ego-functions, importance of,
34–5
Ego-ideal, 155–7, 271, 293; formation, 272; leaders and, 166;
see also Super-ego
Ego-impulses, reactive, 296
Egoism, in speaker, 203
Ego-libido, 306; and pain, 262;
polarity, 310; psychical development, 271; *see also* Libido
Ego-unity, 325
Endogamy, 384, 389
Energy, mental, quantitative
aspects, 155–6
Environment, imagined, 54–5
Epilepsy, 235
Erogenicity: development of,
232; genitalization of, 269–70

Erotic experience, confluence of, 266–7
Erotogenous zones, in infant, 266
Erotamania, 243, 353
'Eternal' factor, in art, 82
Ethics, medical, 29
Euphoria, in mania, 284
Exaltation, 260
Examples, and quotations, difference, 39
Excitation, 305–6
Exogamy, 384
Expiation, lifelong, 124

Face, human, beauty of, 83
Fashion, and aesthetic appreciation, 76
Father, ambivalence towards, 122
Father-identification, in quotations, 38
Fear: and anxiety, 319; Freud on, 55; Jung on, 229; nature of, 55; and ugliness, 85–6
Feed-back process, 179
Ferenczi, S., 22, 27, 34, 38, 50, 161, 262, 265, 274, 275, 313, 346; quoted, 78, 269
Fetishism, 330
Film actresses, 84
Fits, 131
Fixation, 50, 244–5, 276–7, 326; in dementia praecox, 248; and mechanism, 256–7; at oral stage, 287; in paranoiacs, 242
Fixation points, 225; in manic-depressive disease, 258; of neuroses, 329; in obsessional neurosis and melancholia, 280; and sexual aims, 258
Flight, from tension, 254
'Foreign body' in works of art, 74
Forepleasure, and orgasm, 347
France, analysts, 184
Free Association, see Association
Freedom of movement, degree of, 210
Freud, Sigmund, 50, 53, 55, 70, 88, 116, 133, 163, 167, 171, 180, 197, 274, 276, 305, 330; as analyst, 60; and death, 99–100; and groups, 220; and homeostasis, 198; and infantile sexuality, 168; and instinct, 303; invention of analytic technique, 62, 148; and Jung, comparison, 32–6; and mechanism of psychosis, 226 ff.; obituary appreciation of, 95–104; his papers, 191; personal impression of, 59–60; quotation of, by analysts, 38; quoted, 76, 221, 226, 239, 241, 247, 249, 304; on repression, 244–5; and Schreber case, 237 ff.; theory of dreams, 150–151
Frigidity, 124
Frustration, 46, 151–2, 158; as cause of neurosis, 289; and nipple withdrawal, 267–8; toleration of, 128; and wish-phantasies, 241

General practitioner, training of, 105–6
Genital stage, 269–70, 276–7; failure to attain, 22
Genitality, infantile, 153
Genitals, changes in, in degenitalization, 22
Germany, analysts, 184
Gesture: magical, 275; omnipotence of, 320
Glover, James, 276 n.
Goitein, Hugh, 293 n.
G.P.I., 346
Grandeur, delusions of, 234; in mania, 253; see also Megalomania
Graphic impulse, development, 80–1
Gratification : aim-inhibited, 299; and body zones, 276; through hallucination, 256; organ –, 271; from self, 271
Grief: and anxiety, 321; and depression, 249; and melan-

Grief—(continued)
choly, 278–80; see also Mourning
Group cohesiveness, 191
Group dynamics, 167; Freud and, 180; opposition to, 185–6; psycho-analysis and, 185–9
Group psychology, Freud and, 198; see also Psychology, multi-person
Group therapy, 134; forms of, 165; two meanings of, 165
Groups: and individuals, 166; no 'infancy' in, 166, 168; phases in, 169; psycho-dynamics of, 167
Growth, defective, and ugliness, 73
Guilt: aggressiveness and, 123, 160; capacity for, 57; and day-dreams in common, 78; depressive and persecutory, 121–3; and growth of social capacity, 123; psycho-pathology and, 119 ff.; reactions to, 123–4; sense of, 299; as tension with behaviour code, 120
Guilt feelings, 62, 65, 73, 91, 160, 260; in children, 126; in depression, 251, 285; removal of, 125–6
Gynaecology, psycho-analysis and, 22

Hallucination, 228, 230, 235, 248, 256, 311; in delirium tremens, 259 n.; in neonate, 274
Hate, in anal stage, 269
Health service, national; preparation for, 113–14; and psycho-analytical clinic, 177
Helplessness, 319, 326–8
Herd instinct, 167; and super-ego, 292
'Here and now', 117, 133, 188–9, 219
Heterosexuality, 128; development, 232

History, patient's: eliciting, 110; in psychiatric interview, 138
Holiday breaks, in analysis, 129
Holland, analysts, 184
Homeostasis, 198
Homes, broken, and guilt, 126
Homosexual: ideas, intolerable, 228; impulses, in dementia praecox, 248
Homosexuality, 161, 242
Horde, primal, 384; quotation and, 39 n.
Horde psychology, 167
Hug-Hellmuth, Dr., 264
Hungary, analysts, 184
Hypnosis: abandonment of, 148, 151; and origins of psycho-analysis, 62; and quotations, 38–9; and super-ego, 157
Hypochondria, 100; description and differential diagnosis, 349–50; and libidinal distribution, 262; masked expression of, in mania, 284; in melancholia, 279, 281; in psychoses, 262–3
Hypoglycaemia, 131
Hypothesis, minimum, principle of, 32 n.
Hysteria, 229; anxiety, see Anxiety hysteria; characterology in, 230–1; childhood, 235; conversion, see Conversion hysteria; Jung on, 231; libido in, 246; in pregnancy, 23; repression in, 227, 259

Id, 157, 305–6; function of passion, 306; see also Ego
Ideas: 'borrowing' of, 200; for communication, classification, 197–8; creation of new, 198; horizon-moving, rearranging, and transplantation, 197–9; see also Communication
Idées inconscientes, 147
Identification, 297, 298–9; with aggressor, 73; and bad up-

bringing, 302; with parents, 288, 308; and ugliness, 73
Identity, thought- and perception-, in dreams, 77
Illness, organic, desexualization in, 262
Impotence, 124; and shell-shock, 317
Incest-impulse, 388–9
Incorporating stage, 269
Incorporation, 387; oral, 290
Infantile gratifications, in mania, 253
Infantilism, 289 n.
Inhibition(s): and aesthetic appreciation, 76; in depression and mania, 253; in development, 289; of impulses, 313; locus of, 324
Inner-Outer, antithesis, 310–11, 337
Insecurity, mental, 56
Instinct(s); child's, and crime, 46; conflict of, in war neuroses, 93; and ego, 293–4; Freud and, 303–4; psycho-analytical view of, 247; see also Discharge
Institute of Psycho-Analysis, 64
Instruction, medical, see Education
Integration, 166; in analysis, 129; failure, in criminals, 47–8
Intellect, education of, 27
Intelligence tests, 209
Intercourse, horror of, 22–3
Interpretation, 168; see also Dreams
Interpretations: group, 168–9; mutative, 168
Interruptions, in analysis, 129
Interview: medical, 108 ff., 145, 163; psychiatrist's role in, 138–40, 210, 211; student and, 113; two kinds of facts in, 140–1; two-level discourse in, 212–13
Introjection, 269; and aesthetics, 70; of parent, 272, 297
Introjection phase, 275

Irreversibility, 127, 129, 130, 143, 215
Irruption, see Repressed, return of
Isolation, 322
Itching, 264–5

Janet, Pierre, 62, 147
Jealousy, 243, 353
Jones, Ernest, 69, 70, 80, 161, 239, 273, 291 n., 357
Joy, in psycho-therapy, 134
Jung, C. G., 32–6, 160–1, 229–231, 248, 343; quoted, 229, 230, 231
Jungian method, depreciative of personality, 35–6

Klein, Melanie, 50, 56, 65, 79, 161, 388; and aesthetics, 70
Kleptomania, plagiarism as, 42
Kraepelin, Emil, 145, 328–9, 357
Kretschmer, Ernst, 145

Labour, see Parturition
Latency period, 300; and aesthetic response, 71
Law: and medical profession, 29–30; and super-ego, 293
Lay analysis, 26–31
Lay analyst, see Analyst
Leaders, veneration for, 166
Leadership: role, of speaker, 200–1, 203; in scientific societies, 195–6
Leuret, 147
Lewin, Kurt, 220
Libidinal impulse, aim and object, 277
Libidinal organization, development of, 264 ff.
Libido: desexualization of, 306; detachment of, 246–7; development, 225, 232, 241 ff.; developmental stages, 276 ff.; ego – and object –, 261–2; in ego-ideal activity, 273; limited toleration of, 289; shifting con-

Libido—(*continued*)
centration, 287; *see also* Ego-
libido
Libido theory: development,
152–4; extension, 154–5; and
psychoses, 232
'Light, Inner', 386
Listening, to patient, art of, 109,
149
Love: capacity for, loss of, 56;
derivation of social, 299; and
thought, contrast, 27
Love impulse, in criminals, 45
Love object, choice of, 263–4 n.

Magical words and thoughts,
275
Mania: and depression, 252–3;
infantile character, 284; melancholia and, 283–5
Manic-depressive disease, 249,
258; Abraham and, 161, 249;
description and differential
diagnosis, 353–4; guilt in, 124
Masculine protest, 49
'Masked' psychosis, 334
Masochism, 43, 124; in depressives, 252
Masturbation: and hypochondria, 350; and neurasthenia,
349
Materialism, dialectical, 74
Mathematician, schizophrenic,
345
Mathematics: metrical and non-
metrical, 209; and pathology,
216
Mechanism(s): psychical, 255–7;
and symptom, 257 n.
Medical profession, law and, 29
Meetings: analytic, 194 ff.; of
small groups, 201
Megalomania: 234–5, 239, 244,
246, 309, 344 n.; in foetus,
274; in melancholia, 279; of
quiet type, 284; secondary,
260
Melancholia, 259, 278–91, 309;
causes of, 291; end of attack,

291; and grief, 278–80; and
mania, 283–5; narcissism in,
281–3; oral libido in, 285 ff.;
repression in, 259; sense of sin
in, 57; transference and, 280
Melancholic, causes of illness,
289
Memory image, 229; and percep-
tion, distinction, 311
Mendel, Gregor, 356
Methodology, in psychiatry,
207 ff.
Meyer, Adolf, 145
Mimicry, 43–4
Mind, oscillation between libi-
dinal and ego-cathexis, 27
Money, 277
Morale, and delivery of papers,
191
Morality, sphincter- and genital-,
299
Mother, unity of presentation of,
269 n.
Mother-identification, in quota-
tions, 38
Mott, 231
Mourning: capacity for, 128; and
detachment of libido, 246; *see
also* Grief
Mysticism, magical words and,
275
Myths, and racial history, 29

Narcissism, 155, 242, 257, 261 ff.,
297, 305, 317; in criminals,
50; and hypochondria, 263; in
melancholia, 279, 281–3; and
omnipotence, 276; in paranoia, 246; primary and secondary, 273; secondary, 306
Narcissistic neuroses, 329
Narcosis, 131
Needs, 254
Negativism, 314
Nervous system, central, cathexis
of, 268 n.
'Nervousness', 351
Neurasthenia, description and
differential diagnosis, 349

Neurologists, psycho-phobia of, 28

Neurosis (-es): anxiety, *see* Anxiety neurosis; and art appreciation, 74–5; classification, 328 ff.; criminality as, 49–50; guilt and, 124–5; obsessional, *see* Obsessional neurosis; origins of, 233; relation to ego, 308 n.; self-cure of, 289–90; self-punishment in, 47; transference, *see* Transference neurosis; traumatic, *see* Traumatic neurosis

Neurotic, and normal person, compared, 64

Newton, Sir Isaac, 96, 99

Nipple, relation to self, 265 n., 267–8

Nosogenesis, 334

Number: 218 ff.; in individual and group dynamics, 165 ff.; in psychology, *see* Psychology

Nunberg, H., 336

Oaths, Quakers and, 386

Object: double, 57; good and bad, 158, 160; good, Quakerism and, 388–90; introjected, in mania, 285

Object cathexis, 226; loss of, and libido distribution, 279

Objectivity, development of capacity for, 311 ff.

Object-relations, perception of, 26

Object-relationship, 155; animistic, 158; conscious and unconscious, 56; development of, 157–60, 265; disturbance of, 116; early, and Quakerism, 387; three stages, 257; types of, 226

Observation, analyst's use of, 202

Obsession, 226

Obsessional: diagnostic doubts regarding, 280; gestures in, 275

Obsessional neurosis, 227, 250, 259; description and differential diagnosis, 352; ego and super-ego in, 301; and melancholia, 280–1; repression in, 259; transference and, 280

Obstetrician, preference for male, 24

Obstinacy, anal origin, 50

Oceanic feeling, 156

Oedipus complex, 69, 154, 166, 208, 220, 296, 308–9; positive and negative, 309; religion and, 384

Oedipus conflict, in *Hamlet*, 80

Oedipus situation: and criminal, 46; and melancholia, 290

Officers, society, progressive abdication, 205

Omnipotence: feeling of, 274–6; unconditioned, 274

Omnipotence phase, education and, 28

Onanism: and dementia praecox, 236; in Schreber case, 240; *see also* Masturbation

Opposition: to psycho-analysis, 185–6; public and professional, 187

Oral libido, in melancholia, 285 ff.

Oral sadism, 286

Oral stage, 232, 264–8, 276–7; sucking and biting phases, 286, 287

Oral tradition, in psycho-analysis, 202 ff.

Orality, infantile, 153

Organization, at meetings, dislike of, 200

Orgasm, 346–8

Originality, pride in, 200

Osmics, 71

Over-estimation, mutual, 234

Pain, 52, 321; and discrimination between good and bad, 274; ego-libido and, 262; influence of, and research,

213; relief of, by psychical mechanisms, 255

Papers: preparation of, 192; presentation of, 190 ff.; prior circulation, 191–2; reading of, 190

Paralysis, hysterical, 90 ff.

Paranoia, 257–8; chronic, 227–8; compensation in, 353; decomposition in, 239; and dementia praecox, 248; description and differential diagnosis, 352–3; form of symptoms in, 227; Freud on mechanism of, 241 ff.; megalomaniac, 352; persecutory, 352–3; repression in, 227, 259

Paraphrenic: delusions of, 337; restitution in, 344; sense of desolation in, 57

Parent(s): libidinal bond with, and quotations, 39; as love-objects, 287; not a unified figure, 295 n.; relation to, and ego, 156–7; relation with, and guilt feelings, 122; rivalry with, 294, 298

Parent-love, and ego-ideal, 272

Paresis, hysterical, 23

Parody, 41–2

Part-love, stage of, 278, 323

Parturition: abnormal resistance in, 24; function of obstetrician in, 24; neurotic manifestations in, 23

Passivity, fear of, 43

Pathology, medical, 216

Pathoneurosis: cerebral, 346; description and differential diagnosis, 355

Patient: and doctor, relation, 106 ff., 113–14; and psychiatric interview, 139–41; and student, 111–12; see also Analyst; 'Concern'; History

Patients, transfer of, 30

Pattern: termination criteria as, 129–30; transmission of sense of, 211

Pattern making, 209 ff., 217

Payne, Sylvia M., 291 n.

Pelvic floor, weakness of, 22

Penances, 301

Penis, 270; and endogamy, 389

Perineum, danger of laceration, 24

Persecution feelings: in dementia praecox, 234; and guilt, 121

Persecution mania, 243

Personality structure: change in, 143; study of, 134, 135

Perversion, negative of neurosis, 330

Petö, E., 71

Phallic phase (stage), 269–70, 276–7; regression from, 322

Phantasies: aroused by mutilated statues, 72–3; infantile, 66–7; sadistic, 47; seduction, 103, 154; sexual, and dementia praecox, 232; special kind, in paraphrenics, 344–5

Phobias, 324

Physical disorders, psychic factors in, 23

Placebos, 157

Plagiarism, 42

Pleasure: in infant, 265–7; physiology of, 22; sensuous, and art, 79–80

Pleasure-ego, 311

Pleasure-objects, infant's, 266–7

Pleasure principle, 293, 298; and repetition-compulsion, 318

Potency, sexual, 346

Power, will to, 160

Power-words, 231

Preconscious, 307

Prediction, limitations of, 221–2, 223

Pre-genital activities, and culture, 299–300 n.

Pregnancy, hysteria in, 23

Pre-history, 29

Preoccupations, libidinal and intellectual, 28

Pre-psychotic conditions, 334

Priggishness, 42

Primal horde, *see* Horde
Primal scene, 385
Probability, in unconscious, 323
Problems, patient's, priority of, 222
Profession: nature of, 181–2; psycho-analysis as, 182
Projection: 157, 158, 227, 244, 246, 255; and aesthetics, 70; in depressive psychosis, 250–1; and paranoia, 256, 333–4
Projection phase, 275
Prolapse, cause of, 22–3
Propitiation, 124
Psychiatrist(s): active and passive roles, 210; description, 210; mathematical, 212; optimum ratio to population, 183
Psychiatry: basic sciences of, 215; development, 144 ff.; functions of, 131–2; role of psycho-therapy in, 135; social, future of, 137–8; as specialty, 110–11
Psycho-analysis: aim of, 115; alleged vagueness of, 255; description, 61; development, 146 ff.; early history, 61–2; first use of term, 227; general practitioner and, 61 ff.; and hospital in-patients, 115 ff.; opposition to, 185–8; principles of, 115–16; relation to other disciplines, 28, 175–6; as science and art, 204; use of, 64–6; *see also* Analysis
Psychology: clinical, divergent aims in, 53; field of study, 53; four-person, 207–9, 215, 220; multi-person, 166–7, 180, 207–209, 215, 221–2; normal, 110; one-person, 166–7, 180, 207–209, 215, 218–19; research areas, 179–80; three-person, 166–7, 180, 207–9, 215, 220; two-person, 166–7, 180, 207–209, 215, 219
Psycho-pathology, 110, 216–17
Psychosis (-es), 327; classifica-tion, 328 ff.; Freud and mechanism of, 226 ff.; genesis, 309; guilt and, 124–5; 'masked', 334
Psycho-synthesis, 35
Psycho-therapy: definition, 131; future of, 136; as joint undertaking of doctor and patient, 132; reasons for influence of, 132; role of, 135–6; task of, 141–2; technique of, 133
Psychotic conditions, early stages, 332–4
Psychotics, and psycho-neurotics, 333
Publications, analytical, 189
Punishment, *see* Self-punishment
Pygmalion legend, 76

Quacks: definition of, 113 n.; protection from, 30
Quakerism, 385 ff.
Quantity, concept of: in psychodynamics, 197; in psychoses, 258
Quotation(s): in analysis, 37 ff.; compulsive, 40; and early recollections, 37; and hypnosis, 38–9; 'improved', 41; motives for making, 38 ff.; and primal horde, 39 n.; and submission to authority, 43–4; virtuosity in, 40

Rage reactions, 209
Rank, Otto, 261
Rationalizations, 272
Reaction formation, 322
Reading-in, 196
Reality: inability to adapt to, 289; sense of, 310 ff.
Reality testing, 27, 133, 310
Reckoning-operations, unconscious, 27
Recollection, regression in, 228
Reflex arc, 253–4
Reflexes, conditioned, 208
Reformers, 155, 187–8
Register, professional, 182

Regression, 91, 228, 242, 322
Reich, Wilhelm, 347 n.
Rejuvenation tendency, 261
Relationships, deeper-than-personal, 33; personal, development of, 46
Religion: attitude to guilt feelings, 124–5; interest in, 124; psycho-analysis and, 384 ff.
Remission, in melancholic and obsessional, 281
Reparation, and creativeness, 85
Repetition-compulsion, 314, 318
Repressed, return of the, 227, 245, 248, 259
Repression, 246, 311; actual and primal, 321–2; aggression and, 51, 124; in criminality, 49–50; in dementia praecox, 259; in early psycho-analysis, 62, 226–7; and guilt, 121; in hysteria, 259; mechanism of, 244–5; in melancholia, 259; in obsessional neurosis, 259; in paranoia, 227, 259; in Schreber case, 247; super-ego and, 294
Reproduction of past situations, 325–6
Research: in psycho-pathology, 54; pure and operational, 134–135; and therapy, relation, 109, 115, 135, 213–14; two kinds, 213
Research workers, reports of, 196
Resistance, 62, 248–9, 307
Responsibility, doctor's, for patient, 181 n.
Restitution, 123–4, 160, 353; in paraphrenia, 344
Restitution symptoms, 260
Retardation, assessment of, 110
Rivers, W. H. R., 55, 223
Róheim, Géza, 223

Sachs, Hanns, 78
Sadism, 43, 46–7, 288, 297; in melancholia, 281; positive and negative tendencies, 280; repressed, in depressives, 251

Satisfaction: loss of, from object, 56; of need, 254
Schizophrenia, 343; see also Dementia praecox
Schmideberg, Dr., 388
Schoolmen, 195–6
Schreber, 230, 236 ff., 245–6, 247, 248–9, 335, 336
Science, growth of, effects, 96
Scientific stage, 275
Scoptophilia, and self-criticism, 302
Scotland, analysts, 185
Seating, arrangement of, 201
Security, loss of, 55–6
Seduction episodes, imaginary, 103, 154
Self-criticism, 302
Self-love, 263; erotic element in, 263
Self-preservation, 264, 266
Self-punishment, 128; in criminal, 47; in melancholia, 57, 301; need for, and pelvic pains, 23; in obsessional, 281
Self-reproach, 279, 282
Sensory stimuli, in infant, 265
Sexual instinct, aims, 225, 258
Sexual perversion, guilt and, 124
Sexual relations, exogamous, 299, 300
Sexuality, infantile: and adult, 153; Freud and, 97–8, 169, 197
Sharpe, Ella, 81
Shock theory, 316
Short term therapies, 143
Sibling rivalry, 208, 220
Sin, sense of, 57; in depressives, 285; see also Guilt
Size of audience, effects of, 203–204
Skin sensitiveness, in manics, 274 n.
Smelling, in baby, 265
Smells, 71
Smoking, 333
Social feeling, type of, 330–2
Social instincts, development of, 242

Social psychiatry, *see* Group psychiatry
Social relations, origin of, 232
Societies, analytical, membership statistics, 206
Society: opinion of, sensitiveness to, 299; stability of, and psycho-analysis, 188; and super-ego, 293, 299
Society, analytical: organization of, 170 ff.; suggested maxims for, 205
Socio-dynamics, and psycho-analysis, 189
Sociology: of analysts, 182 ff.; implications of psycho-analysis in, 172
'Span' of observer, 222 n.
Speech: and omnipotence, 275; organ, 343, 345
Sphincter play, pleasure in, 294–295
Split, mental, in criminals, 47, 49–51
Stages: in development of libido, 276 ff.; of life, 110
Stanislavsky, K., 139
Statues, incomplete, 71–2
Stimuli: instinctive and individual, 254; sources of, 254
Stoddart, W. H. B., 274 n.
Stories, use in conversation, 40
Strachey, J., 168
Student, medical, and patient, 111–13
Stupor, in depressives, 252
Sublimation, 232, 297; in depressives, 252
Substitution, 227
Subtlety, lack of, in mania, 284
Sucking, 264–6
Suffering, mental, 52
Suicide, 304
Super-ego, 157, 159, 197, 291 ff., 308–9; and aesthetic response, 71; as artist's 'inner audience', 78; beginning of operation, 293; and conscience, 122; decline of, 299–301; disorders, 301–3; and group psychology, 198; and id, 307; infantility of, in women, 300 n.; introduction of concept, 186; in mania and melancholia, 283–4; mechanisms relating to, 293; narcissism of, 282–3; phallic stage, 296–8; post-phallic stage, 298–299; pre-phallic stage, 294–6; stages of development, 293–9; two types, 288; is unconscious, 293; what it is not, 292–3
Super-objectives, 139
Surprise, element of, at meetings, 200
Surrealism, 77
Surroundings, comprehension of, in mania and melancholia, 284
Suttie, Ian D., 190
Switzerland, analysts, 184
Symbolism, 275
Symptom, *see* Mechanism
Symptom-action, locus of, 324–5
Symptom-derivatives, 325
Symptoms, at beginning of analysis, 130
Synthesis, in medical education, 106
Synthesizing element, in psyche, 33

Tact, and the analyst, 186
Tattooing, 345
Tavistock Clinic, 178
Tavistock Institute of Human Relations, 178
Technique, new, acquirement of, 326
Tension: crime as removing, 45; elimination of, by psychical apparatus, 254; group, psycho-analysis and, 188–9; id as reservoir of, 306
Termination of analysis, criteria for, 127–30
Thanatos and Eros, 100
Therapy: non-analytical, and psycho-analysis, 116–17; rank

Therapy—(*continued*)
order in, 134, 143; *see also*
Psychotherapy; Research
Thinking, while speaking, 202–3
Thinking-apparatus, 313
'Third party' in therapeutic
situation, 152, 157, 209
Thought: and orgasm, 346; *see
also* Love
Tic, 330
Time, need for unlimited, in
occasional cases, 136
Time limits, earliest, in formation of disease, 332
Topology, 209
Totemism, 384
Toxic states, 259
Trainees, lay, for non-therapeutic work, 176–7
Training: analyst's, 64 – effects
of, 175; future use of, 178
Transference, 168: analysis of,
and genital disorders, 25;
capacity for, 280; ego's synthetic power in, 35; explanation, 63, 116, 149; Freud and
the, 97, 197; handling by
Freud and Jung, 32 ff.; and
hypochondria, 262; and in-
patients, 116–17; narcissism
and, 261; repetition element
in, 33, 34; as research instrument, 102
Transference neuroses, 327, 329
Transference phenomena: manipulation of, 131, 133; and
termination of analysis, 128,
129
Transference situation: behaviour in, 172–3; two-body
psychology and, 219
Transience, does not comport
irrelevance, 55
Transplantations, 198–9
Traumatic neurosis, description
and differential diagnosis, 355
–356

Ugliness: and mutilation phan-

tasies, 72–3; what it is, 85–8
'Ugly', definition, 70
'Unbearable' ideas, 54 ff., 226–7,
316; clinical view of, 55 ff.; in
normal person, 57
Unconscious, 64, 65, 150, 159,
307; element in ego, 308;
linking of cathexes in, 155;
and response to stimuli, 254;
see also Collective unconscious
Undoing, 322
Unfinished work, and ugliness,
74
United States, analysts, 184
Unpleasant ideas: acceptance of,
312–13, 314; negation of, 311–
312
Unwin, J. D., 190
Upbringing, bad, and super-ego,
302
Urine, as object, 265
Uterus, weakness of suspending
ligaments, 22
Utraquism, 313

Vaginismus, 23; and perineal
laceration, 24
Vigilance, in analyst, 173
Violence, 47; *see also* Aggressiveness

Ward, training in, 111
Washing ceremonial, 301
Week-end break, in analysis,
129
Whitman, Walt, quoted, 137
Winnicott, Dr., 220
'Wish' aetiology, 317
Wit, 253
Withdrawal, 275
Woman, super-ego in, 300 n.
Word-Association tests, Jung's,
229
Word-presentations: and con-
sciousness, 307; and patient's
organs, relation, 343
Work: activity and passivity in,
48; capacity for, 128; crimi-
nals and, 48–9